IC3
Global Standard 5

Certification Guide

Using Microsoft® Windows® 10 & Microsoft® Office 2016

Computing Fundamentals
Key Applications
Living Online

CENGAGE
Learning·

Australia • Canada • Mexico • Singapore • Spain • United Kingdom • United States

Cengage Learning has partnered with CCI Learning to bring you:
IC3® Certification Guide
Using Microsoft® Windows® 10 & Microsoft® Office 2016!

With this partnership, you'll have access to:

SAM and MindTap Reader eBook

SAM (Skills Assessment Manager) is a robust assessment, training, and project-based system that enables students to be active participants in learning valuable Microsoft® Office skills. The MindTap Reader version of *IC3® Certification Guide Using Microsoft® Windows® 10 & Microsoft® Office 2016* works within the SAM environment to teach Office and computer concepts skills. Let SAM be an integral part of your students' learning experience! For more information, please visit *cengage.com/sam*.

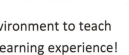

MindTap

Typical courses often require students to juggle a variety of print and digital resources, as well as an array of platforms, access codes, logins, and homework systems. Now all of those resources are available in one personal learning experience called MindTap. MindTap is a cloud-based, interactive, customizable, and complete online course. More than an e-book, each MindTap course is built upon authoritative Cengage Learning content, accessible anytime, anywhere.

Instructor Materials

Included with this product are instructor support materials. These include:

- Data files
- Solution files
- PowerPoint Presentations
- Lesson Notes
- Cognero test banks

These can be accessed at *login.cengage.com* with your instructor SSO account.

Certiport Approved

This product has been approved for the IC3® Certification! It fulfills the basic requirements for all three IC3 Internet and Computing Core Certification Exams. Included in the back of this book is an IC3 Courseware Mapping.

IC3® Certification Guide Using Microsoft® Windows® 10 & Microsoft® Office 2016
CCI Learning

SVP, GM Science, Technology & Math: Balraj S. Kalsi

Senior Product Director: Kathleen McMahon

Product Manager: Amanda Lyons

Associate Product Manager: Sarah Marks

Senior Director, Development: Julia Caballero

Senior Content Development Manager: Leigh Hefferon

Associate Content Developer: Abigail Pufpaff

Product Assistant: Cara Suriyamongkol

Marketing Director: Michele McTighe

Marketing Manager: Stephanie Albracht

Marketing Coordinator: Cassie Cloutier

Senior Content Project Manager: Stacey Lamodi

Senior Art Director and Cover Designer: Diana Graham

Digital Content Specialist: Laura Ruschman

Cover image(s): Mictoon/Shutterstock.com

For product information and technology assistance, contact us at
Cengage Learning Customer & Sales Support, 1-800-354-9706

For permission to use material from this text or product, submit all requests online at www.cengage.com/permissions. Further permissions questions can be e-mailed to **permissionrequest@cengage.com**

Library of Congress Control Number: 2016962892

ISBN: 978-1-337-56417-5

Cengage Learning
20 Channel Center Street
Boston, MA 02210
USA

Cengage Learning is a leading provider of customized learning solutions with employees residing in nearly 40 different countries and sales in more than 125 countries around the world. Find your local representative at **www.cengage.com**.

Cengage Learning products are represented in Canada by Nelson Education, Ltd.

To learn more about Cengage Learning, visit **www.cengage.com**

Purchase any of our products at your local college store or at our preferred online store **www.cengagebrain.com**

Notice to the Reader

Printed in the United States of America
Print Number: 02   Print Year: 2017

IC3

CCI Learning

Internet and Computing Core Certification Guide

Global Standard 5

Using Windows 10 & Microsoft® Office 2016

Computing Fundamentals

Key Applications

Living Online

July 2016
© CCI Learning Solutions Inc.

Internet and Computing Core Certification Guide

This courseware is prepared by CCI Learning Solutions Inc. for use by students and instructors in courses on computer use and software applications. CCI designed these materials to assist students and instructors in making the learning process both effective and enjoyable.

The information in this courseware is distributed on an "as is" basis, without warranty. While every precaution has been taken in the preparation of this courseware, neither the author nor CCI Learning Solutions Inc. shall have any liability to any person or entity with respect to any liability, loss, or damage caused or alleged to be caused directly or indirectly by the instructions contained in this courseware or by the computer software and hardware products described therein.

Courseware Development Team: Irina Heer, Sue Wong, Kelly Hegedus, Kevin Yulo

    Copyright © 2016 CCI Learning Solutions Inc.

    ISBN: 978-1-55332-463-8

    All rights reserved.

    Printed in Canada.

    CCI Courseware#: 7500-1

Working With the Data Files

The exercises in this courseware require you to use the data files provided for the book. Follow the instructions shown to download the data files for this courseware.

1. Launch your browser and navigate to the CCI Web site location http://www.ccilearning.com/data.

2. Enter: 7500 in the Courseware # box and click **Find Data**.

3. Click **Run** in the File Download – Security Warning window. (Alternatively, you can choose to Save the file to a location on your computer.)

4. In the Internet Explorer – Security Warning window click **Run** again.

5. In the WinZip Self-Extractor dialog box, use the **Browse** button to specify the Windows Desktop as the location to unzip the file and then click **Unzip**.

    The *7500 Student Files* folder containing the required student work files has now been downloaded to your desktop. It is recommended that you rename the folder using your own name before starting the exercises in this courseware. You can reinstall and use the work files as many times as you like.

Table of Contents

About This Courseware

Course Description xv
    Course Series xv
    Course Prerequisites xv
    System Requirements xv
    Classroom Setup xvi
Course Design xvii
Course Objectives xvii
Conventions and Graphics xix

Lesson 1: Operating Systems

Lesson Objectives 1
What is an Operating System? 1
    Evolution of the Modern OS Interface 2
    Proprietary and Open-Source Operating Systems 2
Desktop Operating Systems 3
    Operating System Versions and Editions 3
    Popular Desktop Operating Systems 3
Common Operating System Features 5
    User Accounts 5
    User Profiles 6
    Built-In Power Off Procedures 7
Understanding Windows Power Options 8
Looking at the Windows 10 Desktop 9
    Navigating Around the Desktop 10
    Using the Start Button and Start Menu 11
    Using the Taskbar 13
Global and Profile-Specific Settings 17
    The Settings App 17
    The Windows Control Panel 18
Changing Global Settings 21
    Changing the Screen Resolution 21
    Changing Password Protection 22
    Changing Power Management Options 22
Customizing Profile-Specific Settings 23
    Customizing the Desktop Display 23
Mobile Operating Systems 28
    Touch Screen Navigation on Mobile OS 28
    Power On / Off 29
    Lock Screen 29
    The Home Screen 30
    The Mobile Settings App 31
    Virtual Personal Assistants 31

Operating System Updates 32

    Automatic Updating – Previous Versions of Windows 33

    Automatic Updating – Windows 10 33

    Benefits and Drawbacks of Automatic Updating 34

    Updating a Mobile Operating System 34

Lesson Summary 35

Review Questions 35

Lesson 2: Hardware

Lesson Objectives 37

What Makes Hardware Tick? 37

    Device Drivers 37

    Firmware 38

    Platform 38

About the Numbers 38

    Measuring Capacity 39

    Measuring Frequency 39

    Measuring Bandwidth 40

The Basics – What's Inside? 40

Memory and Storage 41

    Random Access Memory (RAM)w 41

    Storage 42

Identifying Types of Computers 44

    Servers 44

    Desktop Computers 45

    Laptop (or Notebook) Computers 47

    Chromebooks 49

    Tablets 49

    Smart Phones 50

Keyboards, Mice, and Touch Screens 51

    Keyboards 51

    Pointing Devices 52

    Touch Screens 53

Typical Smart Phone Hardware 54

    Subscriber Identity Module (SIM) 55

    Smart Phone Keyboard / Dial Pad 55

Power Plans 56

    Working with Power Plan Settings 56

Connecting Peripherals 59

    Video Ports and Connectors 59

    Network Ports and Connectors 62

    Audio Ports and Connectors 62

    USB Ports and Connectors 63

Wireless Connection Technologies 66

    Bluetooth 66

    Infrared 67

Lesson Summary 67

Review Questions 67

Lesson 3: Networks and Mobile Devices

Lesson Objectives 69
What is a Network? 69
    Infrastructure Is Everything 69
Why Network? 70
    Internet Connection Sharing 70
Basic Network Technology 71
    TCP/IP 71
    LANs and WANs 71
    IP Addresses 72
Obtaining Internet Service 74
    Service Providers 74
    Which Service Should You Use? 75
Connecting the Internet to Your LAN 78
    Broadband Modems 78
    Broadband Routers 78
    Public and Private IP Addresses 79
Wired Connections – Ethernet 80
    Ethernet Standards and Cables 81
    Network Interface Card (NIC) 81
    Advantages and Disadvantages of Wired Connections 82
    Adding a Shared Printer to the Wired LAN 83
Wireless Connections – Wi-Fi 85
    Adapters, Signals and Bands 86
    Wireless Security 87
    When Should You Use Wireless Connections? 87
    Connecting Your Computer to a WLAN 87
    Connecting Your Handheld Device to a WLAN 88
    Wi-Fi Protected Setup (WPS) 89
    Adding a Network Printer to the WLAN 89
Cellular Networks 90
    Cellular Generations – All About the G's 91
    Cellular Carriers 91
    Network Coverage 92
    How Cellular Service Differs from Internet Service 92
Obtaining Cell Service 92
    Contract Services 92
    Pre-Paid Services 93
Cellular Service Plans 94
    Plan Add-Ons 94
Cellular Devices 94
    Smart Phones 95
    Basic Cell Phone 95
    Cellular-Enabled Tablets 95
    Mobile Data 96

Hard-Wired Phones 97

    Advantages and Disadvantages..98

    Private Branch Exchange (PBX)..98

    Business Telephones...98

Voice Mail 99

    Configuring Your Voice Mail 99

    Voice Mail on Your Mobile Phone 100

    Leaving a Clear Voice Mail Message 100

Lesson Summary 101

Review Questions...101

Lesson 4: File Management

Lesson Objectives 103

Understanding Folders and Directory Structure...103

    Drive Letters 103

    Folders and Subfolders...105

    Directories and Paths 105

    Connecting "Smart" Devices 105

    File and Folder Permissions 106

    Understanding Local and Remote Locations 107

Using File Explorer...107

    Moving a Window..110

    Sizing a Window...110

    Using Scroll Bars..111

Working with Files and Folders..112

    Creating Folders 112

    Renaming a Folder...113

    Creating a Shortcut to a Folder...113

    Working with Folders and Folder Options 116

    Understanding File Types and File Name Extensions 119

    Windows 10 and File Extensions 122

    Selecting Files and Folders...123

    Copying and Moving Files and Folders 125

    Renaming Files 127

    Searching for Files..128

    Looking at the Recycle Bin 130

Understanding Default Locations 132

    Scanners...132

    Web Site Items 132

    Pictures 133

    Pictures on Smart Phones 133

Managing Electronic Media..134

Sharing Files 135
    Removable Media 135
    Public Folders 135
    Shared Folders 136
    Network Shares 137
    Email Attachments 137
    Compressing Files 139
Lesson Summary 143
Review Questions 144

Lesson 5: Software

Lesson Objectives 147
Why Use Software? 147
    Locally-Installed vs. Cloud-Based Software 147
Obtaining Software 148
    Platform Considerations 148
Managing Software 149
    Installing a New Program 150
    Uninstalling Programs 153
    Repairing Software 154
    Reinstalling a Program 155
    Updating Software 156
Configuring Software 156
    Customizing Toolbars 156
    Specifying Program Defaults 157
Working with Windows Apps 159
    Operating System App Stores 159
    Windows Store 159
    Finding an App in the Store 162
    Downloading and Installing an App 163
    Deleting an App 164
    Signing out of the Store 165
Messaging Applications 165
    Text Messaging 166
    Chat 167
    Instant Messaging 170
Lesson Summary 177
Review Questions 177

Lesson 6: Cloud Computing

Lesson Objectives 179
Cloud Computing Concepts 179
    Benefits of Cloud Computing 180
    Accessing Hosted Services 180
Cloud Accounts 181
    Cloud Account Management 182
    Cloud Storage on Google Drive 183
    Google Drive Mobile Apps 192

Microsoft OneDrive...192
    Cloud Storage on OneDrive...192
    The Local OneDrive folder..194
    OneDrive Web Apps...198
    OneDrive Mobile Apps...202
iCloud..202
    iCloud for Windows..203
Dropbox..204
Other Types of Cloud-Based Applications...206
    Learning Management System (LMS)..206
    Customer Relationship Management (CRM) Software......................................207
Mobile Notifications..208
    Configuring Notifications in the App..208
    Configuring Notifications through Mobile OS...209
Lesson Summary..210
Review Questions..210

Lesson 7: Security and Maintenance

Lesson Objectives..213
The Need for Security..213
User Names and Passwords...213
    Keeping Your Account Safe...214
Identifying Risks..215
    Viruses...215
    Trojans...216
    Malware (Spyware / Adware)..216
    Network Connections...217
    Using Public Computers...217
    Social Engineering..218
    Phishing...219
Protecting Yourself..220
    Antivirus Software..220
    Firewalls...222
    Monitoring Software...223
    Conducting Safe E-Commerce Transactions...224
    Virtual Private Networks (VPNs)...225
Backup and Restore...226
    Backing Up Your Personal Files..226
    Backing Up PC System Files and Settings...231
    Backing Up Your Mobile Data..233
    Using Factory Reset Options for PC...234
    Resetting Mobile Devices...234
Troubleshooting..235
    Is it Hardware or Software?..236
    Troubleshooting Connection Issues...237
Lesson Summary..238
Review Questions..238

Lesson 8: Apps and Applications

Lesson Objectives 241

Understanding Apps and Applications 241

Application Programs 242

    Word Processing 242

    Desktop Publishing 243

    Spreadsheets 244

    Graphic Design and Image Editing 244

    Web Development 245

    Video Editing 246

    Presentation 246

Web Apps 247

    Google Drive 248

Local Apps 250

    App Stores 250

    Accounts and Access 251

    Browsing an App Store 251

    Searching in the App Store 256

    Obtaining an App 256

    Deleting an App 258

    Recovering a Deleted App 259

Limitations 260

Lesson Summary 261

Review Questions 261

Lesson 9: Using Microsoft Word

Lesson Objectives 263

Identifying Common Features 263

    Starting an Application 264

    Exiting an Application 264

    Understanding the Backstage View 264

Looking at the Edit Screen 265

    Accessing Commands and Features 266

Entering and Editing Text 268

    Using the Rulers 268

    Selecting Text 269

Managing Files 269

    Saving Documents 269

    Starting a New Document 272

    Closing a Document 273

    Opening a Document 273

Manipulating Text 280

    Customizing the View 281

    Using Undo 282

    Using Repeat or Redo 282

    Using Cut, Copy, and Paste 282

Applying Formatting 285
    Enhancing Text Characters 285
    Enhancing Paragraphs 286
    Understanding Tab Settings 287
Formatting the Document 289
    Changing the Paper Size 289
    Changing the Orientation 289
    Changing Margins 289
    Adding Page Numbers 291
    Applying Columns 292
Preparing the Document for Printing 293
    Proofing the Document 293
    Finding and Replacing Items 295
    Printing the Document 296
Working with Pictures 298
    Manipulating Objects 300
Using Tables 303
    Inserting a Table 303
    Formatting Text in the Table 304
    Inserting & Deleting Rows/Columns/Cells 304
    Adjusting the Width or Height 305
    Merging and Splitting Cells 305
Tracking Changes 307
Lesson Summary 308
Review Questions 308

Lesson 10: Using Microsoft Excel

Lesson Objectives 311
Looking at the Excel Screen 311
    Understanding Basic Terminology 312
    Entering Data in the Worksheet 313
    Moving Around the Worksheet 314
Managing Workbooks 314
    Creating a New Blank Workbook 314
    Creating a New Workbook from a Template 315
    Saving Workbooks 316
    Opening Workbooks 317
    Closing Workbooks 318
Manipulating the Contents 320
    Selecting Cells 320
    Using Undo or Repeat 321
    Copying and Moving Data 321
    Changing the Column Widths 322
    Adjusting the Row Height 323
    Manipulating Rows, Columns, or Cells 323

Creating Simple Formulas 325
    Using Common Built-In Functions 325
    Using Absolute and Relative Addresses 326
What Does Formatting Mean? 329
    Formatting Numbers and Decimal Digits 330
    Changing Cell Alignment 330
    Changing Fonts and Sizes 330
    Applying Cell Borders 330
    Applying Colors and Patterns 331
Working with Charts 333
    Selecting Chart Types 334
    Changing the Chart Layout 336
Working with Lists and Databases 338
    Sorting Data 339
    Filtering Information 339
    Understanding Excel Databases 342
Working with Tables 343
    Modifying Table Data 343
    Formatting Table Data 343
Finalizing the Print Output 348
    Printing the Worksheet 348
Lesson Summary 349
Review Questions 350

Lesson 11: Database Concepts

Lesson Objectives 353
What is Data? 353
What is a Database? 353
    Spreadsheet Databases 353
    Relational Database Management Systems (RDBMS) 354
    Multiple, Related Tables 354
Database Tables 356
    Table Metadata 356
    Primary Key 357
    Table Relationships – Foreign Keys 360
    Database Metadata (Database Schema) 362
Database Queries 363
Database Forms 364
Where Are Databases Used? 366
    Databases and Web Sites 366
    Have I Used Queries on the Web? 367
    Have I Used Forms on the Web? 368
Lesson Summary 369
Review Questions 369

Lesson 12: Using Microsoft PowerPoint

Lesson Objectives 371
What is PowerPoint? 371
    What Does a Presentation Include? 371
    Looking at the Edit Screen 372
Working with Presentations 373
    Creating Presentations 373
    Saving a Presentation 375
    Closing a Presentation 376
    Opening a Presentation 377
    Displaying Information in the Presentation 377
Managing the Slides 381
    Inserting New Slides 381
    Changing the Slide Layout 382
    Changing the Slide Background 382
    Deleting Slides 382
    Rearranging the Slides 383
Managing Slide Objects 385
    Using Select versus Edit Mode 385
    Manipulating Text 386
    Inserting Pictures 388
    Inserting Media Objects 390
Animating Objects 392
    Customizing the Animation 393
    Applying Slide Transitions 394
Setting up Slide Shows 397
    Viewing the Slide Show 398
Sharing the Presentation 400
    Using the Share Tab 400
    Using the Export Tab 401
    Create Handouts in Word 402
    Publishing the Presentation 402
    Printing the Slides 403
Lesson Summary 408
Review Questions 409

Lesson 13: Looking at the Internet

Lesson Objectives 411
A Connected Community 411
Introducing the Internet 412
    Backbone 412
    Hardware 412
    Public Networks 413
    Private Networks 413
    Specifying a Network Connection Type 414

Finding Computers on the Internet 415
    IP Address Review 415
    DNS 415
Understanding Domain Names 416
    DNS Domain Levels 417
Understanding URLs 418
    Protocol Identifier 418
    Path and Filenames in URLs 419
What is the World Wide Web? 419
What Exactly is a Web Page? 419
    HTML 420
    CSS 420
    Hyperlinks 421
Meet the Browser! 422
    Getting Where You Want to Go – The Address Bar 422
    Browser Scroll Bars 423
    Browser Windows (Tabs) 424
    Hyperlinks in the Browser 425
    Popular Browsers 425
Browser Navigation Tools 429
    Back, Forward, and Refresh Buttons 429
    Home Page and Start Page 429
    Settings 430
Browser Functions and Features 433
    Uploading and Downloading 433
    Searching from the Address Bar 435
    Favorites/Bookmarks 437
Browser Preferences and Settings 443
    Handling Pop-ups 443
    Cookies 444
    AutoFill/AutoComplete 446
    Browser Cache 446
    Browsing History 447
    Private Browsing 449
Extending Browser Functionality 450
    Plug-ins/Add-ons 450
    In-browser Apps 450
Web Standards 451
    Site Home Page 451
    Navigation Bar 453
    Widgets 453
    "Standard" Pages 454
    Using a Mouse on the Web 454
Lesson Summary 456
Review Questions 456

Lesson 14: Managing Media Literacy

Lesson Objectives 459
Searching for Information 459
Using Search Engine Technology 460
    Using Search Engines 461
    Narrowing the Search Results 463
    Searching Social Media Sites 464
Researching Information 469
    Validating Resources 471
Understanding Copyrights Issues 474
    Intellectual Property 474
    Copyright 475
    Licensing 476
    Piracy 478
    Censorship and Filtering 478
    Plagiarism 479
Lesson Summary 481
Review Questions 481

Lesson 15: Digital Communication

Lesson Objectives 483
Digital Communication Technologies 483
    Real-Time (Synchronous) and Delayed (Asynchronous) Communications ... 483
Asynchronous Communications Tools 484
    Electronic Mail (Email) 484
    SMS Text Messages 484
Real-Time Communication Technologies 486
    Phone Calls 487
    Conference Calling 489
    WebEx 489
Skype – More than Just IM 490
    Adjusting Your Status 491
    Managing Your Skype Profile 492
    Group Conversations 495
Checking Out Google Hangouts 499
Online Conferencing 500
    VoIP Conferencing 500
    Video Conferencing 505
Collaboration Tools 508
    Office 365 508
    SharePoint 509
    Skype for Business 510
Distance Learning Technologies 512
Streaming 512
    Business Applications 513
Lesson Summary 514
Review Questions 514

Lesson 16: Understanding Email, Contacts, and Calendaring

Lesson Objectives 517

Working with Email 517

Using an Email Program 518

    Creating New Messages 520

    Receiving and Replying to Messages 523

    Using Signatures 527

    Working with Attachments 528

    Managing Spam 531

    Archiving Messages 533

    Using Contacts 533

Using the Gmail Calendar 536

    Creating an Appointment 537

    Working with Multiple Calendars 539

Lesson Summary 545

Review Questions 545

Lesson 17: Your Life Online

Lesson Objectives 547

We Are Social Beings 547

    How Do We Share Information? 547

Social Media Networks 549

    Building the Network 550

    Popular Social Media Networks 551

Open vs Closed Social Media Networks 551

    Advantages of Closed Networks 552

Taking a Look at LinkedIn 553

    Creating a LinkedIn Account 554

    Creating Your LinkedIn Profile 554

    Inviting Connections 558

Managing Your Digital Identity 559

    Digital Footprints 559

    Why Is Your Digital Identity Important? 560

    Personal Identity and Professional Identity 561

Online Behavior 562

    Cyber Bullying 562

Computers and Your Health 563

    Coping with Change 563

    Disengaging 564

    Ergonomic Best Practices 565

Lesson Summary 567

Review Questions 567

Appendices

Appendix A: Courseware Mapping .... A 2

Appendix B: Glossary of Terms .... A 8

Appendix C: Index .... A 13

Course Description

This courseware is designed to illustrate what it means to be digitally literate, and to demonstrate what can be accomplished using a computer. The participant will progress to using popular software application programs to process typical documents found in a business or school environment. Participants are also introduced to what the Internet is and what makes it so popular for communicating and sharing information with others.

This courseware is targeted towards people who are new to computers or who have had limited exposure to a computer prior to taking this course. The intent of this courseware is to impart knowledge and skill sets that a participant can apply to tasks he/she may want to perform using a computing device.

Note: To recognize some of the components that make up a computer, it is preferable to have access to these actual components, wherever possible.

Course Series

This courseware is a composite of three different modules targeting specific skill sets:

- Computing Fundamentals
- Key Applications
- Living Online

The IC^3 Global Standard 5 (GS5) courseware contains exercises that students can use to learn each of the topics and features discussed.

Teacher Resources are available and are produced specifically to assist a teacher in preparing to deliver the course using the CCI materials. Contact your coordinator or administrator, or call your CCI Account Manager for information on how to access these resources.

Course Prerequisites

This courseware was designed to provide the essential skills for computer literacy, using application programs commonly found in school and business environments. It is intended for those who have not used a web browser, word processor, spreadsheet, presentation, database or email program previously, or for those who have minimal experience. Some familiarity with using a mouse and keyboard can be helpful.

System Requirements

This courseware was developed using specific software and hardware configurations. In order to complete this courseware, you will require the following minimum requirements:

Hardware Requirements

- 1GHz or faster 32-bit (x86) or 64-bit (x64) processor
- 4GB RAM
- DirectX 10 or later graphics card with WDDM 1.0 driver
- 1280 800 screen resolution
- A hard drive 1GB of free space
- Ethernet port or wireless adapter for Internet access

Note: Internet access is required to perform many of the hands-on exercises.

- Mouse or other compatible pointing device
- 101 enhanced keyboard
- A headset with a microphone for each student for performing conference call and video conferencing exercises
- An integrated (or connected) web cam for each student for performing video conferencing exercises
- Printer (must have access rights to print)

Software Requirements

- Microsoft® Windows 10 Professional (Note: Each student should have a user account with administrative privileges or access to an account name and password that will supply sufficient rights for installing software and adjusting hardware settings.)
- Microsoft® Office 2016 Professional
- Windows® Internet Explorer 11.0, and Microsoft Edge (Note: Google Chrome will be installed as part of Lesson 5.)

The objectives outlined in each lesson can be achieved by properly using the material and exercises in this courseware, and by paying close attention to your teacher. You should not hesitate to ask questions if you have problems in working through the material. To help you understand how some tasks or actions are performed in a business environment, CCI builds many of the exercises around a fictional company named Tolano.

All software programs used in this courseware are large and powerful programs, with more features than you can master in a single course. This courseware presents a tremendous amount of material in a simple, easy-to-learn format. You should read ahead during the course; you should also reread regularly. This will increase your retention of important concepts and skills, and will help you cope with the size and power of these programs as you continue to learn.

Classroom Setup

The explanations in this courseware are based on the default settings established during the installation of the Microsoft Windows 10 and Microsoft Office 2016 programs on a networked computer. Your computer (or the computers in the classroom lab) may be configured differently. If so, please check with your teacher (where applicable), or consult the appropriate User's Guide to change the setup.

If you are using another version of Word, Excel, or PowerPoint, or a different office suite such as Open Office or Google Docs, you will find that all of the concepts are the same; there may however be differences in some of the steps required to accomplish the task.

To assist with the learning process, CCI has designed exercises for a variety of business and personal activities. All names of people referenced in the exercises are fictional and created for the purpose of the CCI Learning Solutions only.

Course Design

This courseware was developed for instructor-led training and will assist you during class. Together with comprehensive instructional text and objectives checklists, this courseware provides easy-to-follow hands-on lab exercises and a glossary of course-specific terms.

This course book is organized in the following manner:

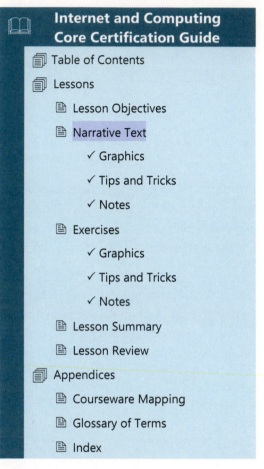

When you return to your home or office, you will find this course book to be a valuable resource for reviewing exercises and applying the skills you have learned. Each lesson concludes with questions that review the material. Lesson review questions are provided as a study resource only and in no way guarantee a passing score on a certification exam. Appendices in the back of this course book provide additional information.

Course Objectives
Computing Fundamentals

The Computing Fundamentals exam covers subjects needed for a foundational understanding of computing, including knowledge and use of computer hardware, software, and operating systems. In this module you will:

- Learn about the features and functions of modern operating systems and access various operating system features and settings.
- Examine different types of computers and learn about various types of computer hardware.
- Learn about connectors and ports.
- Learn about telephone, data, and cellular networks and about service subscription and contract requirements.
- Learn how to configure and use voice mail and how to manage mobile data usage.
- Use Windows File Explorer to find, move, open, and manage files; and navigate a directory and follow a path.
- Learn about various ways to share files with other users.
- Install and configure software and Windows apps.
- Use messaging applications.
- Create and use cloud accounts.
- Identify the need for security and describe risks presented by malware, social engineering, and phishing exploits.
- Learn methods for protecting yourself against risks.
- Understand why, how, and when to back up your data.
- Learn basic troubleshooting techniques.

Key Applications

The Key Applications exam includes questions covering three applications (word processing, spreadsheet, and presentation,) and includes questions on common features of all applications and questions on basic database concepts and uses. In this module you will:

- Learn about a wide variety of apps and applications and identify which types are best suited for particular tasks.
- Use an app store and install, delete, and recover apps.
- Examine the common features shared between the applications in Microsoft Office 2016 and explore basic techniques for working in an Office application.
- Learn some of the basic skills required to create simple documents (including letters, reports, and a brochure) using Word.
- Be introduced to the basic skills for working with a spreadsheet application, including how to enter and format text and formulas, navigate and manage worksheets, filter and sort data, create and modify charts and set printing options.
- Learn basic database concepts and learn how databases are used on the World Wide Web.
- Learn basic skills for working with an application designed to manage presentations, set up presentations, and create and edit slides that include text, images, charts, tables, or multimedia.

Living Online

The Living Online exam covers aspects of working in a networked environment and on the Internet. The exam includes questions on basic knowledge of the Internet, skills in specific applications such as electronic mail software and web browsers, skills required to find and evaluate information, and understanding issues related to using the Internet being at work, home or school. In the module you will:

- Learn about the nature of the Internet and about the role and function of web browsers

- Learn about how web sites are organized, identify common web page elements, and learn how to perform basic tasks using a web browser.

- Conduct research and evaluate the information you find on the Internet.

- Learn about and use various digital communication technologies

- Use electronic mail and calendaring and work with contacts.

- Examine the practices of good digital citizenship and online safety, and learn to manage your online identity.

- Recognize and learn to avoid health risks associated with computing.

Conventions and Graphics

The following conventions are used in CCI learning materials.

File Names or Folder Names	File names or database field names are indicated in *italic* font style.
Exercise Text	Content to be entered by the student during an exercise appears in `Consolas` font.
Procedures	Procedures and commands you are instructed to activate are indicated in **bold** font style.
Features or Command Options	Menu options and features are listed in the left hand column and corresponding descriptions are in the right hand column.

Numbered objective from the IC3 GS5 exam being covered in the topic is indicated in bold text. Refer to the Appendix for a complete listing of exam objectives.

Notes and **Tips** point out exceptions or special circumstances that you may find when working with a particular procedure, when there may be another way to perform a task, or as a reminder on how to complete the task.

Exercise

Exercise graphics signal the start of step-by-step, hands-on exercises or other activities.

Lesson 1: Operating Systems

Lesson Objectives

In this lesson, you will learn about the features and functions of modern operating systems. You will also learn how to start the computer and how to access various features of the operating system. Upon completion of this lesson, you will be familiar with:

- ☐ the function of an operating system
- ☐ popular desktop operating systems
- ☐ user accounts and profiles
- ☐ power on and power off procedures
- ☐ power options
- ☐ using the Start button
- ☐ navigating the Windows Desktop

- ☐ using the taskbar
- ☐ accessing the Settings app
- ☐ accessing the Control Panel
- ☐ customizing the Windows Desktop
- ☐ the features of mobile operating systems
- ☐ operating system updates

What is an Operating System?

Throughout this course, you will learn about using computers. A computer is essentially a collection of electrical and mechanical parts referred to as *hardware*. Each hardware part performs its own function, and in order for all the parts to work together, they must be able to communicate. Instead of communicating directly with one another, the various components communicate via an operating system.

- The *operating system* (or OS) is a computer program.

- A *program* is a sequence of instructions that guides the computer through the performance of a specific task or sequence of tasks.

- The individual lines of instruction are referred to as *code*.

- The term *software* refers to any program that makes a computer run – including operating systems and application programs.

Note: Software developers write source code for their programs in a human-readable format. In order to prepare a program to be installed and used on a computer, the source code is converted into an executable format through a process called *compiling*. Compiling changes source code into machine code.

Every computer requires an operating system in order to function. Think of an operating system as the central manager of communication, coordination, and control.

Application programs, on the other hand, allow you to be productive – to create documents or complete specific tasks such as creating a budget, removing red-eye from a photograph, searching the Internet or scheduling a meeting.

Application programs use the operating system to control the hardware functions of the computer, and you, as a computer user, interact with the operating system whenever you log on to the computer, or type on the keyboard, tap on a touchscreen, or use an application program such as an email program or a word processor.

It works like this:

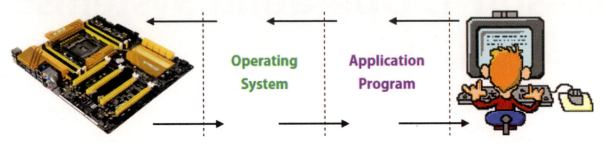

As you work in an application program, the program interacts with the operating system behind the scenes.

The operating system:

- manages hardware devices, and
- controls communication among hardware devices, and
- controls communication between application programs and hardware devices, and
- manages files stored on the computer.

Evolution of the Modern OS Interface

Since the early days of personal computing, operating systems have evolved from simple monochrome text screens to full-color point-and-click (or tap) interfaces.

An *interface* is a point where two systems (or people, or networks, or devices) meet and exchange information. Anytime you use a computer, join a network, or plug in a device, you communicate with it through an interface.

Today's modern operating systems communicate with you through a graphical user interface (GUI), or "gooey." A *GUI* lets you use menus and clickable buttons or icons to start programs, move files, or perform other tasks. This makes it easy for users to work with the operating system and get things done.

Proprietary and Open-Source Operating Systems

Software is sold and/or distributed with a particular type of software license. When you purchase a program, you are purchasing the right to use it. The ways in which you can legally use it are defined by the license that comes with it.

Proprietary Software

Most commercial software programs are proprietary. That is, they are owned by an individual or a company, usually the person or company that created it. The owner sells an executable copy of the software to users for use on their own systems, and includes a license with the program. The owner also controls how the software can be used, if and how the source code can be inspected and/or modified, and under which conditions (if any) it can be redistributed.

Additionally, most commercial software is closed-source. The software is released only in a compiled form and the source code is not released or made available. (However, sometimes vendors will release sections of the source code to third-party developers who create enhancement routines or add-ons.)

When you install software you must agree to the terms of the end user license agreement (*EULA*). In most cases the license agreement is quite restrictive. For example, the license determines the number of systems on which you can install the software, and it usually prohibits you from copying and distributing the software to other users. You are also restricted from attempting to de-compile or reverse-engineer the code back into a human-readable format. You are restricted from making changes of any kind to the software.

All versions (including mobile versions) and editions of Windows, Mac OS X and UNIX are proprietary.

Open-Source Software

In contrast to the restrictive licensing terms of proprietary programs, an open-source software license makes the source code of the software freely available. Users are permitted to study, change, and distribute the software to anyone for any purpose.

Most open-source software is distributed freely without charge, although open-source software does not necessarily need to be free. It is considered open-source because the source code is freely available.

Linux, FreeBSD, Open BSD, and ReactOS are examples of open-source operating systems. Mobile operating systems based on Linux (for example, various versions of Android) are open-source, but are often bundled with a substantial amount of proprietary software as well.

Desktop Operating Systems

There are many types of operating systems in wide use today because there are many types of devices. In this course, you will focus on desktop operating systems and mobile operating systems.

A desktop operating system is one that is used on desktop and laptop computers. A desktop operating system is a large and robust program. It offers many features, and provides a great deal of power and control over how the computer runs.

Operating System Versions and Editions

Operating systems are released in various versions and editions. An operating system version refers to the specific code base that was used to develop the operating system. For example, Windows 7 and Windows 8 are different versions of the Windows operating system. An operating system edition determines which features are available. For example, various versions of the Windows operating system are released in varying editions such as Home, Professional, or Enterprise.

Popular Desktop Operating Systems

Today, you can choose from several operating systems. You might like Windows, while your friend prefers Mac OS X, and your teacher or colleague likes Linux.

Almost all operating systems include a *Desktop* which is the screen that opens once you log on and are ready to begin working. Operating system Desktops usually include colorful backgrounds, icons or buttons for accessing commands, and a status bar to show which programs are open and running. The Desktop is the central place from which a user interacts with the computer.

Some of the most popular operating systems include:

Windows

Windows operating systems are designed by Microsoft. Recent versions are:

- Microsoft Windows 10
- Microsoft Windows 8
- Microsoft Windows 7

The Windows 8 and Windows 7 Desktops are shown here:

You will see the Windows 10 Desktop later in this lesson.

Mac OS X

Mac OS X is designed by Apple for Macintosh computers. Recent versions are:

- Version 10.9 – Maverick
- Version 10.10 – Yosemite
- Version 10.11 – El Capitan

The Mac OS X Yosemite and Maverick Desktops are shown here:

Linux

Linux is a free and open-source operating system. You can find Linux installed on supercomputers – such as those used by Google and NASA. But it is also installed on millions of home and business computers. Because anyone who uses Linux can modify it, it is very popular with programmers.

Versions of Linux are called distributions – or "distros" for short. Some popular distros are:

- Knoppix
- Ubuntu
- Gentoo

The Knoppix and Ubuntu Desktops are shown here:

UNIX

UNIX was one of the earliest operating systems and was first designed for use on large mainframe computers and servers. Modern versions are available for desktop systems, and include a GUI; however, the GUI is separate from the operating system.

Common Operating System Features

Objective 1-3.5

No matter which operating system you use, certain features are common among all of them.

User Accounts

Accounts
Your accounts, email,
sync, work, other users

In addition to managing communication, devices, and file storage, an operating system keeps track of who is using the computer. This is accomplished through user accounts.

You can think of an account as a special area on the computer where you can work and keep your files, separate from other users. For example, an entire family can share a Windows PC, and each family member would have a distinct account with his or her own user name, password, and account settings.

An account name (and usually a password) is associated with each account. Before you can run programs, open files or use the computer to accomplish any type of work, you must log on using a valid user account.

When you first power on a Windows computer, one of two things can happen:

- If you are the only user on the computer and your user account does not require a password, then you will be automatically logged on to your account and the Desktop appears.

- If you are using a computer on which multiple user accounts have been set up, or if your user account requires a password, then Windows displays an icon and account name for each user account and you must log on to your account by clicking your account icon and entering your password.

Account Types

Operating systems allow for the creation of different types of user accounts. In Windows, there are two readily-available account types: standard user accounts and administrator accounts.

Administrator account	Enables you to make changes to the system that will affect other users. Administrators can change security settings, install and uninstall software and hardware, and create or make changes to other user accounts on the system.
Standard user account	Enables you to use most of the capabilities of the computer. You can use most programs that are installed on the computer and change settings that affect your user account. However, you can't install or uninstall some software and hardware, you can't delete files that are required for the computer to work, you can't access other users' files stored on the computer, and you can't change settings that affect other users or the security of the computer.

Each type of account has a specific level of permission associated with it. *Permissions* are rules associated with objects on a computer, such as files, folders and settings. Permissions determine whether you can access an object and what you can do with it. Everyone has permission to read/write (create, edit, view or print) files for their own account; however, only someone with an Administrator account can see files created by other users on the system.

An administrator account is created automatically when Windows is installed on a computer. If you are using your own computer, the account you create the first time you start up your computer is an administrator account. You can then create additional administrator and standard user accounts.

If you use a computer at your school or office, the system administrator will likely have already created an account for you. Your account may be an administrator account or a standard user account.

Note: Computers you use in a school, library, or workplace are usually part of a computer domain. A *domain* is a network of computer systems that are controlled by a network administrator. Your ability to perform certain tasks (such as installing software, changing your password, or installing updates) on a domain system can be tightly controlled by the administrator, regardless of your account type.

Account Options

It is considered best practice to protect your computer and documents if you are going to be away from the system for any length of time. Two recommended practices are signing out of your account, or locking your computer whenever you are away so that other people passing by cannot see or access any of your files.

You can perform either of these tasks by clicking your user icon in the Start menu, and then selecting the desired option.

Change account settings

Lock

Sign out

If you select Lock, Windows displays an image on the monitor and you must enter the logon password before you can resume working. Locking the system is different than logging off (signing out). When you lock the system, all your programs and files remain open and ready so you can resume working quickly.

If you select Sign out, all your programs and files are closed and you return to the Windows log on screen.

User Profiles

Each user account is associated with a profile. A *profile* is a collection of settings that make the computer look and function in a particular manner. A profile includes settings for elements such as the Desktop background, lock screen, screen saver, pointer preferences, date and time format, and so on.

When you log on to a user account, the settings in the associated profile are loaded and affect what is displayed on the Desktop.

When you make customizations, such as changing the Desktop background or applying a sound scheme, those changes are saved in your profile so that the next time you log on to your account, all of your customizations are in effect. You will customize your profile later in this lesson.

Built-In Power Off Procedures

Powering on and powering off a computer are two different processes. When you first power on (start) the computer, you press the power button. The computer runs a set of self-diagnostic programs to ensure that critical hardware is working properly, and then it loads the operating system into memory. Once the operating system is loaded, you are either logged on to your account automatically or you log on manually.

Although you simply press the power button to turn the system on, you should never simply press the power button to turn the system off. You should always use the operating system's Power Off or Shut Down option. This option ensures that any changes you have made to the system are properly saved, and that any temporary files, which are no longer needed, are deleted.

Starting a Windows Computer

On many desktop computers, the power switch is located at the front or top of the system case. The most commonly used icon for a power button is shown here.

Do not try to feel for the power button the first time you want to start the computer – locate it visually.

1.   Turn on devices that are connected to the computer (such as the monitor, speakers and printer) first.

2.   Press the power button on the computer to turn it on.

The computer performs a start-up test and then loads the operating system files into memory. This process is also referred to as *booting*.

When the operating system is loaded, Windows will display either a Welcome screen followed by the Desktop, or a logon screen from which you must select your account (and perhaps enter your password). After you log on to your account, the Desktop displays.

Powering Off a Windows Computer

When you are done working, you should save your work, close any open programs, and then power off the system.

Each operating system includes built-in power-off procedures which you should use to ensure that files and programs are closed and that internal services are properly exited before the electrical power is cut off. In Windows 10, various options are presented in the Power menu.

Sleep
Shut down
Restart
⏻ Power

To properly power off a Windows 10 computer:

1.   Click the **Start** button then click **Power** to display the Power menu.

2.   In the Power menu, click **Shut down** to power off the system. The computer closes all files and programs, closes the operating system and turns off the power completely.

Note: In Linux, the power off options are named: halt, power off, reboot, and shutdown. In Mac OS X, the options are named: sleep, restart, and shut down.

Understanding Windows Power Options

Objective 1-2.6

Power options affect the way your computer uses energy. Because we are often called away from our computers for various periods of time which fall inside our "regular working hours," most operating systems provide options for reducing the amount of power the system uses. For example, if you take an hour for lunch, you can use one of the power options on your computer to conserve power without having to shut the system off.

Reducing power consumption is good for the environment, and it prolongs battery life on a system that is running on battery power.

Windows 10 provides several power options from which to choose. These options include:

Sleep	Clicking *Sleep* leaves the computer on, but puts it into a mode where it uses less power than when it is awake. The screen turns off and often the computer fan stops. Windows puts your work into memory. Sleep mode is similar to pausing a DVD movie. It is useful when you won't be using your computer for a short period of time.
	When you wake the computer, the screen will look exactly as it did when you put the system to sleep. On some systems you can wake the computer by moving the mouse or pressing a key on the keyboard; on others, you must press the Power button. On a desktop computer, the Sleep command may be listed as Standby.
Hibernate	This option is found on laptops only. When you click *Hibernate*, the computer writes your open files and programs to a storage location and then turns off the system. Hibernate mode uses no power. Hibernate mode is useful if you will not be using your laptop for an extended period of time, but you do not want to close your documents.
	When you press the power button on a laptop in hibernation, the system starts back up and puts your files and programs back into memory. You can start working again right where you left off.
	By default, the Hibernate option does not appear in the Power menu, but you can customize the operating system to include this option.
Shut Down	The computer closes all files and programs, closes the operating system and turns off the power.
Restart	Windows closes all open files and programs, exits the operating system and restarts the computer without turning off the power. Sometimes when a computer starts to behave strangely or seems to get "lost" or "stuck" restarting it will make it run properly again. Restarting clears the memory and reloads the operating system, but does not cause the computer to perform the start-up tests again.

Exercise 1-1: On, In, Out, and Off

In this exercise, you will turn on the computer to start the operating system. You will also log on to Windows and explore various power options. If you require assistance finding objects on the screen, ask your teacher for help. Navigating the Desktop will be covered in detail later in this lesson. For now, you will simply explore power options.

1. Identify where the power buttons are located on the computer and monitor.

2. Turn on the monitor, then press the power button to turn on the computer.

3. Watch the monitor to see the messages that display.

4. If a Windows logon screen appears, click the icon for your user account and enter your password to log on to Windows. When you have successfully logged on to Windows, the Desktop displays.

5. Click the **Start** button in the lower left corner of the Desktop to open the Start menu.

6. In the Start menu, click **Power** to view the power menu, then click **Sleep** to put the computer to sleep. The screen either goes dark or displays a picture or the log on screen.

7. Press a key on the keyboard or press the power button to wake the computer. Depending on how the computer has been set up, you may need to click the icon for your user account and/or enter your password to return to the Desktop; otherwise you will be returned to the Desktop immediately.

8. Click the **Start** button to open the Start menu.

9. Click **Power**, then click **Restart**. Windows shuts down and then starts again without performing the startup tests that run when you first power on the computer.

10. When the log on screen displays, click the icon for your user account and enter your password to access the Desktop.

11. Click the **Start** button, click your user icon at the top of the Start menu, then click **Sign out** to log out of Windows and display the log on screen.

12. Click the icon for your user account and enter your password to return to the Desktop.

13. Click the **Start** button, click **Power**, then click **Shut down** to power off the system.

14. Press the power button on the computer to start the system.

15. Log on to Windows.

Looking at the Windows 10 Desktop

The Windows Desktop is the main screen on which program windows, icons, menus, and dialog boxes appear.

Your Windows 10 Desktop should look similar to the following screen. You will notice several objects or icons on the Desktop: these vary from one system to another, depending on how the computer is configured.

The Desktop includes several types of objects that you use to move around and get work done.

Desktop icons	The "shortcuts" you can click to open frequently used programs, folders, or files.
Mouse pointer	The arrow that follows the movement of the mouse (or touchpad) and highlights icons on the screen when you point to them.
Start button	Click to start programs, open documents, find items on your computer, and get help. You also use the Start button to power down the system.
Taskbar	The long horizontal bar at the bottom of the screen that includes three main sections: the Start button and search box; the middle section (which displays the buttons for open programs and files); and the notification area (which includes a clock and icons that communicate the status of certain programs and settings). The taskbar is an integral part of Windows' multitasking feature.

Navigating Around the Desktop

Using a Pointing Device

You use a pointing device such as a mouse or the touchpad to move the mouse pointer:

- To select an item, move the mouse pointer (arrow) over top the item and then click the left mouse button once; this is called a single-click.

- To activate an item, point the arrow at the item and then press the left mouse button twice quickly; this is called a double-click.

- To display a shortcut menu with more options, point the arrow at the item and then click the right mouse button once; this is called a right-click.

Using the Keyboard

A number of features can be accessed through the keyboard. For example, press the WINDOWS button to open the Start menu, press ESC to cancel an action, or press TAB to move to the next field in a dialog box.

Using a Touch Screen

If you have a touch screen device, you can:

- Tap to open, select, or activate an item; similar to a single-click.

- Double-tap to open a file or folder; similar to a double-click.

- Press and hold (long press) to show information or open a short-cut menu; similar to a right-click.

Note: Windows 10 has been designed to work with touch screen devices as well as it works with a traditional mouse and keyboard, and provides the ability for the user to work in Tablet mode. In this course, however, you will use a mouse and keyboard.

Using the Start Button and Start Menu

To work in Windows 10, you begin at the Start menu. To open the Start menu, you can:

- Click the **Start** button, or

- Press the WINDOWS key.

The Windows 10 Start menu includes a classic pop-up menu on the left, and a panel of application shortcuts called "tiles" in the middle.

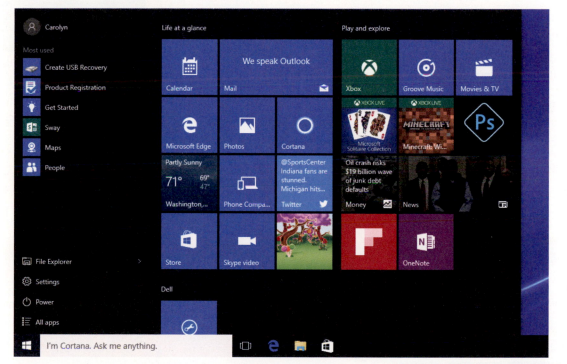

Your user account icon (and name) display at the top left of the Start menu. Click your user name to access commands to lock the screen, sign out, or change your account settings.

Along the left side of the Start menu are shortcuts to the most used and most common programs, apps, and settings. Click an item to launch the program or access the setting. Some items display a right-facing arrow. Click the arrow to open a sub-menu of application-specific tasks or items.

Click **All apps** at the bottom of the Start menu to see all your apps and programs.

Click an app or program from this panel to launch it. Some items display a down-facing arrow. Click the arrow to open a sub-menu of tools or options. To return to the main Start menu, click **Back** at the bottom of the All apps pane.

You can also right-click the Start button to display a shortcut menu to various commands and features.

In the middle of the Start menu, tiles represent apps and programs. The tiles are movable and sizable. You can drag new tiles in from the All apps pane. Click a tile to launch an app or a program. You can also right-click a tile or an item in the left pane to access additional options which allow you to pin or unpin the item in the Start menu or task bar.

About Apps and Application Programs

Both apps and application programs are software and both can be installed on various computing devices. An application program is software designed to perform a variety of functions, whereas an app is software designed to perform a single function.

Application programs are large and usually require a fair deal of system resources (such as RAM and processing power). They are designed to be used with a mouse and keyboard. Apps are small, and light-weight and are designed primarily for use on mobile touch-screen devices.

Windows 10 refers to application programs as "Desktop apps." For example, "OneNote 2016 Desktop app" refers to the installed application program, while "OneNote" refers to the app designed for the touch screen interface.

You will learn about apps and application programs throughout this course.

Search Box/Cortana

Just to the right of the Start button is the search box.

Search the web and Windows

Click in the search box and begin typing. Windows will display topics and file names that match what you type.

When you first use Windows 10 the search box may display a circle icon and the text "Ask me anything."

◯ Ask me anything

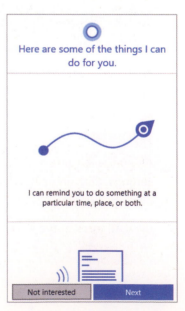

These elements are part of *Cortana*, the Windows 10 personal assistant. If you click in the box, the Cortana feature will open for initial setup. To use Cortana, you must sign into the system with a personal Microsoft account.

You can click **Not interested** to turn the feature off. For this course, you will not use Cortana.

Using the Taskbar

The *taskbar* appears at the bottom of the Windows Desktop (although you can move it to either side or to the top of the window).

It includes the items described below:

Taskbar buttons	A button displays in the taskbar for each open application program, for some built-in Windows applications (such as Microsoft Edge or File Explorer), and for any applications which you have "pinned" to the taskbar. Click a taskbar button to activate a program or window.
Task View	Task view is a new view in Windows 10 that shows small windows of all your running applications in the middle of the screen and displays a command for creating virtual Desktops.
Notification area	Displays the time and date and provides quick access to items such as the volume control or a wireless network connection. It can also display information about the status of the power level of a laptop battery or whether operating system updates are available. You can also control which icons are visible.
Action Center	Click this button to open the Windows Action Center.
Show Desktop	Point at this button to make all open windows transparent so you can see the Desktop for a moment, or click it to instantly minimize all open windows on the Desktop. You can restore all the windows to their previous state by clicking it again.

Task View

New in Windows 10, *Task View* shows small windows of your running applications and a New desktop icon.

You can click a window to bring that particular application to the front of your screen, or you can point the mouse pointer over a window to display a Close button ☒. Click the **Close** button to close the application.

You can also click **New desktop** to create a *virtual Desktop*. In computing, the word virtual refers to the way a particular component or environment appears to a user. For example, a virtual Desktop is a software implementation of a physical Desktop – it does not exist physically, but you can use it (and organize your work on it) as if it did exist physically.

Click the virtual Desktop to bring it front and center. You can launch different applications on this Desktop and then alternate between your open Desktops to keep your workspace uncluttered. You can create as many virtual Desktops as you like, and you can move applications between Desktops.

When you are finished working with a virtual Desktop, display Task View, point the mouse pointer over the Desktop you want to close to display a Close button.

Click, the **Close** button to close the Desktop.

Action Center

When you click the Action Center button in the notification area, the Windows 10 Action Center opens as a sidebar.

You can read and respond to (or clear) notifications, access system settings through the Settings app, or turn specific features such as Bluetooth or Airplane mode on or off. Appointments and alerts you set in Windows calendar also appear here.

The buttons that appear in the Action Center are called *Quick Actions*, and you can control which quick Action buttons display by configuring the notification settings.

Key Fact: You can also display the Action Center by pressing WINDOWS+A or by swiping in from the right on a touch screen.

Taskbar Buttons

When you open a program, an underlined button for that application appears in the taskbar as a visual clue that the program is running. If you point the mouse pointer over a taskbar button, Windows displays a preview window for each file that is open within that application.

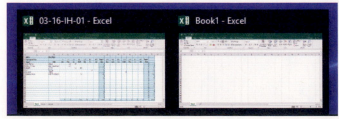

Exercise 1-2: Exploring the Start menu and Taskbar

In this exercise, you will explore areas of the Desktop, Start menu, and taskbar.

1. If necessary, start the computer and log into Windows.

2. When the Desktop appears, put your hand on the mouse and then slide the mouse along your desk and observe that the mouse pointer follows the movements you make with the mouse.

3. On the keyboard, press WINDOWS to open the Start menu.

4. On the keyboard, press ESC to close the Start menu.

5. Click the **Start** button to open the Start menu again.

6. Click in the search box. If the box displays elements of the Cortana personal assistant, click **Not interested**, then click the **Start** button again. Otherwise, proceed to Step 7.

7. In the search box, type: notepad. Notice that a list of possible matches for the term you typed displays at the top of the menu.

Best match

    Notepad
    Desktop app

Store >

    Notepad Classic

    ColorNote **Notepad** Notes

Photos >

    notepad.png

    notepad-window.png

Web >

    notepad

    notepad++

    notepad2

    notepad-plus-plus

    notepad online

    notepad free

notepad

8. At (or near) the top of the menu, click **Notepad Desktop app** to open the Notepad application window on the Desktop.

9. Click the **Close** button at the upper right corner of the Notepad window to close the application.

10. Click **Start**, then click **All apps** to display the All apps pane, then click **Calculator** to open the calculator app. Notice that the calculator displays inside its own window. All programs run inside their own dedicated windows. Notice that a button for the calculator app now displays in the taskbar.

11. In the taskbar, click the **File Explorer** button (it looks like a yellow file folder) to open a File Explorer window. You use File Explorer to view and manage files on your computer.

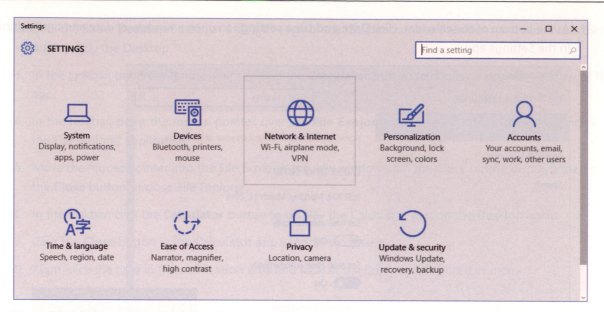

From this window, you can browse the categories or use the search box at the upper right corner to find what you are looking for, including advanced options on specific pages in the Control Panel.

Note: You can also right-click on the Desktop and click either **Display settings** or **Personalize** to open specific settings windows in the Settings app.

The Windows Control Panel

The Control Panel is the area in Windows where you can access features to customize settings for devices on your system.

You can access the Control Panel by:

- Right-clicking **Start**, then clicking **Control Panel** in the shortcut menu; or
- selecting an advanced feature in the Settings app.

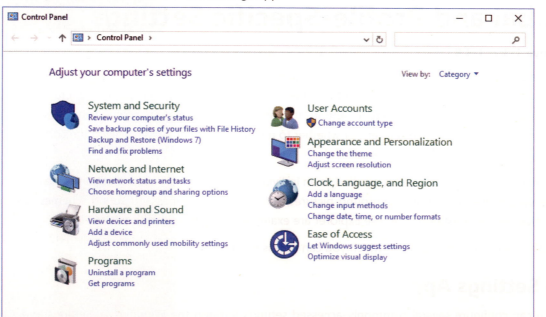

The default view for Control Panel topics is Category view. The categories are described below:

System and Security	Provides options for firewall settings, power options and file history (backups).
Network and Internet	Set up or modify how your system connects to a network or the Internet, and to share files with others.
Hardware and Sound	Set up or modify devices such as printers, speakers and monitors.
Programs	Provides access to system management tasks such as installing and uninstalling programs.
User Accounts	Provides options for setting the computer up to be used by more than one person.
Appearance and Personalization	Customize your screen with screen savers, desktop backgrounds, and so on.
Clock, Language, and Region	Change the format of dates, times, currency, or numbers to reflect regional standards or languages.
Ease of Access	Provides options for changing accessibility specifications, such as turning on voice recognition or altering visual displays.

Clicking a category opens a particular page or window in the Control Panel, and each screen provides links to other pages. Click various links to drill down to the command or feature you want to access.

Note that in the preceding figure, a small down-facing arrow displays to the right of the word Category. This arrow denotes that a *drop-down list* or drop-down menu is available. When you click the arrow, a list opens and drops down on the screen, allowing you to click an option.

You can use this drop-down menu to change the display in the Control Panel from Category to view either Large icons or Small icons. The Large icon view is shown in the following figure.

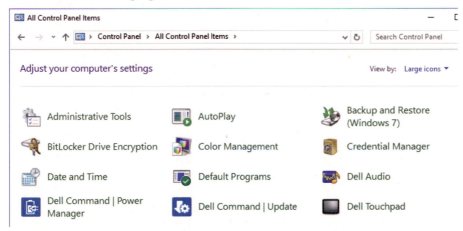

When you drill down to a page where you configure settings, you can use the various menu options on the page. The following figure shows a portion of the Power Options > System Settings page in the Control Panel. This figure features three other types of menu options used in Windows.

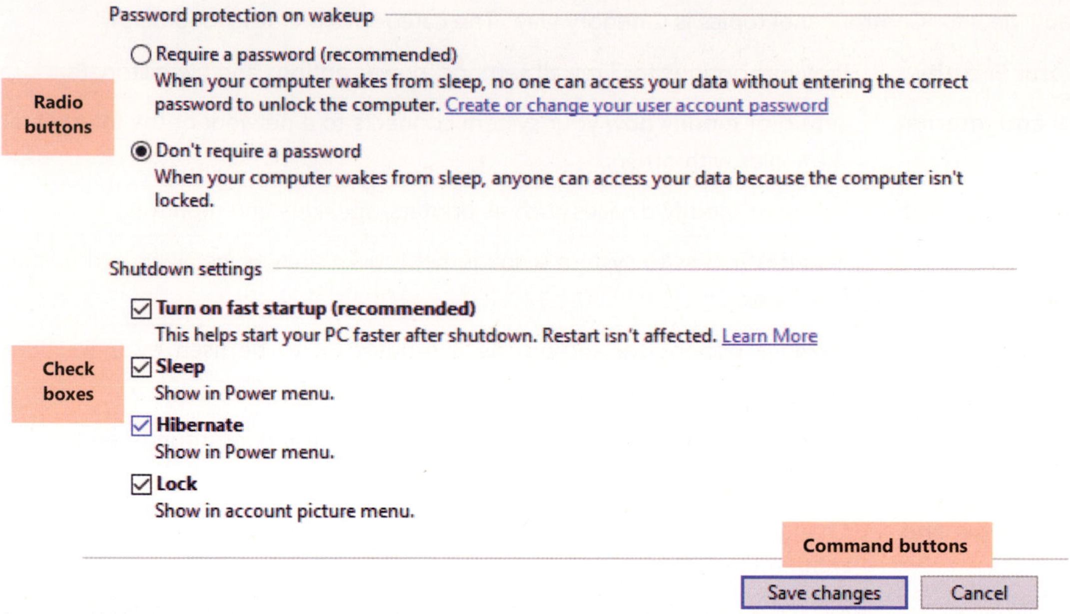

Password protection on wakeup

Radio buttons

○ Require a password (recommended)
When your computer wakes from sleep, no one can access your data without entering the correct password to unlock the computer. Create or change your user account password

⊙ Don't require a password
When your computer wakes from sleep, anyone can access your data because the computer isn't locked.

Shutdown settings

Check boxes

☑ **Turn on fast startup (recommended)**
This helps start your PC faster after shutdown. Restart isn't affected. Learn More

☑ **Sleep**
Show in Power menu.

☑ **Hibernate**
Show in Power menu.

☑ **Lock**
Show in account picture menu.

Command buttons

Save changes   Cancel

Radio buttons	Force a user to select one option out of a group of options. When you select a radio button, any previously selected radio button within the same group is automatically unselected.
Check boxes	Allow users to turn one or more option choices on or off.
Command buttons	Enable a user to either save (and apply) or abandon configuration setting choices. For example, after you select the options you want to enable, you would click Save changes to keep your changes, or you could click Cancel to discard the changes you made.

Dialog Boxes

In Windows, you often specify settings through dialog boxes. A *dialog box* is a window that displays on top of all other windows. It is designed to accept user input, and it remains open until you close it. The following figure shows a typical Windows dialog box. This dialog box includes several tabs on which you can specify settings. Notice that the tab shown in the figure includes radio buttons, check boxes and command buttons.

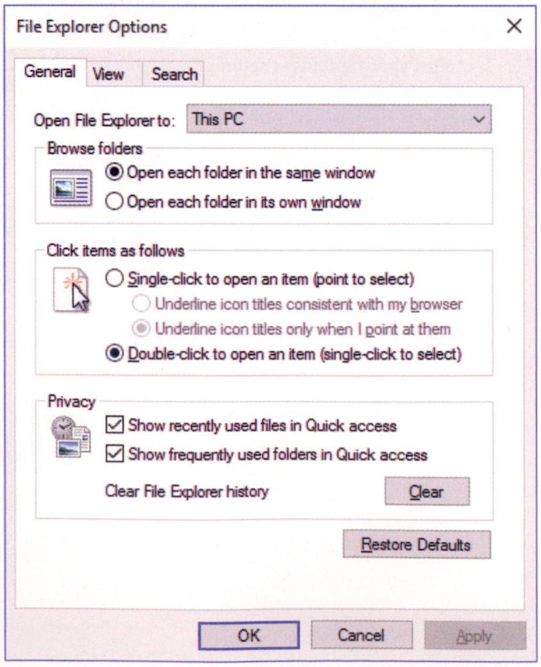

You cannot access any other items on the Desktop or in a program while a dialog box is open.

File Explorer Options   ✕

General | View | Search

Open File Explorer to: This PC   ⌄

Browse folders
⊙ Open each folder in the same window
○ Open each folder in its own window

Click items as follows
○ Single-click to open an item (point to select)
    ○ Underline icon titles consistent with my browser
    ⊙ Underline icon titles only when I point at them
⊙ Double-click to open an item (single-click to select)

Privacy
☑ Show recently used files in Quick access
☑ Show frequently used folders in Quick access

Clear File Explorer history   Clear

                            Restore Defaults

            OK   Cancel   Apply

Changing Global Settings

Objective 1-3.3

You can use the Control Panel or the Settings app to customize many operating system settings, including global settings.

Some features, specifically those that affect how the computer functions or those that can affect other users, may not display in the Control Panel if you are using a system that belongs to a company or school domain.

Note that even if you have the ability to change certain settings, the options may not be readily available in the Control Panel. However, you can make these options available by clicking a link that says **Change settings that are currently unavailable**.

🛡 Change settings that are currently unavailable

Changing the Screen Resolution

Screen resolution refers to the degree of clarity with which text and images appear. Screen resolution is measured by the number of pixels (or dots) the screen can accommodate, and the measurements are given as width by height. For example, a resolution of 1024 x 768 displays 1024 pixels horizontally on the screen and 768 pixels vertically.

Most displays work best at their maximum resolution setting, and most systems are automatically set to use the highest resolution setting. However, you have the ability to adjust the resolution. If you reduce the resolution (for example, if you change it from 1024 x 768 to 800 x 600), items displayed on the screen will appear bigger but you may not be able to see all the items on the screen.

The screen resolution is a global hardware setting (it affects all user accounts on the PC). You can access the resolution setting on the Advanced Display Settings window in the Settings app:

← Settings

⚙ **ADVANCED DISPLAY SETTINGS**

Identify   Detect   Connect to a wireless display

Resolution

| 1366 × 768 (Recommended) |
| 1360 × 768 |
| 1280 × 768 |
| 1280 × 720 |
| 1024 × 768 |
| 800 × 600 |

You can also access it from the Display > Screen Resolution page in the Control Panel.

Changing Password Protection

By default, Windows 10 systems are configured to require a user to re-enter the log on password when waking the system from sleep. However, you can reconfigure this option through the Accounts window of the Settings app.

Alternately, you can change this setting on the Power Options > System Settings page of the Control Panel.

Changing Power Management Options

Hibernate mode, which is available on laptops, is not included in the Power menu by default. You can however, specify to add this option to the Power menu through the Power Options > System Settings page in the Control Panel as well.

Exercise 1-3: Working with global settings

In this exercise, you will examine global settings that affect power options and password protection.

Note: Depending on how your system is configured, you may not have the ability to change certain settings. In such cases, simply read along.

1. Right-click **Start**, then click **Control Panel**.

2. At the top right, click the arrow for View by and click **Category**, if necessary. Then click **Hardware and Sound**.

3. Under Power Options, click **Change what the power buttons do**.

4. At the top of the window, click **Change settings that are currently unavailable**.

5. In the Password protection on wakeup section, click the **Don't require a password** radio button. Notice that when you click this option, the option above it (Require a password) becomes de-selected.

6. At the bottom of the window, in the Shutdown settings section, select the check box for **Hibernate**. (This option will be listed only if you are using a laptop. If you are using a desktop PC, skip to Step 7).

7. Click **Save changes**.

8. Close the Control Panel by clicking its **Close** button.

9. Click **Start** to open the Start menu.

10. Click **Power**. If you selected the Hibernate check box in Step 6, the Hibernate option now appears in the menu.

11. In the Power menu, click **Sleep** to put your PC to sleep.

12. Press the power button to wake your computer. Notice that you do not have to enter your password to resume working right where you left off.

Now, return your system to its original setting.

13. Right-click **Start**, then click **Control Panel**, **Hardware and Sound**.

14. Under Power Options, click **Change what the power buttons do**.

15. At the top of the window, click **Change settings that are currently unavailable**.

16. In the Password protection on wakeup section, click the **Require a password (recommended)** radio button.

17. At the bottom of the window, in the Shutdown settings section, clear the check box for **Hibernate**. If applicable.

18. Click **Save changes**, then close the Control Panel by clicking its **Close** button.

Customizing Profile-Specific Settings

Objective 1-3.3

Profile-specific settings allow you to customize the look and feel of your PC to make your working environment truly yours. Changes that you make to these settings are saved with your profile and do not affect other users on the same computer.

Customizing the Desktop Display

You can customize your Desktop by changing the background picture, configuring a screen saver, changing window colors, applying themes and configuring sounds.

To access these customization settings through the Settings app, use one of the following options:

- Click **Start**, **Settings**, **Personalization**; or
- right-click an empty area on the Desktop, then click **Personalize**

You can use the tabs within the Settings app window to make your customizations. A few of the links for advanced settings take you to an appropriate page in the Control Panel.

To access these customization settings directly through the Control Panel:

- Right-click **Start**, then click **Control Panel**, **Appearance and Personalization**, **Personalization**.

In Windows 10, a theme is a combination of pictures, colors and sounds. Each theme includes a Desktop background, a window border color, sounds and a screensaver.

My Themes	Themes you have customized, saved or downloaded. When you make changes to a theme, the new settings appear in this section as an unsaved theme.

Windows Default Themes	Themes that are included with Windows 10. The Windows 10 and Flower themes include a Desktop background slide show. You can go online to Microsoft.com to browse, download and install additional themes.
Installed Themes	Themes that are created by computer manufacturers or non-Microsoft providers. Not every system includes installed themes.
High Contrast Themes	Themes that are designed to improve computer performance or to make items easier to see. These themes do not include transparency effects.

Click any theme to select it. For the selected theme, you can change the window color, sounds and screen saver settings. Simply click the theme component at the bottom of the Personalization window to access the configuration settings.

To customize the Desktop:

- Use the **Desktop Background** option to display the Background tab of the Personalization window in the Settings app. (This window is shown in a preceding figure.) You can select one of the pictures shown in the window, or you can browse to a different location on your computer and select a saved picture to display on the Desktop.

- Use the **Color** option to display the Colors tab of the Personalization window in the Settings app. Click a color square to specify an accent color. You can also tell Windows to automatically select an accent color based on colors in your background picture.

- Use the **Sounds** option to apply a specific sound scheme to the theme. The sound scheme determines which sounds play when particular Windows events (such as closing a program or minimizing a window) occur.

- Use the **Screen Saver** option to select and apply a screen saver. If the screen saver includes configurable options, you can set those too.

Exercise 1-4: Customizing the Desktop

In this exercise, you will customize the Desktop and configure and apply a screen saver.

1. Close any open screen elements, if necessary, then right-click an empty area on the Desktop, and click **Personalize** in the shortcut menu to open the Background tab of the Personalization window in the Settings app. The Background setting should currently be set to Picture.

2. Click the drop-down arrow for the Background setting, then click **Solid color**. Notice that the display in the Preview area changes to reflect the current selection.

3. Click a color square in the Background colors section and observe the effects in the Preview area.

4. Display the Background drop-list again and click **Slideshow**. Notice that options for choosing a picture album and setting a time interval for changing the background picture become available in the window.

5. Display the Background drop-down list once more and click **Picture**.

6. In the Choose your picture section, click an image that you want to use as your Desktop background.

7. In the left pane of the window, click **Colors** to display the Colors tab. You can use this tab to select an accent color for the tiles and menu options that display in the Start menu.

8. Click a color square for the color you would like to use as your accent color.

9. Scroll to the bottom of the window to view the remaining options. You can specify to show your accent color on the Start button, taskbar, action center and in the title bars of individual windows. You can also specify whether to make the Start menu, taskbar and action center transparent.

10. In the left pane of the window, click **Lock screen**. The lock screen is the image that displays when you lock your system, or when you wake your computer and you require a password upon waking. The available settings are Windows Spotlight (which features changing images chosen by Microsoft), picture (which lets you select a picture that does not change), or slide show (which allows you to specify a folder on your computer where you have images that can be used for a lock screen slide show).

11. In the left pane of the window, click **Themes** to open the Themes tab, then in the right pane, click **Theme settings** to open the Personalization page in the Control Panel.

12. At the bottom of the page, click **Screen Saver** to open the Screen Saver Settings dialog box.

13. Display the Screen saver drop-down list, then click **Ribbons**. A preview of the Ribbons screen saver should display at the top of the dialog box.

14. Ensure that the Wait time is **1 minute**, click **Apply**, and then click **OK**.

15. Do not touch your mouse or keyboard for at least 1 minute so that you can view the screen saver.

16. Once the screen saver displays, move your mouse slightly and notice that the screen saver disappears.

17. Change the Wait time to **20 minutes**.

18. Close the Control Panel.

19. Close the Settings app.

Mobile Operating Systems

Smart phones (and some tablets) use mobile operating systems. Mobile operating systems are optimized for touch screen technology, small screen size, fast file transfer, and accessing cellular networks. Even though they run on small devices and are streamlined so that they do not use excessive battery power or system resources, they can accomplish an amazing array of tasks including phone calling, video calling, streaming audio and video, Internet browsing, texting, connecting to Wi-Fi, and pairing with Bluetooth devices. Some of the most widely-installed mobile operating systems are:

- **Android** – is from Google, is based on Linux and is open-source. Android releases are named for sweet confections; for example, version 4.3 is Jelly Bean, 4.4 is KitKat, 5.x is Lollipop, and 6.x is Marshmallow. Releases prior to 2.0 were used exclusively on mobile phones. Android 2.x releases are used on phones and some tablets. Android version 3.0 is used on tablets only. At the time of this writing, the current Android version is 6.0. It has the largest install base in the world and runs on phones manufactured by a wide variety of vendors including Samsung, HTC, Google, Sony, Motorola and LG.

- **iOS** (previously known as iPhone OS) – is from Apple. It is closed-source and proprietary and is derived from OS X. The Apple iPhone, iPod Touch, iPad, and second-generation Apple TV all use iOS. The more recent versions allow for the installation of third-party applications. In previous versions, you had to "jail break" your phone in order to install third-party apps. iOS smart phones are developed by Apple and manufactured primarily by Apple partners, such as Foxconn.

- **Windows 10 Mobile** (formerly called Windows Phone) – is from Microsoft. It is closed-source and proprietary and it is integrated with Microsoft services such as OneDrive and Office, Xbox Music, Xbox Video, Xbox Live and Bing. It is also integrated with non-Microsoft services such as Facebook and Google accounts. Most Windows phone devices are made by Nokia, HTC and Samsung.

- **BlackBerry 10** – is from BlackBerry and is closed-source and proprietary. It runs only on phones and tablets manufactured by BlackBerry.

Touch Screen Navigation on Mobile OS

Various phones and mobile operating systems recognize specific actions and gestures for navigating and performing tasks on a touch screen. Generally, you can use the following motions and gestures to interact with a smart phone or tablet:

- Tap (lightly tap items with your finger tip)
  - Tap keys on the onscreen keyboard to enter characters and text
  - Tap an item to select it
  - Tap an app icon to launch an application
- Touch and Hold (touch an item with your finger and maintain contact)
  - Touch and hold a widget to move
  - Touch and hold a field to display a pop-up menu of options
- Swipe or Slide (lightly drag your finger vertically or horizontally across the screen)
  - Swipe the screen to unlock a device
  - Swipe the screen to scroll through Home screen options or menu options

- Drag (touch and hold on an item, and then move it to a new location)
  - Drag a shortcut to add it to a Home screen
  - Drag a widget to place it in a new location on a Home screen
- Pinch and Spread (pinch the screen using your thumb and forefinger, or spread by moving your fingers apart)
  - Pinch or spread to zoom in or out while viewing a picture or a web page
  - Pinch or spread to zoom in or out while taking a picture

Power On / Off

To turn on a smart phone or tablet, press and hold the power button until the device starts up. On most phones the power key is also the lock key – you can press it to lock the device.

The first time you turn on your device, a welcome screen displays and you are guided through the basic steps required to set up your phone (such as choosing a default language, connecting to a Wi-Fi network, setting up accounts associated with the device, and so on).

To turn the phone off, press and hold the power/lock button until the device options menu displays, then tap the power off option. The figure to the right shows the options on an Android phone.

The Options menu allows you to put the device into one of several modes. You can turn the phone off, restart it, put it into airplane mode (in this mode the phone disconnects from all networks and turns off features for phone calling and Wi-Fi access) or put it into emergency mode (this mode is designed to conserve battery power by disabling apps and functions that use a lot of power; however, you can still send messages, use contacts, and make emergency calls.)

Lock Screen

Mobile operating systems on smart phones and tablets typically use a gesture-based lock screen. A lock screen on a mobile device is similar to the lock screen in Windows – this screen displays until the user performs the required gesture, or enters the correct information (similar to entering

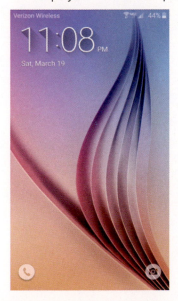

your user account password in Windows). The following figure shows an Android lock screen. Notice that there are no shortcut icons displayed on the lock screen; you must unlock it before you can access any of the device's features.

Lock screens protect your devices from unintended access (that is, you can't accidentally launch an app or make a call while the phone is in your pocket or purse), and can also protect your phone from illicit access by others. Until you unlock the phone, there is very little you can do with it.

By default, most phones lock automatically when the screen times out. You can also manually lock your phone at any time by pressing the power/lock key. Generally, a mobile operating system can use the following lock screen types:

- **Swipe** – unlock the phone by swiping the screen. This option provides no security.

- **Pattern** – you create a pattern by dragging your finger across a grid of dots, and you re-enter that pattern to unlock the phone. This is considered a medium-level security setting.

- **PIN** – set and then enter a personal identification number (PIN) of at least four digits. This option provides medium to high security.

- **Password** – you create a password for unlocking the screen. This option provides high security.

- **Fingerprint** – you can use fingerprint recognition to unlock the screen. This option provides medium to high security.

- **None** – you can set your phone to never use a lock screen.

If you choose one of the secure lock screen options, you can also specify whether to show or hide content and notifications on the lock screen.

It is always a good practice to lock your phone. Smart phones often contain a lot of private information, such as account numbers and electronic ID cards and more. Locking the phone can help prevent illicit use even if your phone is stolen.

The Home Screen

Instead of featuring a Desktop as the place from which to launch programs and perform other tasks, mobile operating systems are designed around a Home screen. (Some mobile operating systems refer to the Home screen as the Start screen.)

The Home screen displays links or shortcuts (in the form of icons or buttons) to applications, settings, features, and notifications, and generally display as much status information as possible within a very small space.

Home screens differ from one mobile operating system to the next, but for the most part the Home screen consists of a grid of shortcuts that can be arranged over multiple pages. The following figure shows the Home screen on an Android phone.

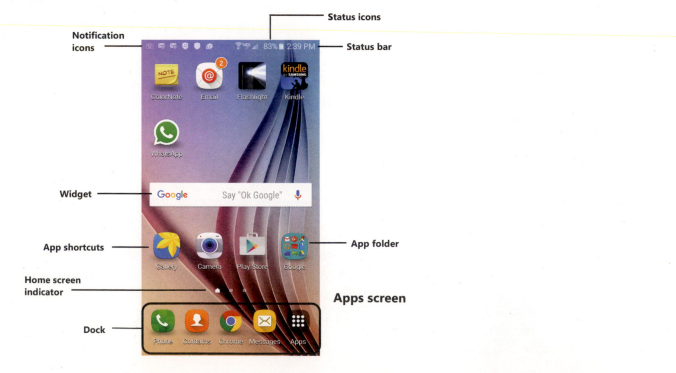

The Home screen shown in the preceding figure includes the following features:

Notification icons	Displays new messages and emails notification, information about available software updates, and so on.
Status icons	Displays information about the state of the phone hardware, including signal strength, battery level, the current time, and so on.
Status bar	Bar across the top of the phone that displays the status icons (on the right side) and notification icons (on the left side).
App shortcuts	Shortcuts to installed apps. Tap once to launch the app.
App folder	Several apps can be grouped into a folder.
Widget	Self-contained application (not a shortcut) that runs on the Home screen. There are widgets for clocks, calendars, Internet bookmarks, stock prices, weather, and even those that display the number of unread messages in your email Inbox.
Home screen indicator	Indicates which Home screen is currently displayed. In the preceding figure, there are three Home screen pages (indicated by the three icons). The first Home screen page is currently displayed. You can tap an indicator icon to move to that Home screen page, or swipe left or right to access the various Home screen pages.
Dock	An area along the bottom edge of the screen (in the figure, the dock contains icons for Phone, Contacts, Chrome, Messages, and Apps) which displays on all Home screen pages.
Apps screen	Allows quick access to all the installed apps, including the Settings app.

The Home screen is highly customizable; you can add wallpapers, apply themes, add apps and widgets, create folders, affect the display of the date and time, and so on.

The Mobile Settings App

The Settings app provides access to basic device settings for a smart phone or tablet. In most mobile operating systems, the icon for the Settings app is a gear (or set of gears). Tap the **Settings** app icon to display the main settings page, which allows you to configure several elements of the phone hardware and the operating system. The arrangement of the settings may differ from one mobile operating system to another, but for the most part you will find settings that affect:

- Wireless and cellular network connections
- Phone hardware (for example, sounds and notifications, storage, battery)
- Personalization settings (themes, wall paper, accounts, and so on)
- System settings (such as date and time, accessibility settings, OS version and system updates)

Notice that these are the same types of settings that you can configure in a desktop operating system.

Virtual Personal Assistants

Many mobile operating systems include virtual personal assistants, which are voice-activated services that use a natural language user interface to answer questions, make recommendations and perform actions by delegating requests to a set of web services. You speak natural language voice requests and commands in order to operate your smart phone and its apps.

For example, you can say, "OK Google, show me some maps of Mesa, Arizona." Or you can say, "Siri, remind me to take the turkey out of the freezer tonight at 8pm."

In order for the virtual assistants to work, they need access to items such as your location, contacts, voice input, browser history (a history of web sites you have visited), search history, calendar details, information from text messages and email messages, and so on. The first time you launch the assistant, you will be prompted to allow access. Note that most of these functions and services require a connection to either a Wi-Fi or a cellular network.

Popular virtual assistants include:

- **Siri** – from Apple. Siri is integrated with services such as Yelp, OpenTable, Google Maps, Taxi Magic, MovieTickets.com, and so on. Siri is turned on by default. To talk to Siri, hold the Home button until you hear a prompt and then ask Siri a question or ask Siri to perform a task, such as emailing or texting.

- **Google Now** – from Android. You activate Google Now by tapping the microphone in the Google widget or by saying, "Okay, Google." You can use Google Now to search the Internet, set alarms, make calls, take a picture, set reminders and more.

- **Cortana** – from Windows. You must turn Cortana on in order to use the feature. Once it is turned on, Cortana asks questions to learn what is important to you, and you can tell Cortana what name you want her to call you. Microsoft collects and uses information obtained through Cortana to improve personalized speech and speech recognition services.

- **BlackBerry Assistant** – from BlackBerry. You can tap the icon or activate the assistant by voice. BlackBerry Assistant displays icons for common tasks, and as you use it, it customizes which tasks it displays.

Operating System Updates

Objective 1-3.1

Operating systems are routinely updated for the purposes of increasing security, fixing bugs and adapting to new hardware and technology standards. Updates can be released in various forms. These include:

- **Patches** – a patch is a file of programming code that is inserted into an existing program to fix a known problem, or bug. Patches are designed to provide an immediate solution to a particular programming problem. Patches are intended to be only temporary solutions until problems can be permanently repaired.

- **Updates** – an update is a file or collection of software tools that resolves security issues and improves performance. Updates are released when necessary.

- **Service Packs** – a service pack is a collection of updates that is typically released after enough updates have accumulated to warrant the release. Service packs typically contain all previous updates, which include security patches, bug fixes, and new features.

Microsoft provides updates for the Windows operating system (and web browser) through a service called *Windows Updates*. The updates can be downloaded from the Windows Update web site. Apple provides updates in the Mac App Store and on the Apple Support Downloads site.

There are different kinds of updates. Security updates or critical updates protect against security vulnerabilities and viruses and spyware. Other updates correct errors that are not related to security, or they enhance functionality and improve performance.

Automatic Updating – Previous Versions of Windows

The Windows Update web site was first made live when Windows 95 was launched, and users would check the web site and manually download and install updates. Since that time, Microsoft has continually made the update process more streamlined and automated.

In Windows 7, Windows 8 and Windows 8.1, Windows Update is a service that continuously checks for updates automatically. Users can configure the service to run in one of three ways: You can automatically check for and install the latest updates. You can also set Windows Update to check for and download updates and then alert you that updates are ready to be installed. You can even set it not to check for updates at all. Users can also manually check for (and install) available updates at any time.

Update Categories

Users can configure the Windows Update service by specifying actions for different categories of updates. Updates are categorized based on their importance. There are three categories for updates:

- **Important** – these updates include security and critical updates.
- **Recommended** – these updates include software updates and new or improved features. Depending on how you set up Windows Updates, recommended updates can be shown together with important updates, or with optional updates.
- **Optional** – these updates include software that you can install manually, such as new or trial Microsoft software or optional device drivers from Microsoft partners.

Windows 7 and 8 users often configure their systems to automatically install critical updates and then decide whether to install feature updates on a case by case basis

Automatic Updating – Windows 10

In Windows 10, Windows Update automatically downloads and installs that latest updates, drivers and patches released by Microsoft.

On a Windows 10 system, Windows Update will automatically download and install important and critical updates by default. Optional updates and updates that require you to accept new terms of use are downloaded, and then Windows Update will let you know that these are ready to be installed.

Windows 10 does not allow you to selectively install updates; you can choose only whether your computer will reboot automatically to install updates when the system is inactive, or whether you prefer to be notified to schedule a reboot.

Manually Checking for Updates

Microsoft releases important updates every second Tuesday once per month. However, updates can be released at any time. You can manually check for and install these updates by opening the Settings app and clicking **Update & security**. Windows Update is the first tab in the Update & Security window.

The current status of the system is shown in the right pane. In the preceding figure, the current status is "Your device is up to date." Notice that the message also shows when Windows Update last checked for available updates.

Click **Check for updates** to have Windows Update check for, download, and install any available updates.

Exercise 1-5: Checking your update status

In this exercise, you will see when updates were last installed.

1. Click **Start**, then click **Settings** to open the Settings app.

2. Click the **Update & security** category.

3. Ensure that the Windows Update tab is selected in the left pane. When was the last time Windows Update checked for updates?

4. At this point, you could click **Check for updates** to have Windows Update check again for updates right now. In this exercise, however, we will not check for updates.

5. Close the Settings app.

Benefits and Drawbacks of Automatic Updating

Keeping your system updated ensures that you have the latest security schemes and technologies as well as the latest features.

However, not all updates are necessary, and at times, updates can cause unexpected conflicts and even failures. This is especially true in workplace or school settings where computer systems must often interact with old hardware or old applications.

Updating a Mobile Operating System

When mobile phone manufacturers create updates for their devices, they decide when those updates will be pushed out to their customer base. Users will see a notification on their devices that an update is available and ready to be installed. You can also check manually for updates.

To look for updates for your Android phone:

1.   Connect to Wi-Fi.

2.   Tap **Settings** (or if necessary, tap **Apps**, then tap **Settings**).

3.   Tap **System updates**.

4.   Tap **Check for new system update**.

To look for updates for your iPhone:

1.   Connect to Wi-Fi.

2.   Tap **Settings** > **General** > **Software Update**.

3.   Tap **Download and Install**.

Note: It is always a good idea to back up your personal data before installing an update. You will learn how to back up your mobile data in an upcoming lesson.

Lesson Summary

In this lesson, you learned about the features and functions of modern operating systems. You also learned how to start the computer and how to access various features of the operating system. You should now be familiar with:

- ☑ the function of an operating system
- ☑ popular desktop operating systems
- ☑ user accounts and profiles
- ☑ power on and power off procedures
- ☑ power options
- ☑ using the Start button
- ☑ navigating the Windows Desktop
- ☑ using the taskbar
- ☑ accessing the Settings app
- ☑ accessing the Control Panel
- ☑ customizing the Windows Desktop
- ☑ the features of mobile operating systems
- ☑ operating system updates

Review Questions

1.   The ability for different people to use the same computer is made possible through:

   a.   Open-source software

   b.   Desktop elements

   c.   User accounts

   d.   Settings app

2.   Which of the following is the collection of stored settings that ensure your customizations are in effect whenever you log on?

   a.   Your user profile

   b.   Your domain

   c.   Your lock screen

   d.   Your permission level

3.   Kelly has several documents open on her laptop, and is working concurrently in each one. She is about to leave for several hours to attend an off-site social function, but will return to her documents later in the day. Which option below would save the most power and still ensure that she can pick up right where she left off?

   a.   Hibernating the laptop.

   b.   Putting the laptop to sleep.

   c.   Shutting down the laptop.

   d.   Displaying the lock screen.

4. From which of the following areas in Windows 10 can you access Desktop customization settings?

    a. Desktop drop-down list   c. Calculator app

    b. Desktop Customization wizard   d. Control Panel

5. Which of the following Windows dialog box features allows you to select several options?

    a. Drop-down lists   c. Check boxes

    b. Radio buttons   d. Command buttons

6. Which of the following is an example of a global setting on a Windows system?

    a. Desktop background picture   c. Accent color

    b. Screen resolution   d. Screen saver

7. Which mobile operating system feature helps you avoid accidentally placing a call or taking a picture?

    a. Virtual personal assistant   c. Dock

    b. Pinch gesture   d. Lock screen

8. Which of the following is a function of the operating system?

    a. To compose and send email.

    b. To edit photographs and other high-resolution images.

    c. To control communication and manage files.

    d. All of these are operating system functions.

9. What is the best way to shut down a computer?

    a. Press the power button on the computer case.

    b. Click Start, Power, Shut down, then let the process complete.

    c. Press CTRL+ALT+DEL twice.

    d. Press ESC.

10. What is a service pack?

    a. A collection of software updates.

    b. A form of spyware.

    c. A power mode designed to provide emergency power during a power outage.

    d. A collection of Desktop backgrounds, sounds and themes that you can find online and then download and install on your system.

Lesson 2: Hardware

Lesson Objectives

In this lesson, you will look at different types of computers, learn about various types of computer hardware and examine ways to connect devices. On completion you should be familiar with:

- [ ] the relationships among hardware device drivers, firmware, and platforms
- [ ] common measurements used in computing
- [ ] standard internal computer components
- [ ] memory and storage
- [ ] identifying different types of computers
- [ ] keyboards, microphones and touch screens
- [ ] typical smart phone hardware
- [ ] Windows power plans
- [ ] connecting peripheral devices
- [ ] wireless connection technologies

What Makes Hardware Tick?

Objective 1-2.7, 1-2.8

As you learned in another lesson, a computer is a collection of electrical and mechanical parts referred to as hardware. Hardware are the pieces you can see and touch; hardware performs the physical work of the computer.

Software programs (including operating systems, application programs, and device drivers) control the hardware and make it useful, and within the device itself, firmware provides basic functionality.

Device Drivers

Operating systems use small programs called *device drivers* to communicate with installed hardware devices. Device drivers are software that allows your computer to communicate with and control the devices connected to it. Device drivers actually control the hardware, and the operating system communicates with the device drivers. Without drivers, devices will not function properly.

Device drivers are developed and released by hardware manufacturers. For any given piece of hardware, device drivers are developed for use on a specific operating system (and usually, a specific version of that operating system). Many devices include drivers for numerous operating systems. For example, if you purchase a printer, the printer most likely will ship with drivers for Windows and Mac OS X.

Some devices include drivers that will work on only one operating system. For example, a particular wireless network adapter may work on Windows 7, Windows 8, and Windows 8.1, but not support Mac OS X or Linux. Always read the product labeling before purchasing hardware to make sure that it is compatible with your operating system.

Operating systems generally include drivers for various devices that you may want to connect. These generic drivers will provide basic functionality, but in order to utilize the full features of a device, you should install the drivers that ship with the device, or download and install drivers from the manufacturer's web site. As you update your programs and your operating system over the course of time, you should check periodically for driver updates.

Firmware

Firmware is built-in programmable logic (software) that is embedded in a piece of hardware and controls how the device functions. Firmware is device-specific: it is developed for one particular model and release of a device.

The firmware on a smart phone, for example, is the code needed to control the phone hardware itself and run the base operating system. Firmware, however, is separate from the operating system. For example, you may be running the Android version 5.1.1 (Lollipop) mobile operating system on your phone, and be running firmware build number G920VVRU48OK7.

Smart phone manufacturers decide which phones will receive an update, and send the update to the various mobile network providers (for example, T-Mobile, Verizon, Vodafone, and so on) who sell their phones. The mobile provider can then add network-specific elements (such as branding or provider-specific features) and test the updates to ensure the best user experience. At the proper time (as determined by the mobile provider) the firmware update is pushed out to the devices that are part of their cellular network.

Different mobile providers push out firmware updates at different times. For example, if you and your Aunt Mary both own a Samsung Galaxy S5 and you are on the Verizon network and she is on the T-Mobile network, she might receive a firmware update in October, but you might not receive it until March.

Platform

Software applications (and mobile apps) run on a hardware device within an environment created by the operating system. This environment is referred to as the *platform*. The platform is an interface between the application (or app) and the operating system, and is what makes it possible for apps to run on a device.

Think of a platform as a foundation. The operating system (and device drivers and firmware) work together to control the basic functionality of the hardware. An application sits on top of this foundation (which is already in control of the hardware). The application performs its own special functions and then sends specific requests to the operating system to make sure that the necessary hardware tasks are performed. The functionality and syntax of these requests is built into the platform.

About the Numbers

Before we examine different types of hardware and how various devices compare to one another, you must understand how speed and storage capacity are measured.

All the measurements revolve around the binary digit or bit. A bit is the smallest unit of data a computer can understand. A bit can have one of two values: a 0 or a 1. Bits are grouped in sequences of 0s and 1s to represent data.

A group of eight bits is called a *byte*. The smallest unit of data humans can understand is represented by one alphanumeric character ('a' to 'z', or 0 to 9); an alphanumeric character requires a full byte of space in either the computer memory or a storage device.

Measuring Capacity

Storage capacity (that is, the amount of space available to store data either on disk or in memory) is measured in bytes. Because a byte represents such a small amount of data, these capacities are measured in thousands, millions, billions and trillions of bytes. Notice that a byte is indicated by a capital "B" in the abbreviation. The following table shows standard capacity measurements:

Measurement	Abbreviation	Equal to ...
Bit		A single binary digit
Byte	B	Eight bits
Kilobyte	KB	1,024 bytes (a thousand bytes)
Megabyte	MB	1,024 KB (a million bytes)
Gigabyte	GB	1,024 MB (a billion bytes)
Terabyte	TB	1,024 GB (a trillion bytes)
Petabyte	PB	1,024 GB (a quadrillion bytes)

Measuring Frequency

Inside every computer is at least one *microprocessor*. The microprocessor is a silicon chip that performs calculations and logical operations in the computer. The microprocessor is also referred to as the Central Processing Unit (CPU) or simply as the processor.

The CPU controls everything that happens in the computer. All the hardware, all the memory and all the software send information to and receive commands from the CPU.

Different CPUs process information and instructions at different speeds, and processor speed is measured in units called hertz. Silicon chips oscillate (or cycle) when electrical current passes through them. One hertz is equal to 1 cycle (or oscillation) per second. Because processor chips are very fast, this measurement is commonly used with the prefixes shown in the following table.

Measurement	Abbreviation	Multiplies by	Equal to ...
Hertz	Hz		1 cycle per second
Kilohertz	KHz	One thousand	1,000 cycles per second
Megahertz	MHz	One million	1,000,000 cycles per second
Gigahertz	GHz	One billion	1,000,000,000 cycle per second
Terahertz	THz	One trillion	1,000000,000,000 cycles per second

Faster processors give better performance than slower ones, so the higher the hertz, the more powerful the processor.

Most desktop systems available today include processors with speeds between 3 and 4 GHz. Most laptops include processors in the 2 GHz to 3GHz range. When you purchase a computer you will find the processor speed listed in the product description.

Measuring Bandwidth

Network connections (for example, those in a cellular network or in an IP network such as the Internet) move data from one location to another at a particular volume per unit of time. The measurement of this volume is called *bandwidth*, and it is expressed in bits per second (bps).

Synonyms for bandwidth include: capacity, bit rate, transfer speed, data transfer rate, and throughput. As with storage capacities, bandwidth is usually expressed in terms of thousands, millions, and even billions of bits per second, as shown in the following table.

Measurement	Equal to ...
bps	Bits per second
Kbps	Thousand bits per second
Mbps	Million bits per second
Gbps	Billion bits per second

The greater the bandwidth, the greater the capacity for transferring data, and the greater the network performance.

Exercise 2-1: Comparing measurements

For each selection of two measurements, circle the one that is larger.

932,000	bytes	or	3 MB
4,000,000	KB	or	2.8 GB
145,000	KB	or	200 MB
8,000,000,000	bytes	or	900 MB
3,020	MB	or	2 GB

The Basics – What's Inside?

Regardless of whether your computer is a large desktop tower or an ultra-portable tablet, the basic "anatomy" is the same. Every computer includes at least:

- a **system board** – this is a printed circuit board that contains most of the computer's circuitry and provides pathways for communication among all the components and connected devices. Internal components are seated on or otherwise attached to the system board. It also provides ports for connecting external devices, such as a mouse, speakers, a charger, and so on.

- one or more **processors** – the silicon chips that control the hardware components and manage the flow of data and instructions

- **input devices** – these allow you to send information to the computer. Examples include a keyboard, or touchscreen.

- **output devices** – these allow the computer to send information to you. Examples include a monitor, or a display screen.

- **storage devices** – these include memory chips and other storage media

- a **power supply** – converts AC current from a wall outlet into low-voltage DC power for the components. In portable devices, the DC power is stored in a rechargeable battery.

In the next several sections, you will examine some of these internal components.

Memory and Storage

Objective 1-2.2

In order to run programs and create and use files, a computer needs both memory and storage space. Every file used by a computer has a specific byte size, and there must be sufficient memory to "hold" the file when it is in use, and sufficient storage space to store the file when it is not in use.

Random Access Memory (RAM)w

For a computer to process information, it must include a certain amount of installed system memory. This type of memory is also called *Random Access Memory (RAM)*.

RAM is used for the temporary storage of information. Data and programs are read into memory from a storage location and then passed from memory to the CPU. Without RAM, a computer could not run programs or be used to create or edit files.

Note: RAM can store data only while the computer is on. Any information stored in RAM "vanishes" when the computer is turned off. When you close a program or save and close a file, the information is cleared from memory, and the memory becomes available to store other information.

Physically, memory consists of chips located inside the system unit. The number of memory chips in the computer and the capacity of each chip determine the amount of available memory.

How Much RAM Do You Need?

All software (including operating systems) requires RAM, and lists the minimum amount required to run the program successfully. Some programs use very little memory (for example, Notepad can run with less than 1MB of memory), while some programs require significant amounts. For example, Adobe Photoshop requires a minimum of 2GB (although 8GB is recommended); AutoCAD 2016 requires a minimum of 4GB (8GB is recommended).

Determining how much RAM you will need depends on which programs you want to run. The general rule of thumb is, the more RAM, the better.

Every time you launch a program or open a file, you use RAM. The more files or programs you have running, the more RAM you are using. Having sufficient (or better still, more than sufficient) memory keeps the system performing at top speed, and gives you the ability to run several application programs simultaneously, and/or to have multiple browser windows open without experiencing a slowdown in performance.

Storage

A computer loads software programs into RAM while you are working; however, the software programs must be stored on the computer when they are not in use. Additionally, any files that you create using a software program must also be stored if you want to be able to retrieve them in the future.

Local and Remote Storage Locations

Programs and user files are saved to storage devices. These devices can be internal (inside the computer) or external (storage devices attached to your computer). All internal storage devices, and all external devices attached directly to your computer are considered local storage locations.

You can also save your files to remote storage locations. Folders on other computers in your network, or folders in a cloud storage server are examples of remote locations.

How Much Storage Do You Need?

All software (including operating systems) requires storage space, and lists the minimum amount required to install the program. Some programs are quite large. Windows 10, for example can require up to 20GB of storage space. Determining how much space you need depends on which programs you want to install, and (perhaps more importantly) on the anticipated size and number of the user files you plan to store.

Different types of files require different amounts of storage space. For example, word processing documents (even long ones) are relatively small files. However, they increase in size if you add media such as images or audio/video. Image files can be large depending on the file format. Audio files can be quite large, and video files can be tremendous – for example, a 60-second video saved in Blu-ray format might be 420MB, while a 60-minute video could be 25GB.

If you plan to store and edit videos or high-resolution photographs on your system, you should be sure to purchase a system with sufficient storage, or you can quickly use up your internal storage space.

The more storage space you have, the less stringent you have to be regarding which files to save.

Common Storage Devices

Commonly-used storage devices include hard disks, external drives, flash drives and memory cards.

Hard Disks

The term "hard disk" and "hard drive" are used to refer to a central storage location inside a computer. Hard disks are the primary storage location for both data and programs. Software programs must be installed on a hard disk before you can use them. The operating system must also be installed on a hard disk.

Some computers use magnetic hard disk drives (HDDs), which include moving parts. A magnetic hard drive stores data on platters, which are metal or plastic disks that are coated with magnetic material. A motor spins the platters around a spindle, while read/write heads (small recording/playback devices) hover close to the surface of the platters and read or write data to the magnetic coating.

Some computers use solid state drives (SSDs), which do not have any moving parts. A solid state drive stores data on a set of interconnected flash memory chips that save the data even when the power is off.

Flash memory chips can be installed directly on the system board, installed on a card that plugs into the system board, or housed inside a 2.5-inch box that fits into the slot where you would otherwise install a magnetic hard disk drive.

External Drives

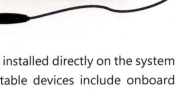

External drives are hard drives contained in a case and attached to a computer with a cord as a peripheral device. External drives provide extra storage capacity for user documents, pictures, video, etc. You do not, however, install software on external drives.

Flash Memory Storage in Tablets and Phones

Because flash memory chips (the technology used in solid state drives) can be installed directly on the system board, this type of storage is used in tablets and smartphones. Most portable devices include onboard storage memory.

Flash Drives

Flash drives (also called jump drives or thumb drives) are portable mass storage devices that use flash memory chips.

Flash drives are small (averaging between 2½" (60mm) and 2¾" (70mm) long and around ½" (16mm) to ¾" (20mm) wide), weigh less than 1 oz. (28g) and can store gigabytes of information. They are durable and reliable because they do not contain moving parts and can last for several years.

While the technology is basically the same, the flash memory chips used in a USB thumb drive are slower and less reliable than those used in solid state drives. That is the reason solid state drives cost more than thumb drives of the same capacity.

Secure Digital Cards (SD cards)

SD cards are small, high-capacity flash memory storage devices. You use an SD card in the same way you would use a flash drive – insert it into the designated slot on your device. A card reader/writer is integrated into the device that uses the SD card. You can write (store) data on the card, and then retrieve (read) it. You can also pop the card out of one device and insert it into a reader on another device for the purpose of transferring files from one device to another. SD cards are popular storage devices for digital cameras, camcorders, cell phones, tablets, MP3 players, and GPS systems.

Optical Discs and Drives

Optical disc drives are designed to read Compact Discs (CDs) and Digital Versatile/Video Discs (DVDs). The drive spins the disc and a laser reads the data stored on the disc.

A CD-ROM (Compact Disc Read Only Memory) or DVD-ROM drive is similar to a player in an audio/video entertainment system. The information is written (or burned) onto the surface and retrieved with a laser beam and you can only read the data.

An optical writer drive, also known as a burner drive, uses special software which allows you to "burn" or write data onto a disc.

New desktop systems are usually equipped with at least one optical drive, usually a DVD optical drive or a CD/DVD optical writer drive. Laptops used to include an optical drive, but more and more often newer models do not. You can, however, use an external optical drive that connects to the laptop through a USB cable.

iMac Desktop

Windows compatible Desktop

Desktop computers are stable and powerful and most include ample storage space (500GB – 1TB on average), a fair amount of installed memory (4GB - 8GB on average), the ability to read data stored on a wide variety of storage media, and the ability to play music and video. They include several USB ports for connecting external devices, and may include one or more slots for reading and writing to SD cards. Many are equipped with powerful video and sound cards. They usually include a network port for a wired network connection, and many include built-in wireless networking ability as well.

They are also easily upgradeable – you can pop open the case to access the internal components and there is generally enough "working room" to easily replace or upgrade components such as a video, audio, or network card. You can also easily add more storage space.

Common Set-up

A typical desktop setup includes the PC on or under the desk and a keyboard and mouse either on the desk or on a pull-out tray 4-5 inches below the desktop. The keyboard and mouse may be wired or wireless. Most people use large flat-screen computer monitors or TVs that can accept PC input; these large displays allow you to easily work with large spreadsheets, drafting programs or graphics editing programs.

Users often attach speakers for playing sound, and some even opt for a "surround-sound" setup with high quality speakers and separate sub-woofer for extra bass. Depending on your sound card and the available space, you have quite a bit of freedom in setting up your system.

A desktop system can be a comfortable place for long work periods and is usually the most accommodating for working extensively with documents. When you are working on that novel, a desktop might be just the place for you.

Disadvantages

The primary disadvantage of a desktop system is that it is not portable because it must always be plugged in to an electrical outlet while you are using it. You can, of course, move them from one location to another; however, this requires time to "tear down" the workstation at one location and set it up again (plug in the monitor, mouse, and keyboard) at the new location.

Generally Used By

Traditionally, people who work at one dedicated desk for the duration of the workday (for example, office workers, secretaries, accountants) have used desktop systems. However, as portable computers have become more powerful and less expensive, many workers now use laptop systems as their primary computing device.

More and more often in the workplace, only those who require significant memory, processing power, video resolution or storage space use desktop systems, while the rest of the employees use laptops for their day-to-day work. For example, people who use design software (such as AutoCAD or Autodesk Revit) or photo and video editing software (such as Adobe Photoshop or Adobe Premier) are more likely to use desktop systems.

Laptop (or Notebook) Computers

Laptop (or notebook) computers are designed to be portable. They are small and light enough to sit on your lap. They are also self-contained; everything you need (display, keyboard, camera, speakers, pointing device) is included in one unit.

Laptops run the same operating systems as their desktop counterparts, and include the same internal components such as a hard drive and installed memory. Laptops also include a rechargeable battery that is charged from an AC adapter.

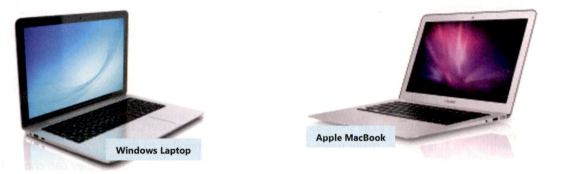

Windows Laptop

Apple MacBook

Laptops are very popular with students and business people alike because of their portability. For example, students can bring a laptop to class and take notes, then take it home to do homework and other assignments.

Aside from their portability, laptops are popular because:

- They are available in PC and Mac models.
- They are powerful enough to run most productivity and entertainment software. That is, they can run Office and play movies and stream audio, just as well as a desktop system. This makes them well-suited for the needs of most users.
- They usually include built-in wireless networking capability.
- In some cases, the power consumption is considered a "greener" alternative to desktops.
- You can purchase a number of accessories to enhance your laptop computing experience and make it more like a desktop computing experience. For example, you can connect to a larger monitor, add an external full-size keyboard with a number pad, or connect a mouse if you don't like using the built-in touchpad.

Disadvantages

- They generally are not as robust as desktop systems; they come with less storage space, less memory and lower-power graphics cards. This can make them poorly suited for running specialized software like graphics manipulation and video-editing programs that require extra computing or graphics power. However, high-end models can be well suited to running larger programs.
- Laptops generally have a shorter lifespan than their desktop counterparts.

> Working on your novel on a tablet might be a little more taxing than using a desktop or laptop. The screens are smaller and use different illumination technologies, and your eyes may become fatigued if you read documents on them for a long stretch of time. Even though you can attach an external keyboard, most people do not use their tablets in this fashion. Depending upon the operating system and the storage space, you might not even be able to open a large Word document on your tablet.

2-in-1s

Tablets have become so popular that many laptops now offer tablet-style features. These 2 in 1 "convertible" devices are laptops with special touch-screen displays that you can fold all the way back (360 degrees) so that you can use the laptop like a tablet.

Such devices offer the power, comfort, and document-editing capability of a laptop with the high-definition, high-speed streaming, touch screen capabilities of a tablet.

Smart Phones

Smart phones are hand-held devices that combine the features of a standard cell phone with those of a personal computer. They are widely used by people of all ages for a wide variety of purposes. You can use them to make calls, send text messages, download music or electronic books from the web, take pictures or video, check your email, browse the Internet, access cloud storage, open and edit documents, use GPS navigation, make mobile payments and watch movies – all in the palm of your hand.

> While you can open email attachments and read documents on a smart phone, you would probably not want to spend a lot of time doing so. Even though you can install the Microsoft Word app on a smart phone and use it to edit your document, it would probably become a tiring experience after a relatively short time. Additionally, internal storage space on a smart phone is limited.

Unlike traditional cell phones, smart phones allow users to install, configure, and run a tremendous variety of application programs called apps. They run mobile operating systems and are highly customizable.

Smart phones come complete with built-in cameras, video cameras, system memory and support for memory cards for storing data, and include software for organizing appointments and contact lists, or for writing notes. Most models incorporate touch screen technology as well as the option to connect to a desktop or laptop computer and synchronize files (such as photos, music files or contact lists).

You will learn more about smart phone hardware later in this lesson.

Exercise 2-2: Selecting the right device

For each scenario described below, select the most practical device to use from the options shown in the parentheses.

1. Dan is in line at the airport waiting to go through Customs. He has three suitcases with him. Which device would he most likely use to check his email while is he standing in line? (desktop, laptop, smart phone)

2. Jamey has to edit three large video files. Which device will she use? (server, desktop, tablet)

3. Mariette needs to make 127 e-books available for download to students at her school. What will she use? (server, laptop, smart phone)

4. Iain and his six-year-old sister are waiting for their mom at the dentist's office. Which device did Iain bring with him so that his sister could watch a movie? (server, desktop, tablet)

Keyboards, Mice, and Touch Screens

Objective 1-2.14

Users interact with a computer through input and output devices. An input device allows you to send information to the computer; output devices display (or otherwise send) information from the computer to you.

Keyboards and pointing devices are basic input devices. Monitors, printers, and speakers are basic output devices. Touch screens serve as both input and output devices because you can touch the screen to input information, and the screen displays the output.

Keyboards

The keyboard is the primary tool for sending information to the computer. You use it to enter data or to run commands in an application. Keyboards can by physical or virtual. In computing, a *virtual* device is one that does not physically exist, but is made to appear and act as if it exists by software. Virtual keyboards (and dial pads) are presented on screen in touch screen devices; the user "types" or dials by tapping the virtual keys that appear on the screen.

Physical keyboards can be external devices that connect to a computer, or they can be integrated into a system.

They come in many sizes and configurations. Some are ergonomically designed to protect against repetitive strain injuries such as carpal tunnel syndrome. Many include buttons for enhancing your multimedia experience.

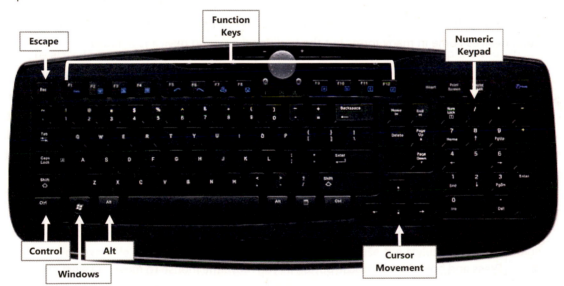

The preceding figure shows a standard Windows keyboard, which includes the following types of keys:

Key Type	Used for
Typewriter keys	Use these keys to type text and enter commands.
Modifier/ Extender keys	These keys are used in combination with other keys as shortcuts to commands, menus or functions. On a Windows keyboard, these include the WINDOWS key, the ALT key and the CTRL key. On a Mac keyboard, these include the COMMAND key, the OPTION key and the CONTROL key.

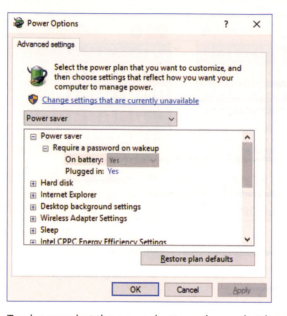

To choose what the power buttons do or what happens when you close the lid of the laptop, click the **Choose what the power buttons do** or **Choose what closing the lid does** option from the panel at the left of the main Power Options window. Options set here determine what happens with the power for Standby/Sleep, Hibernation, or Shut Down mode.

Define power buttons and turn on password protection

Choose the power settings that you want for your computer. The changes you make to the settings on this page apply to all of your power plans.

🛡 Change settings that are currently unavailable

Power and sleep buttons and lid settings

	🔋 On battery	🔌 Plugged in
⏻ When I press the power button:	Sleep	Sleep
◐ When I press the sleep button:	Sleep	Sleep
💻 When I close the lid:	Sleep	Sleep

Password protection on wakeup

◉ Require a password (recommended)
When your computer wakes from sleep, no one can access your data without entering the correct password to unlock the computer. Create or change your user account password

○ Don't require a password
When your computer wakes from sleep, anyone can access your data because the computer isn't locked.

Exercise 2-3: Examining power plan settings

In this exercise, you will examine power plan settings.

1. Right-click **Start**, then click **Control Panel**.

2. Click **Hardware and Sound**, then click **Power Options**.

3. If necessary, click the arrow for **Show additional plans**.

4. Review the power plans on your system. Is there a plan from the computer manufacturer?

5. Click **Change plan settings** for the Power saver plan.

6. Display a few of the drop-down lists to see the available settings, but do not change any settings.

7. Click **Change advanced power settings** to open the Power Options dialog box.

8. Scroll through the box to examine the settings categories.

9. Double-click an item to view its options.

10. Click **Cancel** to close the Power Options dialog box.

11. Click **Cancel** to exit the Edit Plan Settings page.

12. Close the Control Panel.

Connecting Peripherals

Objective 1-2.3, 1-2.4

Peripheral devices are connected to a computer system by a cable or by using wireless technology.

Cables are attached to the devices at one end, and the "free" end is terminated in a specialized connector designed to attach to the system unit through a special socket called a *port*. Most computer systems include (at least some of) the following ports:

- **Video ports** – these allow you to connect monitors, projectors, and even televisions to the computer for the purpose of displaying output.

- **Network ports** – these allow your computer to connect to various networks.

- **Audio ports** – deliver sound from the sound card to external speakers or headphones. These ports are sometimes called jacks.

- **Universal Serial Bus (USB) ports**– these allow you to attach a wide variety of devices (printers, scanners, cameras, flash drives, keyboards, mouse devices, and so on) to the computer. Because USB ports also deliver electrical power, they can be used to power peripheral devices or to re-charge the batteries of connected devices.

Video Ports and Connectors

Video ports allow you to connect a monitor, projector, or television to a computer in order to display video output. Most desktop systems include at least two video ports. High performance systems and gaming systems often include more. Standard computer video ports include:

- Video Graphics Adapter (VGA)
- Digital Video Interface (DVI)
- High-Definition Multimedia Interface (HDMI)

An HDMI port and cable are shown here.

9. If your teacher says it is okay to print, click **Print**, otherwise click **Cancel**.

10. Click the **Close** button in the Notepad window and click **Don't Save** to discard your changes.

Digital Cameras

Digital cameras encode images and video into digital files that are stored and can later be edited and played back. Files are stored on an SD card.

Many digital cameras can connect directly to a computer for the purpose of transferring captured images and video.

USB is the most commonly used connection for this type of file transfer. When you connect a camera to a PC via USB, the camera's internal storage system is treated as an accessible storage location. The PC will assign it a drive letter, and you can navigate it as you would any storage device.

Newer cameras also commonly include wireless capabilities and can use Wi-Fi or Bluetooth or infrared connections to transfer pictures and video to a PC or to smart phones. Smart phones can use cellular networks to transfer and share photos, and many mobile operating systems provide for automatic uploading to cloud storage.

Another alternative for transferring image and video files from a camera to a computer is to remove the SD card from the camera and insert it into a card reader slot on the computer. In this manner, you are using the SD card like a flash drive.

Wireless Connection Technologies

Objective 1-2.7

Wireless connections use radio waves and free space instead of physical wires or cables. The short-range wireless connections discussed in this section (Bluetooth and infrared) are used to connect devices (such as computers and phones) to accessories (such as headsets, mice, keyboards, and so on.) These technologies are not related to Wi-Fi. Wi-Fi connections will be discussed in an upcoming lesson.

Bluetooth

Bluetooth is a wireless technology used to allow devices (such as computers and phones) to work with Bluetooth-enabled accessories (such as headsets, mice, keyboards, and so on).

Bluetooth devices and accessories must be "paired" with each other before they can communicate. You can pair devices by following these steps:

1. Turn Bluetooth ON on your device. (Bluetooth requires quite a bit of energy, and accordingly, most people keep Bluetooth turned off on their battery-powered devices until they need it.)

2. Put your accessory into discovery mode; this allows your accessory to broadcast its availability and other Bluetooth devices within range can discover it. The specific steps required to change to discovery mode depend on the accessory. On many accessories, you hold down a button for several seconds until a light starts flashing. A device will remain discoverable for only a few minutes in order to save power.

3. On the device that you want to connect the accessory to, view the Bluetooth settings screen to see a list of nearby devices that are in discovery mode. (This screen also shows accessories that are already paired to the device.)

4. Pair the devices by selecting the accessory in the list. You may be prompted to enter a PIN code to pair the devices. The required code will be displayed on the device's screen. For example, if you are pairing your phone with your computer, you will see a PIN on the phone's screen and you will type it into your computer. After Bluetooth devices are paired they should automatically see each other and communicate when they are both powered on and have Bluetooth enabled.

Note: Bluetooth is also commonly used to enable hands-free phone calling by using a car's stereo system to make or receive calls without touching the phone, and to transfer files between devices that are in close proximity to each other.

Compatibility Considerations

It is important to understand that devices and accessories must be compatible. In other words, just because a device and an accessory are Bluetooth-enabled, it does not necessarily mean that they will work together.

For example, iPads and iPhones support an array of Bluetooth accessories such as headsets, remote controls, and keyboards; however, they do not support Bluetooth mice.

Infrared

Infrared wireless (or IR wireless) technology uses a beam of invisible light to transmit information. The sending and receiving devices must both contain infrared ports, and must be within fairly close proximity (for example, in the same room) in order for a connection to succeed.

Infrared technology is used in TV remotes, cordless microphones, wireless mice, cameras and audio devices. Infrared transmitters on smart phones allow you to use your smart phone as a TV or Set Top Box remote control.

Lesson Summary

In this lesson, you learned about various types of computers and computer hardware, and you examined ways to connect devices. You should now be familiar with:

- ☑ the relationships among hardware device drivers, firmware, and platforms
- ☑ common measurements used in computing
- ☑ standard internal computer components
- ☑ memory and storage
- ☑ identifying different types of computers
- ☑ keyboards, microphones and touch screens
- ☑ typical smart phone hardware
- ☑ Windows power plans
- ☑ connecting peripheral devices
- ☑ wireless connection technologies

Review Questions

1. Which internal component performs calculations and logical operations?

   a. Microprocessor   c. System board

   b. RAM chips   d. Power supply

2. Why is RAM used for temporary storage?

    a. It is not big enough to be used for permanent storage.

    b. It disappears when the computer is turned off.

    c. It is too slow to be used for permanent storage.

    d. It wears out after a few uses.

3. Which of the following is likely to have the greatest internal storage capacity?

    a. Chromebook   c. Server

    b. Tablet   d. Smart phone

4. Which of the following is a disadvantage of using a desktop PC?

    a. It is not portable.

    b. It probably does not have a lot of storage capacity.

    c. It probably does not have a lot of RAM.

    d. All of these are disadvantages of using a desktop PC.

5. Which of the following is a disadvantage of using a touch screen keyboard?

    a. It becomes uncomfortable after a period of time.

    b. It does not include symbols.

    c. It does not include numbers.

    d. All of these are disadvantages of using a touch screen keyboard.

6. Madge is going to connect a printer to her laptop computer. Which type of port is she likely to use?

    a. A video port   c. A USB port

    b. An audio port   d. There is no way to tell

7. Adam stores video files on a 1TB hard disk. Which computing device is he most likely using?

    a. A desktop   c. A Chromebook

    b. A tablet   d. A smart phone

8. Which piece of smart phone hardware identifies a GSM phone to its carrier network?

    a. The lock screen   c. The SIM card

    b. The widget   d. The infrared transmitter

9. Gary is going to connect an external monitor to his laptop. Which of the following ports is he most likely to use?

    a. Ethernet port   c. USB port

    b. HDMI port   d. Line In port

10. Harlene wants to pair her Bluetooth headset to her laptop. Which of the following is a step she must take?

    a. Connect the headset to a USB port.

    b. Change power plan on her laptop to High Performance.

    c. Put the headset into discovery mode.

    d. Turn off the wireless networking card because it interferes with Bluetooth.

Lesson 3: Networks and Mobile Devices

Lesson Objectives

In this lesson, you will examine different types of networks, explore subscription and contract costs, and examine connection technologies and hardware. You will also learn how to configure and use voice mail and how to manage mobile data usage. On completion you should be familiar with:

- [ ] the benefits of networking
- [ ] basic data network concepts
- [ ] how to obtain Internet service
- [ ] broadband technologies and speeds
- [ ] LAN hardware and addressing
- [ ] Ethernet connections

- [ ] Wi-Fi connections and wireless security
- [ ] basic cellular network concepts
- [ ] how to obtain cellular service
- [ ] how smart phones and tablets connect to the Internet
- [ ] basic telephone network concepts
- [ ] how to configure and use voice mail

What is a Network?

There are networks all around us – transportation networks, cellular networks, data networks, cable television networks, and the telephone network. At its very simplest definition, a *network* is a system for moving objects or information.

In computing, a network is simply an arrangement of computers (and additional computing devices) that are connected in such a way that they can communicate and share information. Individual networks can also be connected to other networks, and this practice is referred to as *internetworking*.

A network can consist of two or three computers in a single room, while an *internetwork* can consist of millions of computers connected across the globe.

Infrastructure Is Everything

Networking technologies have been in a state of constant development and improvement since the late 1960s. However, networking becomes practical and desirable and adopted into widespread use only when the proper infrastructure is in place.

Infrastructure is the basic underlying physical structure or framework needed for the operation of a service or an enterprise. In the case of networking, infrastructure is the hardware that supports high-speed communications and data transfer. Infrastructure is millions of miles of fiber-optic cable, high-powered cell relay towers dotting the landscape, over a thousand communication satellites in orbit around the earth, high-speed routers and servers and exchange points strategically positioned along the Internet, and consumer devices capable of participating in modern networks.

It has taken over fifty years and billions of dollars to build the infrastructure that our modern networks rely on today. And today, modern networking technologies and networks evolve and expand at an amazing rate because now (finally) there is sufficient infrastructure in place to support that type of growth.

Connectedness is Key

In this lesson, you will learn about different types of networks. Even though these networks are distinct from one another, they also inter-connect with each other. Cellular networks, the telephone network, and the Internet all inter-connect, and since our private (within our homes or schools or businesses) networks and computers and computing devices tap into these large networks, we are all inter-connected.

Why Network?

Networks are in wide use today because they are practical and useful. They enable users to share many things, including:

- Files – for example, Betty can create and store a file on her computer, and her fellow network user Barney can open and work with Betty's file without having to obtain a copy of the file.

- Resources – printers and scanners are commonly shared on a network. An entire office can share one or two printers, eliminating the need to purchase and attach a printer to each computer.

- Internet connections – networks within a home or office allow several users to share an Internet connection.

Internet Connection Sharing

Multiple computers in your home or office can share an Internet connection – but what about all those other familiar Internet-enabled devices we use daily? Smart phones, tablets, video game consoles, Blu-ray players and widescreen TVs all connect to the Internet as well. All these devices can share in that single Internet connection too.

For this reason, even a single person living alone can benefit from creating a small home network that is connected to the Internet. With a simple home network, you can:

- Stream audio and video to various devices.

- Share stored media (such as audio files, or photographs) among your devices.

- Share and backup files (including documents, pictures, scans, and so on.)

- Play games online.

Even though your devices are sharing a connection, each device can access the Internet independently. That means, the laptop in the kitchen might be surfing the Internet, while a tablet in the next room is streaming a video, and the Xbox 360 in the living room is being used for multi-player gaming.

About Streaming and Downloading

Before getting too far into our networking discussion, you should have a clear understanding of the difference between streaming and downloading. When most people talk about downloading and streaming they are usually talking about audio and video files accessed through sites like YouTube or Netflix, or songs and movies that they have purchased from an online store.

Downloading is the process of copying a file (any type of file) from a server on the Internet to your device. When you download a file, you can access it (play it) any time you like, even when you do not have an Internet connection.

Downloading, however, takes time. Video files can be quite large, and high-definition (HD) or ultra-high definition (UHD) movies border on tremendous, weighing in at several gigabytes. Depending on your Internet connection, files of this size can take hours to download. You also must have sufficient storage space on your device for the downloaded file.

Streaming is the process of having a file delivered to your device in a constant and steady stream. Streaming is like listening to a song on the radio – you can listen to it as soon as the stream starts (no waiting), but once the song is over, the task is complete. The file is not copied to (and stored) on your device. That is, you cannot save streamed content. Streaming requires an Internet connection.

Basic Network Technology

Objective 1-3.11

Home networks, school networks, business networks, and even the Internet are data networks. They transport data from one location (computing device) to another. This data is prepared for transport through a process called packetization – that is, the data is broken down into multiple pieces called *packets*. These individual packets are sent across the network, and when they arrive at their destination, they are re-assembled into their original form.

TCP/IP

The mechanism that controls the process of breaking data down into packets, sending it across the network, and re-assembling it when it reaches its destination is a networking protocol called Transmission Control Protocol/Internet Protocol or TCP/IP.

Don't let the word protocol intimidate you. A *protocol* is simply a set of rules that enable devices to communicate with one another in an agreed-upon manner.

All major operating systems (Windows, Mac OS X, Linux and UNIX) use TCP/IP as their networking protocol. TCP/IP is the international standard protocol for both local and wide area networking, and it is the networking protocol used on the Internet.

LANs and WANs

There are two basic types of networks relevant to our discussion – local area networks (LANs) and wide area networks (WANs).

Local Area Networks (LANs)

A *local area network (LAN)* is a private, local set-up. Your home network, or a small office or school network is a LAN. LANs are <u>private</u> networks. LANs come in different sizes, but are generally confined to one geographic location.

Wide Area Networks (WANs)

Wide area networks (WANs) are networks that connect computers in multiple locations using communication lines owned by a public carrier (such as the phone company or an Internet Service Provider).

For example, XYZ Company might own a LAN in their Boston office and a LAN in their Philadelphia office. In order to connect these two LANs, XYZ Company might lease high-speed lines from the phone company. Or, XYZ Company might use the Internet to connect their two LANs.

Whenever LANs are connected to one another using the lines of a public carrier, a WAN is formed. The Internet is the largest WAN in the world – it connects individuals and networks from around the world to one another using public communication lines. WANs are <u>public</u> networks.

IP Addresses

In order for the computers connected to a network to communicate with one another, each computer requires a unique address. This address is called an Internet Protocol (IP) address. Each computer on the local network (and each computer on the Internet) has an IP address that distinguishes it from all other computers on the network.

A typical LAN IP address looks like this:

>   192.168.1.104

On the Internet, each web site has its own IP address which is associated with an easy to remember text address called a *URL*. For example, the URL www.yahoo.com is associated with the IP address 98.138.252.30.

IPv4 and IPv6

There are two versions of Internet Protocol (IP)—version 4 (IPv4) and version 6 (IPv6). IPv4 is used predominantly in North America and Europe, while IPv6 is used in Asia and other countries. Because the number of available IPv4 addresses is rapidly running out, support for IPv6 (even in countries where IPv4 is currently used) is a requirement.

IPv4 addresses are written in decimal form as a series of four decimal numbers, separated by periods. The LAN IP address shown previously is an IPv4 address.

IPv6 addresses are written in hexadecimal form as a series of 8 hexadecimal numbers separated by colons. A typical IPv6 address looks like this:

>   805B:2D9D:DC28:0000:0000:FC57:D4C8:1FFF

Since 2011, all major operating systems for personal computers and servers include built-in support for IPv6. Cellular providers use IPv6 addresses in all their 4G networks, which means that all cell phones (and other computing devices) with 4G capability, operate using IPv6 addressing (with optional support for IPv4).

Finding Your IP Address

If you are having connection difficulties and need to request help from your IT department or from your ISP, you may need to find your IP address.

An easy way to find your computer's private IP address is to use a command line tool called ipconfig. This tool (run within a command prompt window), displays a wealth of information about your system's network settings. The following figure shows a computer that has two network connections – one is a wired (Ethernet) connection, and the other is a wireless (Wi-Fi) connection.

```
Ethernet adapter Ethernet:

   Connection-specific DNS Suffix  . :
   IPv6 Address. . . . . . . . . . . : 2600:8800:2300:527:5993:143d:f408:f1c9
   Temporary IPv6 Address. . . . . . : 2600:8800:2300:527:e1b5:e922:ded3:6711
   Link-local IPv6 Address . . . . . : fe80::5993:143d:f408:f1c9%13
   IPv4 Address. . . . . . . . . . . : 192.168.1.142                          ← IP address
   Subnet Mask . . . . . . . . . . . : 255.255.255.0
   Default Gateway . . . . . . . . . : fe80::4af8:b3ff:fecd:db05%13
                                       192.168.1.1

Wireless LAN adapter Wi-Fi:

   Connection-specific DNS Suffix  . :
   IPv6 Address. . . . . . . . . . . : 2600:8800:2300:527:20b7:c46e:26a4:2407
   Temporary IPv6 Address. . . . . . : 2600:8800:2300:527:856b:52b0:85d6:8a90
   Link-local IPv6 Address . . . . . : fe80::20b7:c46e:26a4:2407%12
   IPv4 Address. . . . . . . . . . . : 192.168.1.125                          ← IP address
   Subnet Mask . . . . . . . . . . . : 255.255.255.0
   Default Gateway . . . . . . . . . : fe80::4af8:b3ff:fecd:db05%12
                                       192.168.1.1
```

You can also view your IP address from the Windows Network and Sharing Center. Right-click **Start**, **Control Panel**, then click **View network status and tasks** to open the Network and Sharing Center. Your connection(s) display in the right side of the screen.

Click a connection to open a connection status dialog box.

Click the Details button to view specifics about the connection, including the IP address.

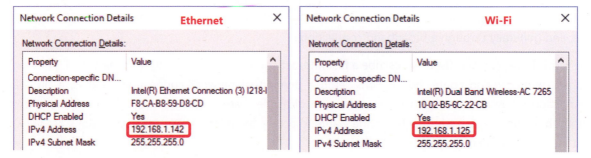

❙ Exercise 3-1: Finding your IP address

In this exercise, you will view your IP address.

1. Click **Start**, and click **Control Panel**. Then click **View network status and tasks** to open the Network and Sharing Center. Your connection(s) will be listed in the right side of the window, under the View your active networks heading.

2. Click your connection to open a connection status dialog box.

3. Click the **Details** button to view your IP address. Write down your IP address.

4. Click **Close** twice to close the open dialog boxes.

5. Close the Control Panel.

6. As a class, list your IP addresses on the board. Are they similar to one another?

Obtaining Internet Service

Objective 1-2.11

Accessing the Internet from your school or office is easy because the Internet service is already running, and you can access it either through Ethernet or Wi-Fi. However, at some point, someone at your school or office had to decide which service to purchase, and then arrange to have it set up.

If you want to add Internet service to your home, you will need to decide which type of service you want, how fast you need that service to be, and how much you would be willing to pay for it.

Service Providers

If you want to access the Internet from within your home, you must obtain Internet service from an Internet Service Provider (ISP). An ISP is a company that provides Internet connections to the public for a fee. Typical service providers include:

- phone companies
- cable TV companies
- satellite TV companies

These telecommunications companies provide an Internet connection, usually for a monthly subscription rate, and generally through a broadband connection.

The term "broadband" is used to describe a fast Internet connection (technically, at speeds of 1.544 Mbps or higher). A broadband connection is considered a permanent network connection. That is, a broadband connection is always "on." (This is in contrast to old-style dial-up connections, which require a user to establish a connection each time he or she wants to access the network. Dial-up connections are very slow and are no longer in wide use.)

Typical broadband technologies in wide use today include:

- **Digital Subscriber Line (DSL)** – provided by the phone company. This service runs over copper telephone wiring and provides speeds of up to 3Mbps. You must live a certain distance from a phone company switch in order to use DSL, and for this reason, the service is not available in all areas. Most providers offer DSL service of $30-$50 USD per month, and may offer special "package" rates for combining with landline phone service.

- **Broadband Cable** – provided by cable TV companies. This service runs over the copper coaxial cable that is part of the cable TV (CATAV) system. Cable provides speeds up to 30Mbps, depending on the provider, and monthly subscription rates hover between $30-$50 USD. Many providers offer discounts for subscribing to multiple services such as cable TV, Internet, and Internet-based phone services. Subscribers in the same neighborhood share a connection with their neighbors, and often experience a slowdown in service when other subscribers connect to the network.

- **Fiber Optic Service (FiOS)** – provided by several telecom companies (such as Verizon FiOS, AT&T and CenturyLink). This technology runs over fiber optic cable. This service is also called Fiber to the Home (FTTH) and is just starting to become available. FiOS offers speeds of 3Mbps up to 50Mbps, and pricing from $30 USD to up to about $100 USD per month, depending on the provider and the package. In your home, the fiber optic line connects to an optical network terminal (ONT), which can split the signal to provide services for Internet, television and telephone. (The function of the ONT is the same as the function of a broadband modem.)

- **Satellite Internet** – this technology is provided by satellite communications providers such as HughesNet and ViaSat, Inc. This technology involves three satellite dishes; one at the service provider's hub, one in space, and one attached to your home. Wireless signals are sent from the ISP to outer space to you; or from you to outer space to the ISP. Satellite providers offer speeds from 5Mbps to 15Mbps, and cost from $50 USD to $100 USD per month depending on which tier of service you choose.

  - Satellite connections are useful if you live in an area where you do not have another broadband choice. However, satellite connections do not support VPN and satellite plans must adhere to a monthly data allowance. If you exceed the monthly allowance (for example, if you stream a lot of HD video), the provider will slow down your service.

Blurred Lines

At one time, there was a clear-cut distinction between service providers; you got phone service from the phone company, and television service from the cable company, and so on.

Today, however, partnerships among TV, Internet and phone providers makes it possible to bundle services that provide one-stop-shopping. For example, you can purchase television, Internet and phone services from DirecTV (a satellite television provider), or from Cox Communications (a cable TV provider), or from CenturyLink (a phone company).

Which Service Should You Use?

It would be great to be able to simply purchase the fastest Internet service available. However, Internet service can be expensive, and sometimes you need to find a balance between what you want and what you need. Additionally, not all types of services may be available in your area.

In order to make an intelligent choice about finding a suitable Internet service package, you should understand a few things about broadband speeds, and about determining how much speed you actually need.

Upload Speed and Download Speed

The terms uploading and downloading refer to the process of sending information from your computer to a server (uploading), and the process of receiving information from a server (downloading). Most users download much more information than they upload. Accordingly, most service providers offer service with two speeds:

- **Downstream (download)** – Data moves downstream as it reaches you from a web server. When your browser loads a web page, or when you stream a movie to your laptop, you are downloading. Downstream services are usually tremendously faster than upstream services.

- **Upstream (upload)** – Data moves upstream when you send or upload information. When you enter a URL into your browser address bar or you fill in and then submit an online form, you are uploading.

Typical Broadband Speeds

Broadband providers advertise their top download speed with the words "up to." This is because the top speed is almost never experienced by subscribers. Even though each broadband technology is defined by a specification that lists its top speed, that speed is theoretical, meaning, if all network conditions were perfect, the technology could operate at the cited top speed.

Several factors affect network performance. The conditions of the wires in your neighborhood affect the speed, as does the network equipment you are using in your home. If you subscribe to a shared service, such as broadband cable or satellite, you will experience slower network response time when more subscribers access the network.

The following table summarizes typical broadband speeds and general monthly subscription costs. Remember that pricing can vary widely and that you can often achieve more affordable rates if you bundle services.

Technology	Speeds	Pricing	Comments
DSL	Up to 3Mbps	$30-$50USD per month	Not available in all areas
Cable	Up to 30Mbps	$30-$50USD per month	Shared service
FiOS	3Mbps – 50Mbps	$30-$100USD per month	Not widely available
Satellite	5Mbps – 15Mbps	$50-$100USD per month	Data allowance enforced by provider

How Much Speed Do You Need?

Determining how much speed you need is really about considering what you want to do. Do you want to play online games? Do you want to stream audio and watch streaming HD video through Netflix and Hulu? Or are you more the type to send a few emails and play Solitaire and Mine Sweeper?

If you want to stream HD movies from Netflix, for example, Netflix recommends that you use a 5Mbps connection for a good quality 1080-pixel stream. This amount of bandwidth is sufficient for one user; however, if you have multiple users streaming video to different devices, then you need more. If you want to stream ultra-high-definition (UHD) videos, then you need a 25Mbps connection.

The Federal Communications Commission (FCC) in the United States suggests that a 10Mbps – 25Mbps connection is reasonable for households that stream video. If you are a heavy data user, you may want to increase your connection to 50Mbps.

Choosing a Provider

When it is time to choose a provider, there are several things you can do to ensure you make a good choice:

- Determine your service requirements. If you know how much bandwidth you really need, you know which services you can rule out. For example, if you don't plan to simultaneously stream three UHD movies to three separate devices in your house, then you probably don't need to pay the extra money for a FiOS connection.

- Find out which services are available in your area.

- Do some homework:

  - Look at various provider web sites to view their pricing plans, or call and talk to a representative.

  - Investigate whether bundling different types of services can save you money.

  - Most plans are on a subscription basis, but some may have contract requirements. That is, you may be required to maintain service for a set amount of time (such as a year or two years), and may have to pay a fee for breaking the contract early.

  - Watch for data caps – a data cap is a limit on monthly broadband usage. While satellite providers have capped usage for quite a while, some cable and DSL providers have begun imposing caps (some as low as 50GB per month) on their plans. If you stream a lot of video, you may exceed the cap, and you may be charged an overage fee.

Testing Your Connection Speed

Once you have subscribed to a broadband Internet service, you can check the speed of your connection at any time. Most providers maintain tools on their web sites that test and report connection speed. You can also go to a third party connection speed testing site such as speedtest.xfinity.com or testmy.net.

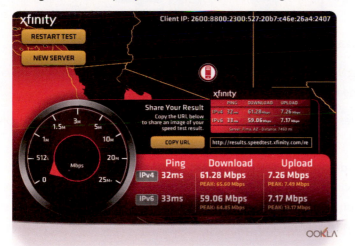

Exercise 3-2: Testing your Internet connection

In this exercise, you will test your connection speed.

1. In the taskbar, click (**Microsoft Edge**) to open the Microsoft Edge browser.

2. In the Search or enter web address box, type: `testmy.net` and press ENTER to navigate to the Testmy.net Internet speed test web site.

3. Near the top-right of the web page, click **Test My Internet+** to reveal the test options. You can test your download speed, your upload speed, or both.

4. Click **Combined** to test both upload and download speed, then let the test run. It may take a few minutes.

5. What is your download speed? What is your upload speed? Are they significantly different from one another?

6. If time permits, click the **Result Details** tab and the **Understanding the Results** tabs.

7. Close your browser.

Connecting the Internet to Your LAN

Objective 1-2.11, 1-3.11

Regardless of the technology used to get the Internet connection to your premises, the setup inside your home is pretty standard: you use a modem to connect to the service provider's network.

Broadband Modems

A broadband modem converts the incoming signal (from your phone line, cable line, fiber optic line, or satellite dish) into a digital signal that can be sent to a computer (if you do not have a home network), or to a broadband router (if you have set up a home network).

The modem is the place where the private LAN connects to the public WAN. The modem is a connection point which has two sides or "faces."

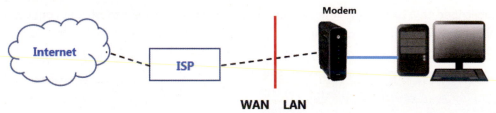

The WAN side of the modem faces your provider's network. The LAN side of the modem faces your private network, and you connect your LAN systems to the modem using Ethernet cable.

In many implementations, a modem includes only a single Ethernet port, which allows you to connect only one computer system to the Internet service.

However, in other implementations, a modem may also include wireless functionality – allowing other systems within your LAN to connect. Sometimes these devices are referred to as wireless gateways. These types of modems include built-in routing functions (and are actually modem/router combinations). You will learn about this type of functionality in the next section.

Broadband Routers

If your broadband modem provides only a single Ethernet port (and does not support wireless connections), and you want to share your Internet connection among multiple systems in your LAN, then you must add a broadband router to your network.

Most broadband routers include at least four Ethernet ports for wired connections, and they have built-in wireless functionality, allowing additional systems to connect wirelessly. In setups where you use a broadband router, you would plug the router into the Ethernet port on the modem, and then connect the computer systems to the router.

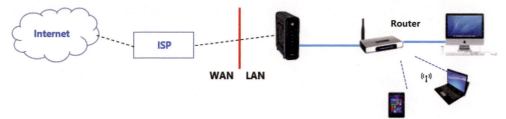

Notice that in this configuration, the router comes between the modem (which provides the link to the public network – the Internet) and the computer systems/devices on the private LAN. Part of a router's function is to connect different networks.

Broadband routers come in wired-only and wired/wireless versions. Wired-only routers function as a hub for the devices in your wired network but cannot provide services for wireless devices.

Wireless routers, on the other hand, combine a wired network router with a wireless access point. These devices include four or more Ethernet ports for wired connections, and they have a built-in Wi-Fi transmitter/receiver, which enable them to serve as wireless access points to the network for wireless devices.

Public and Private IP Addresses

There are two types of IP addresses. A public IP address (also called an Internet-addressable address) is one that will be unique on the Internet. You must use a public IP address to participate on the Internet.

A private IP address is one that is used within the LAN. There are three ranges of IPv4 addresses that are reserved for private use. The most commonly-used range is 192.168.0.0 to 192.168.255.255.

Private addresses within a LAN must be unique – but only within the LAN itself. That means, any network can use these addresses. Systems within your private LAN may use the exact same addresses as those in your next-door neighbor's private LAN without causing any problem because these are not the addresses that your network actually uses to access the Internet.

I Have a Private Address – How do I Connect to the Internet?

When you purchase Internet service from an ISP, you get one Internet-addressable (public) IP address included with the purchased service. The Internet service comes into your home through your broadband modem or modem/router combination.

Remember that broadband modems/routers have two faces. One face connects to the Internet and the other face connects to your private LAN. The broadband modem/router also has two IP addresses: one for the external or wide area network (WAN) Internet connection, and one for local devices to connect to across the local area network (LAN).

On the WAN side, the modem/router gets the public WAN-IP address when it connects to the ISP. (You can find your public IP address by visiting a Web-based IP address lookup service, such as WhatIsMyIPAddress.com.)

On the LAN side, the modem/router performs several functions, including (but not limited to) the following:

- It assigns private network addresses to the systems connected to it (usually 192.168.1.x), thus establishing an internal LAN.

- It uses a technology called network address translation (NAT) to replace the private IP address used by a system on the LAN with the Internet-addressable IP address that was provided with the purchase of Internet service.

Private network addresses are also commonly used inside corporate LANs. A corporation may lease several public IP addresses that can be used on the Internet, and then translate private network addresses into public ones when Internet access is required. Network address translation occurs in the same way as it does on a home network, although a corporate LAN might use different hardware (proxy servers, firewalls, etc.).

Viewing Your Public IP Address

If you want to view the public IP addresses your system uses while on the Internet, there are several web sites that will report your IP address to you. For example, you can visit http://get-site-ip.com or you can visit www.myipaddress.com.

Exercise 3-3: Viewing your public IP address

In this exercise, you will view your public IP address.

1.   Open a browser and navigate to www.myipaddress.com.

2.   What is your public IP address?

3.   Compare your results with your classmates. Do you all have the same public IP address?

4.   Close your browser.

Important Points about IP Addresses

These are the important things to understand about IP addresses:

- An IP address is not permanent; IP addresses are assigned to computers on the network for a specified period of time. In other words, an IP address is leased to a computer. If you were to move a computer from one network to another, its IP address would change.

- An IP address provides information about the computer it is leased to and about the network that the computer is participating in.

- A computer must have an IP address to connect to the Internet.

- An IP address must be unique within the network. When a system is connected to the Internet, its IP address must be unique on the Internet.

Wired Connections – Ethernet

Objective 1-2.4, 1-2.9, 1-2.10, 1-2.11

A wired connection to a LAN is called an Ethernet connection because it uses a networking cable called an Ethernet cable. Using a wired connection provides the fastest, and most secure connection possible within the LAN.

Ethernet Standards and Cables

Ethernet is a network-cabling protocol for transmitting data across a LAN. You use Ethernet cables to connect computers and other devices to wired connection points in your network, such as LAN ports in a wall plate, or on a router.

An Ethernet connection can transmit data at one of three standard speeds:

- Gigabit Ethernet moves data at 1Gbps
- Fast Ethernet moves data at 100Mbps
- 10Base-T Ethernet moves data at 10Mbps

Except for the older 10-Mbps Ethernet standard, Ethernet networks are faster than most wireless networks, and they are more stable (because you do not have to worry about signal interference), and more secure (because the signals are not sent through the air where they can be intercepted).

Ethernet connections are recommended for transmitting important and sensitive data. They are also ideal for high-volume streaming, such as streaming high-definition video from the Internet.

Cables

Ethernet cables are manufactured in different numbered grades or categories. Each cable grade is referred to by its category and number, for example, Category 5 or "Cat" 5. Ethernet cables can reliably transmit signals over a cable length of about 300 feet (100 meters). If you need to cover more distance, you can use two cables with an Ethernet switch in between them. The following cables are most commonly used:

- Cat 5 – supports data transfer at 10Mbps, and 100Mbps
- Cat 5e – supports data transfer at 10Mbps, 100Mbps, and 1Gbps
- Cat 6 – supports data transfer at 10Mbps, 100Mbps, 1Gbps, and 10Gbps
- Cat 6a – same as Cat 6 but designed for reduced signal interference

Network Interface Card (NIC)

In order to make an Ethernet connection between your computer and your home, school, or company wired LAN, your computer must include a network interface card (NIC). A NIC sends and receives data back and forth between your computer and the network, and it includes its own Ethernet port.

NICs are manufactured to support various data transfer rates, such as 10Mbps, 100Mbps, and 1Gbps. The faster NICs are backward-compatible meaning that they can slow down to match the speed of other equipment on the network.

Note: The speed of a single network connection is only as fast as its slowest link. This means that if you have 50Mbps Internet service, a high-speed router and Cat 5e cable, but your NIC is an ancient 10Mbps version, your connection speed will be 10Mbps.

A NIC may be built into a device (as it is in most desktop computers and some laptops), or it can be added to a device (either internally or externally).

- You can add an internal NIC to a desktop system by opening the case and inserting the NIC into a slot on the system board.

- You can add an external NIC to a computer by connecting one to an available USB port.

Connecting to the wired network is as easy as plugging in the cable. Most devices you connect via Ethernet automatically detect the network connection and will perform any necessary configuration (such as obtaining an IP address) automatically.

When you use a wired connection, a wired network icon 🖥 will display in the Windows 10 taskbar.

Advantages and Disadvantages of Wired Connections

On the plus side, wired connections are faster than wireless connections, they are secure, and they are reliable. Wired connections are ideal for handling a large volume of traffic.

The main drawbacks to using wired connections are that they require cabling – and cabling can get messy and can get in the way. Stringing cables across the middle of the floor is never a good idea because you can trip over them and pull them out of their connection ports. This makes it necessary to run cables behind walls or under the carpet, or through the attic. These are tasks most home owners are reluctant to undertake on their own.

Additionally, wired connections are not portable. For example, if you must connect your laptop to a port on the router in your living room, you will not be able to take your laptop to another room or out to the patio to work if you want to maintain your network connection.

In short, Ethernet connections are not convenient.

When Should You Use an Ethernet Connection?

Although Ethernet connections are not convenient, there are times when using this type of connection makes sense:

- If your computer (or other Internet-enabled device) does not include wireless capability, then the only way you can participate in a network is to use a wired connection. Even if the router is a wireless router, it will still have Ethernet ports on the back.
- If you require the fastest speed possible, wired connections are faster. A Gigabit Ethernet connection is more than twice as fast as the fastest wireless connection. This makes wired connections a good choice for:
  - Streaming video – if you want to stream HD videos to your Internet-enabled wide screen TV, a wired connection will give you better performance.
  - Downloading or uploading large files, such as digital photos, or video files.
  - Playing high-performance real-time online games.
- If you require guaranteed reliability, wired connections are not subject to the type of interference that wireless signals encounter.
- If you require security for transmitting sensitive and/or private information, wired connections are secure. Even though you can take steps to secure a wireless network, they are inherently insecure, and financial institutions and large corporations usually do not allow wireless connections in their networks.

Exercise 3-4: Examining your network connection

In this exercise you will locate the hardware that connects your system to the Internet, and view your data transfer speed.

First, determine whether you use an Ethernet connection.

1. If the physical location of your computer permits, try to locate your network interface card (NIC). Ask your teacher for assistance if necessary. Does your system use a wired connection for networking?

2. If your connection uses a wire, where does the wire connect to the network? Is there a box with connection ports near your desk? Do you plug into a wall jack?

    If your computer uses a wireless adapter and connects wirelessly, can you see the wireless broadband router or modem? If not, how far away do you think it might be located?

3. If your computer uses a wired connection, look at your NIC. Does it include a light that flashes on and off periodically? Most NICs include an indicator light to let you know that the device is sending and receiving data.

Next, examine the properties of your connection.

4. Right-click the network icon in the Windows taskbar, then click **Open Network and Sharing Center**. Your connection(s) will be listed in the right side of the window, under the View your active networks heading.

5. Click your connection to open a connection status dialog box. Your current connection speed is listed in the dialog box.

6. What is the speed of your network connection?

7. Close any open dialog boxes, then close the Control Panel.

Adding a Shared Printer to the Wired LAN

Within a LAN, a shared printer is one that is directly connected to one of the computers in the LAN. For example, if you have a printer connected via USB to your desktop PC, you can share that printer with the other computers on the LAN, regardless of whether those other computers connect via Ethernet or via Wi-Fi.

Any computer on the LAN that shares a resource, such as a connected printer, or a file storage location, is referred to as a *host*.

Sharing a printer is a simple matter of enabling printer sharing on the host computer. To activate printer sharing in Windows 10, navigate to the Network and Sharing Center, then click the **Change advanced sharing settings** link.

Change sharing options for different network profiles

Windows creates a separate network profile for each network you use. You can choose specific options for each profile.

Private (current profile) ⌄

Guest or Public ⌄

Domain ⌄

All Networks ⌄

The advanced sharing page provides access to different network profiles on your computer. Click the arrow to display the options for the **Private** network profile. Scroll to the File and printer sharing section and select **Turn on file and printer sharing**.

Change sharing options for different network profiles

Windows creates a separate network profile for each network you use. You can choose specific options for each profile.

Private (current profile)

Network discovery

When network discovery is on, this computer can see other network computers and devices and is visible to other network computers.

● Turn on network discovery
  ☑ Turn on automatic setup of network connected devices.
○ Turn off network discovery

File and printer sharing

When file and printer sharing is on, files and printers that you have shared from this computer can be accessed by people on the network.

● Turn on file and printer sharing
○ Turn off file and printer sharing

Click the **Save changes** button at the bottom of the dialog box to save the settings.

Next, navigate to the Control Panel home page, then click **View devices and printers** to open the Devices and Printers page, which allows you to view and configure the devices connected to your computer. Right-click the printer you want to share, then click **Printer properties** to open the printer Properties dialog box. Click the **Sharing** tab, then click the **Share this printer** check box.

Canon MP280 series Properties

| General | Sharing | Ports | Advanced | Color Management | Security | Maintenance |

You can share this printer with other users on your network. The printer will not be available when the computer is sleeping or turned off.

☑ Share this printer
Share name: Canon MP280 series

☑ Render print jobs on client computers

Drivers

If this printer is shared with users running different versions of Windows, you may want to install additional drivers, so that the users do not have to find the print driver when they connect to the shared printer.

Additional Drivers...

When you elect to share a printer, you may choose to install additional printer drivers on your system. Doing so makes the drivers available to other users who want to connect to your printer. Click **Apply**, and then click **OK** to save your settings.

You should understand that when you share a printer, other computers connect to that printer through your computer. Your computer must be turned on and logged in to the network in order for anyone else to use the printer.

You can clear the Share this printer check box at any time to stop sharing the printer.

Connecting to a Shared Printer

To connect to a shared printer, open the Devices and Printers page of the Control Panel and click **Add a printer**. Windows will look for printers on the network. Select the printer to which you want to connect, then click **Next**. Windows connects to the printer and installs the required drivers. When a successful connection is made, Windows displays a success message, allows you to specify this printer as your default printer, and gives you the option of printing a test page.

Click **Finish**.

Once you have successfully connected to a shared printer, the printer will appear in the Print dialog box in any application that you use.

Disconnecting a Shared Printer

To disconnect a printer (that is, to remove it as an option on your PC), open the Devices and Printers page, click the printer you want to remove, click **Remove device** in the in the toolbar at the top of the page, then confirm that you want to remove the printer by clicking **Yes**.

Wireless Connections – Wi-Fi

Objective 1-2.5, 1-2.9, 1-2.10, 1-2.11

Wireless networking is a form of networking wherein systems use their Wi-Fi capability to send and receive radio transmissions over the air instead of over wired cabling. Wireless networking occurs in two distinct modes:

- Ad-hoc – systems communicate with one another directly using their Wi-Fi capability. This mode is highly insecure, and it does not provide access to the Internet.

- Infrastructure – systems connect to the network through a wireless router (or access point), and communicate with each other and with other systems on a wired Ethernet network through the router. This mode of communication can be secured, and it provides Internet access.

Most modern broadband routers include wireless capability, which means they can be used to create wireless networks. These are infrastructure mode networks: all wireless devices that join the network communicate with the router, not directly with one another.

Because the router is also a central connection point in the LAN, this type of network is called a Wireless LAN (WLAN). Devices connected to the WLAN can communicate (through the router) with one another and with systems that are connected to the LAN via Ethernet.

Additionally, because the router is connected to the broadband modem, the WLAN has access to the Internet.

Adapters, Signals and Bands

Devices that participate on WLANs must include a wireless adapter, which is the device that transmits and receives the radio signals. When you power on a wireless device, it picks up signals from all the wireless networks within the vicinity and displays the name of each available network.

Most handheld devices like smart phones and tablets have a wireless adapter built in. For computers and laptops that do not contain one, you can either install one in a slot on the system board, or you can connect one through a USB port.

A USB wireless adapter looks almost like a flash drive.

Devices on WLANs use one of two different radio frequency bands: the 2.4GHz band or the 5GHz band. The 2.4GHZ band is also used by many other types of wireless devices (such as cordless phones and baby monitors), and these devices can sometimes cause interference with WLAN signals.

Radio signals also weaken as they get farther away from the transmitter. As you move near the edge of a transmission range, your wireless networking connection will get slower. Objects (such as walls or floors) through which a signal must pass can also reduce its range.

Wireless Standards

Wi-Fi (short for wireless fidelity) is the consumer-friendly name we use to refer to a family of standards for wireless equipment and transmission technologies. These standards are part of the 802.11 wireless networking standard.

There are several Wi-Fi standards, and each offers a different level of performance.

Wi-Fi Standard	Top Speed	Frequency Band
802.11a	54Mbps	5-GHz
802.11b	11Mbps	2.4-GHz
802.11g	54Mbps	2.4-GHz
802.11n	450Mbps	2.4-GHz and 5-GHz
802.11ac	1.3Gbps	5-GHz

Wireless equipment that is compatible with multiple Wi-Fi standards is often identified by multiple suffixes. For example, you might see a laptop ad that includes the spec "802.11b/g/n wireless." This means that the built-in Wi-Fi adapter will work with 802.11b, 802.11g, and 802.11n.

As is the case with advertised broadband speeds, the top speeds are theoretical maximum rates. The throughput rates you experience will be lower than the maximum rates.

Wireless Security

Because wireless networks use radio waves to send and receive information, they are susceptible to eavesdropping, interception, and unauthorized access. For this reason, it is highly recommended that you secure your wireless transmissions and use secure wireless networks whenever possible.

Wireless transmissions are secured using the following mechanisms:

Wired Equivalent Privacy (WEP) 64-bit	The was the first security mechanism available for wireless networks. It does not offer strong protection and today is considered obsolete. However, some very old wireless hardware will not support more advanced security schemes, and so WEP is the only option.
Wi-Fi Protected Access (WPA)	This was the first phase of improved wireless security and it works with many older wireless devices.
Wi-Fi Protected Access 2 (WPA2)	WPA2 provides the most secure wireless transmissions, but it requires modern wireless equipment. All new wireless networking hardware supports WPA2 (and some older hardware supports it as well).

You should always use the strongest level of wireless security supported by your wireless hardware.

Whenever you connect to a secure wireless network, you must provide a passkey (also called a pass phrase or a network security key). This is the wireless equivalent of a password.

When Should You Use Wireless Connections?

The beauty of wireless connections is that they are so convenient – there is no cable to string through a room or route behind a desk, and wireless connections allow you to work anywhere you like – on the sofa, in your bedroom, or out in the back yard (assuming the signal is strong enough). In most instances, using a wireless connection is a matter of choice.

The only time you might find yourself forced to use a wireless connection is when you have a device that includes wireless capability, but does not include an Ethernet port, and does not include a connection port (such as a USB) port where you can attach an external NIC. Most tablets fit this description.

Connecting Your Computer to a WLAN

Your wireless adapter will scan the area for nearby wireless networks. In Windows 10, available wireless networks display in a pop-up window when you click the available networks icon in the taskbar.

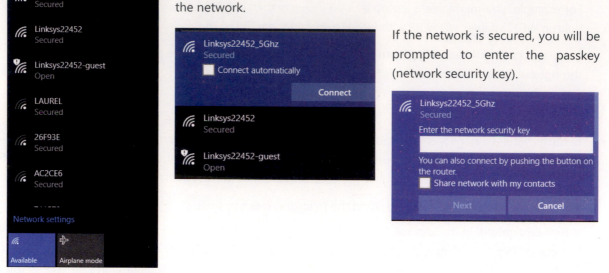

Click a network to select it, and then click the **Connect** button to connect to the network.

If the network is secured, you will be prompted to enter the passkey (network security key).

Type the network security key in the box, then click **Next** to have your system authenticate with the wireless router. When you have successfully connected to a wireless network, the network icon in the taskbar displays like this: .

Once you connect to a WLAN, Windows keeps the settings and configures the connection to connect automatically whenever the network is in range. You will not be prompted to enter the passkey again, unless the network administrator changes the passkey, or you specifically tell Windows to forget the connection settings.

To connect to a WLAN on a Mac, follow these steps:

1. Click the **Wi-Fi** symbol on the toolbar at the top of the screen to display a list of available networks.

2. Select your network from the list.

3. When prompted, enter the passkey for your network, and click **OK**.

Connecting Your Handheld Device to a WLAN

Tablets and smart phones include a built-in wireless adapter that allows them to connect to a Wi-Fi network when one is in range. Connecting your device is as easy as turning Wi-Fi on, selecting the desired network in the list of available networks, and then entering the appropriate passkey if the network is secured.

Public Wi-Fi hotspots are generally not secured, which means that you can connect to them without entering a passkey. Complimentary wireless service at a hotel often requires a passkey, which is provided to you by the hotel staff when you check in.

To connect an Android device, follow these steps:

1. Tap **Apps**, tap **Settings**, then tap **Wi-Fi**. The available networks should display on your screen. (Secure networks display a lock icon . You must enter a passkey to connect to a secure network.)

2. Tap the network you want to connect to and enter the passkey if prompted.

3. After you type the passkey, tap **Connect**.

Once you have been authenticated, "Connected" displays below the network name.

To connect an iOS device, follow these steps:

1. From your Home screen, go to Settings > Wi-Fi.

2. Turn on Wi-Fi. Your device will automatically search for available Wi-Fi networks. Secure networks display a lock icon 🔒.

3. Tap the name of the Wi-Fi network that you want to join and enter the passkey if prompted.

4. Tap Join.

After you join the network, you'll see a check mark ✓ next to the network and Wi-Fi connected indicator 📶 in the upper-left corner of the display.

Smart phones and tablets remember your WLAN connections and their associated security keys. The next time the same WLAN is in range, your handheld device will be able to connect automatically.

Wi-Fi Protected Setup (WPS)

Most wireless routers include setup capability through Wi-Fi Protected Setup (WPS). WPS is a wireless networking standard that used to connect wireless devices to your WLAN by pressing a button on the router.

The WPS button is usually designated by two opposite-facing arrows, such as the ones shown in this image.

WPS works only on WLANs that use WPA or WPA2 for security. Both the router and the device must be WPS-enabled for the process to work.

Press the WPS button on the router, and then press the WPS button on the device. They identify each other and make all necessary configuration settings automatically. This is especially useful for adding devices such as network printers to a WLAN – it is not always a straight-forward process to advance through the configuration screens on a printer in order to enter a WLAN passkey. WPS makes the process fast and easy.

Adding a Network Printer to the WLAN

Unlike a shared printer (which is directly connected to a host computer on the network), a network printer is connected to the router. All systems on the network can connect to the network printer through the router.

In order to be set up as a network printer, the printer itself must include either a wireless adapter or an Ethernet port (or both). Most printers sold today have wireless capability built in.

With most newer printers, the setup is very simple: you take the new printer out of the box, turn it on and perform the normal first-time setup steps such as removing any internal packaging and inserting ink or toner, and then wait for the printer to automatically detect and connect to the WLAN.

Some older printers may require that you first connect via USB to one of the network computers and run an installation utility, and enter the printer's IP address and enter the network security password. If both your printer and your router support WPS, then you can press the WPS button on the router and press the WPS button on the printer and wait for them to establish a connection automatically. Once the printer has successfully joined the WLAN, you can disconnect the USB cable.

Connecting to a Network Printer

Once the printer has joined the wireless network, it should appear as a printing option for all computers on the network.

For some older models, it may be necessary to manually install the drivers that shipped with the printer on each computer that will use the printer.

Cellular Networks

Objective 1-1.1, 1-2.10

Cellular networks carry voice, text, and digital data through the transmitting and receiving of radio frequency (RF) signals. At its heart, a mobile phone is a two-way radio, and it sends and receives signals as it moves through a network of transmitters and receivers. Think of all the cell towers you see as you travel to and from work or school each day. These towers are part of the cellular network infrastructure. Cellular carriers (or providers) own and operate these towers and the networks they form.

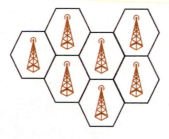 Each cellular network is divided into thousands of overlapping geographic areas called *cells*. You can think of it as a mesh of hexagonal cells (like honeycomb). Each cell has its own base station at the center and the cells overlap at the edges to ensure that users always remain within range of a base station.

This layout makes it possible to maintain a call as you travel out of one cell and into another.

The base station at the center of each cell acts as a network hub only for that cell – not for the entire network. Radio signals transmitted by a phone are received by the base station, where they are then re-transmitted from the base station to another mobile phone. The base stations are connected to one another and calls are automatically transferred from one base station to another as callers move between cells.

Each base station is also connected to the landline telephone network, and can relay mobile calls to landline phones. Cellular networks are also connected to the Internet at various points where different large networks exchange traffic, enabling you to access the Internet on your smart phone through your cellular provider.

Cellular Generations – All About the G's

In almost any discussion about mobile phones, you hear "G." G stands for generation. Mobile phone technology is continually evolving as more cell towers and relay stations are put into place (providing the required infrastructure to support newer standards and faster speeds) and as more sophisticated phones are developed and put into widespread use.

Modern generation cellular networks are:

- **3G** – third generation. 3G networks transfer data at up to 2Mbps (almost as fast as DSL), which makes it practical to use a mobile phone to surf the Internet and use web-based applications. 3G is considered the minimum requirement for using a smart phone today. That is, if you want to use your smart phone for anything other than voice calls and text messages, you must be on a 3G network.

- **4G** – fourth generation. Things start to get a little sticky here. The 4G standard promises speeds in excess of 1Gbps when you are stationary and 100Mbps when you are highly mobile (such as when you are using your phone while traveling in a car). However, at the time of the release of the 4G specification, these speeds were unheard of. At the time of this writing, there are no true 4G cellular networks.

- **LTE / 4G LTE** – fourth generation. LTE stands for Long Term Evolution. LTE devices were originally marketed as 4G technology, but they delivered nowhere near the promised 4G speeds. They are, however, significantly faster than 3G, and the telecommunications governing body (the International Telecommunication Union or ITU), determined that LTE products could be marketed as "4G." LTE is the fastest cellular technology currently available, and the average speed of today's 4G LTE networks in the USA is around 24Mbps (nearly as fast as cable), which is fast enough to stream audio and video and give a satisfactory user experience. Note that 4G LTE coverage is available in large metropolitan areas, but outside the coverage area, a 4G LTE phone falls back to 3G.

Cellular Carriers

A cellular carrier is a cell phone company that provides cellular service to mobile phone users. In the USA, the four biggest cell carriers are AT&T, Sprint, T-Mobile, and Verizon. There are, of course, numerous others in the states, and worldwide there are over 30 large carriers who each service hundreds of thousands of subscribers.

A carrier uses either the Global System for Communication (GSM) radio system or the Code Division Multiple Access (CDMA) radio system for its cellular network. These systems differ in technology, but offer the same services.

Carrier Types

There are different types of cell carriers:

- **GSM Carriers** – these cell companies use GSM networks, and their phones identify with the carrier network through the use of a SIM card. This makes it easy for users to swap GSM phones and retain their phone number and account information. AT&T and T-Mobile are GSM carriers.

- **CDMA Carriers** – these cell companies use CDMA networks, and CDMA phones use an ESN (Electronic Serial Number) to identify with the carrier network. If a user wants to change to another CDMA phone, he or she must contact the carrier and perform an ESN change. Sprint and Verizon are CDMA carriers.

Cellular Service Plans

Because cellular service provides for voice, text and data, service plans include these three elements in their pricing points, depending on which plan you choose. Generally, these are referred to as:

- **Talk** – refers to sending and receiving voice calls. Some plans allot a certain number of free talk minutes per month, and then charge a specific amount per minute for every minute that exceeds the allotted number of minutes. Other plans allow for an unlimited number of voice calls every month.

- **Text** – refers to the sending and receiving of text messages (SMS) and picture and video messages (MMS). Some plans allow for a certain number of text messages per month, and charge a fee for each text message that exceeds the allotment. Other plans allow for unlimited text messaging every month.

- **Data** – refers to information that you upload and download to and from the Internet. This includes app updates, notifications, GPS information, as well as email, uploading or downloading large files, streaming audio and streaming video. Most carriers provide several options for data plans, each allowing a certain amount of data (measured in GB) per month for a per-month fee. If you download more than your allotment, you will be charged for each additional GB of data. Some carriers also offer plans that allow for unlimited data usage.

Note: If you use a basic cell phone as opposed to a smart phone, you are not required to purchase a data plan. However, if you use a smart phone, you must buy a data plan as part of your service package, unless you sign up for a "Wi-Fi Only" smart phone plan. On this type of plan, you will pay for ANY and ALL data that you download over the cellular network.

You can purchase a plan for each phone, or you can purchase one of many family plans that allows all the lines of service on a particular account to share plan minutes, text and data.

Most carriers offer plans for smart phones, basic phones, and data devices such as cellular-enabled tablets. These devices can access the cellular network (because they have their own line of service) but cannot be used to make phone calls.

Plan Add-Ons

Many carriers also offer add-on features that you can purchase for each line of service, including international calling plans, extra data, insurance plans that protect against theft and damage, and the ability to use your phone as a mobile hotspot.

Cellular Devices

Objective 1-1.2, 1-1.3

Cellular devices connect to your carrier's cellular network. Each device must be recognized by the carrier network (either through a SIM card or an ESN number programmed into the device).

Devices include basic cell phones, smart phones, and cellular-enabled tablets.

Smart Phones

We have already discussed smart phones to a certain extent in a previous lesson. In this lesson, the thing to consider about smart phones is that they are designed to keep you connected – 24/7. An average user installs and enables apps on a smart phone that broadcast location and GPS information, receive notifications night and day from email and Instagram and Facebook, look for Wi-Fi networks, look for Bluetooth devices and so on. They are active devices, and usually need to be recharged every night.

We use them for doing work. We use them for communication. We use them to "carry" our insurance cards and coupons and address books and phone books. We use them for entertainment. We use them for social activities like taking pictures and video. We use them for shopping, and we use them to pay at the cash register.

It can be argued that smart phones are more like computers with voice call capability than they are like phones with computing capability. They are complex, expensive, and, if we are not vigilant, they can consume enormous quantities of our time precisely because they keep us connected. They bring an endless stream of information to our hands and sometimes they are difficult to put down. They can make it difficult for us to disengage.

Basic Cell Phone

The basic cell phone (think of the old model flip phone) is designed primarily for making and receiving voice calls. The call quality is sometimes better than what you can find on a smart phone. The basic phone is also less expensive, more durable (they can survive quite a few falls without becoming unusable or cracking a screen), and a single charge can last from three days to a week.

Additionally, they are smaller than smart phones, simple to use because you need only flip it open to answer it, and flip it closed to hang up., and secure because they cannot be used to store a lot of personal information (like banking account and credit card information) the way smart phones can.

Although you can use a basic phone to access the Internet, the functionality is quite limited since they are not designed with large color displays and touch screen capability. To check your email, you can use the phone's built-in email client (if it has one) or you can use a web browser and navigate to a web-based email site such as Gmail, Yahoo, or Hotmail.

For people who do not wish to be connected all the time, a basic phone is a viable choice.

Cellular-Enabled Tablets

A cellular-enabled tablet looks and feels like a standard tablet, and it can even connect to Wi-Fi just like a "regular" tablet. But it has the extra capability of connecting to your carrier's cellular network.

A cellular-enabled tablet includes a SIM (or is programmed with an ESN) so that it can connect to the carrier network. To use a cellular-enabled tablet you must purchase a separate line of service for the tablet and a data plan. In some cases, you may be able to share a data plan between your tablet and your phone; it depends on your carrier. The tablet will be assigned a phone number for identification purposes (although you won't be able to use it to make voice calls).

Cellular-enabled tablets run a mobile operating system, such as Android or iOS, and can run the same apps they run while they are using Wi-Fi.

For a set monthly service fee, you can call anyone in your calling area without additional charge. Calls outside your local calling area are considered long-distance and usually incur an extra charge based on the duration of the call.

Advantages and Disadvantages

Landline phones require voltage for ringing and dialing, and this power is delivered from the telephone network through the phone line itself. For this reason, you can use a landline phone to place a call even during a power outage. VoIP phones, which use the Internet, are dependent upon routers and modems (which all require AC power). You cannot use a VoIP phone during a power outage.

Another advantage of landline service is that the service is extremely reliable and provides excellent sound quality. In fact, landlines are so reliable, residential and business alarm systems are tied in to a landline and place a call to the alarm company and/or to emergency services when a break-in is detected.

An obvious limitation of a landline phone is that the service is not portable. The phone must be connected to the telephone jack.

Private Branch Exchange (PBX)

To save money on leasing public telephone lines for each employee, many businesses lease a few lines from the phone company for making out-going calls, and use a private branch exchange (PBX) to manage internal calls among their telephones. A PBX is a private telephone switch; it allows businesses to create their own internal telephone-numbering scheme and to keep all internal calls separate from the telephone network.

Businesses can also save money on phone lines using an IP version of a PBX; this is called an IP PBX and performs the same functions as a PBX, except that it is designed to work with IP phones.

If your business, school, or organization uses a PBX, then you (may):

- Use short code dialing (that is, you dial only the extension) to reach anyone within your office or campus
- Dial an access code (such 9 or 0) to access an outside line to make a call outside your office or campus

Business Telephones

Because businesses typically use more advanced phone features than home users, business phones have a different design and appearance from residential phones.

The buttons and specific key press sequences for performing certain tasks differ from one make and model to another, but for the most part you can perform the following functions by taking the described actions:

- **Put a call on hold** – press the Hold button. When you are ready to resume the call, press the Hold button again.
- **Transfer a call** – On most business phones you can transfer a call by selecting the line you want to transfer, pressing the Transfer button (this puts the caller on hold), waiting for a dial tone and then dialing an internal extension. You would then wait for the party to answer, then press Transfer again, and then hang up.)

  On phones that do not include a Transfer button, you press the Flash button, wait for a recall dial tone (3 beeps and then a dial tone), dial the number to which you want to transfer the call, wait for the party to answer, and then hang up. If the person you are trying to reach does not answer, you can press the Flash button again to return to the caller.

- **Create a conference call** – a conference call involves at least three parties. While you are on an active call, press the Conference button, dial the number of a party you want to add to the call, then press Conference again so that all three of you can converse on the call.

Voice Mail

Objective 1-1.4

A voicemail system is a centralized system used in businesses for sending, storing, and retrieving audio messages. Residential and cell phone service plans also often include voice mail capabilities.

In a business phone system, each extension is usually linked to a voice mailbox. When a party calls a number and the line is not answered or is busy, the call is sent over to the voice mailbox. The caller will hear a greeting message previously recorded by the user. This message can give instructions to the caller to leave a voice message, or may provide other options, such as paging the user or being transferred to another extension or to a receptionist.

Voice mail systems also provide notifications to the user to alert them when they have received new voice mail messages. Most systems provide multiple ways for users to check their voice mail, including accessing the voice mailbox through a PC, or from a landline phone or even a mobile phone.

Configuring Your Voice Mail

Voice mail systems guide you through a menu of options and choices. Listen to the voice prompts and follow the instructions. At various points you will be asked to record information, after which you are usually given the options to keep your recording, or to discard and record again. You indicate your choice by pressing a specific key on the dial pad, for example, you might be instructed to press 1 to keep your recording, or 2 to discard it and record again.

The first time you configure your voice mail, you may be prompted to state your name slowly and clearly, and to create and confirm a PIN code that you will use later to access your messages, and configure your greeting messages.

Follow the voice prompts to record a general greeting, and any supplemental greetings, such as an out of office message. The voice mail configuration program will guide you through setting up greeting messages and turning specific ones on or off.

A suitable business voice mail greeting should include the following information:

- Your name, department, and company name
- A brief apology that you cannot take a call right now
- An invitation to leave a message
- An indication of when the caller can expect a return call
- Any additional options that might be available to a customer, such as your web site address or the name and number of an associate within your company.

Retrieving Your Messages

Most phones show a notification when you have new, unheard voice mail messages. On some phones, a red light illuminates, on others a voice mail message icon displays.

You may need to dial a specific number, or press a button to call the voice mail system. You may then be required to enter a PIN to access your messages.

Follow the voice prompts to play your messages. After you have listened to a message you are usually given the option to erase the message or save it in the message archive. You can retrieve and replay archived messages at any time.

Voice Mail on Your Mobile Phone

Cellular plans also include voice mail. The voice mail phone number is usually included in the default list of contacts. You can access your voice mail through the Contacts list or by dialing the number directly. (Often, this is a shortcut number, such as *86.)

As with business phone systems, the voice mail system on a mobile phone uses voice prompts to guide you through the menu options. The first time you call the voice mail system, you will be prompted to create and confirm a numeric password, and to record a greeting.

If a caller cannot reach you on your mobile phone, he or she is sent to your voice mailbox. However, if you have not set up your voice mailbox, the caller will be informed that the mailbox has not been set up, and the caller will be unable to leave you a voice mail message.

Many cellular providers offer a form of visual voice mail, which lets you see and manipulate your voice mail messages on the screen. However, there is often a monthly fee associated with using visual voice mail.

Personal or Business

Obviously, a voice mail greeting for a personal phone number can be less formal than one that you use for a business number. However, if you use your mobile phone for both business and personal calls, you should ensure that your greeting is suitable for both types of callers.

Retrieving Messages

Your mobile phone will display an icon when you have new, unheard voice messages waiting for you. You must call the voice mail system and log in (enter your password) to access your mailbox. You can play your unheard messages, discard them, or archive them. You can also record greetings, and configure pager settings from within the voice mail system.

Mailbox Full

If you receive a high quantity of voice mail messages and do not clear out your voice mailbox, the mailbox will become full and callers will not be able to leave new messages. The mailbox will remain full until you listen to and clear out the existing messages.

Leaving a Clear Voice Mail Message

Many people freeze up when prompted to leave a voice mail message (especially when making a business call), and hang up the phone instead! A little preparation can help alleviate this issue.

Before you place your call, prepare in advance a sentence or two that summarizes the nature and purpose of your call. A clear and understandable voice mail message is much more likely to get a response than one that rambles on and on.

Additionally, plan to include the following items in your voice mail message:

- Identify yourself by first and last name, and if appropriate, state the name of your company.

- State the number (or numbers) at which you can be reached, and if appropriate, during which time frames. You might also provide your email address if you are willing to accept a response via email.

- Mention the date and time you are calling.

- Briefly describe the nature and purpose of your call.

- Ask the person to call you back at their earliest convenience (or in whatever time frame is required).

- Repeat the number at which you can be reached.

- Thank them for their time.

It is not difficult to leave a clear, concise message, and it is usually greatly appreciated.

Lesson Summary

In this lesson, you examined different types of networks, explored subscription and contract costs, examined connection technologies and hardware. You also learned how to configure and use voice mail and how to manage mobile data usage. You should now be familiar with:

☑ the benefits of networking

☑ basic data network concepts

☑ how to obtain Internet service

☑ broadband technologies and speeds

☑ LAN hardware and addressing

☑ Ethernet connections

☑ Wi-Fi connections and wireless security

☑ basic cellular network concepts

☑ how to obtain cellular service

☑ how smart phones and tablets connect to the Internet

☑ basic telephone network concepts

☑ how to configure and use voice mail

Review Questions

1. Which protocol is required to access the Internet?

    a. 802.11a   c. 802.11ac

    b. TCP/IP   d. TKIP

2. Which of the following is an example of a private network?

    a. The Internet.

    b. The telephone network.

    c. Your carrier's cell network.

    d. Your company's LAN.

3. Which of the following broadband technologies is the fastest?

    a. DSL   c. Broadband cable

    b. Satellite   d. 3G cellular

4. Ann's cable modem has only one Ethernet port and does not support wireless connections. What must she add to her network in order to share her Internet connection with her laptop, tablet and smart phone?

   a. A wireless broadband router.   c.   An optical network terminal.

   b. A network printer.   d.   A satellite dish.

5. How fast is Fast Ethernet?

   a. 10 Mbps   c.   1,000 Mbps

   b. 100 Mbps   d.   10,000 Mbps

6. Which two frequency bands are used by wireless LANs?

   a. The 88MHz band and the 206MHz band.

   b. The 800MHz band and the 1.2GHz band.

   c. The 2.4GHz band and the 5GHz band.

   d. The 54MHz band and the 300GHz band.

7. Which Wi-Fi standard is the fastest?

   a. 802.11a   c.   802.11g

   b. 802.11ac   d.   802.11n

8. Which wireless standard simplifies the process of adding a device to a WLAN?

   a. WPA   c.   WEP

   b. WPA2   d.   WPS

9. Which cellular network is fastest?

   a. 1G   c.   3G

   b. 2G   d.   LTE

10. Sue made a big bowl of popcorn and is planning to stream four hours of Disney movies to her cell-enabled tablet. Why has she opted to use Wi-Fi for her movie night?

   a. Wi-Fi gives a clearer picture.

   b. Using Wi-Fi won't impact her data plan.

   c. Wi-Fi provides for true surround-sound.

   d. No special reason; Sue is just being whimsical.

Lesson 4: File Management

Lesson Objectives

In this lesson, you will learn to use Windows File Explorer to find, move, open, and manage files. You will work with windows, learn about default locations, learn about file types and file permissions. Upon completion of this lesson, you should be able to:

- navigate a directory and follow paths
- understand rights and permissions
- use File Explorer
- work with windows
- recognize different types of files
- work with files and folders
- find files
- work with the Recycle Bin
- describe default file locations
- share pictures on a smart phone
- manage electronic media
- share files with other users
- zip and unzip files

Understanding Folders and Directory Structure

Objective 1-3.6

Computers are designed to store and manage information. In order to do that successfully, they must provide a logical storage methodology and an interface that allows a user to see and work with the stored data.

All computer storage devices are arranged into a logical, hierarchical structure that makes it possible to store and retrieve data. It does not matter if you are working with a hard disk inside your PC, a flash drive connected to a USB port on your laptop, an SD card inserted into a card reader slot, or a storage location on a server somewhere in cyberspace – all storage locations can be traced through a logical, hierarchical path.

Drive Letters

On a personal computer, each storage device (or location) is referred to by a drive letter. This applies to internal storage devices, mapped network folders, and externally connected storage devices as well.

The hard drive in a PC is drive C. This is where the operating system and application programs are installed.

Note: In the early days of personal computing, the letters A and B were reserved for disk drives that accommodated removable storage media called floppy disks. Hard drives did not become available until sometime later, and when they did, the letter C became the standard drive letter for hard disk drives.

When you write a designation for a drive letter, you follow the letter with a colon (:). For example, you would write C: to refer to drive C.

Additional Internal Storage Devices

Computers can accommodate multiple internal storage devices, and each is assigned a drive letter when it is installed. Usually, the next available alphabet letter is used. Consider the following examples:

- if your PC has two hard drives: the primary hard drive is drive C and the secondary hard drive is drive D.

- if your PC has one hard drive and an internal DVD drive, the hard drive is drive C and the DVD drive is drive D.

- if your PC has two hard drives and a DVD drive, the primary hard drive is drive C, the secondary hard drive is drive D, and the DVD drive is drive E.

The drive designation of an internal storage device does not change unless you manually change it.

Mapped Network Locations

If you have access to shared network locations, you can create shortcuts to these locations by "mapping" a particular location and assigning it a drive letter. The process of drive mapping is simply a matter of tracing the path to a particular network location and telling the operating system that you want to refer to this location using a particular drive letter. The process is manual, and you can select whichever available letter you want to use.

The following figure shows a graphical representation of a PC with one internal hard drive (C:), and two mapped network locations (H: and L:).

Connected Storage Devices

When you connect an external storage device to your PC (for example, through a USB port or an SD card slot), the operating system automatically assigns the next available drive letter to that device. The following figure shows a PC with one hard drive, two mapped network drives, and two connected flash drives (D: and F:) and an inserted SD card (E:).

Because external storage devices are constantly connected and then disconnected, drive designations for these devices are assigned each time a device is connected. A particular flash drive may be drive E on Monday, and drive G on Wednesday, depending on whether other external devices are connected on Wednesday before the flash drive is connected.

Folders and Subfolders

You can store files in the root folder of a drive; however, it is more efficient to store files in folders. A *folder* is a container for files and provides a method for organizing information; it's something like a hanging folder in a file cabinet within which you can organize other folders and files. A *subfolder* is simply a folder contained within another folder, and the terms folder and subfolder are often used interchangeably.

A folder that you create is represented by a yellow icon that looks like a file folder 📁. You can create folders using Windows or an application program.

Additionally, Windows provides a feature called libraries to help you access files quickly. A library is a collection of items, such as files and folders, assembled from various locations and presented in one central location. A library looks and acts like a folder, and they are often referred to as folders. For example, the Documents library is often called the "Documents folder." The libraries in Windows 10 are: Camera Roll, Documents, Music, Pictures, Saved Pictures, and Videos.

Directories and Paths

The organization of files and folders on a disk is called a *directory* or a directory tree. The highest level of any directory on a disk is the root folder, or *root directory*. The root directory is always represented by the drive letter and a colon, followed by a backslash (\). For example, the root directory of the hard drive is represented as C:\.

Every file on a computer is stored in a particular location on a disk, and that location is described by its *path*. A path indicates the exact route to follow to get to the location of a file. When you write a path, you separate each folder level with a backslash.

Consider the directory structure shown at the right:

- The structure shows the Documents library with two folders: one called 7500 Student Files, and another called Annual Reports.

- The Annual Reports folder contains two subfolders; one called 2015 and one called 2016.

- Stored within the 2016 folder are four files named: Balance Sheet, Budget 2016, ComputerSales, and Meeting Minutes 4-26-16.

📄 Documents
　📁 7500 Student Files
　📁 Annual Reports
　　📁 2015
　　📁 2016
　　　📊 Balance Sheet
　　　📊 Budget 2016
　　　📊 ComputerSales
　　　📄 Meeting Minutes 4-26-16

If you were to verbally describe how to find the Balance Sheet file, you could say, "Go to Documents, then Annual Reports, then the Balance Sheet document is inside the 2016 folder."

If you were to write your description of how to find the file in "path notation", it would appear as follows: Documents\Annual Reports\2016\Balance Sheet.

Connecting "Smart" Devices

Objective 1-3.6

When you connect a smart device to a PC, the device appears as a location/folder. A smart device is one that includes its own operating system. Smart phones, tablets, and eReaders are examples of smart devices. You can connect a smart device to your PC using a USB cable, usually for the purpose of copying or moving files from the device to your computer.

Once the device is connected, you can navigate its internal storage system just as you can a folder within your PC. The following figure shows part of the internal storage system of an Android tablet (identified as QMV7B) connected to a PC.

File and Folder Permissions

Objective 1-3.6, 1-3.10

File permissions are rules that determine whether you can access a file and what you can do with it. Let's begin our discussion by defining two basic file permissions:

Read	You can view the names of files and folders on the network, view the contents of files, and execute application program files.
Write	You can view the names and contents of files and folders, and can create new files and folders, modify the contents of files, and delete files and folders.

As a standard user, you can create, edit, view or print files for your own user account. You cannot, however, work with files and folders created by another user on the system. In fact, you will not be able to access folders stored under another user's profile – if you try to navigate to another user's folder, the operating system denies you access.

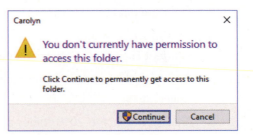

Only a user with an Administrator account can work with files stored under another user's profile.

Additionally, the operating system may restrict you from saving or altering files in certain locations. For example, if you want to paste a file into the root directory of the hard drive, administrator level privileges are required.

Network Access

If you work on a network, for example at your school or within your organization, there may be areas of the network that you cannot access. The network administrator controls which users can access specific network resources, such as printers, or servers, or files stored in network folders. One of the primary job roles of a network administrator to protect an organization's assets. This is generally accomplished by providing the least amount of access privileges required for users to perform their daily tasks.

For example, a user in data entry who spends all day entering customer orders into the company database does not require access to the company web server, except perhaps to request web pages on the company intranet. The web server administrator on the other hand, requires access to the web server, but does not require access to confidential documents handled by the Human Resources department.

By restricting access to resources or folders that contain sensitive information, network administrators keep the organization's data secure.

If you need to access files stored in a specific network location, the network administrator will set specific permissions for those files that control what you can do with them. For example, you might have access to a document in a network folder, but even though you can read the document, you might not have permissions to make changes to it.

Additionally, you may be able to view the contents of some network folders, but not be able to create or save files to those folders. There might also be some folders that you cannot access at all.

If you need to work in a specific file or folder stored in a network location, but do not currently have sufficient permissions, you should contact the network administrator so that he or she can adjust your rights accordingly.

Understanding Local and Remote Locations

In terms of computing, a *local location* is a drive or folder on a storage location within the computer or immediately attached to the computer (for example, a folder on a connected flash drive or an SD card).

A *remote location* is one that you access over a network (either wired or wireless). Computers you connect to over the Internet, storage locations in the cloud, and shared network folders on your organization's LAN or on another computer in your private LAN or Windows Homegroup are all examples of remote locations.

Using File Explorer

Objective 1-3.3

The graphical representations of locations, directories and files that you have seen so far in this lesson are part of the interface of File Explorer. File Explorer is the file management interface of Microsoft Windows. It provides a GUI for accessing and working with files.

Like any other task you perform on your PC, every interaction you have with File Explorer takes place inside one or more windows. You use different types of windows depending on what you are doing, but all windows share similar features.

To open File Explorer:

- click the File Explorer icon in the taskbar; or
- click **Start**, then click **File Explorer**; or
- double-click a folder on the Desktop; or
- press WINDOWS+E.

The following figure shows a typical File Explorer window.

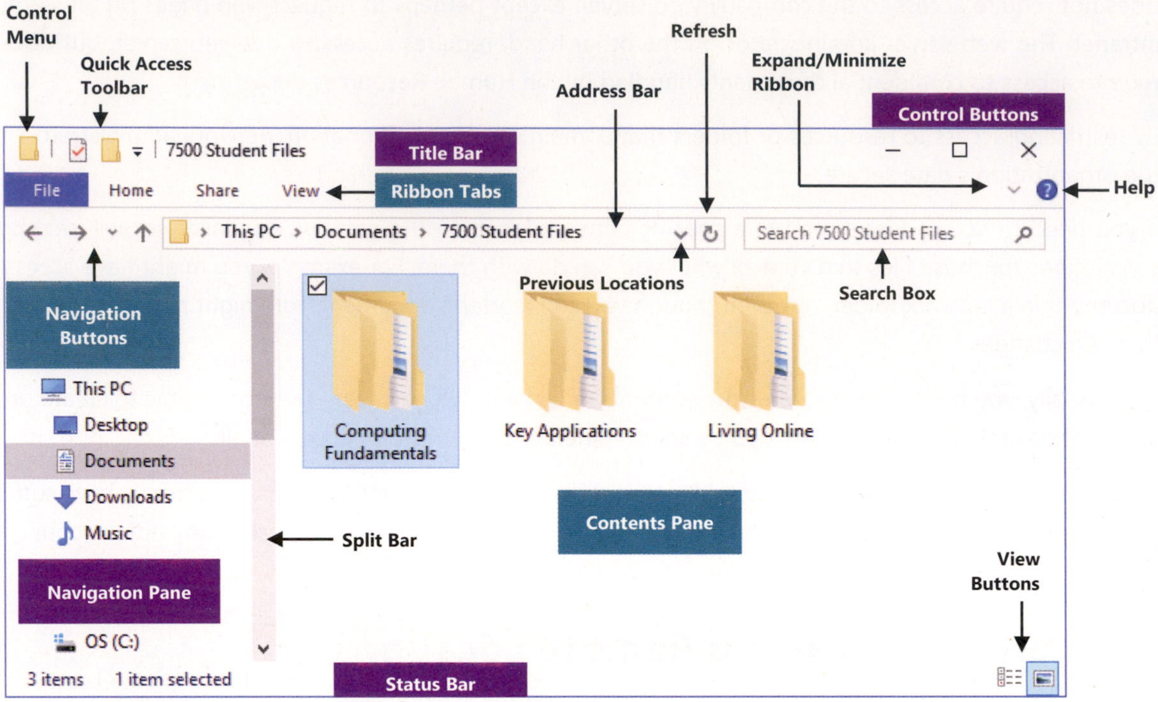

Control Menu	Click to display options to restore, move, size, minimize, maximize, or close the window.
Quick Access Toolbar	Contains buttons for frequently used commands. By default, it displays the Properties, New Folder, and Customize Quick Access Toolbar buttons. However, you can add the Undo, Redo, Delete, and Rename commands to the toolbar. You can also specify to show the toolbar below the ribbon.
Title Bar	In File Explorer, the title bar displays the name of the currently selected folder. In an application window, the title bar displays the name of the application and the name of the active file.
Control Buttons	Change the way currently open windows are displayed, as follows: • ― (**Minimize**) Temporarily closes the window, replacing it as a button on the taskbar. Click the button on the taskbar to open or restore the window. • ▢ (**Maximize**) Displays the window full screen. • ▱ (**Restore Down**) Restores the window to the size it was before it was maximized. • ✕ (**Close**) Closes the window.
File Menu	Displays options for working in the current folder. For example, you can open another window that shows the contents of the current folder, or you can open a command prompt window or a Power Shell Tools window. You can also open a dialog box that allows you to configure options for the current folder.

Ribbon Tabs	File Explorer windows include ribbons for working with files. When you click on a tab, the ribbon expands to display the available commands. When you click a command on the ribbon, the ribbon minimizes again. The File Explorer ribbon tabs are: • The Home tab includes commands for copying, moving, and renaming files. • The Share tab includes commands for emailing, printing, sharing, or compressing files. • The View tab includes commands for changing the display of the contents in the current folder. Some ribbons are contextual and, when appropriate, display on a Manage tab. For example, if you are working in a folder that contains image files, the Manage tab appears and displays a Picture Tools ribbon which includes commands for rotating images, setting an image as a background, or displaying images in a slide show.
Expand or Minimize the Ribbon	Click ⌄ (**Expand the Ribbon**) to expand the ribbon and keep it expanded, even after you click a command. When the ribbon is expanded, this button changes to ⌃ (**Minimize the Ribbon**), which you can click to minimize the ribbon at any time.
Help	Click ❓ to open the browser to a page of Help topics related to using Windows 10 File Explorer.
Navigation Buttons	Use ← (**Back**) or → (**Forward**) to navigate back and forth among previous views of files and folders. Click ⌄ (**Recent Locations**) to display a list of locations recently visited in File Explorer. Click a location in the list to jump to it. Click ↑ (**Up One Level**) to move up one level in the path.
Address Bar	Indicates the current location and facilitates quick and easy navigation. This feature allows you to click the name of any folder visible in the path so that you can go to that folder, or click the arrow that appears next to any item and see other items at the same level in the folder hierarchy. The Address Bar is also known as the Breadcrumb Bar.
Previous Locations	Click ⌄ at the right end of the path to open a drop-down list of previously visited locations. Click a location in the list to jump to it.
Refresh	Click ↻ to refresh the display in the Contents pane.
Search Box	Use this box to search for a file for folder within the current folder (and its subfolders).
Navigation Pane	Displays drives and folders in a tree view. Click a drive or folder in the Navigation pane to view its contents in the Contents pane. The contents of the Navigation pane are commonly called the *Folder list*.
Contents Pane	Displays the contents of the drive or folder currently selected in the Navigation pane. Double-click a file or folder in the Contents pane to open it.
Split Bar	The split bar separates the Navigation pane from the Contents pane. Click and drag the split bar to show more or less of the Navigation pane.
Status Bar	Displays properties or details about the item(s) currently selected in the Contents pane.
View Buttons	Affects the display in the Contents pane. Click ▦ to view details about each file or folder; or click ▤ to view thumbnails of each file or folder.

Exercise 4-1: Viewing File Explorer windows

In this exercise, you will practice working with File Explorer windows.

1. In the Window taskbar, click the **File Explorer** icon.

2. Click the **Maximize** button at the top right corner of the window.

3. Click the **Minimize** button. The File Explorer window disappears from the screen. Notice that the File Explorer icon now displays with a line beneath it, indicating that it is a button. You can access the File Explorer window from its taskbar button.

4. Click the **File Explorer** button on the taskbar to redisplay the maximized File Explorer window.

5. Click the **Restore Down** button at the top right corner of the window to reduce its size.

6. In the Navigation pane, under the Quick Access heading, click **Desktop** to view the contents of the Desktop in the Contents pane. (It is okay if only the 7500 Student Files folder displays in the File Explorer window.)

7. At the bottom right corner of the Contents pane, click each of the two view buttons to compare the views. Ensure that thumbnails are displayed before proceeding to the next step.

8. Click the **View** tab to display the ribbon, then in the Layout group, click **List**. Now the names of the files and folders display in a list. Notice that the ribbon minimized as soon as you clicked a command.

9. Click the **Close** button to close the File Explorer window. The window is removed from the screen, and the File Explorer button in the taskbar becomes an icon (without an underline) once again.

Moving a Window

You can move a window anywhere on the desktop using the mouse or keyboard.

- Position the mouse pointer anywhere on the title bar and then drag the window to a new location.

- With the keyboard, press ALT+SPACEBAR to open the control menu. Press the DOWN ARROW key to select the Move command and press ENTER to put the window into move mode. Using the arrow direction keys, move the window to the new location and then press ENTER again to exit move mode.

🗗	Restore
	Move
	Size
–	Minimize
🗖	Maximize
x	Close Alt+F4

Maximized windows cannot be moved because they occupy the entire screen. You can only move a restored (that is, not maximized) window.

Sizing a Window

On occasion you may want to change the size of the window so that you can see more or less of the information inside it, or so that you can view that information in multiple windows. You can use the mouse or the keyboard to size a window.

- Position the mouse pointer anywhere on the border (side) to be sized. When you see the mouse cursor change to a ↕ (vertical double-headed arrow) for the top or bottom border, or ⇔ (horizontal double-headed arrow) for the left or right border, drag the mouse to the desired size.

- To size the vertical and horizontal sides at the same time, position the mouse cursor on any corner of the window, and then drag to the desired size for the window when you see ⤢ or ⤡ (diagonal double-headed arrow). Some windows are set to a specific size and cannot be altered.

- With the keyboard, press ALT+SPACEBAR to activate the control menu. Press the DOWN ARROW key to select the Size command and press ENTER. Using the appropriate arrow direction key for the side you want to size, press that direction key until the window is the size you want, and then press ENTER to exit resize mode. You will need to repeat this action for every side to be sized.

Using Scroll Bars

If a window is too small to display all its contents, scroll bars will automatically appear vertically on the right side of a window, and/or horizontally at the bottom.

A scroll bar consists of three parts: an arrow button at each end of the scroll bar, a scroll box, and the scroll area. The scroll box is also called a thumb or an elevator. The position of the scroll box within the scroll area provides an approximate gauge of where the information currently displayed in the window is in relation to the entire window's contents.

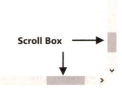

Use one of the following methods to move around with the scroll bars:

- Click in the lighter shaded area above or below the scroll box to display the previous or subsequent screen of information.

- Click the arrow at either end of the vertical scroll bar once to display a line of information in that direction.

- Click the arrow at either end of the horizontal scroll bar once to display a column of information in that direction.

- Click and hold down the mouse button on the arrow at either end of the scroll bar to have the screen scroll in that direction.

- Drag the scroll box to a specific area in the scroll area to move directly to that location. Depending on the program, you may also see a tip showing where the cursor will be placed when you release the mouse button.

Exercise 4-2: Moving and sizing windows

In this exercise, you will move a window around the screen and resize it.

1. Click the **File Explorer** icon in the taskbar.

2. If the window appears full screen, click the **Restore Down** button.

3. Position the mouse pointer in the title bar of the window, then click and drag the window to a new position on the desktop.

4. Practice moving the window around to several different locations.

5. Move the mouse pointer to the right edge of the window and hold the mouse over the border until the pointer changes to a horizontal double-headed arrow.

6. Drag the border to approximately one inch (2.5 cm) from the right side of the screen.

7. Move the mouse pointer to the lower right corner of the window and drag the corner of the window until the window is approximately half the current size.

Click **Browse** to open the Browse for Files or Folders dialog box.

Click locations and folders in the dialog box until you work your way to the folder you want to set as the target of your shortcut.

Click **OK** to set the shortcut target. Click **Next** in the wizard, type a name for your shortcut, then click **Finish**.

Exercise 4-3: Working with folders

In this exercise, you will create, and rename folders and, create shortcuts to folders.

Note: The following exercise requires that you have downloaded the student data files. If you have not already done so, please follow the data file instructions in the Preface before proceeding.

1. On the Desktop, double-click the **7500 Student Files** folder.

2. In the Contents pane, double-click **File Mgmt**. You are now viewing the files for this lesson.

3. Click **New folder** in the Quick Access toolbar to create a new item near the top of the Contents pane.

4. Type your first and last name for the new folder and press ENTER.

5. Double-click your new folder to view the contents (it should be empty).

Now, create some subfolders within your folder.

6. In the Contents pane, right-click to display the shortcut menu, click **New**, and then click **Folder**.

7. Type: Personal and press ENTER. You have created a new folder that resides within the folder with your name in the *File Mgmt* folder.

8. Move up one level by clicking **File Mgmt** in the Address bar, as shown in the following:

    > 7500 Student Files > File Mgmt > Lucy Lee >

    You should now be looking at the contents of the *File Mgmt* folder. You can use the path in the Address bar to help you navigate quickly to a specific location.

9. Double-click the folder with your name once again to move back down one level.

10. In the Contents pane, right-click, click **New**, and then **Folder**.

11. Type: Worksheets as the name of the new folder and press ENTER.

12. Repeat steps 10 and 11 to create the *Documents*, *Misc*, and *Slide Shows* folders. When you are finished, your folders should display as shown:

    Documents
    Misc
    Personal
    Slide Shows
    Worksheets

    Tip: When adding new folders, be sure to right-click in a blank area of the Contents pane. If necessary, make the window larger to show a blank area.

Now, try renaming a folder.

13. In the Contents pane in the File Explorer window, right-click the **Documents** folder, then click **Rename** in the shortcut menu.

14. Type: Docs and press ENTER. The folder is renamed.

Now, try creating a shortcut on the Desktop that will take you to the *Personal* folder inside the folder with your name.

15. In the Navigation pane in the File Explorer window, under This PC, click **Desktop**. The desktop contents display in the Contents pane.

16. Right-click in a blank area of the Contents pane, click **New**, and click **Shortcut**.

17. Click the **Browse** button.

18. In the Browse for Files or Folders dialog box, click **This PC**, then click **Desktop**, then click **7500 Student Files**, then click **File Mgmt**, then click **<your name>**, then click **Personal** and click **OK** to set the target for the shortcut.

19. In the Create Shortcut wizard, click **Next**.

20. Type: JustMe in the Type a name for this shortcut box, to specify a new name for the shortcut.

21. Click **Finish**. Windows creates the shortcut on the Desktop.

22. Minimize the File Explorer window.

23. On the Desktop, double-click the **JustMe** shortcut. Windows opens a new File Explorer window and shows the contents of the *7500 Student Files\File Mgmt\<your name\Personal* folder.

24. Close all open File Explorer windows.

Tiles

Displays files and folders as medium-sized icons with the file names to the right of the icon. The file format and file size also display.

LucyLee	**Annual Sales Report** Microsoft Word Document 17.0 KB
Awards Rich Text Format 43.0 KB	**Budget 2015** Microsoft Excel Worksheet 11.4 KB
Budget 2016 Microsoft Excel Worksheet 11.4 KB	**Car Expenses - Personal** Microsoft Excel Worksheet 11.2 KB
Computer Sales Microsoft Excel Worksheet 13.6 KB	**Department Budget** Microsoft Excel Worksheet 11.3 KB

Content

Displays any properties or reference information about the contents of the file.

LucyLee	Date modified: 5/23/2016 11:11 AM
Annual Sales Report	Date modified: 4/27/2016 2:13 PM Size: 17.0 KB
Awards	Date modified: 4/27/2016 2:14 PM Size: 43.0 KB

You can click the Sort by button in the View tab to arrange files by Name, Date modified, Type, Size, Date created, Authors, Categories, Tags or Title. You can specify Ascending or Descending order.

Additionally, whenever you can see the column headings in the Contents pane, you can use them to sort the contents or to manipulate the view further, as follows:

- To adjust the width of a column, position the mouse pointer over the vertical line at the right edge of the column you want to adjust; the mouse pointer changes to display ↔. Click and drag to the left or right to make the column narrower or wider.

- To sort the contents by item type, click the **Type** column heading. An ⌃ up-facing arrow symbol indicates the items are sorted in ascending order (that is, A–Z or 0–9); a ⌄ down-facing arrow symbol indicates the items are sorted in descending order (that is, Z–A or 9–0).

Exercise 4-4: Working with views

In this exercise, you will use different views in File Explorer.

First, you will change the location that is displayed automatically when File Explorer launches.

1. Click the **File Explorer** icon in the taskbar to open File Explorer. By default, File Explorer opens to show Quick access. (Windows keeps track of your recently used files and folders and adds them to the Quick access list.) You can, however, specify that you want File Explorer to open to This PC.

2. In the File Explorer window, click the **File** menu, then click **Change folder and search options**.

3. At the top of the General tab of the Folder Options dialog box, display the Open File Explorer to drop-down list and click **This PC**.

4. Click **Apply**, then click **OK**.

5. Close and then re-open File Explorer. Now, File Explorer opens to This PC.

Now, use a shortcut to open a folder in File Explorer.

6. Close the File Explorer window again.

7. On the Desktop, double-click the **JustMe** shortcut to display the folder in File Explorer.

8. In the Address bar, click **File Mgmt** to jump to that folder.

Now, try some different views.

9. Right-click a blank area in the Contents pane, point to **View**, then click **Tiles** to display the contents of the folder as tiles.

10. Click the **View** tab, then in the Layout section, click **List**.

11. Click the **View** tab, then in the Layout section, click **Details**.

12. Click the **Date modified** column heading to sort the contents by date.

13. Click the **Type** column heading to sort the contents by file type.

14. Try changing the view a few more times to see what you like.

15. Make **Name** the last heading sort and **List** the last view style you apply.

Understanding File Types and File Name Extensions

A *file name extension* is a suffix added to the base name of a computer file, and separated from the base name by a dot (.). Operating systems and application programs use file name extensions to recognize the format of a file and to identify which program created the file and which program may be used to open the file successfully.

Most operating systems automatically recognize common file name extensions, and associate particular application programs with particular extensions. These associations make it possible for you to double-click a file to open it. The operating system launches the necessary application and then opens the file within the application.

Additionally, Windows displays an application icon to the left of the file name, indicating which application is associated with the file type. In general, the icon is a visual reminder of the software program used to create or access the file. If Windows displays a generic file icon, then it does not know which application to use to open the file. In most cases, this is because you do not have an application installed that is capable of opening and editing the specific type of file.

There are thousands of file types and applications. The following sections introduce a few of the most common types, and the applications often associated with them.

Audio Files

Audio files are generally produced using specialized applications, but can be played through freely available applications called "players." Common audio players include Windows Media Player, Windows 10 Groove music app, Winamp2, Winamp3, and iTunes. When you double-click an audio file, the associated player opens and begins playback of the file. Common audio types include:

.aiff	Audio Interchange File Format – developed by Apple Computer, but most browsers can play AIFF files.
.mp3 or .m4a	Motion Picture Experts Group MPEG – requires a player application such as iTunes, Apple QuickTime or Windows Media Player.
.wav	Waveform Audio File Format – this is the native sound format for Windows. Most browsers include built-in support for WAV files. This is also the format used on audio CDs.
.wma	Windows Media Audio – developed by Microsoft, this format produces much smaller files than the .wav format.

Video Files

Video files are generally produced using specialized applications, but can be played through freely available applications called "players." Common video players include Windows Media Player, the Windows 10 Movies & TV app, and Apple QuickTime. When you double-click a video file, the associated player opens and begins playback of the file. Commonly-used video file formats include:

.avi	Audio Video Interleave – standard video files for Windows. AVI files play in Internet Explorer through the Windows Media Player. Apple QuickTime player can also open this format.
.mov or .qt	Standard video formats for Apple QuickTime movies, and the native format for Macintosh operating systems. Opens with Apple QuickTime player.
.mpg, .mpeg, and .mp4	Motion Picture Experts Group – standard format for video files on the Internet. Opens with MP4 players, Windows Media Player and Apple QuickTime player.
.swf	Animation file created with Adobe Flash and played in web browsers through the Flash Player plug-in.
.wmv	Windows Media Video – a compressed video file format originally designed for Internet streaming applications.

Note that not all media types are compatible with all players. For example, if you download a movie clip and then receive an error message when you try to play it back, it may be due to the fact that the player does not support that particular video format. You can look online to find which player is required and then download and install it.

Graphics Files

Graphics files are images. Many graphics formats are supported in web browsers and most operating systems include built-in graphics viewers. Graphics can be imported to a system from a digital camera or scanner, or can be created on a computer using a dedicated graphics creation and manipulation program such as Microsoft Paint, Paintshop Pro or Adobe Illustrator. When you double-click a graphics file, the image displays in either a dedicated graphics editing program, or in a viewer. If the file is not supported, Windows will prompt you to select an application to use to open the file. Common graphics formats include:

.gif	Graphics Interchange Format – graphics format used for line drawings and illustrations.
.jpg or .jpeg	Joint Photographic Experts Group – graphics format used for photographs and complex graphics.
.png	Portable Network Graphics – graphics format commonly used on web pages.
.tif or .tiff	Tagged Image File Format – graphics format commonly used for desktop publishing and medical imaging.

Document Files

Document files can be created using specialized applications, such as those found in the Microsoft Office suite, in OpenOffice, or in web apps such as those you can access on Google Drive or OneDrive. Some formats can be opened and edited in simple text editors such as Notepad. Some formats, such as PDF and RTF, are designed to be cross-platform compatible. That is, you can open them on Windows systems or Apple systems, or UNIX systems. Double-clicking a document file opens it in an application that can support it (if one is installed on the system).

Document file formats include:

.asc	ASCII – a standard text format for all computers, regardless of operating system.
.doc	The default document format for Microsoft Word (prior to version 2007) or Windows WordPad.
.docx	The default document format for Microsoft Word 2007 and above.
.htm or .html	Hypertext Markup Language – the document format used in web pages and supported by all web browsers.
.one	The default format for Microsoft OneNote
.pdf	Portable Document Format – document format supported on all operating systems through the use of the Adobe Reader plug-in. A full version of Adobe Acrobat is required to edit a PDF file. Microsoft Office files and documents created in Google Drive can be saved to PDF format to make them cross-platform compatible.
.ppt or .pptx	The default presentation formats for Microsoft PowerPoint.
.rtf	Rich Text Format – a document format that supports text and images. This format is supported by most word processing applications across many operating systems.
.txt or .text	Document format that supports plain text only, without formatting. Double-clicking a .txt file on a Windows system will open the file in either NotePad or WordPad.
.xls or .xlsx	The default spreadsheet formats for Microsoft Excel.

Executable Files

Executable files are files that launch a program or procedure. Take great care when opening executable files that you receive via email or that you download from web sites with which you are not familiar. When you open an executable file, your PC can automatically run any number of operations without your explicit approval. Executable file formats include:

.bat	Batch file – found on old DOS systems.
.cgi	Common Gateway Interface – script file used to generate web content.
.cmd	Windows command file.
.com	DOS command file.
.dll	Dynamic Link Library – these files are not executables, but are libraries of code that are referred or called by executable programs.
.exe	Windows executable program; these files are typically self-extracting compressed files.
.msi	Windows installer file – these executables are used to automate software installation on Windows systems.
.vbs	Visual Basic – script files created in the Visual Basic programming language. VBS scripts have been used to spread viruses.

Archive/Compressed File Formats

Archives are compressed file formats. Used primarily on the Internet, the compressed file format reduces the amount of time necessary to download a file. Archives can contain any type of file – images, documents, executables, and so on. A compression utility is required to compress and decompress the files. Archived file formats include:

.bz or .bz2	Archive files used by the Bzip/Bunzip application.
.rar	A compression standard that is platform-neutral (can be used on various operating systems). On UNIX systems, the RAR application is used. On Windows systems, the WinRAR application is used.
.tar	Compressed file used on UNIX systems.
.zip	Compressed file used by the PKZIP and WinZip applications.

Exercise 4-5: Recognizing file types

In this exercise, you will match the file type with an appropriate software program that could be used to view or edit the file.

a.	.docx	_____	iTunes
b.	.swf	_____	WinZip
c.	.pptx	_____	Internet Explorer
d.	.jpg	_____	Windows Media Player
e.	.mp3	_____	Word
f.	.avi	_____	PowerPoint
g.	.htm	_____	Photoshop
h.	.zip	_____	Flash Player

Windows 10 and File Extensions

Windows automatically recognizes common file name extensions, and associates particular application programs with particular extensions. For example, if you are using a file management tool such as File Explorer, and you double-click a file with a .pdf file name extension, Windows will try to open the file in Adobe Reader, which is the program used to read PDF files. The operating system launches the necessary application and then opens the file within the application.

If you try to open a file for which there is no associated application installed, Windows displays a window similar to the one shown:

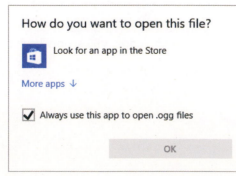

Click **More apps** to display a list of installed apps.

In some cases, you can choose a program that is already installed on the computer to try and open the file. If you cannot find an application that will successfully open the file, you can search in the Windows store for a suitable app.

Viewing the File Extensions

To keep things simple and keep the display uncluttered, you may want to hide file name extensions in file Explorer. Displaying file name extensions can be useful, however. For example, you can display extensions to show which picture files use the .jpg, .gif, or .tiff format.

Viewing file extensions is also useful for differentiating between two files with the same name but different file formats, such as .xlsx versus .csv. Both of these file types can be opened in a spreadsheet program such as Microsoft Excel. However, a .csv file is not a native Excel file type and will not appear in a list of available files when you try to open a file from within Excel.

By viewing the file name extension of audio or video files, you can quickly identify which program you can use to open the file. Another good reason for displaying the file types is to help you easily identify executable files. These files are used to launch a program (or other code that will carry out commands). You should take care before launching any executable file. While in most cases these files launch legitimate programs, they can also be used to install a virus on your computer.

To display the file extensions at all times, open a File Explorer window, click the **File** menu, then click **Change folder and search options** to open the Folder Options dialog box. Click the **View** tab and in the Advanced settings list, uncheck **Hide extensions for known file types**.

When you need to see hidden files, you can uncheck the **Hide protected operating system files (Recommended)** option. Important files such as system files or the data file for your email program are hidden to prevent them from being deleted or changed inadvertently. Protected system files may be displayed when a technical support person is working on your computer and needs to view them; it is recommended that you hide the system files once he/she has finished.

Selecting Files and Folders

Before performing any actions such as copying, moving, or deleting, you must select the file or folder. Consider the following traditional methods of selecting files or folders. These methods work in all versions of Windows:

- To select one file or folder, click it.

- To select all files and folders within a location, click the **Home** tab, and click **Select all** in the ribbon or press CTRL+A.

- To select multiple files or folders that are consecutive, point to the first file or folder in the list, press and hold the SHIFT key, and then point to the last file or folder in the list.

- To select files using the lasso method, point at the right of the first file or folder to be selected, then click and drag up or down to select the rest of the files or folders in the selection. A box will appear as confirmation of the selection, along with the files or folders being highlighted.

- To select multiple files or folders that are non-consecutive, point to the first file or folder to be selected, press and hold the CTRL key, and then point at each file or folder to be selected.

- At any time as files or folders are selected, if you need to change any part of the selection, use either the SHIFT or CTRL key to deselect specific parts of the selection.

To de-select or turn off the selection of files or folders, click anywhere away from the selection.

Note that in Windows 10, items in File Explorer display a check box when you point at them and display a check in the check box when they are selected.

Click the check box for the file you want to keep. If you elect to keep both copies (by selecting the check boxes for both files) Windows will create a file with a number at the end of the filename to indicate that it is a copy. In this example, the original file will be named Balance Sheet.xlsx and the copy in the same location will be named Balance Sheet (2).xlsx.

Exercise 4-7: Copying files

In this exercise, you will use the copy and paste features to copy files.

1. Ensure you are viewing the contents of the *File Mgmt* folder.

2. Press CTRL+A to select everything in the folder.

3. Now press and hold CTRL and click the folder with your name in order to de-select it. Now everything except the folder with your name is selected.

4. Click the **Home** tab, then in the Clipboard group, click **Copy**.

5. In the Contents pane, double-click the folder with your name to open it.

6. Click the **Home** tab, then in the Clipboard group, click **Paste** to paste the copied files from the student files folder to your folder.

Moving Files or Folders

When you move a file or folder, it is cut (deleted) from its original location and copied into the destination location. When you move a folder, all the contents within that folder (subfolders and files) move as well.

After selecting the files or folders to move, use one of the following methods:

- Click the **Home** tab, and then click **Cut** in the ribbon, move to the new location, click the **Home** tab again if necessary, and then click **Paste**, or

- press CTRL+X, move to the new location and then press CTRL+V, or

- right-click the selection and then click **Cut**, move to the new location, right-click and then click **Paste**, or

- drag the selected files or folders to the new location on the same drive. For different drives, Windows will automatically copy the selection unless you press the SHIFT key as you drag.

If after completing the move action the file or folder is not in the location you intended, it is possible you may have moved the file or folder to the folder above or below the one you wanted. Click in the folder on either side to see if the file or folder is there, then move it into the appropriate location.

Exercise 4-8: Moving files

In this exercise, you will move files to various locations.

1. Ensure you are in your folder.

2. Change the view to **Details**, and sort the files by the **Type** column.

3. Select all the Microsoft Word files and then press CTRL+X to cut them from the current location.

4. In the Contents pane, double-click the **Docs** folder to open it, then press CTRL+V to paste the copied files into this location.

5. Click your folder in the Address bar.

6.   Repeat steps 3-5 moving the Microsoft Excel files into the *Worksheets* folder.

7.   Select the Microsoft PowerPoint files, then drag the selected files into the *Slide Shows* folder.

8.   Move the remaining files into the *Misc* folder.

Suppose you want to move your folder to another location, such as the Desktop.

9.   Click **File Mgmt** in the Address bar to move up one level. If necessary, click your folder to select it, then drag to the left so that it hovers over Desktop in the Navigation pane.

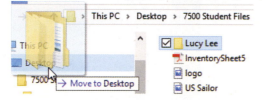

10. Release the mouse button when Desktop is highlighted, as shown in the preceding figure. You have successfully moved your folder to the Desktop.

Now move your folder back to where it was.

11. In the Navigation pane, click the **Desktop** folder, then in the Contents pane, click your folder to select it.

12. Press CTRL+X to cut it and remove it from the Desktop.

13. In the Contents pane, double-click **7500 Student Files**, then double-click *File Mgmt*, then press CTRL+V to paste your folder back into its original location.

Renaming Files

As with folders you can rename a file to make it more descriptive using the Edit mode.

To activate the Rename feature use one of the following methods:

*   Select the file and then press F2, or

*   select the file and then click once in the file name, or

*   right-click the file and then click **Rename**.

Remember the two limitations of file and folder naming conventions: a maximum of 255 characters; and the following characters \ / : * ? " < > | cannot be used in the file or folder name.

Be very careful not to rename any program files or folders, or the application program may not be able to find them.

Exercise 4-9: Renaming files

In this exercise, you will copy and then rename a file.

1.   In the File Explorer window, navigate to the *File Mgmt* folder.

2.   Right-click the **Letter to Joan Woods** file, then click **Copy**.

3.   Right-click in an empty area of the Contents pane, then click **Paste** to paste the file into the current folder. Windows pastes the file and adds "- Copy" to the end of the file name.

4.   Right-click **Letter to Joan Woods – Copy**, then click **Rename** to enter edit mode.

5.   Type: Letter from <your name> and press ENTER to rename the file.

Searching for Files

You can use two methods for finding files and folders on your system. You can use the Windows Search box/Cortana feature, or you can search from within File Explorer.

Using Windows Search Box/Cortana

The Windows Search box is located in the Windows taskbar, just to the right of the Start button. When you use the Windows Search box, Windows displays results from your system and the Internet. You can use the Search box to find help, apps, files, images, settings, and so on.

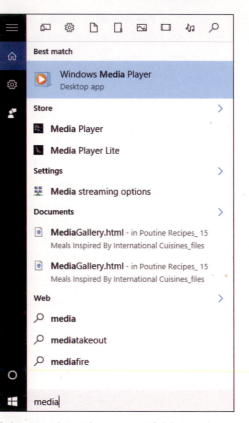

Click in the box and begin typing a search term. Windows will display suggestions and answers to your questions in a panel that appears above the search box.

Notice that the results in the previous figure are grouped by installed apps, store apps, settings, documents, and web. Windows will group the results it gathers depending on what it finds. Simply click on a result to access it.

You can also press the WINDOWS key and begin typing to use the Windows Search box.

Note: On a Mac, you can use the built-in Spotlight feature by clicking the Spotlight icon or by pressing COMMAND+SPACEBAR.

Searching within File Explorer

When you search from within File Explorer, you limit the scope of the search to the current folder and any subfolders below it in the directory hierarchy. Windows will not search folders outside the given path, nor will it search the Internet.

Click in the **Search** box within a File Explorer window and begin typing a search term. As you type, documents that match the search term display in the window.

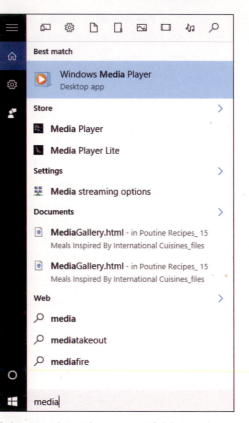

Windows lists all files that include the search term in the file name and that include the search term within the file contents. For example, in the preceding figure, the three Excel files contain the word "budget" in the file name. The word document includes the word budget somewhere within the document text.

Additionally, the Search Tools ribbon becomes available and you can use it to fine-tune your search.

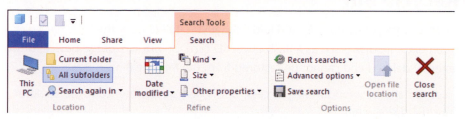

Notice that you can specify whether to include subfolders, or whether to filter the results by a variety of characteristics, such as the date the file was modified, or the approximate file size.

Windows also keeps track of your search history, allowing you to perform a previous search again. You can also clear the search history.

Exercise 4-10: Finding files

In this exercise, you will search for files.

1. Ensure that you are viewing your folder in the File Explorer window.

2. Click in the **Search** box in the top-right corner of the window and type: budget. Windows displays four files that match the search term.

Now, refine your search.

3. Click the **Search** tab if necessary, then in the Refine group, click **Size**, then click **Tiny (0 - 10KB)**. Now, no files display.

4. Click the **Search** tab if necessary, then in the Refine group, click **Size**, then click **Small (10 – 100KB)**. Now the four files are listed again.

Clear the search criteria and begin a new search.

5. Click in the **Search** field and click ✖ at the right end of the search box to clear the search field, then click the Search tab if necessary and in the Refine group, click **Other properties**, click **Tags**, then type: vintage. Now the US Sailor picture displays in the results list.

6. Click ✖ to clear the search criteria.

Begin a new search and change the search scope.

7. Click in the **Search** field and type: sale. Several results are listed.

8. In the Search tab, in the Location group, click **Current folder**. Now, no results are listed.

9. Clear the Search field.

10. On the Search tab, in the Options group, click **Recent searches**, then click **Clear search history**.

11. Close the File Explorer window.

Looking at the Recycle Bin

The Recycle Bin is a temporary storage area for files and folders that you delete from the local hard disk. Files and folders deleted from an external disk (such as a flash drive, SD card, or virtual storage device) or from a network drive are permanently deleted and cannot be restored from the Recycle Bin.

The Recycle Bin has an icon on the desktop for easy access, but is also accessible from File Explorer. Two icons are used to represent the Recycle Bin:

 Indicates there are files in the Recycle Bin that can be restored or the Recycle Bin can be emptied. 　　 Indicates the Recycle Bin is empty.

If the computer is shared by multiple users, a separate Recycle Bin exists for each user account on the computer.

To permanently delete a file and bypass the Recycle Bin, press and hold the SHIFT key while deleting the file.

Deleting Files and Folders

When you no longer need files or folders, you can delete them.

Always check the contents of a folder before you delete the entire folder. This is especially crucial if the folder is stored on a network drive or external disk, as these are not moved to the Recycle Bin.

To delete a file or folder, select the file or folder and then use one of the following methods:

- Click the **Home** tab, and then click **Delete**, or
- select the file or folder and then press DELETE, or
- right-click and click **Delete**, or
- drag the item to the Recycle Bin icon on the Desktop.

Restoring a File or Folder

You can restore a deleted file or folder to its original location. Double-click the Recycle Bin on the Desktop to open it.

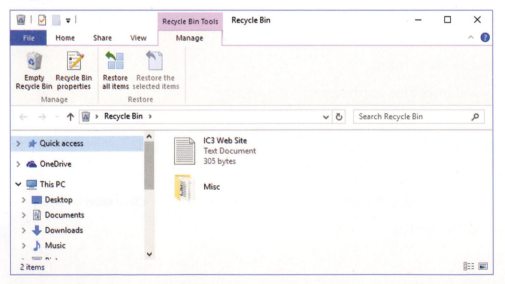

You can restore only an entire folder (including all its contents), not individual items that were deleted with the folder.

To restore a file or folder from the Recycle Bin, use one of the following methods:

- Select one or more files or folders to be restored, click the **Manage** tab, and then click **Restore the selected items**, or

- if you want to restore all items, click the **Manage** tab, and then click **Restore all items**, or

- right-click the selected files or folders, and then click **Restore**.

Emptying the Recycle Bin

Deleted files remain in the Recycle Bin until you empty it or it becomes full; in the latter case, Windows will automatically delete older files and folders to free up space for new items. When a file or folder is deleted from the Recycle Bin, it is permanently deleted.

To empty the Recycle Bin, use one of the following methods:

- Double-click the Recycle Bin on the desktop to open it, click the **Manage** tab, and then click **Empty Recycle Bin**, or

- right-click in a blank area of the Recycle Bin window and click **Empty Recycle Bin**, or

- right-click the Recycle Bin icon on the desktop and then click **Empty Recycle Bin**.

Use this option only when you are sure that you will not want to restore anything from the Recycle Bin.

Exercise 4-11: Using the Recycle Bin

In this exercise, you will delete files and folders and work with the Recycle Bin.

First, you will delete a file and a folder.

1. Ensure that you are viewing your folder in the File Explorer window.

2. Open the *Misc* folder, select the *IC3 Web Site* file, then press DELETE to delete the file and move it to the Recycle Bin.

3. Move up one level to your folder, then right-click the *Misc* folder and click **Delete** in the shortcut menu to delete the folder and move it to the Recycle Bin.

Now, restore the folder.

4. On the Desktop, double-click the **Recycle Bin** icon to open the Recycle Bin.

5. Select the **Misc** folder, then click the **Manage** tab and click **Restore the selected items**. The Misc folder is restored to its previous location.

6. Close the Recycle Bin, then in the File Explorer window, navigate to your folder if necessary to verify that the Misc folder has been restored.

7. In the Address bar, click *File Mgmt* to move up one level.

Next you will delete your folder and the Desktop shortcut and then empty the Recycle Bin.

8. Right-click your folder, then click **Delete**. Your folder is deleted and moved to the Recycle Bin.

9. On the Desktop, right-click the **JustMe** shortcut, then click **Delete**. Your shortcut is deleted and moved to the Recycle Bin.

10. On the Desktop, right-click the Recycle Bin, then click **Empty Recycle Bin**. Click **Yes** to confirm that you want to permanently delete the contents of the Recycle Bin.

11. Close the File Explorer window.

Understanding Default Locations

Objective 1-3.7, 1-3.9

Although Windows provides tools to help you locate files on your system, it is helpful to understand that different types of files have default locations to which they are saved, depending on the program that you are using.

Generally, it is not difficult to locate documents you are creating because you purposefully save them to a specific folder when you create them. But have you ever scanned a picture and wondered where it went? Have you downloaded a user manual from the Internet and then you could not find it? Have you taken a picture with your integrated laptop or tablet or phone camera and then been unable to find it?

Scanners

A *scanner* is a device that converts a printed page into an electronic format. Most modern all-in-one printers include a scanning function that allows you to scan one or more pages and then save them as image files or as PDF documents.

Some scanners include *optical character recognition* (OCR) functionality which allows the scanner to convert the scanned image into editable electronic text and save that editable text as a document. Many also include functionality that will allow you to scan one or more pages, save the output as an email attachment, and then send the email message.

Most scanners automatically create a folder for all scanned output within your PC's Pictures folder. Each time you scan a page using the scanner's software, the scanner creates a subfolder within its own folder and names that new subfolder with the current date. Generic, sequentially-numbered file names are assigned to all scanned files. In the following figure, the *MP Navigator EX* folder and its dated subfolder (and its files) were created by a Canon scanner.

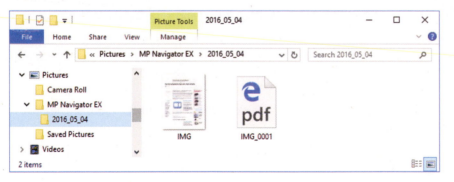

If you use the Windows Fax and Scan utility included in Windows 10, scanned images are automatically saved to the *Documents\Scanned Documents* folder.

Web Site Items

Any file that you copy from the Internet and save to your computer is saved in the *Downloads* folder, regardless of whether it is an image file, a document, a user manual, or an executable file. In certain situations, you will be prompted to save a file you want to download and you can specify where you want to save the file.

However, if you save a file or image from the Internet and are then unable to find it, check the *Downloads* folder.

Pictures

Windows uses the *Pictures* folder and subfolders for saving picture files. Certain actions save image files in specific default locations. For example:

- When you use the Windows 10 Camera app to take pictures on your laptop, those pictures are saved automatically in the *Pictures\Camera Roll* folder.

- If you take screen shots using the WINDOWS+PRINT SCREEN command, these are saved in the *Pictures\Screenshots* folder.

- If you take screen shots using the Windows Snipping tool, these are saved in the *Pictures* folder.

Additionally, if you use the Windows 10 Photos app to import pictures from a digital camera to your PC (via a USB cable), these are imported by default into the *Pictures* folder as well.

Keep in mind that these are default locations. In many situations, you can specify a different location in which to save your pictures. However, if you take some action that results in the saving of a picture file and you don't pay attention to where it is saved, you can check these default locations first.

Pictures on Smart Phones

We all love to take pictures (or even shoot video) using our smart phones – and once we grab that fantastic shot we want to share it with our friends and family. Usually, we want to share it right then and there.

Fortunately, smart phone apps make it easy to point, click and share.

Photos that you take with your smart phone are stored in a picture gallery. When you access the picture gallery, you can click any picture to view it full screen. Tap the picture to make the picture options visible. The following figure shows options for a photo taken on an Android phone:

The icons at the bottom of the screen allow you to adjust, share, edit, or delete the photo. To share the photo, tap the Share icon to bring up a menu of apps you can use to share the picture.

There are a wide variety of apps you can use to share pictures. Apps that appear as sharing options depend on the apps you have installed on your device and on the types of accounts you have – for example, social media accounts, email accounts, and so on.

When you use an app to share a photo (or other type of file), the app handles the transfer and will prompt you to enter any necessary information. For example, if you want to send a photo via email (which you can do as long as you have an email account configured on your phone), you will be prompted to enter the name or address of your recipient. You can type a brief message and then click Send to send your picture on its way.

Notice also that you can send the file to a variety of cloud locations (such as Google Drive, Instagram, or Facebook). Simply tap the appropriate app icon, and then confirm that you want to proceed.

Using Hardware to Share Photos

You can also share photos with other users using hardware methods for transfer. You can:

- Save your photos to an SD card, remove the card and give it to another user.

- Connect to a PC using a USB cable, navigate the phone's directory structure and then copy the desired photos. Most smart phones store photos in the *DCIM\Camera* folder. (DCIM stands for *Digital Camera Images*.)

- Use Bluetooth sharing if both devices support it. Put both devices into discovery mode, then when your phone detects the device to which you want to send your picture, tap the device in the list of detected devices and tap the send command. Your recipient will need to accept the file transfer.

Managing Electronic Media

Objective 1-3.6

Electronic media (or digital media) refers to media that is stored and played or viewed electronically. Music, movies and books are widely available in electronic format, and you play these formats within a player app designed for the content.

That is, you play movies on your Windows 10 laptop in a movie player app such as 5KPlayer or Movies & TV player for Windows 10. (On a Mac or iPad, you might use iMovie.) You play music on that same laptop in a music app such as Groove Music. You read eBooks on an eReader (such as Kindle, Nook, Kobo, or Sony Reader) or on a device on which an appropriate app has been installed.

These players and player apps are designed to handle digital content that is freely available and re-distributable as well as content that is protected by *digital rights management* (DRM) software. DRM is designed to prevent the unauthorized use, or redistribution of the media to which it is applied. DRM restricts the way you can copy content that you have purchased.

For this reason, you cannot directly manage digital media using File Explorer or other computer file management utilities.

In many cases, you cannot even see the digital content using File Explorer; you need to access and manage your titles using the player or player app.

Consider the following pair of figures. The background image shows eight eBooks that are downloaded to the PC and read using the Kindle app. The foreground image shows the storage location for the books that have been downloaded to the PC. The recognizable titles are for free books (and are stored in MOBI format). The others are for books which were purchased for the Kindle, and they are saved in a format which supports DRM.

Of the 16 files shown, can you tell which one is for the Wireless Networking book? The app knows how to interpret the file names and supporting information and display it in a way that is meaningful to you.

Let us go one step further and compare a partial listing of eBooks on an Amazon Kindle Fire (the figure in the background) to a file listing of the internal storage directory on the same Kindle Fire (the figure in the foreground). Do you think you could find a particular book by title?

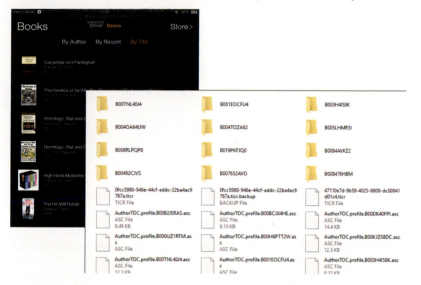

Players and player apps are essential tools for working with and managing digital media. Most include built-in search features that help you find just the file you want.

Sharing Files

Objective 1-3.6, 1-5.1

The available methods for sharing files have evolved over the years. Shortly, we will examine sharing files in the cloud. In this section, we will review a few "old school" methods for sharing files which are still used today.

Removable Media

Perhaps the oldest method of sharing files with other users to is copy them to removable media (such as a USB flash drive) and then deliver the media to someone else, who can then plug in the drive and copy the requisite files from the drive on to their own system.

Public Folders

Although standard users cannot see files created by other users on a given PC, you can place files that you want to share into one of several public folders located in: *This PC\OS (C:)\Users\Public*.

All users on a computer system have access to the public folders.

If you want to make some of your files available to other user accounts on the computer, save or copy them into one of the public folders.

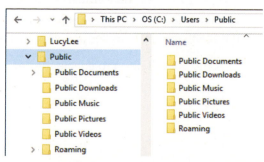

Shared Folders

If you want to share a file or folder only with a specific user (and not everyone else on the system), you can do so by setting the sharing properties for that file or folder.

In File Explorer, right-click the file or folder you want to share, click **Properties** to open the Properties dialog box, then click the **Sharing** tab.

Click the **Share** button to access a screen where you can enter the names of users with whom you want to share.

Type the user's name and click **Add** to add the user to the list of people who have access to the shared file.

If applicable, click the **Permission Level** arrow to adjust the permissions you want to extend to the other user. The default permission level is Read, but you can change it to Read/Write if you want the user to have the ability to edit your files or add or delete the contents of a shared folder.

Click the **Share** button to enable the new settings. Then click **Done**.

×

← 🔲 File Sharing

Your folder is shared.

You can e-mail someone links to these shared items, or copy and paste the links into another program.

┌─ Individual Items ──────────────────────────────── ^ ─┐
│ 📁 2016
│   \\CCI-IHEERL\Users\LucyLee\Documents\Annual Reports\2016
│
└──┘

⚠️ Shared items aren't accessible when your computer is asleep.
Show me all the network shares on this computer.

[Done]

The user with whom you shared your file or folder will be able to navigate to and access your shared file or folder using File Explorer the next time he or she logs on to the system.

If you want to share a file or folder with another user on the same network (but not a different user account on the same system), you can copy the share link that displays in the box and paste it into an email message and send it to the person with whom you want to share your file or folder. As long as that user is on the same network as you, he or she can simply click the link and access your file or folder.

Conversely, you can stop sharing a file or folder with a specific user (or with all users) by removing that user's name from the share properties, or by turning off sharing.

Note: You must be logged on with an Administrator account to enable sharing. If you try to enable sharing while logged on with a standard user account, you will be prompted to enter an administrator user name and password to enable sharing.

Network Shares

Another way to share files or folders is to place them in a network share. A *network share* (also called a network drive or a network folder) is simply a location on a server that is available over a network. Network shares are used within the private confines of a LAN. Network administrators often set up shares so that students or employees can access files that are stored in a central location.

As you learned earlier, the network administrator controls who can access what, and what they can do with it once they access it.

Email Attachments

It is easy and convenient to share files with other users by sending those files as attachments to an email message.

All email programs (whether locally installed or web-based) enable you to attach and send files with a message. As you are composing a new message, you can click an attachment button (or icon) and a dialog box will open which you can use to navigate to and select one or more files you want to attach to your email message. The specific name of the dialog box varies from one email client to the next, but all of them function in the same way.

- When you attach a file to an email message in Gmail, for example, you use the Choose File to Upload dialog box.

- In Outlook.com you use the Open dialog box, and in the Outlook Desktop app, you use the Insert File dialog box.

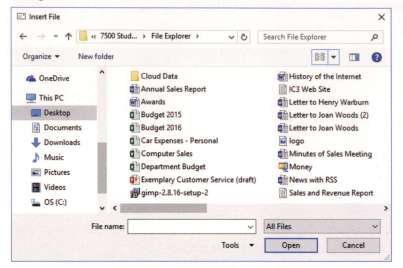

When you receive a file as an email attachment, you can save the attachment to your computer and then access it using File Explorer.

Limitations on Email Attachments

While sending all the files you want to share as email attachments might seem like an easy solution, there are certain limitations to using email for sharing files.

- Many email programs limit the size of file attachments – email must traverse networks, and very large files cause network congestion and can slow network performance. They also occupy a lot of space on email servers.

  - The maximum attachment size in Gmail is 25MB, in Outlook the limit is 20MB and in Yahoo the limit is 25MB.

  - Even if your particular email service allows very large attachments, your intended recipient's email service might not.

  - If you need to send many files, it might be best to send them in a series of email messages to avoid hitting the file size limit. You might also want to consider "zipping" the files into a compressed format. (We will discuss this in the next section.)

- Many email providers and network administrators restrict certain types of file attachments:

  - Executable files (.exe, .bat, .cmd, .com, and so on), script files, and various file types related to programming have been used to harbor computer viruses and other types of malicious code. Messages that contain files of these types will be rejected.

  - Database files (.mdb) cannot be sent as email attachments either.

  - Documents that contain macros are also commonly rejected.

- In most cases you cannot get around the file type restriction by zipping the files into a compressed format; however, you may be able to send your file as an attachment if you manually change the file name extension. (Your recipient will need to change it back to the correct extension after saving the file to his or her system.)

Compressing Files

When you need to reduce the size of one or more files, you can use a file compression utility. *Compressing* one or more files is also referred to as zipping, much like when you stuff a tote bag as full as possible and then press everything down to make it fit prior to zipping (closing) the bag.

Some files are larger than others, simply by the nature of the type of file. For example, video files are usually very large and should be converted to a compressed format (such as .avi) so they can be shared. Music files in .wav format are generally converted to .mp3 format to make them smaller for sharing. Picture files with a .tif or .bmp file type tend to be large in size and are compressed to a .png or .jpg format. The image, audio and video files you encounter on the Internet are already in a compressed format, which reduces the time required to download them to the temporary storage folders on your hard drive utilized by your web browser.

You are probably already familiar with popular "zip" programs that compress text and images. WinZip and PKZIP are third-party utilities that have been used to easily and successfully compress and un-compress files for decades, and a built-in zip utility has been included with Windows since Windows XP.

Zipped files are also called *archives*. Computers running Windows, Mac OS X, Linux and UNIX can handle zipped archive files.

To compress (zip) a file or folder:

1. Locate the file or folder that you want to compress.

2. Right-click the file or folder, point to **Send to**, and then click **Compressed (zipped) folder**.

    Money   5/4/2016 7:56 PM   49 KB   Compressed (zipped) Folder

To extract (unzip) compressed files and folders:

1. Locate the compressed folder from which you want to extract files or folders.

2. To extract a single file or folder, double-click the compressed folder to open it. Then drag the file or folder from the compressed folder to a new location, or

    To extract the entire contents of the compressed folder, right-click the folder, click **Extract All**, specify a destination folder for the extracted files, then click **Extract**.

10%
Setup progress

✓ Account Created

🎓 Learn how to use Gmail

📱 Get Gmail for mobile

🖼 Choose a theme

👤 Import contacts and mail

👤 Change profile image

0 GB (0%) of 15 GB used
Manage

Terms - Privacy

13. The modern Gmail Inbox is divided into three tabs – Primary, Social, and Promotions. Ensure that you are on the Primary tab. A welcome message from Andy from Google should appear in your Inbox.

Now, find an exercise partner and send an email message with a file attachment.

14. Exchange Gmail addresses with a person sitting near you. For the sake of this exercise, this person will be your partner.

15. Click the **Compose** button to open a New Message window.

16. In the New Message window, in the **To** field type your partner's Gmail address.

17. In the New Message window, click in the **Subject** field and type: A file for you.

18. Click in the empty space below the Subject field and type: Please look this over and tell me what you think. Thank you!

19. In the toolbar at the bottom of the new message window, click the 📎 **Attach files** button to open the Choose File to Upload dialog box. (If a window opens asking you to try inserting files using Google Drive, click **Maybe next time**.)

20. Navigate to the *7500 Student Files\File Mgmt* folder, click the **Letter from <your name>** file then click the **Open** button to add the file as an attachment to the email message.

A file for you

cccicarolyn@gmail.com

A file for you

Please look this over and tell me what you think. Thank you!

Letter from Lucy.docx (17K) ✕

Send A 📎 △ $ 📷 🔗 😊   🗑 ▾

21. Click **Send** to send the message.

Now, retrieve the file attachment you received.

22. When you receive the message from your partner, click it to open it.

23. Position the mouse pointer over the letter attachment. Notice that three icons appear. You can download the file, save it to Google Drive, or edit it in Google Docs.

24. Within the attachment, click the **Download** button, then in the notification bar that appears at the bottom of the browser window, click **Save**.

> Do you want to open or save **Letter from Lucy.docx** (16.8 KB) from **mail-attachment.googleusercontent.com**?   Open   Save ▼   Cancel   ×

25. When the file has been successfully downloaded, the notification bar presents different options.

> The Letter from Lucy.docx download has completed.   Open ▼   Open folder   View downloads   ×

26. Click **Open folder**. File Explorer opens to show the file in its current location. Notice that the file was automatically saved in your *Downloads* folder.

27. Close the File Explorer window.

28. At the top of the Gmail window, click your account icon (usually a blue circle with the first letter of your email address), then click **Sign out**.

29. Close your browser.

Lesson Summary

In this lesson, you learned to use Windows File Explorer to find, move, open, and manage files. You worked with windows, learned about default locations, and learned about file types and file permissions. You should now be able to:

☑ navigate a directory and follow paths

☑ understand rights and permissions

☑ use File Explorer

☑ work with windows

☑ recognize different types of files

☑ work with files and folders

☑ find files

☑ work with the Recycle Bin

☑ describe default file locations

☑ share pictures on a smart phone

☑ manage electronic media

☑ share files with other users

☑ zip and unzip files

Review Questions

1. Which letter is commonly used to refer to the storage device where the operating system is installed on a computer?

   a. A   c. C

   b. B   d. D

2. What happens when you connect a flash drive to a USB port on your computer?

   a. The operating system assigns the next available drive letter to that device.

   b. You are asked to download and install a device driver to handle USB drives.

   c. The operating system asks you which drive letter to assign to the device.

   d. A shortcut to the device is automatically created and added to your Desktop.

3. What do you call the organization of files and folders on a disk?

   a. Directory or directory tree   c. File management

   b. Path   d. Root directory

4. When you connect your smart phone to your PC using a USB cable, what can you do?

   a. Navigate the device's internal storage system.

   b. Assign the smart phone a drive letter.

   c. Organize the installed apps on the phone.

   d. Install a mobile operating system update on the phone from your PC.

5. Who can work with files stored under another user's profile?

   a. A user with an Administrator account.

   b. A standard user with Read permissions.

   c. A standard user with Write permissions.

   d. A standard user with Read/Write permissions.

6. Which are the four control buttons you can use to adjust the display of a window on the screen?

   a. Minimize, Maximize, Restore Down, Close

   b. Help, Minimize, Maximize, Close

   c. Program Icon, Minimize, Maximize, Close

   d. Help, Program Icon, Restore Down, Close

7. Which method would you use to move a window?

   a. Click in the title bar for the window and drag to a new location.

   b. Click at the left or right border of the window and drag to a new location.

   c. Click at the top or bottom border of the window and drag to a new location.

   d. Click in the title bar for the window and press ENTER.

8. How can you identify which program you might need to modify a file?

   a. From the icon at the left of a file name.

   b. From the name of the file.

   c. From the arrow at the lower left corner of the file name.

   d. From the folder icon at the left of a file name.

9. Which key can you use to edit or rename a file or folder?

   a. F2   c. F1

   b. F4   d. F9

10. What do you call the suffix added to the base name of a computer file?

    a. File name extension

    b. Program application

    c. File name path

    d. Operating system identifier

11. Which is the default setting for viewing file extensions in File Explorer?

    a. Hide the file name extensions.

    b. Show the file name extensions.

12. Before you can perform any action on a file or folder, what must you do?

    a. Select the file or folder.

    b. Log into the computer again.

    c. Start File Explorer twice.

    d. Create a shortcut for the file or folder.

13. Once a file or folder has been selected, which keyboard shortcut can you use to move it from its original location?

    a. Press CTRL+X.   c. Press CTRL+V.

    b. Press CTRL+C.   d. Press CTRL+W.

14. Which character cannot be used as part of a file name?

    a. \   c. ,

    b. .   d. -

15. When you use the Windows Search box/Cortana to search for a feature, where do the results appear?

    a. In the panel above the search box.

    b. In a new search window.

    c. Within File Explorer.

    d. In a text file.

16. Which feature allows a scanner to convert a scanned image into editable electronic text?

    a. OCR   c. GSM

    b. PDF   d. SCR

17. By default, in which folder are items you copy from the Internet stored?

    a. Downloads   c. Desktop

    b. Documents   d. Libraries

18. Which folder does Windows 10 use as the default folder for images?

    a. Pictures   c. Scanned Documents

    b. Quick access   d. Documents

19. What does digital rights management software do?

    a. Prevents unauthorized use or redistribution of media.

    b. Allows you copy content that has been purchased.

    c. Enables others to download the digital content from your device.

    d. Enables you to manage digital media using File Explorer.

20. Which folder would you use to make certain files available to all other user accounts on your computer?

    a. Public   b. Shared

21. Which of the following file types can be sent as an attachment?

    a. .png   c. .bat

    b. .exe   d. .mdb

22. Why might you want to use the Send to Compressed (zipped) folder command before sending four pictures to a friend via email?

    a. You need to reduce the size of the picture files for email purposes.

    b. It's faster to send one file instead of sending four files in the one email.

    c. The friend has a web-based email program.

    d. The picture files are stored on the cloud.

Lesson 5: Software

Lesson Objectives

In this lesson you will learn how to obtain, install, manage and configure software. You will also install and manage Windows apps and use messaging applications. Upon completion of this lesson, you should be able to:

- ☐ describe the benefits of software
- ☐ install, uninstall, repair and update apps and applications
- ☐ set software preferences
- ☐ work with Windows apps
- ☐ use messaging applications

Why Use Software?

Objective 1-1.3

While hardware is what makes our computers powerful and capable machines, it is software (programs) that makes our computing devices useful. The operating system provides an interface with the hardware itself, and software programs are what we use to get work done.

Software programs enable us to produce documents and charts; solve complex equations; calculate rocket trajectory; make online purchases; edit digital movies; decode the human genome; and so on. Additionally, light-weight apps can keep us on schedule, remind us of appointments, or help us find our way to a location when construction crews block our familiar path. Software and apps keep us productive and empowered.

> **Important Info: Apps and Applications**
> These are terms that describe the software we use to accomplish various tasks. The terms are used loosely, making it difficult to distinguish an app from an application. In this lesson, applications (or application software) are complex programs you install from removable media or from the Internet. Apps are small, light-weight programs you obtain from an app store. In Microsoft's terminology, applications are "Desktop Apps," and the light-weight programs are "Windows Apps."

Locally-Installed vs. Cloud-Based Software

Locally-installed software is installed on a device and runs directly on that device. These programs are designed to work with specific operating systems and with hardware that meets certain minimum requirements.

Cloud-based software on the other hand runs on a dedicated server (not on your computer) and is designed to be accessed over the Internet. You will learn about cloud-based software in an upcoming lesson.

In this lesson, you will work with locally-installed software.

If you are downloading software from the Internet, always save it (if you are given the option) to a designated location such as the desktop and scan it for viruses prior to installing it. It is rare that software from a reputable vendor will have problems; however, if you download software from a site that is not the vendor's official web site, there could be spyware or viruses included in the download file.

Installing a New Program

You can install programs from a number of different locations such as a network drive, an optical drive, a USB drive, or the Internet. How you purchase the software will determine the installation process.

One of the more traditional methods for installation is installing from optical media. You insert the installation CD or DVD and the process either begins automatically, or you can launch the process yourself. Another "tried-and-true" method is to purchase software over the Internet, and then download and run the installation program.

A more modern method for installing software is to stream the installation files from a server. For example, Microsoft has been using a setup and installation technology called "Click-to-Run" or "C2R Installer" for delivering Office setup files since Microsoft Office 2010. This type of installer streams Office setup files from Microsoft servers to your system, which allows you to start using Office even before the entire Office suite is installed on the system.

Regardless of the method of installation, most installation routines lead you step by step through the installation process. For example, the following sequence of screens shows the installation process for an open-source application called Notepad++:

15. Close the Notepad++ application window.

Now, install the free Google Chrome browser.

16. Open the Internet Explorer browser, click in the Address bar and type: www.google.com/chrome/browser and press ENTER to navigate to the download page for the Chrome browser.

17. Click **Download Chrome**.

18. Read the Terms of Service, clear the Set Google Chrome as my default browser check box, then click **Accept and Install**. Click **Run** if prompted.

19. Click **Yes** in the UAC (or enter an administrator user name and password) if prompted. The Chrome browser installs and then opens.

20. Close the Chrome browser.

21. Close the Internet Explorer browser.

Uninstalling Programs

You can uninstall a program when you no longer need it. Usually, the best way to uninstall a program is to use the Uninstall a program command on the Programs and Features page in the Control Panel.

Once you select the program you want to uninstall, click the **Uninstall/Change** button in Control Panel, then follow the prompts in the uninstall routine as they appear onscreen.

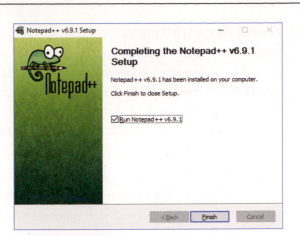

To advance through each stage of the installation process, click **Next**. When the installation is complete, click **Finish** to close the installer.

User Account Control (UAC)

The User Account Control (UAC) is a feature in Windows that issues notices (called *elevation prompts*) when a program is about to make a change that requires administrator-level permissions. For example, if you are logged in with an administrator account, the UAC displays the following prompt when you install a program.

Click **Yes** to proceed with the installation.

If you are logged in as a standard user and try to install software, the UAC will prompt you to enter the user name and password for an administrator account.

Entering an administrator user name and password in this UAC prompt has the same effect as clicking Yes in UAC prompt that displays when you are logged in as an administrator.

EULA and Registration

Once the installation process begins, you will be asked to agree to an End User License Agreement (EULA); depending on the vendor, this may appear in a separate screen or it may be a link you should click in order to read the contents of the agreement. Typically, you agree not to make illegal copies of the software to distribute to others, and you agree not to hold the software vendor liable for any damage or expenses that may occur from misuse or improper use of the software, such as putting incorrect entries into an income tax preparation program which results in an audit by the tax collector.

When the installation is complete, you will usually be asked to register or activate your copy of the program. Performing this last step ensures that you will be notified of any updates to the program. It also usually provides the option to call technical support should you require technical assistance.

Exercise 5-1: Installing software

In this exercise, you will install a program called Notepad++ which is designed to help programmers (coders) create and keep track of their code. You will also install the Google Chrome browser. This exercise assumes you have sufficient rights to install software on your system. If not, please read the steps to gain some familiarity with installing and uninstalling programs on your system or watch a demonstration provided by your teacher.

First, view some simple web page code in the standard Notepad text editor.

1. In File Explorer, navigate to the *7500 Student Files\Software* folder.

2. Right-click the *hello-world* document, click **Open with**, then click **Notepad** to open the document in the Notepad editor. The document contains some simple HTML code for a web page.

3. Close the Notepad application.

Now start the installer for Notepad++.

4. In File Explorer, double-click **npp.6.9.1.Installer** to start the installation program.

5. In the UAC, click **Yes** to allow the installer to make changes to the system (or enter an administrator user name and password.)

6. Select your language, then click **OK** to display the first screen of the setup wizard.

7. Click **Next**.

8. Read the EULA, then click **I Agree**.

9. Click **Next** twice.

10. Select the **Create Shortcut on Desktop** check box, then click **Install**.

11. Click **Finish**. Notepad++ opens and displays release notes pertinent to the current version in a document called change log.

12. Press CTRL+W to close the change log document.

Now, view the web page code in Notepad++.

13. In the Notepad++ window, click **File**, **Open**, navigate to the *7500 Student Files\Software* folder, then double-click *hello-world*. Notice that this editor displays tags in blue and numbers each line of code.

14. Press CTRL+W to close the hello-world document.

Alternatively, you can use the program's uninstall option (if one is included). Most antivirus applications are best uninstalled using the included uninstall routine. Either of these options helps ensure that the program is properly and completely removed from the system.

You should never simply delete program files using File Explorer. When you install a program, configuration information is added to the Windows Registry so that the operating system will identify this program. The Windows Registry is an operating system database that stores settings for installed applications. If you delete program files improperly, the obsolete configuration information is left behind in the Registry. This can lead to problems with other software programs or if you try to reinstall this program at a later date, or if you try to upgrade this program with a new version.

Exercise 5-2: Uninstalling an application

In this exercise, you will uninstall Notepad++.

1. Right-click **Start**, then click **Control Panel**.

2. With the Control Panel options displayed in Category view, click **Uninstall a program** beneath the Programs heading.

3. Scroll in the list until you see the *Notepad++* program and then click to select it.

4. Click the **Uninstall/Change** button in the blue toolbar above the listed programs.

5. If prompted, click **Yes** in the UAC (or enter an administrator user name and password.)

6. Click **OK** in the Installer Language box.

7. Click **Uninstall** to begin the uninstallation.

8. When the Uninstallation Complete message displays, click **Close**. Notepad++ no longer displays in the Control Panel.

9. Close the Control Panel.

Repairing Software

Sometimes an installed application program stops working correctly. Sometimes restarting the program will fix the problem. If that does not work, you can try repairing it.

The Microsoft Office suite includes a repair utility that you can access through the Programs and Features page in the Control Panel. Click the suite in the list box and then click **Change** to access the repair tool.

Organize ▾	Uninstall	Change			
Name		**Publisher**	**Installed On**	**Size**	**Version**
Intel® PROSet/Wireless Software		Intel Corporation	3/4/2016	203 MB	18.11.0
Intel® Rapid Storage Technology		Intel Corporation	3/4/2016	22.5 MB	14.5.0.1081
Intel® Security Assist		Intel Corporation	2/14/2016	2.36 MB	1.0.0.532
Microsoft Office 365 ProPlus - en-us		Microsoft Corporation	5/8/2016	1.18 GB	16.0.6741.2033
Microsoft SQL Server 2012 Data-Tier App Framework		Microsoft Corporation	4/13/2016	12.8 MB	11.0.2316.0
Microsoft SQL Server 2012 Data-Tier App Framework		Microsoft Corporation	4/13/2016	12.3 MB	11.0.2316.0
Microsoft SQL Server 2012 Transact-SQL ScriptDom		Microsoft Corporation	4/13/2016	9.06 MB	11.0.2100.60
Microsoft SQL Server Compact 4.0 SP1 x64 ENU CTP1		Microsoft Corporation	4/13/2016	27.4 MB	4.0.8854.1
Microsoft System CLR Types for SQL Server 2012		Microsoft Corporation	4/13/2016	2.31 MB	11.0.2100.60
Microsoft System CLR Types for SQL Server 2012 (x64)		Microsoft Corporation	4/13/2016	3.53 MB	11.0.2100.60
Microsoft Visual C++ 2012 Redistributable (x64) - 11.0...		Microsoft Corporation	2/14/2016	20.5 MB	11.0.61030.0

Microsoft Corporation Product version: 16.0.6741.2033
Size: 1.18 GB

You can specify:

- **Quick Repair** – this runs faster but only detects and then replaces corrupted files.

- **Online Repair** – does an uninstall and complete reinstall but takes longer.

Click an option, then click **Repair**.

The following series of screens shows a repair in progress.

When the repair operation has completed, click Close to exit the utility. Be aware that you may need to restart the system after running a repair routine.

Reinstalling a Program

Sometimes, a program may not work correctly (or at all) after installation, or it may work for a while and then stop working. If a repair is not available for the application, you can try uninstalling and then reinstalling the program.

Most vendors allow you download and install or reinstall a program on the same system numerous times without any fees. Generally, once you have paid for a software program, you can reinstall it as often as needed.

Sometimes, Windows detects that a program is running improperly, or detects that a program has been installed improperly. In such cases, Windows will display the Program Compatibility Assistant, which may give you the option to reinstall or to verify that the program has been installed correctly.

You can also check online user groups, knowledge bases, blog sites and forums to see if other users have experienced similar problems and you may find solutions there.

When you click the **Options** tab, you open the Options dialog box.

The Options dialog box also contains several tabs: General, Display, Proofing, Save & Backup, Send to OneNote, Audio & Video, Language, Advanced, Customize Ribbon, Quick Access Toolbar, Add-ins, and Trust Center. These provide access to various settings that control how the program functions on your system.

For example, you can use the General tab to set a default font for all new pages you create in OneNote. Or you can use the Save & Backup tab to specify how often to back up your OneNote notebooks.

Different commands and settings are available in different programs in the Office suite; however, these settings are always accessed through the tabs of the Options dialog box.

Exercise 5-3: Setting software preferences

In this exercise, you will open Microsoft Word and explore some of the available customizations.

First, customize the Quick Access toolbar.

1.   Open File Explorer, navigate to the *7500 Student Files\Software* folder, then double-click **Customizations** to open this document in Microsoft Word.

2. In the Quick Access toolbar, click **Customize Quick Access Toolbar**, then in the menu, click **Quick Print** to add a button to the Quick Access toolbar that sends a document to the default printer with a single click.

3. In the Quick Access toolbar, click **Customize Quick Access Toolbar**, then in the menu, click **Print Preview and Print** to add another button to the toolbar. This one opens the Print tab in Backstage view, allowing you to specify what to print, and which printer to print on.

4. In the Quick Access toolbar, click **Print Preview and Print** to preview the document, then at the top of the Backstage tabs, click the **Back** button to return to the document.

Now, return the Quick Access toolbar to its original configuration.

5. In the Quick Access toolbar, click **Customize Quick Access Toolbar**, then in the menu, click **Print Preview and Print** to remove the button.

6. In the Quick Access toolbar, click **Customize Quick Access Toolbar**, then in the menu, click **Quick Print** to remove the button.

Now, explore some of the options you can set for the application.

7. In the ribbon, click **File** to open Backstage view, then in the Backstage tabs, click **Options** to open the Options dialog box.

8. Click each of the tabs in the Options dialog box, read the available settings and note the type of settings you can configure for Microsoft Word. How customizable do you think this application is?

9. When you have finished examining the tabs, click **Cancel** to close the dialog box.

10. Close the Microsoft Word application window.

Working with Windows Apps

Objective 1-2.8, 1-3.12, 1-6.5

In addition to using application software on your system, you can also use apps that you obtain from an app store. Per our definition at the beginning of this lesson, apps are small and light-weight programs. They are generally optimized for use on a touch-screen interface.

Operating System App Stores

An *app store* is a digital platform for distributing software. Just like full-featured application programs, apps are written for specific operating systems such as iOS, Mac OS X, Windows, or Android. For this reason, different platforms utilize different apps stores.

An app for accessing the appropriate app store is usually built in to the operating system. For example, the Windows Store app is built into Windows 10, while the Mac App Store app is built into OS X v10.6.6 or later.

Windows Store

Windows 10 comes with built-in apps including OneNote, Mail, Groove Music, Movies & TV, Photos, Camera, Games, People, Maps, Calendar, Money, and Alarms, but you can get more at the Windows Store. Click the ▦ (**Store**) icon in the taskbar to open the Store app and browse the store.

If you want to download and install apps, you will need to sign in with a Microsoft account.

What is a Microsoft Account?

A *Microsoft account* is an ID composed of an email address and password. You use a Microsoft account to log in to Microsoft web sites and services, such as Hotmail, Xbox Live, Outlook.com and OneDrive. A Microsoft account also gives you access to apps and games from the Windows Store, and lets you see your settings and personal files across multiple Windows 10 devices.

If you use an email address to sign in to Outlook.com, Hotmail, Windows 10 Mobile (or Windows Phone 8), or Xbox LIVE, then you already have a Microsoft account. If not, then you can create a free Microsoft account.

Exercise 5-4: Creating a Microsoft Account

In this exercise, you will create a Microsoft account. If you already have a Microsoft account, skip this exercise.

1. Open the Internet Explorer browser and navigate to `https://account.microsoft.com`.

2. Click **Sign in**, then below the Sign in button, to the right of No account?, click **Create one!**

3. Enter your Hotmail or outlook.com email address and password, or click the **Get a new email address** link to create a new account/email address. Fill out the rest of the form (ask your teacher for help if you need to), then tap or click **Create account**. Your Microsoft account is created and you are signed in. (If prompted, do not let the browser save your password.)

4. Be sure to record your Microsoft ID.

5. Click your user icon in the upper-right corner of the window, then click **Sign out**.

6. Close your browser.

Signing in to Store

Once you have created a Microsoft account, you can use your ID to sign into the Store app. Click **Store** in the taskbar to open the store app, then click ⋏ **Sign In** at the upper-right corner of the store window to open the Sign In menu.

In the menu, click **Sign In** to open the Choose an account screen.

Click **Cortana** if you want to use your personal Microsoft account. (If you have a Microsoft account associated with your school or business and you want to use that account instead, click the Work or school account option.)

Enter your Microsoft ID, then click **Sign in**. Windows will prompt you to use this account to sign in to your device. Signing in to your computer or device using a Microsoft account enables you to sync settings across your devices. However, in this course, you will not use your Microsoft account for signing on to your computer.

To sign only into the Store app using your Microsoft account, click **Sign in to just this app instead**.

Your account icon displays as ⦷ when you are signed in.

Exercise 5-5: Signing into the Store App

In this exercise, you will sign into the Store app with your Microsoft account.

1.   In the taskbar, click **Store** to open the Store app.

2.   In the upper-right corner of the window, click **Sign In**, then in the menu, click **Sign In**.

3. In the Choose an account screen, click **Cortana**.

4. Enter your Microsoft ID and click **Sign in**.

5. Click **Sign in to just this app instead**. You are now signed into the Store app.

6. Minimize the Store window.

Finding an App in the Store

The Windows Store is your gateway to apps, games, music and TV and movies. Top picks or featured items are presented on the first page; and you can click or tap options that allow you to browse by category. The following figure shows some of the categories for apps:

Categories			
Books & reference	Food & dining	Medical	Personal Finance
Business	Government & politics	Multimedia design	Personalization
Developer tools	Health & fitness	Music	Photo & video
Education	Kids & family	Navigation & maps	Productivity
Entertainment	Lifestyle	News & weather	Security

When you click a Category here the results show in the window, and a panel along the left side allows you to refine which apps are displayed in the window.

Home **Apps** Games Music Movies & TV				Search
Refine	**Top free • News & weather**			
Chart				
Top free	The Weather Channel ★★★★★ Free	Flipboard ★★★★☆ Free	MyRadar ★★★★★ Free*	Police Radio Scanner 5-0 ★★★★★ Free*	USA TODAY ★★★★☆ Free	AccuWeather - Weather for Life ★★★★☆ Free*
Top paid				
Best-rated				
New and rising				
Category	CNN App for	Fox News	NPR One	Associated Press	NBC News	CBS News
News & weather ✕				

In addition to browsing the categories, you can type the name of a specific app in the Search bar and search for it. The Store will display the best matches.

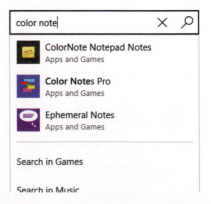

Downloading and Installing an App

When you find an app that you are interested in, click or tap it to open its detail page. The detail page lists (among other things) ratings and reviews, the price of the app (if any) and similar apps.

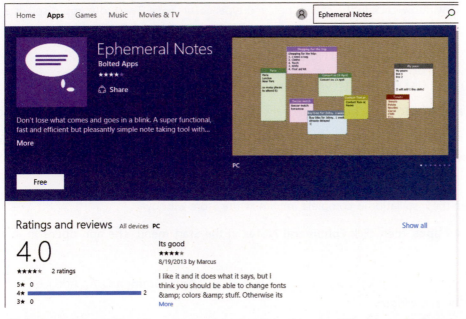

Click the price (or "Free") to begin downloading the app. Windows will download the app and acquire a license for it automatically. When the download is complete, the app will display an Install button. Click it to install the app.

When the installation is complete, the app will display an Open button.

You can click **Open** to launch the app from within the Store. Note that some apps require you to accept certain terms and conditions, and some will ask for permission to access particular features (such as a built-in camera, or your location information) before they open for the first time. Once you have accepted the terms and granted appropriate permissions, the app will run.

You can launch an installed app at any time from the Start menu: click **Start**, click **All apps**, then click or tap the app to launch it.

Exercise 5-6: Obtaining Windows Apps

In this exercise, you will explore the Windows Store and download and install a Windows app.

1.   Restore the Store window.

2.   At the top of the window, click **Apps** to see the top apps.

3.   Scroll to the bottom of the page, then in the Categories, click **News & weather** to view news and weather apps.

4.   In the Refine panel, click **Best-rated**.

5. In the Refine panel, click **New and rising**.

6. In the Refine panel, click the **X** to the right of News & weather to remove the category filter.

7. In the Refine panel, scroll the category list and click **Productivity** to view productivity apps.

8. Near the top of the window, click in the search box and type: color note. The Store app displays a few apps that might be what you are looking for.

9. In the search results list, click **Ephemeral Notes** to open the detail page for this particular app.

10. In the description area, click **More** to read a little more, then click **Less** to close up the description.

11. Read the ratings and then scroll to the bottom of the page to read about the app's approximate size.

12. Scroll back up and click **Free** to begin downloading the app from the Store. Notice that Windows automatically downloads the app, and acquires a license for it. Notice that the app displays the text: You own this product and you can install it on this device.

13. Click **Install**. When the installation is complete, minimize the Store window.

14. Click **Start**, click **All apps**, then click **Ephemeral Notes** in the Start menu. The app opens in its own window.

15. At the top of the app window, click the menu icon ≡ then click **... App commands**. An Add icon appears at the bottom of the app window.

16. Click **Add** to create a new, untitled note.

17. Type: check out this new app!

18. At the top of app window, click **menu** then click **... App commands** and click **Delete** to remove the note.

19. Close the app window.

Deleting an App

Apps can be easily removed from your PC. Click Start, All apps, then right-click the app in the Start menu and click Uninstall. Confirm that you want to uninstall and Windows removes the app.

Recovering a Deleted App

If you accidentally delete an app, or if you delete it on purpose and then change your mind, you can recover the app without having to pay for it again and without having to download it again.

Sign into the Windows Store, if necessary, and search for the app you deleted. When you click its detail page, the app will display the message: You own this product and you can install it on this device. The Install button will also display in the app, allowing you to install it once again.

Signing out of the Store

If you are using a shared computer, you should sign out of the Windows store. To do so, click the Sign in icon, then click your account at the top of the menu to open the Account window. In the Account window, click your account name to make the Sign out link visible. Click **Sign out**.

Account

ccifred@outlook.com
Cortana
Sign out

+ Add account

Exercise 5-7: Removing Windows Apps

In this exercise, you will delete the app you installed previously.

Delete your app from the Start menu.

1. Click **Start**, then click **All apps**.

2. Locate the **Ephemeral Notes** app, then right-click it in the Start menu and click **Uninstall**.

3. Click the **Uninstall** button to confirm, then click away from the Start menu.

Ensure that it has been removed.

4. Click **Start** and **All apps** and look for the Ephemeral Notes app. The app is uninstalled.

5. Close the Start menu.

Search for the app in the Store.

6. Restore the Store window.

7. Use the Search box to find the Ephemeral Notes app, and click it to open the detail page. Notice that the app displays an Install button.

Sign out of the Store.

8. In the Store window, click the **Sign in** icon, then in the menu, click your account to open the Account window.

9. In the Account window, click your account name to make the Sign out link visible, then click **Sign out**.

10. Close the Windows Store.

Messaging Applications

Objective 1-1.3, 1-1.5

Although personal computing might have begun as a means toward increased productivity, social behavior (connecting with others) has always been part of the evolving process. Message boards, forums, email, and chat rooms have existed since the early days of the modern Internet. We have always wanted, it seems, to be able to use our computers to communicate with each other.

On the cellular side of things, it seems we have always wanted the ability to use our phones for more than simple communication. We want them to entertain us, and allow us to work, and allow us to share files and photos, and video, and more.

And today we have choices. We can work on a hand held or on a desktop. And we can communicate from either place as well. Messaging apps keep us in communication, no matter where we are.

Text Messaging

Text messages (or "texts") are short strings of text sent over a cellular provider's network using a protocol called *Short Message Service* (SMS). Text messages are created and sent from cellular phones (or other similar mobile devices). As the name of the protocol implies, the number of characters allowed per message is limited (about 100 to 200 characters per message, depending on the service provider). The original SMS protocol allowed for a maximum of 160 characters. You can send a text message to one person or to many people. The figure shows five text messages that form a conversation.

In addition to Short Message Service, many cellular providers offer *Multimedia Messaging Service* (MMS), which provides a standard way to send messages that include multimedia content to and from mobile phones or other suitably equipped mobile devices.

This service allows users to send photographs and video to other users, as well as mobile updates such as breaking news or weather updates. As with plain text messaging, you can send multimedia messages to one or more people, but the speed for sending and receiving may be slower depending on the size of the message or the speed of your cellular provider's network.

Text messaging can be useful when no other forms of communication are available or when the intended recipient cannot be reached through a phone call. For example, you can text your boss (who might be at a concert) to let her know that you will be coming into work later than usual tomorrow.

In order to send a text message, you must know the cell phone number of the person you want to text. It is easiest if you enter that person into your Contacts list in your phone.

To send a text, open the messaging application on your phone or tablet, specify one or more contacts who will receive the message, type your message, and then tap the Send button. If your recipient's phone is turned off at the time that you send your text message, he or she will receive the message the next time the phone is powered on.

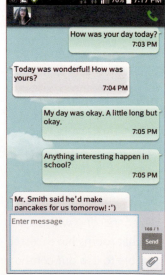

Depending on your cellular text plan, you may be limited to the number of text messages you can send and receive before you start incurring charges. This is especially relevant with pre-paid plans.

Additionally, most providers charge fees for sending/receiving texts to people who live in other countries. For example, if you live in the United States and you travel to Canada and use your mobile phone to send text messages, you will likely find fees assessed on your next mobile bill. Be sure that you understand the terms and conditions of your cellular contract and know in advance how much international messages will cost. Many providers offer special international text packages (for a set fee) that allow for international texting.

Most mobile devices come with text messaging apps preinstalled. If you use Android, Google Hangouts is the default for messaging with other Android users. If you use iOS, the Messages app is built in. However, not all messaging apps play nicely with others. That is, you may run into difficulty sending/receiving messages to users on platforms other than your own. Happily, there are thousands and thousands of apps that can be downloaded to a smart phone – including those that make cross-platform messaging fun and easy.

Non-SMS Messaging Apps

There are many messaging apps today that bypass your cellular carrier's SMS and MMS service, and use Wi-Fi or mobile data instead. Exchanges between users who have the same app installed are free. These include:

- **WhatsApp** – a cross-platform messaging system that supports Android, iOS, Windows 10 Mobile and BlackBerry devices. You can send individual and group text, photo, and voice/video messages using mobile data or Wi-Fi. Messages to any other WhatsApp user are free.

- **Viber** – supports Android, iOS, Windows 10 Mobile and BlackBerry, and includes desktop clients for Windows and OS X, allowing you to send, receive, and manage messages on your computer as well as on your mobile device. All exchanges with other Viber users are free.

- **Facebook Messenger** – allows you to connect with any other Facebook user (there are over one billion active Facebook users) for free, bypassing traditional SMS and MMS channels. The app supports iOS, Android, and BlackBerry and also includes a Windows desktop client that allows you to use your computer for messaging instead of your phone.

Chat

Many social networking sites (such as Facebook or Google+) include built-in "chat" or "messenger" features, and accordingly, most instant messaging clients allow you to connect to and exchange messages with the people you know on social networks.

Additionally, many instant messaging and chat clients are associated with online services, such as a web-based email account (such as a Gmail or Outlook.com account). This association allows you to log into your email account and launch the web-based chat feature from within your mailbox.

You can type text, copy and paste hyperlinks into messages, and send picture files with your chat messages. Gmail chat even lets you draw and send freehand images with your chat messages. You can also send chat messages to a contact who is not currently online. Your recipient will see the message the next time he or she signs in. In this way, a chat service is similar to email; you can send messages to people who are not currently online.

Using Gmail Chat

Gmail includes built-in chat features that you can use, and chat sessions take place on the Google Hangouts platform. The chat "roster" appears on the left side of the page below your name. In order to engage in "real time" chat, you and the person with whom you want to chat must be logged into Gmail. A green circle in the chat roster indicates that a contact is logged in. (If your intended recipient is not logged in, you can send a message to your offline contact, and that message will be seen the next time he or she signs in).

The roster stores previous chat sessions, and you can click one to open it and pick up a conversation where you left off.

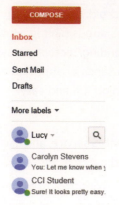

If you have not used Gmail chat before, the chat roster will be empty. To start a new chat, click the 🔍 (**Search**) button and type the name or email address of the person you want to chat with. The first time you chat with a particular contact through Gmail, you will need to send a chat invitation.

Depending upon the other person's prior activity on Google, various options may be presented when you try to open your first chat session, and you may need to investigate icons on the screen in order to invite that person to chat with you.

In the following figure, Fred has searched for *cciethyl@gmail.com*. When he clicks her contact info in the search results, he is prompted to send an invitation.

Fred can simply click **Send Invite** to invite Ethyl to chat with him on Google Hangouts. He will receive confirmation that the invitation was sent, and then he must wait for Ethyl to accept the invitation.

In the meantime, Ethyl will see a notification in her chat roster that Fred has sent a message.

When she clicks the notification, the invitation displays in the lower-right corner of the Gmail window. When she clicks Accept, they can begin chatting.

To use the chat window, click in the Send a message box, type your message, then press ENTER.

As new messages are sent and received, previous messages scroll up in the window

Exercise 5-8: Using Gmail chat

For this exercise, your teacher should divide the class into teams of two. The other person on your team will be your partner. Decide who will be Student A and who will be Student B. In this exercise, you will use the Gmail chat feature to chat with your partner.

This exercise assumes that you have installed the Google Chrome web browser, as Gmail is designed to work best with Chrome. You can use Internet Explorer or Microsoft Edge, however you may need to adjust the steps. For example, you will need to navigate to the Gmail sign-in page; these browsers will not display a Gmail link in the upper-right area of the window.

1. Double-click the **Google Chrome** shortcut on the Desktop to open the Chrome browser. Click the **Gmail** link that displays in the upper-right region of the browser window to access the Gmail sign in page. Sign into Gmail. You should be looking at your Gmail Inbox.

2. **Student A**: Click the search button that appears to the right of your name in the chat roster to open the search box.

3. **Student A**: Enter your partner's email address into the search box, and click his or her contact info in the search results.

4. **Student A**: When the chat invitation displays at the lower-right corner of the window, click **Send Invite**. You should see a confirmation that your invitation was sent. You must now wait for your partner to accept the invitation.

5. **Student B**: When you see a notification in your chat roster that your partner has sent you a message, click the notification to open the invitation.

6. **Student B**: In the invitation, click **Accept**.

7. **Student A**: Click in the Send a message box, type a brief message, then press ENTER. Your message appears in your chat window and in your partner's chat window.

8. **Student B**: Type a response, then press ENTER.

9. **Everyone**: Exchange several messages.

10. **Everyone**: Close the chat window.

11. **Student B**: In your chat roster, click the conversation with your partner to re-open the chat window. Notice that the entire thread of the conversation is preserved.

12. **Student B**: Type and send a new message to your partner.

13. **Student A**: Click the conversation with your partner in your chat roster. Notice that when the window opens, the new message from your partner displays at the bottom of the window.

14. **Everyone**: When you are finished using Gmail chat, close the chat window, sign out of Gmail and close your browser.

Instant Messaging

Sometimes referred to as IM, this type of electronic communication allows two or more participants to "converse" with one another in real time by typing messages in the window of an instant messaging program. Instant messaging programs such as Skype, ICQ, or Yahoo! Messenger enable people to chat with each other, regardless of where they are located. For example, two participants may be working on different floors of the same office building, and they can type messages back and forth to one another as a means of real-time communication.

Most instant messaging programs allow for group conversations, so our two participants could easily add in a third participant who might be working in an office across town. Instant messaging is a very useful means of communication to use when an answer is needed quickly.

In order to use an instant messaging program, you must create an account with a username and password. In the early days of instant messaging, you were required to download and install the program in order to use it. Today, most instant messaging clients include a web-based version, allowing you to sign in and use the program from any computer (regardless of whether the client is installed on the computer you are using).

Using Skype

Skype comes in both business and consumer versions. Skype for Business lets you add up to 250 people to an online meeting and is integrated into Microsoft Office apps, allowing you to schedule online meetings from Outlook. It costs $2 per month per user. Skype for consumers is free.

Because Microsoft owns Skype, you can sign into Skype using a Microsoft account, and you can open instant messaging sessions from your Outlook.com inbox and exchange messages with your contacts as long as you and your contact have Skype accounts.

You can also create a Skype account independent of a Microsoft account, and you can log in to Skype using your Skype name.

You can download and install the Skype for Windows client from the Skype web site, and then sign in to the service.

Exercise 5-9: Creating an account & installing Skype

In this exercise, you will sign up for a Skype account, and then download and install Skype for Windows.

First, create a Skype account.

1. Open the Internet Explorer browser and navigate to: **https;//login.skype.com**.

2. Click **Create new account** to access an online form for creating a Skype account.

3. Fill in the required fields along with the security code requirement at the bottom of the page. Then click **I agree - Continue**. You should now be viewing your Skype account page, which includes a welcome message with your first name. Your account has been created.

4. Be sure to record your Skype name and password.

Next, download and install the Skype client.

Note: Your teacher may have already installed Skype on the classroom systems. If that is the case, press the Windows key on your keyboard, type: Skype, then click **Skype for Desktop** in the Search results pane to open the Skype sign-in window, and then skip to Step 12.

5. In the welcome page, click **Download Skype for Windows**. (Notice that you can elect to download Skype for other devices – there are versions for PCs, mobile phones, tablets, home phones, television, Xbox, etc.).

6. In the message bar that appears across the bottom of the window, click **Save**.

| Do you want to run or save **SkypeSetup.exe** (1.39 MB) from **download.skype.com**? | Run | Save ▼ | Cancel | × |

7. When the message bar changes, click **Run**.

| The SkypeSetup.exe download has completed. | Run | Open folder | View downloads | × |

8. Click **Yes** in the User Account Control dialog box to allow the program to be installed. (Or enter an administrator user name and password.)

9. When prompted, select your language, then click **I agree – next**.

10. You can elect to install Skype Click to Call, which is a browser add-in that allows you to click phone numbers on web pages in order to automatically place a call. For now, clear the **Install Skype Click to Call** check box, then click **Continue**.

11. You can elect to make Bing your default search engine and make MSN your home page. Clear the check boxes for these options, then click **Continue**. It may take a few moments for the installation to proceed, after which the sign-in screen appears.

Sign in to Skype.

12. Click in the Skype name, email or mobile box and type your Skype name, click in the Password box and enter your password, then click **Sign in**.

13. If this is the first time you are signing into Skype, or if you have signed in before but have not configured your account, you will be presented with a series of configuration dialog boxes. Click **Continue** to proceed with the configuration.

14. Click **Test sound** to make sure you can hear.

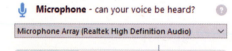

15. Speak to check your microphone.

    🎤 **Microphone** - can your voice be heard?　❓

    | Microphone Array (Realtek High Definition Audio) ▼ |

16. You can use the Video drop-down list to select a camera. Make sure you can see yourself in the video area.

17. Click **Continue**. You are prompted to add a profile picture. A profile picture displays next to your name when you are in an instant messaging session or anytime you are engaged in communication and your video is turned off. A profile picture can also help your friends locate you in the Skype directory. You can use a web cam or integrated camera to take a picture, or used a stored image file. You can add a profile picture now, or later.

18. Click **Add later**. The final setup screen displays:

    | ⓢ Skype™   — □ ✕ |

    Setting up Skype

    You're all set up and ready to add your friends, family and colleagues and start making voice and video calls.

    Lucy Lee
    ✓ Online
    2:05 PM

    [Start using Skype]

19. Click **Start using Skype** to view the Skype home screen.

20. Minimize the Skype window, and close the browser.

Adding Contacts

To send instant messages in Skype, you need to add people to your Contact list.

In the menu bar in the Skype window, click **Contacts**, point to **Add Contact**, then click **Search Skype Directory** to open the Search field. Enter the Skype name (or email address or mobile number) of the person you want to add then click the **Search Skype** button. The results display below the Search field.

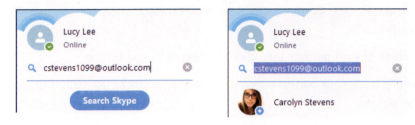

In the Search results, click the contact you want to add. The contact information displays in the central pane in the Skype window along with information about whether this person is in your Contacts list.

Click **Add to Contacts** to open an invitation. You must invite your intended contact before you can add him or her to your Contacts list.

Notice that you can replace the boilerplate text with a message of your own. Click **Send** to send the invitation. A received invitation (shown in the figure) will appear in your recipient's Recent tab.

When you receive an invitation, click it to open it in the Skype window.

Click **Accept** to share your contact details. Once you accept, you are added to the requestor's Contacts list, and that person is added to yours. You can now exchange messages.

Exercise 5-10: Adding Skype contacts

In this exercise, you will add your partner as a contact in Skype. Decide who on your team will be Student A and who will be Student B.

1. **Everyone**: Restore the Skype window.

2. **Student A**: In the Skype menu bar, click **Contacts**, point to **Add Contact**, then click **Search Skype Directory** to open the Search field.

3. **Student A**: Enter the Skype name of your partner, then click the **Search Skype** button.

4. **Student A**: In the Search results, click your partner's Skype name. The contact information displays in the central pane in the Skype window.

5. **Student A**: Click **Add to Contacts** to open an invitation, then click **Send** to send the invitation.

6. **Student B**: After a few moments, you should receive the invitation your partner sent. If necessary, click the **Recent** tab to view your new communications. The pending request should appear in the Recent pane.

7. **Student B**: Click **Accept** to share your contact details. You are now added to your partner's Contacts list, and your partner is added to yours. You can now exchange messages.

8. **Everyone**: Minimize the Skype window.

Exchanging Instant Messages with Skype

You use the message area at the bottom of the Skype window to communicate with your contacts.

Click in the box, type your message and press ENTER or click (or tap) the 🔵 (**Send**) button. As with Gmail chat, as messages are sent and received, they scroll up in the message window.

Notice the via Skype setting above the message box. You can send SMS (text messages) to mobiles from Skype if you have Skype Credit. Click via Skype and change the selection to SMS. If your contact has not saved a mobile phone number in their profile, you'll see the option to enter one. Select the country from the drop-down, type the phone number and click the checkmark.

Type your text message into the message box and click the Send icon. You'll see the icon next to your message when it's been delivered successfully.

You are not limited to sending simple text messages with Skype; you can use Skype to send images, document files, videos, contact cards, and emoticons and Mojis. (Mojis are short video clips you can use to express yourself.)

If the 🔗 (**More**) icon displays in the message area, click it to access the additional tool buttons:

Send image	📷
Send file	📄
Send Video Message	📹
Send contacts	📇
Insert emoticon or Moji	😊

When you send a file or image through Skype, you use the Send File to dialog box to navigate to and select the file you want to include with your message, similar to inserting an attachment to an email message.

The first time you are sent a file, you must specifically accept the file before it will be downloaded to your system. You accept the file by clicking the download file icon that appears in the Conversation window. A download file icon for an Excel workbook is shown in the following figure.

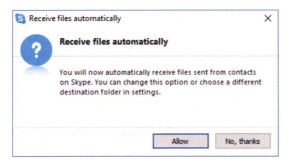

When you accept the first file through Skype, you can then specify whether you want to receive files automatically when they are sent to you.

Although sending files over Skype is safe, you may still want to make a decision on a case by case basis, depending on who is sending you a file. Additionally, when you accept files on a case by case basis, you can specify where you want to save them.

Be very careful not to share or give out passwords or credit card numbers in an instant message. Exchanges made through instant messaging programs travel across the Internet, and these communications are not always secure.

5. If you need to repair a Microsoft Office program, which option completely uninstalls and then reinstalls the software?

   a. Quick Repair

   b. Online Repair

   c. Neither option uninstalls and then reinstalls.

   d. Both options uninstall and then reinstall; one is just faster than the other.

6. Which of the following is an example of configuring an application program?

   a. Setting a default save location and customizing toolbar buttons.

   b. Making an adjustment in the Control Panel that tells the operating system to run the program in compatibility mode so that the application works smoothly.

   c. Making an edit to the Windows Registry so the application starts immediately after the Desktop displays.

   d. Using your Microsoft ID to log in to your computer instead of using a local log in account.

7. What do you need to do before you can download or install apps from the Windows Store?

   a. Sign in with a Microsoft Account.

   b. Update your operating system.

   c. Open an Outlook.com email account.

   d. Create an account on the Windows Store.

8. What was the original size limit for messages sent via SMS?

   a. 160 characters   c. 160 KB

   b. 16 KB   d. 16 MB

9. Which of the following is true regarding Gmail chat?

   a. Chat sessions take place on Google Hangouts.

   b. You cannot use the chat feature from within Gmail.

   c. You must download and install the G-Chat desktop client before you can use Gmail chat.

   d. Messages that you send in Gmail chat are limited to 160 characters.

10. Which of the following items can you send in a Skype instant message?

    a. You can send all of these items via Skype.

    b Document files and images.

    c. Video messages.

    d. Contact cards and Mojis.

Lesson 6: Cloud Computing

Lesson Objectives

In this lesson, you will learn about cloud computing. Upon completion of this lesson, you should be able to:

- understand the benefits and characteristics of cloud computing
- create and use cloud accounts to store, manage, and share files
- describe different types of cloud applications
- configure mobile notifications

Cloud Computing Concepts

Objective 1-6.1, 1-6.2, 1-6.3, 1-6.4, 1-6.5

Cloud computing is a phrase that is used today to refer to a number of different scenarios in which a computing resource, such as a storage location or software, is delivered as a service over the Internet.

Note: Historically, the Internet has been represented in all manner of diagrams as a cloud. (A cloud is remote – off in the distance somewhere – and its contents are generally unknown.) The word "cloud" today refers to almost any type of computing that takes place over the Internet.

In networking, there are client systems (those systems which request services and access to resources) and there are server systems (those systems that supply services and grant access to resources). In order to maintain a network on their own premises, organizations typically invest thousands and thousands of dollars in server systems, server software, and trained IT staff.

However, because high-speed broadband connections are available almost everywhere, network resources and functionality can be delivered quite efficiently and inexpensively over the Internet. Accordingly, companies such as Google, Apple, Microsoft and countless others successfully provide hosted services to millions of users.

A *hosted service* is provided by a server located outside your own network. That is, for example, instead of maintaining its own email server, a company can pay for email services hosted on a Microsoft server. Or, instead of maintaining its own file server, a company can pay for file storage locations hosted on a Google server. For a monthly fee (subscription) companies can carry on business using modern software and hardware without having to purchase and maintain the necessary resources.

You must create a cloud account before you can use cloud technology. Once you sign in to your account, you can access the services and files associated with it.

Most hosting providers offer both consumer and business-grade hosting solutions, and in many cases, consumer solutions are offered free of charge. Consumer accounts generally provide the same basic features (regardless of the provider):

- Cloud storage space
- Apps to connect multiple devices to your account
- Apps to keep all your devices synchronized
- Provision for offline access
- The ability to share files through web links
- The ability to upload and download files to your storage location
- Automatic backup features
- Automatic photo and video uploading features
- Web apps to work with documents and folders
- Ability to collaborate on files

Cloud Account Management

As you can imagine, there are many facets to cloud accounts, and accordingly, most provide a central place from which you can manage your account. In Google, this central location is the My Account page.

From this page you can manage your account and sign in settings, track your log in activity, control connected devices, edit your personal information, add account recovery information, see how much of your allotted storage space you are using, set your account preferences, and more.

To access the My Account page (or any of the Google services) log into a Google service (such as Gmail), click the ▦ (**Apps**) icon in the upper right corner of the window to open the Google Apps menu, and click **My Account**. You can also log in at: https://accounts.google.com to sign in to the My Account page.

Exercise 6-1: Managing your Google account

In this exercise, you will explore options associated with your Google account.

Note: This exercise assumes that you created a Gmail account and installed the Chrome web browser as directed in the previous lesson. If you have not done so already, do so before proceeding.

1. Open the Chrome browser and navigate to **https://accounts.google.com**. Enter your Gmail address in the box provided, click **Next**, and then enter your password and click **Sign in**. (If the page already displays your email address, click in the password box, enter your password, and click Sign in.)

2. You should be on the My Account page. If you are not, click the **Google apps** icon, then click **My Account**.

3. Under Personal info & privacy, click **Activity controls** and scroll the page. Did you have any idea that you could maintain and research your browsing and search history, your location history, your video watching history and your video searching history? Did you know you could use voice controls and access information stored on your devices?

4. Under Account preferences at the left side of the page, click **Your Google Drive storage** to view information on how much of your free cloud storage you are using.

5. Under Sign in & security, click **Device activity & notifications** to see a list of devices you have used to sign in to your account (and when).

6. Spend several minutes exploring the links on this page. Take note of all the facets of your account that you can control, but do not change any settings at this time.

7. When you are finished, click the **My Account** link at the upper-left area of the window to return to the main My Account page.

8. Minimize the browser window.

Cloud Storage on Google Drive

Cloud storage is safe, secure, and accessible from anywhere on any device with an Internet connection. Different providers offer varying amounts of free storage, and all provide options for purchasing additional storage.

The cloud storage associated with a Google account is (interchangeably) called "Google Drive" or simply, "Drive." Drive currently provides 15GB of free storage.

Accessing Your Cloud Drive

To access Google Drive, sign in to your Google account, click the **Google apps** icon to display the Google Apps menu, then click **Drive**. The first time you access Google Drive, you may be greeted by introductory information.

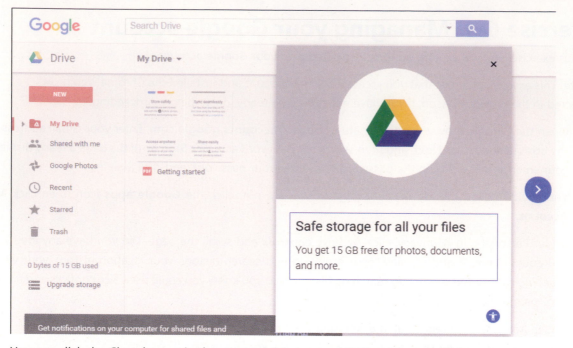

You can click the Close button in the upper-right corner of the introductory PDF to close it, or you can click ⊙ to view the introductory information, then click the **Take me to Drive** button to exit the PDF slide show.

Uploading Content

Because Drive is a cloud location, you copy content into it by uploading files. Uploading is the process of moving data from your device, across a network, to a server.

Note: Drive includes integrated web apps which you can use to create content directly in the cloud. You will use these in an upcoming lesson in the Key Applications module.

You can use the built-in commands to upload files and folders. To upload one or more files, click **NEW**, **File upload** and use the Open dialog box to select file(s) to upload. To upload an entire folder, click **NEW**, **Folder upload**, then navigate to and select the folder using the Browse for Folder dialog box.

If you prefer, you can drag and drop files from File Explorer into the Drive window.

Working with Content on Drive

A command bar displays at the top of the Drive window.

Drive   My Drive ▾

You can use the buttons on the command bar to change the view. You can display items in a list or grid view; sort by various properties; display details about specific files and folders, or about your recent activity on Drive; and access the Settings page for Drive.

When you select a file or folder in Drive, a toolbar displays in the command bar.

Drive   My Drive ▾

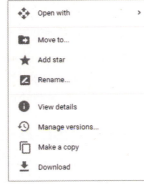

Use the buttons on the toolbar to generate a link for sharing; share a file with specific people; preview a file; or remove a file from Drive.

You can also click the ⋮ (**More actions**) button to access a menu of other options.

Organizing Content on Google Drive

The "root" folder on Google Drive is named **My Drive**. You can create folders in My Drive and move files into the folders just as you can in File Explorer. Click the **NEW** button, then click **Folder**. Type a name for the new folder, then press ENTER. You can then drag and drop files into the folders you create.

You can also use the Move to command to organize your content.

Right-click a file, or select a file and click **More actions**, then select the **Move to** command to open a dialog box you can use to move files into (or out of) folders.

Downloading Content

To copy files from Drive to your computer, you download them. Downloading is the process of copying content from a server, across a network, to your device. To download content from Drive, select the file(s) you want to download, click **More actions**, then click **Download**. In Chrome, a button will appear at the bottom of the window when the download is complete.

Files are automatically saved in the *Downloads* folder. Click the button to open the file. Click the arrow at the right of the button to access options for opening the file, specifying to always open that particular file type when downloading, or showing the file in its current folder location.

Note: If you are using Internet Explorer instead of Google Chrome, use the buttons in the notification bar that appears at the bottom of the window to specify whether you want to open or save the file, and to specify a location for saving the file.

Exercise 6-2: Working with content on Drive

In this exercise, you will upload, organize, and download content on Drive.

1. Restore the browser window. You should be signed in to your Google account.

2. Click the **Google apps** icon, then click **Drive**. Chrome opens a new tab and displays your My Drive storage area.

3. If necessary, view the introductory information, then click the **Take me to Drive** button to exit the PDF slide show.

4. If a *Get notifications on your computer* message displays, close it.

First, upload files using the built-in commands.

5. Click the **NEW** button at the top of the left pane, then click **File upload** to open the Open dialog box.

6. In the dialog box, navigate to the *7500 Student Files\Cloud Data* folder, select the first six items displayed, then click **Open** to upload those six items to Drive.

7. Click the **Close** button in the 6 uploads complete window to dismiss the message.

8. Click **My Drive** at the top of the window, then click **Upload files** to open the Open dialog box again.

9. In the *Cloud Data* folder, double-click **Mobile Devices Info** to upload the document to Drive.

10. Close the upload complete window.

Next, drag and drop a file into Drive.

11. If the Chrome window is maximized, click the **Restore Down** button. Then in File Explorer, navigate to the *7500 Student Files\Cloud Data* folder.

12. Restore the File Explorer window if it is maximized, then position the two windows so that you can see the contents of both on your screen.

13. In the File Explorer window, click the **RockBand** file, then drag it into an empty area in the Drive window, and release the mouse button. The file is uploaded to Drive.

14. Close the upload complete window, then maximize the Drive window.

Now, create a folder for the slide shows and move a file into it.

15. Click **NEW**, then click **Folder**, type: Slides, then press ENTER. You have created a folder on Drive.

16. Click the **Embedding Fonts** file, drag it over the *Slides* folder, then release the mouse button. You have moved the file into the Slides folder.

17. Double-click the **Slides** folder to move into it. The presentation file is here.

Now move the presentation file back to the My Drive location.

18. Click the **Embedding Fonts** file, click the **More actions** button, then click **Move to**. A dialog box opens that shows the file's current position in the Slides folder.

19. Click the **Back** arrow that displays to the left of *Slides* to change the displayed location to My Drive, then click the **Move here** button. The file is moved back to the My Drive location.

20. Click **My Drive** in the path that displays at the top of the window to move back out to the *My Drive* location.

Delete the Slides folder.

21. Click the **Slides** folder to select it, then in the toolbar at the top of the window, click **Remove**. The Slides folder is removed.

Now download a file.

22. Click **Animals.xlsx** in My Drive, click the **More actions** button, then click **Download**. A button with the file name displays in the lower left corner of the window when the download is complete.

23. Click the **Animals.xlsx** button to open the file in Excel.

24. Close Excel.

25. Minimize the browser window.

Apps for a Local Folder

Like most other cloud storage services, Drive includes an app that you can download and install on your PC that adds a local Google Drive folder to your File Explorer window. This folder is linked to your My Drive location, and is set for automatic synchronization.

This means that you can simply drag files into the local Google Drive folder on your PC and those files will be automatically uploaded to your My Drive folder.

You can download apps for your phone and tablet too, which will allow you to get to your files easily from any device. You can also configure these devices to automatically upload files (such as photos) to My Drive.

You can download and install the app right from the Google Drive window in your browser. The installation process may add shortcuts for Google Docs, Google Drive, Google Sheets, and Google Slides to your Desktop. Once you receive a message that the installation is complete, you finish setting up Drive for PC by launching the Google Drive app. You are greeted by a welcome wizard that will guide you through the setup process.

Google Drive also adds an icon to the notification area in the taskbar. You can click it to see synchronization status and to access your Google Drive folder.

- Can view – others can open a file but not change it or comment on it. This is the default setting for link sharing.

To share with specific people:

1. Select the file you want to share, then at the top of the window click ![share icon] (**Share**).

Share with others   Get shareable link 🔗

People

| | ✏ Can edit ▾

Done   Advanced

2. Under People, type the email address of the person you want to share with. A text box opens below the address box, allowing you to type a note.

3. To change the access level, click the down arrow beside the Can edit box and make a selection.

4. Click **Send**. The person you shared the file with will get an email letting him or her know that you have shared a file or folder.

Animals.xlsx   📒   Inbox x   🖨 🖼

Lucy Lee (via Google Drive) <ccilucy2016@gmail.com>   1:32 PM (0 minutes ago) ☆ ↩ ▾
to me ▾

Lucy Lee has shared the following spreadsheet:

X   Animals.xlsx

Open

The recipient can click the link in the email message to open the location where the file is stored on your cloud drive. From there, he or she can access options to open the file, download the file, share the file, and so on.

To share more than one file, move the files you want to share into a folder and then share the folder.

To share using a sharing link:

You can share a file with multiple people without typing in their individual email addresses in My Drive by creating a link that allows anyone (who has the link) to open the file.

1. Select the file you want to share, then at the top of the window click 🔗 (**Get shareable link**).

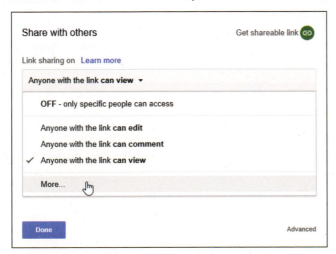

2. When the green light is on, and the shareable link is selected and underlined, it can be copied to the Windows clipboard. Press CTRL+C to copy it.

3. Paste the link into an email (or into a chat message or text message) and send it to whomever you like. The documents will be "read only" unless the person is signed into a Google account.

   To stop sharing, select the file again, click **Get shareable link**, and click the green light to toggle sharing off.

To share a file or folder publicly:

When you share files or folders publicly, anyone on the Internet can search for and access your file.

1. Select the file you want to share, then at the top of the window click ⊕ (**Share**).

2. In the top right of the Share with others box, click **Get shareable link**.

3. Click the down arrow next to Anyone with the link can view, then click **More**.

4. Select **On – Public on the web**, then click **Save**.

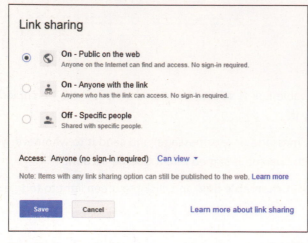

5. Specify the level of access you want to grant, click **Save**, then click **Done**.

Google Drive Mobile Apps

You can download and install Google Drive mobile apps for Android and iOS. Installing the apps and signing in on your mobile device keeps devices synchronized.

You can enable automatic uploading of photos and videos that you take on your device by turning Auto Backup on. Photos are automatically uploaded to *My Drive\Google Photos*.

Microsoft OneDrive

Objective 1-6.1, 1-6.3

OneDrive is a cloud storage location as well as a site that provides built-in online office web apps which you can use to create, edit, share and collaborate on documents. In the following sections, you will use the cloud storage and productivity apps.

Cloud Storage on OneDrive

OneDrive provides 5GB of free storage space. Because OneDrive is hosted by Microsoft, a local OneDrive folder is automatically available in File Explorer in Windows 10.

In the cloud, you can access your OneDrive location by navigating to https://onedrive.live.com, and signing in with your Microsoft account.

The default location is named Files. You can use the items in the left pane for navigation, just as you do in File Explorer.

Uploading, Organizing, and Downloading Content

A command bar displays across the top of the content area in the OneDrive window.

As you select files or folders, different commands become available on the command bar. You work with content in OneDrive in much the same way as you do in Google Drive:

- To create a new file or folder, click **New**, then click the appropriate option in the drop-down menu.

- To upload files, click **Upload** to open the Choose a File to Upload dialog box. Navigate to and select the files you want to upload, then click the **Open** button. You can also drag and drop files from File Explorer into the OneDrive window.

- To change the view in the OneDrive window, use the buttons at the right end of the command bar. You can display items as thumbnails or in a list view; sort by various properties; and display details about specific files and folders, or about your recent activity on OneDrive.

- To select a file, point the mouse pointer at the file until a small circle appears in the upper-right corner, then click the circle. The circle turns blue and a white check mark displays inside it ✅ to indicate the file is selected.

- To download a file from OneDrive, select the file, then click **Download**, then use the buttons in the notification bar that appears at the bottom of the window to specify whether you want to open or save the file, and to specify a location for saving the file.

- To delete a file or folder, select it, and then click **Delete** in the command bar.

- To move a file, select it and then drag it into a folder.

- To open a file in its appropriate web app (if available), click the file.

- To access other options for working with a selected file, click the ••• **Other things you can do with the selected items** button to display a menu of available options.

The Local OneDrive folder

A local OneDrive folder is built into Windows 10. Add files to the local folder so that you can access them from the cloud, and from other devices and still have them on your PC.

The first time you access the local OneDrive folder in File Explorer you are prompted to set up OneDrive by signing in.

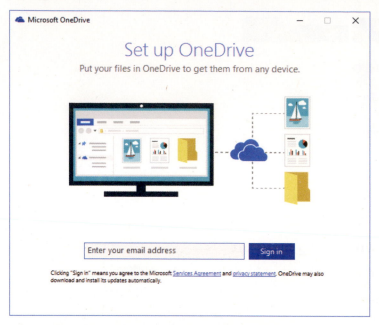

Enter the email address associated with your Microsoft account, then click the **Sign in** button. Enter your password when prompted, and click **Sign in** again.

The default location for your OneDrive folder is *C:\Users\<your name>\OneDrive*, but you can change it if you want to.

Click **Next** to continue.

The default configuration is to sync all files and folders in OneDrive; however, you can specify to sync only particular folders if you want to.

Click **Next**.

Click **Open my OneDrive folder** to access the local folder. (Note that OneDrive may launch a browser and display a Getting Started presentation which you can click through.)

Once you have signed in and configured the options, OneDrive will automatically upload and synchronize files between your computer and your OneDrive folder in the cloud.

Exercise 6-4: Using OneDrive for storage

In this exercise, you will sign into OneDrive, upload files, and activate the local OneDrive folder.

1. Open the Internet Explorer browser and navigate to **https://onedrive.live.com**.

2. Click **Sign in**, enter the email address associated with your Microsoft account, click **Next**, enter your password, then click **Sign in**. You are taken to your OneDrive Files folder. You may see a Welcome message. If so, click the close button. Your OneDrive folder should include a getting started file, a Documents folder, and a Pictures folder.

Upload a file:

3. At the top click **Upload**. The Choose a File to Upload dialog box opens.

4. In the Choose a File to Upload dialog box, navigate to the *7500 Student Files\Cloud Data* folder, then click **Yard Sale** and click **Open**. The file is uploaded to OneDrive and appears in the browser window. (You may need to refresh the screen by clicking F5 in order to see the uploaded file.)

Move the file into the Documents folder.

5. Hold the mouse pointer over the *Yard Sale* document to display a small circle in the upper-right corner, then click the circle to select the file. Notice that several options become available at the top of the window.

6. Drag the selected file onto the **Documents** folder, then release the mouse button.

Move the file back again.

7. Click the **Documents** folder to move into it.

8. Select the **Yard Sale** file, then drag it onto **Files** in the path that displays at the top of the window, then release the mouse button.

9. Click **Files** in the path to move back out to the Files folder.

Download a file.

10. Select the **Yard Sale** file, then click **Download** in the command bar.

11. In the notification bar that appears at the bottom of the window, click the arrow for Save, and select **Save as** to open the Save As dialog box.

12. In the Save As dialog box, navigate to the Desktop, then click the **Save** button to save the file to the Desktop.

13. In the OneDrive window, close the notification that the download has completed.

Delete a file.

14. Select Yard Sale if necessary, then click **Delete** in the Command bar.

Upload files into the Documents folder.

15. Click the **Documents** folder to move into it.

16. Click **Upload**, then in the Choose a File to Upload dialog box, navigate to the *Student Files\Cloud Data* folder, select the first seven files that display in the list, then click **Open** to upload the files.

17. Minimize the browser window.

Set up your local OneDrive folder.

18. Open a File Explorer window and click **OneDrive** in the Navigation pane. If prompted, sign in with your Microsoft account (email address and password), and click **Next** to make your way through the setup screens. When the final screen displays, click **Open my OneDrive folder**. (If your browser opens to display the Getting Started presentation, minimize it.)

19. Within the OneDrive folder, double-click **Documents**. The seven files you uploaded online are here.

Now drag a file into the local OneDrive folder and see it online:

20. In File Explorer, navigate to the *7500 Student Files\Cloud Data* folder, and click the **logo** file to select it.

21. Drag and drop the selected file onto the *OneDrive\Documents* folder, then release the mouse button. A copy of the logo file is added to the local OneDrive folder.

22. Restore the browser window. You should see the logo file; if you do not, refresh the browser window. The logo file was automatically uploaded to your OneDrive folder in the cloud.

Delete another file in the cloud.

23. Select the **logo** file, then click **Delete** in the command bar.

24. Minimize the browser window, then check the local OneDrive\Documents folder. The logo file is deleted from this location as well.

25. Close File Explorer.

26. Minimize the browser window.

OneDrive Web Apps

Web apps are applications that run on the World Wide Web. These apps do not run directly on a device and are not installed; instead, they are accessed over the Internet and provide some of the same functionality as installed versions of the software. Microsoft calls these apps "Office Online."

With only a browser and an Internet connection you can use online versions of Microsoft Excel, OneNote, PowerPoint and Word to read, edit, and create documents, even if you do not have the Microsoft Office suite installed on your computer.

You can click the ⊞ (**Apps**) icon to view all the services that are integrated with your Microsoft account:

Click one of the online apps to open a new browser tab and access templates for specific types of documents.

You can also create and work with web apps directly within OneDrive. Click **New** to display a menu of document types that you can create:

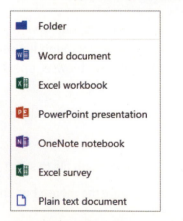

Click the app that you want to use to create a new document. As you work in your document, all changes are automatically saved to OneDrive.

Integration with Desktop Apps

Even though you can use the office online apps without having the Office suite installed on your system, these apps are designed to integrate seamlessly with a locally installed version of Office. Each Office online app provides a command that allows you to open your document in an installed Desktop version of the application, where you can continue your work. When you save your document, your changes are saved to OneDrive.

Sharing Documents on OneDrive

As you can with documents on Google Drive, you can share documents on OneDrive by specifying people to share with or by generating sharing links.

When you select **Get a link**, you generate a sharing link that you can copy and paste into email messages, chat windows and text messages. These links can be forwarded to other users.

When you select **Email**, you send an email message with a sharing link to specific recipients. The recipient must be logged in to the email service in order to access the shared file. OneDrive will authenticate anyone trying to access the shared file.

Share 'Something About Me'

Anyone with this link can edit this item. ˅

Get a link

Email

Manage permissions

To share via email, select the file, click **Share** in the command bar. (You can adjust the permissions by clicking the arrow to the right of Anyone with this link can edit this item and clearing the Allow editing check box.)

Click **Email**. Enter your recipient's email address and an optional message, then click the **Share** button.

← Share 'Something About Me'

Lucy_Lee2016@outlook.com ✕

Here is some personal information about me. Please do not share it with anyone else. Thanks.

Share

When your recipient receives your email message, he or she can click **View in OneDrive** to open the shared document on your OneDrive folder.

I shared "Something About Me.docx" with you in OneDrive

Lucy Lee (lucy_lee2016@outlook.com)   Add to contacts 9:02 AM

To: cstevens1099@outlook.com ˅

Here is some personal information about me. Please do not share it with anyone. Thanks!

Something About Me

View in OneDrive

Exercise 6-5: Using OneDrive office apps

In this exercise, you will use OneDrive office apps. You will work with your partner from previous lessons. Exchange email addresses with your partner in preparation for this exercise.

1. Restore the Internet Explorer browser window.

Begin by creating a new word processing document.

2. Click **New**, then click **Word document** to open a new word processing document named Document1 in Word Online.

3. Type: `My name is` and type your first name.

4. Press ENTER twice to insert a blank line.

5. Type one or two sentences about yourself.

6. Double-click your name, then in the toolbar, click the ⊔ **Underline** button.

7. At the top of the window, click **Document1** to open the field so that you can rename the file.

8. Select the *Document1* text, type: `Something About Me`, then press ENTER to rename the document.

9. Close the browser tab for the *Something About Me* document to return to the OneDrive window. Notice that the new file is visible in the folder.

Now, create a new spreadsheet.

10. Click **New**, then click **Excel workbook** to open a tab with a new, blank worksheet. The rectangle with the border around it shows that the current position of the cursor is cell A1.

11. Type: `Calculus`, then press ENTER. Excel Online enters the text in cell A1, and moves the cursor to cell A2.

12. Type: `Political Studies 1`, then press ENTER.

13. Type: `English Poets`, then press ENTER.

14. Type: `Business Systems`, then press ENTER.

15. Close the browser tab for the worksheet. OneDrive saves the changes and displays the new worksheet as *Book1* in the *Documents* folder.

16. Right-click the *Book1* worksheet, then click **Rename** in the shortcut menu to open the Rename window.

| Rename   ✕ |
| Book1   .xlsx |
| Save |

17. Type: `My Classes`, then press ENTER to rename the worksheet.

18. Click **My Classes.xlsx** to open the worksheet again. Notice that all your changes have been saved.

Now open the document in the Excel desktop app.

---

19. Click the **Edit in Excel** command. If you encounter a security warning, click **Yes** to confirm that you want to open the document. The workbook opens in the Excel desktop app.

20. In cell A5, type: Chemistry, then press ENTER.

21. Press CTRL+S to save the workbook.

22. Close the Excel application window.

23. Close any open message windows. The Excel Online window refreshes. Notice that the changes you made in the desktop app are reflected in the workbook in Excel Online.

24. Close the My Classes browser tab to return to the OneDrive page.

Now, share a file with your partner.

25. Select the **Something About Me** document, then click **Share** in the command bar.

26. Click **Email**, then type your partner's email address (the one associated with his or her Microsoft account).

27. Click in the text box below the email address box, and type: Here is some personal information about me. Please do not share it with anyone. Thanks!

28. Click **Share** to send your message.

Access a shared document on your partner's OneDrive folder.

29. Click the **Apps** icon to view your Microsoft services, then click **Mail** to access your Microsoft Inbox. You should see an email message from your partner.

30. Click the email message to open it, then within the email message, click **View in OneDrive**. Your partner's document should display on your screen in a new browser tab.

31. At the top of the window, click **Edit Document**, then click **Edit in Browser** to open your partner's document in Word Online.

32. Click at the end of the text your partner has written, press ENTER, and then type a sentence in response.

33. Close the Something About Me browser tab.

34. Close the browser tab with the open sharing message. You should be looking at your OneDrive Files\Documents folder.

35. Click **Something About Me** to open the document in Word Online. You should see the text that your partner added to your document.

36. Close the Something About Me browser tab.

37. Click the account icon at the upper-right corner of the window, then click **Sign out** to sign out of OneDrive.

38. Close any open Internet Explorer browser tabs.

Examine your local copy.

39. Open a File Explorer window, then navigate to your local *OneDrive\Documents* folder and double-click **Something About Me** to open the document in Word. Notice that this copy includes the text your partner added to your document. Your local OneDrive folder is synced to your OneDrive folder in the cloud.

40. Close the Word application window, then close File Explorer.

OneDrive Mobile Apps

You can download and install OneDrive mobile apps for Android, iOS and Windows 10 Mobile. Installing the apps and signing in on your mobile device keeps devices synchronized, and enables automatic uploading of photos and videos that you take on your device.

Photos are automatically uploaded to the *OneDrive\Camera roll* folder.

iCloud

Objective 1-6.3

Hosted by Apple, iCloud is integrated with iTunes and other Apple services that are linked to your Apple ID. iCloud connects you and all your Apple devices (iPad, iPhone, iPod touch, and your Mac) and services. Advanced sharing features allow you to share photos, videos, documents, and iTunes Store, App Store, and iBooks Store purchases.

When you set up iCloud on your iOS devices and your Mac, you always have the latest version of your important documents, photos, notes and contacts on whatever device you're using.

You can also install iCloud on your iOS devices. iCloud automatically backs up your iOS device daily over Wi-Fi when your device is turned on, unlocked, and connected to a power source. You can also use your iCloud backup to restore your iOS device or to set up a new device.

Pages, Numbers, and Keynote are Apple web apps that you can use to create and work with content in your web browser.

iCloud Drive is the associated cloud storage location.

Use the icons at the top of the window to create new folders, upload, download, or delete files. You can also drag and drop files into the iCloud Drive window. 5GB of storage space is associated with iCloud Drive.

A local iCloud folder is built into Mac OS X and iOS devices and becomes available when you set up an iCloud account. Drag and drop files into the local folder so that they will be automatically uploaded to iCloud Drive.

iCloud for Windows

If you own iOS devices, but use a Windows PC, you can download and install the iCloud for Windows app on your PC, which will create folders that will sync with your iOS devices. Your photos, videos, mail, files, and bookmarks will then be accessible on all of your devices. iCloud stores your content and automatically keeps it up to date on your iPhone, iPad, iPod touch, Mac, and PC.

Web-Only Access

iCloud is designed to work primarily within the Apple universe; however, if you do not have an iOS device or a Mac, you can still get web-only access to create and share documents using Pages, Numbers, and Keynote by signing into iCloud. 1GB of storage space is associated with a free account.

Go to www.icloud.com, and use one of your existing email addresses to create an account if you do not have an iCloud.com address or an Apple ID.

Click **Don't have an Apple ID? Create yours now**.

Fill out the form, making sure you scroll to the bottom.

Select security questions and answers, deselect check boxes for any email items you do not want to receive, then click **Continue**. Apple will send an Apple ID email verification message to the email address you used to create your account. It may take a few minutes for the email message to arrive. When it arrives, open the message, then enter the code in the verification screen that displays, and click **Continue** once again. Agree to the terms and conditions.

Log in using the email address and password, then on the welcome page click **Start using iCloud**.

If you have web-only access linked to a free iCloud account, the features are a little more primitive. You drag and drop files into the iCloud window with certain limitations:

- in the Pages folder, you can drag and drop Pages, TXT, and Word files
- in the Numbers folder, you can drag and drop Numbers, CSV and Excel files
- in the Keynote folder, you can drag and drop Keynote and PowerPoint files

Dropbox

Objective 1-6.3

Hosted by Dropbox, Inc., Dropbox is a popular cloud storage provider. As with the other types of cloud storage, you can store any type of file you want in Dropbox. You can upload and download content in the web interface, and you can download and install the desktop app which creates a local folder on your hard drive.

Syncing is automatic between the local folder and the cloud location, and if you install and configure the app on your other devices and sign in, then content is synced across all your devices.

You can share the files stored in Dropbox in the cloud by creating and distributing sharing links via email, text messages, or chat. You can also download and install mobile apps for Android and iOS.

To create a free Dropbox account, go to www.dropbox.com and fill in your name, email address and password, agree to the Dropbox terms, and then click the **Sign up for free** button. The account is set up for you and you are prompted to download and install the Dropbox app.

Download the app and then run the installer.

When the Dropbox Setup window displays, enter your email address and password, and click **Sign In**.

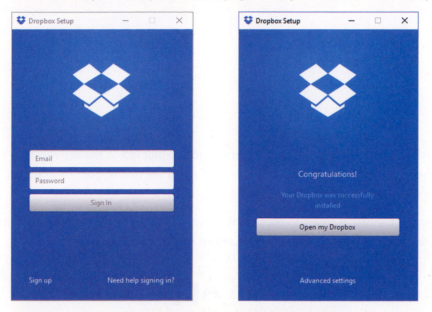

When the setup is complete, click the **Open my Dropbox** button to reach the Welcome screen. Click **Get Started** to view some introductory information; click **Next** to advance through all the screens, then click **Finish** to open your local Dropbox folder in File Explorer.

Drag files here for automatic upload to Dropbox in the cloud.

When you are working in Dropbox.com in your web browser, you can drag and drop files into the browser window, or use the buttons in the web interface to upload, download and work with files and folders.

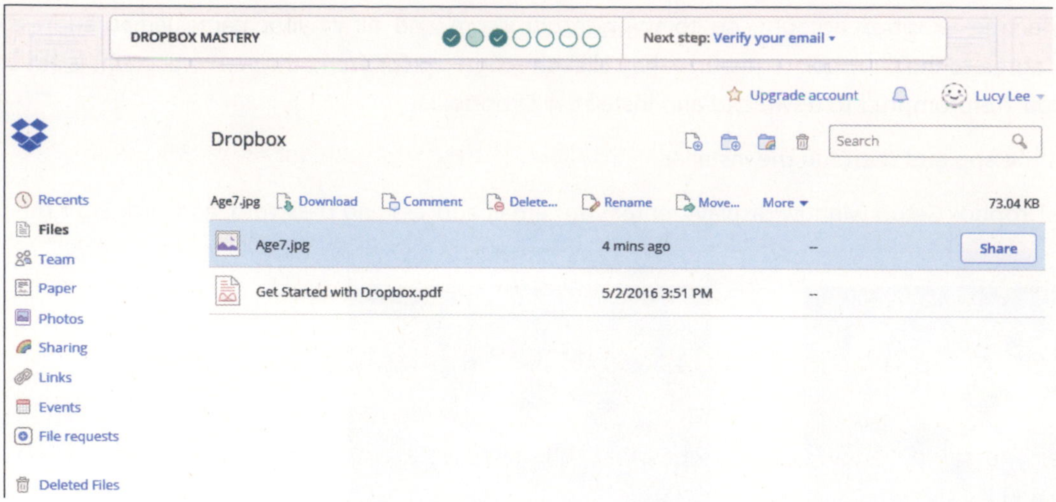

The local Dropbox folder provides offline access, so even if you are not connected to the Internet you can work on your files and save them to your Dropbox folder. The next time you are online, your changes will be synced to the cloud and across all your devices.

Dropbox includes a 30-day version history; in case you accidentally delete a file or want to restore a previous version. It also features automatic photo uploading from your *Camera roll* folder to Dropbox.

Other Types of Cloud-Based Applications

Objective 1-6.4, 1-6.5

The cloud offers much more than simple online storage and online productivity apps. Some of the most widely-used enterprise-level apps include Learning Management System (LMS) apps and Customer Relationship Management (CRM) apps.

Learning Management System (LMS)

A *Learning Management Systems (LMS)* is a software application designed to deliver electronic training courses (also called eLearning), track student progress, and generate performance reports. It is essentially an engine that powers eLearning.

An LMS lets you create content and organize it into courses, deliver the content (as training) online, enroll students, and monitor and assess student performance.

The most common implementation of an LMS includes two parts:

Server component – this is the part that performs the core functions (creates, manages, and delivers courses, keeps track of users and their progress, and so on.)

User interface component – this is the part that runs inside the browser and it is the interface through which administrators, teachers and students interact with the LMS.

When organizations and schools use an LMS to deliver training, each student can study the material online at their own pace. The student signs in to the LMS through a web browser, and reads and interacts with the training material within the browser. Student progress data (lessons read, quiz and exam scores) is stored on the server.

The interface usually includes built-in communication tools such as email, chat and discussion boards. Students can post assignments, chat with each other and send messages to their teachers. While these tools are accessed through the browser, they are hosted on the server.

The integrated monitoring and reporting tools that keep track of each student's progress are also hosted on the server, and facilitators access these tools through the browser.

In an LMS, most of the application is hosted on a server. Users may need to download and install a sign-in tool on their local systems to enable quick access; but generally, that access is made through a web browser.

Customer Relationship Management (CRM) Software

Customer relationship management (CRM) is the practice of managing and analyzing interactions with customers. The goal of CRM is to improve business relationships with customers, thereby increasing customer retention and helping to drive sales growth.

CRM software applications capture customer information across different points of contact, such as the company's web site, telephone calls, live chat sessions, direct mailings, marketing materials and social media. The captured information is consolidated and stored in a CRM database. Sales and marketing staff can then access the database to view detailed information on customers' personal information, purchase history, buying preferences and so on.

CRM software can also be used to record customer interactions with staff (over email, phone calls, or social media for example). It can also automate certain processes. For example, as a sales prospect is entered into the system, the system might automatically send out marketing materials (via email or social media), with the goal of turning the sales lead into a customer.

Popular CRM application vendors include:

Salesforce.com – offers a completely cloud-based CRM product.

Oracle – Oracle Corporation has long been known for its sophisticated relational database products, and they offer several cloud-based CRM products.

Workfront (formerly AtTask) – offers cloud-based CRM Marketing applications and project management solutions.

Traditional CRM implementations were locally hosted on the premises; but modern implementations are cloud-based. This keeps the customer data secure, and it enables employees to access the information from anywhere – thus enabling a mobile or telecommuter workforce.

Who Uses CRM Software?

Almost any business that wants to show their customers that they are a priority can benefit from using CRM software. However, specifically likely users would be:

- Any business with a sales team.
- Any business with a marketing team.
- Any business that generates quotes or invoices.

Essentially, any business with customers is a candidate for CRM.

5. Scroll the list of apps, then tap the app you want to configure.

Click **Notifications**, move the **Allow notifications** slider on or off. Depending on the app, you may be able to turn off particular types of notifications (such as sounds or notifications that appear on the lock screen) as opposed to turning all notifications off for the app.

On iOS, you can use the Notifications Center to turn notifications on or off for a particular app. To access these settings on iOS:

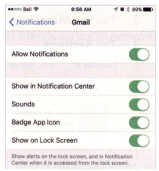

1. Tap **Settings**.

2. Tap Notifications.

3. Find and tap the app you want to configure.

Move the **Allow Notifications** slider on or off. Depending on the app, you may be able to turn off particular types of notifications (such as sounds or notifications that appear on the lock screen) as opposed to turning all notifications off for the app.

Lesson Summary

In this lesson, you learned about cloud computing. You should now be able to:

- ☑ understand the benefits and characteristics of cloud computing

- ☑ create and use cloud accounts to store, manage, and share files

- ☑ describe different types of cloud applications

- ☑ configure mobile notification

Review Questions

1. Which of the following is an example of cloud computing?
   a. Using Gmail.
   b. Using your laptop on an airplane.
   c. Using Wi-Fi to connect to a network printer.
   d. All of these are examples of cloud computing.

2. Which of the following is a benefit of cloud computing?

   a. The ability to make a backup copy of your cloud computing software.

   b. The reliability of locally installed applications.

   c. Reduced hardware costs.

   d. This refers to the number of backups the service will create for your data.

3. Which type of app generally provides the most complete feature set?

   a. Desktop apps.

   b. Browser apps.

   c. Tablet apps.

   d. Smart phone apps.

4. Which of the following is a feature found in most cloud accounts?

   a. Automatic backup.

   b. Cloud storage space.

   c. Apps to connect multiple devices to your account.

   d. All of these are features found in most cloud accounts.

5. How can you upload content to Google Drive?

   a. Click New, File upload.

   b. Click New, Folder upload.

   c. Drag files into the Drive window.

   d. You can use any of these methods to upload files to Google Drive.

6. How can you download content from Google Drive?

   a. Drag files from Drive into File Explorer.

   b. Select a file, click More actions, then click Download.

   c. Create folder called Local in Drive, then move files into the folder; they will be automatically downloaded.

   d. You can use any of these methods to download files from Google Drive.

7. Which of the following is true concerning a local Google Drive folder?

   a. The app for creating a local folder is built into Windows 10.

   b. You create the folder in File Explorer, then configure it to sync with your My Drive location.

   c. It is set for automatic synchronization with your My Drive location.

   d. The app for creating a local folder is built into iOS.

8. Which of the following are levels of access you can set for files that you share on Google Drive?

   a. Can delete, Can edit, and Can comment.

   b. Can edit, Can comment, and Can view.

   c. Can share, Can edit, and Can view.

   d. Can copy, Can download, and Can comment.

Passwords protect your accounts. You should take the following steps to create a strong password:

- Use a minimum of six characters (sometimes a standard is set up by your school or organization); eight or more characters is even better, with 15 characters considered the most secure.

- Include a mixture of numbers, letters, symbols and capital letters.

- Select a password that will be easy for you to remember, but difficult for someone else to guess.

- Avoid using the names of people close to you such as members of your family, or the names of your pets. People who know you well enough can try to guess your password using these names first.

- Avoid using variations of your name or including your name, address, or birthdate in your password.

- Avoid using a variation of a password that may be easy to guess, such as Password-Jan, Password-Feb, password001, password_003, DrewJ12, DrewF12, pa$$w0rd, and so on.

Keeping Your Account Safe

Your account protects your files and your reputation. If you allow someone else to log on with your account, you can be held responsible for actions performed under your account name. For example, if someone sends threatening email from your account, recipients will think the messages came from you. If someone deletes important files on the network using your account, that activity will be traced back to you as well.

In order to keep your account secure, you should protect your user name and password and keep them to yourself. Follow these guidelines:

- Never share your account information.

- If you accidentally share your logon information, change it immediately.

- Do not "hide" your password near your computer. For example, tucking a sticky note under your keyboard or in a desk drawer is not secure. Do not keep password "cheat sheets."

- Do not use the same password for all your accounts – if someone guesses your password, they would have access to multiple accounts.

Changing Your Password

It is good practice to change your password periodically.

To change your Windows 10 password:

1. Click **Start**, then click **Settings**.

2. Click **Accounts**, then click **Sign-in options**.

3. Under Password, click **Change**.

4. Type your old password, then click **Next**.

5. Type your new password, type your new password again as a confirmation, enter a password hint, then click **Next**.

6. Click **Finish**.

Often, if you are a member of a domain network, you will be required to change your password at regular intervals. If you are using a domain account, use these steps to change your logon password:

1. Press CTRL+ALT+DELETE.

2. Click **Change a password**.

3. Type your old password, type your new password, type your new password again as a confirmation, then press ENTER.

Locking the System

Ideally, you should log off your system if you are going to be away from it for any period of time. This practice protects your computer and your documents. However, a more convenient option is to lock the system while you are away.

When you lock the system, all your programs and files remain open and ready so you can resume working quickly. Windows displays an image on the monitor and you must enter the logon password before you can resume working.

To lock the system, click **Start**, click your account icon in the upper right corner of the Start menu, then click **Lock**.

Identifying Risks

Objective 1-7.2, 1-7.4

You should be aware of the potential risks you face when you connect to a network or to the Internet. These risks include becoming "infected" with computer viruses and Trojan horses; these are programs designed with the specific intent of harming computer systems. You should understand how to detect and remove malicious code on your system before it harms your computer, your data, or data on the network to which you connect.

Viruses

A *virus* is a malicious program designed to take control of system operations, and damage or destroy data. Viruses are loaded onto your computer without your knowledge and run without your consent. All computer viruses are human made and are often designed to spread to other computer users through networks or email address books.

Viruses can be transferred via email attachments, program or file downloads, and by using infected disks, CDs, or flash drives. If you pass an infected drive to a co-worker, that co-worker's system can also be infected. Similarly, a colleague might inadvertently send you an email attachment infected by a virus. If you attempt to open or print the file, the virus will engage. Email attachments have long been a favorite way to spread viruses.

A virus can:

- Display harmless messages on the screen.
- Use all available memory, thereby slowing or halting all other processes.
- Corrupt or destroy data files.
- Erase the contents of an entire hard disk.

Worms

A worm is a self-replicating program that consumes system and network resources. The difference between a worm and a virus is that a worm automatically spreads from one computer to another, whereas a virus requires some form of action; for example, a user must pass an infected disk to someone else, or must forward an infected email message.

A worm can reside in active memory and replicate on the network. Worms can spread to all computers connected to a network and are commonly spread over the Internet via email attachments.

Trojans

A *Trojan* (or Trojan horse) is a program designed to allow a hacker remote access to a target computer system. The code for a Trojan is hidden inside seemingly harmless applications, such as games. Trojans are installed on the target system when the user runs the infected application. Unlike worms and viruses, Trojans do not replicate themselves or copy themselves to other files and disks.

Once installed on the target system, the Trojan can allow a hacker to take control of the target system, steal information, install other software (including viruses), download or upload files, or crash the system.

Trojans can be accidentally installed through software downloads (for example, a Trojan might be hidden in a software application downloaded from a network), through Web sites containing active content (that is, in the form of an ActiveX control), or through an email attachment.

Malware (Spyware / Adware)

Spyware is a software application that is secretly placed on your system and gathers personal or private information without your consent or knowledge.

Adware is a software application that automatically displays or downloads advertisements.

Many Internet-based applications contain spyware. Companies with both good and bad reputations have included spyware code in their software. Spyware can also be placed on your system by a virus or by an application downloaded from the Internet.

Once installed, spyware monitors your activity on the Internet and conveys the information to the spyware originator. The originator can then gather Web site usage, email and even password information from your system, then use it for advertising purposes or malicious activities.

Spyware can consume memory resources and network bandwidth. Spyware has the ability to:

- Scan files on hard drives.
- Read cookies.
- Monitor keystrokes.
- Install other spyware applications.
- Change the default home page in Web browsers.
- Automatically send information to the spyware developer.

A cookie is a small text file placed on your computer by a Web server. Although cookies themselves are not dangerous, they can be used to store user names and passwords if you click "Yes" when your browser asks you if you want to store this information. Cookies also track browser activities, such as sites you visit and options you select.

In a normal Internet transaction, cookies are read only by the server that placed them on your system; however, a hacker who gains physical access to your system or successfully installs spyware can steal your cookies, and with them, any stored user names and passwords.

You can download and install freeware spyware/adware applications, or you can use Windows Defender to monitor your system for spyware. Anti-spyware applications are discussed later in this lesson.

Network Connections

Any time you join a network, you open your system up to possible connections from other systems participating on the same network. Infected systems and/or would-be hackers connected to the network always present a risk.

Wired Connections

Generally speaking, if you connect to a wired network within your school or business, you are pretty safe. Network administrators take great pains to ensure that all company/school systems are routinely scanned for infection, and all users must log on to the network using a valid user name and password.

However, the same guarantee is not in place when you plug into a public wired network. For example, some hotels still provide Ethernet connections for Internet access to their guests. There is no way to guarantee that every hotel guest who connects is an honest and upstanding citizen (who would never dream of trying to hack into someone else's system or who would never consider trying to unleash a virus); nor is there a way to guarantee that everyone connecting to the network is using up-to-date antivirus software. You connect at your own risk.

Wireless Connections

These same risks apply to Wi-Fi connections. Anyone can join a Wi-Fi network provided by a public hotspot. Even if you connect to a secured network (one that requires a pass phrase) provided by a hotel for example, you still do not know who else is on the network. No one can guarantee that all the systems connected are virus-free, and no one can guarantee that there is not a hacker lurking in the background waiting to find a system he or she can exploit.

Participating in ad-hoc networks (those which do not use an access point) is dangerous. Wireless systems connect directly to one another in an ad-hoc network; there is no access point at the center to relay signals among the participants. There is also no authentication required. That means anyone within range can connect – with or without your knowledge.

Mitigating Risks

Whenever you connect to a public network, always identify the network to the operating system as a Public network (as opposed to a Work or Home network). Windows automatically limits incoming connections from a public network while still allowing you access to the Internet.

If you use Wi-Fi, always connect to an infrastructure network. Avoid participating in ad-hoc networks.

Using Public Computers

The risks associated with using public computers (such as those found in a library) have to do with protecting your privacy and your personal accounts. Remember that anyone who has physical access to a public computer can access any information stored on it.

Because you do not "log on" to a public computer, all activity is performed under one open account. That means search history, cookies, and any other information that is stored on the computer is accessible.

For this reason, you should take the following steps to ensure your safety when you use a public computer.

Log out of online accounts – if you log into an online account (for example, a banking account or a credit card account, or even a social media account) and then walk away without logging out, anyone who comes along behind you can access those accounts and take action within those accounts because you are still logged in. You are leaving yourself wide open to both monetary theft and identify theft.

Clear caches and cookies – browsers store information (such as browsing history and search history) in storage locations called *caches* (pronounced "cashes") which are located on the hard disk. Browsers also store cookies (small text files that contain information pertaining to web site activity) from sites that you visit. These entries are stored in plain text, so anyone can navigate to and view them. If you want your online activity to remain private, use the built-in features in your browser to clear these entries. (You will learn how to work with browsers in the Living Online module.) Also, do not allow the browser to store your passwords for online sites/accounts.

Log out of the operating system – if you use a shared computer at school or at work that requires a personal log on, always log out when you are finished. Logging out prevents other users from using your account to access personal files stored under your profile. Additionally, logging out prevents an unauthorized user from gaining illicit access to the network.

Social Engineering

Social engineering is the practice of tricking users into giving out passwords or other types of access information. Social engineers pose as fellow employees or classmates, technical consultants or cleaning staff, in order to gain the trust of real employees or students.

Social engineers count on people's desire to be helpful. For example, a social engineer may wait near a secured door that requires a smartcard for access and wait until a legitimate employee is about to enter. The social engineer could then approach the door carrying an armload of boxes. Out of courtesy, the real employee may then hold the door open so the social engineer can enter.

Social engineers also attempt to imitate a legitimate user by confusing a switchboard operator or a security guard. In several instances, a social engineer has called a company, posing as the systems manager. After explaining that he had accidentally locked himself out of the computer, he convinced someone in the company to change administrative access according to his instructions. All the social engineer then had to do was log on to the machine, and he had full administrative access.

Typical targets of the social engineering strategy include anyone who has access to information about systems they do not use, including secretaries, janitors, some administrators and even security staff.

Reducing the Risk of Social Engineering

The best way to guard against becoming a victim of social engineering is to recognize common social engineering practices. Following is a brief list of social engineering strategies:

- Posing as a technician and using that implied authority to cause employees to divulge information, to make configuration changes to servers, or to obtain sensitive information.
- Confusing or intimidating an employee or guard into allowing physical access to a building.
- Sending official-looking email messages to all employees with instructions that cause them to reveal sensitive information.

Phishing

Phishing is the process of trying to gather sensitive information such as a password, or credit card details from an unsuspecting victim by pretending to be a trustworthy entity. Typically, a phisher sends a legitimate-looking email message that appears to come from a legitimate source, such as your bank or credit card company.

The email message generally includes a false alert and instructs you to take a particular action. For example, you might receive an email message alerting you that suspicious activity has been detected on your credit card account. The email will include a link and directions that instruct you to click the link to visit the web site where you will be expected to enter account-specific information. When you click the link, you are taken to a fraudulent web site made to look just like the legitimate site. When you update your personal information (such as password, credit card or bank account numbers) on the fraudulent web site, the phisher captures your information and can then use it for malicious purposes, including identity theft.

To protect yourself against phishing:

- Enable the anti-phishing features in your browsers.
- Check an unknown site manually. (In Internet Explorer, click **Tools**, point to Safety, then click **Check This Website**.)
- Avoid clicking links in email messages. If a message appears to have come from a bank, credit card company or government agency, call the organization directly to discuss the email message. Often you will be informing the genuine company that a fraud scheme is in place so they can send appropriate notices to their clients.
- Before logging in to a secure site, check the Address bar to be sure the address starts with the legitimate site name.

Exercise 7-1: Recognizing risks

In this exercise, you will review two scenarios and identify the risks represented by each.

1. Consider the following scenario:

    Alan is the new receptionist at XYZ Company. Most of the management staff has been at an offsite meeting all day and it is already 4 PM. The phone rings and the conversation proceeds as follows:

    Alan: "Dream Pages LLC, this is Alan, can I help you?"

    Caller: "Alan! Great. Hey, this is Jim from IT. We've been stuck offsite all day, and it looks like we may be here several more hours, and I really need to finish getting all the email accounts moved over to the new server. I can do it remotely, but I left my notes at the office. I can get your account moved over, but I need your user name and password to do it."

    Alan: "You're in the IT department?"

    Caller: "Yes, Alan, this is Jim from IT. I'm in charge of the email server."

    Alan: "Sorry, I'm still new here ..."

    Caller: "Oh, hey, no worries, Alan. Anyway, I can get your account moved over if you could just give me the user name and password. Yours is the last one I need to move, and it would save me a trip all the way back to the office. Can you help me out?"

- Be suspicious of any unexpected attachments you receive with email or instant message transmissions. If you receive an attachment that you did not expect or do not recognize:

    - Do not open the attachment.

    - Try to contact the message sender (using a method other than email) and determine whether the attachment is legitimate.

    - If you are unable to contact the sender or the sender is unaware of the attachment, delete the attachment from the message.

    - Open your Deleted Items folder and delete the attachment from it to permanently remove the attachment from your system.

The best protection is prevention; however, you should understand that most viruses can be removed without causing permanent damage to your system.

Removing Viruses

When an antivirus program is running, it will scan the files you select; when it finds a virus or threat, it will give you the option to quarantine or remove the threat.

- If you elect to quarantine the infected files, the antivirus program will place the infected file in a quarantined or vault area where it cannot infect other files. Quarantined files can usually be deleted at any time.

- If you elect to remove the file, the antivirus program will permanently delete this file from your system. You usually do not need to do anything else.

- If the antivirus finds a virus that cannot be removed, it will still quarantine the infected file. You may be able to find a removal tool for this virus on the antivirus program's web site. Generally, you will need to download a file and then follow the instructions for removing the virus from your system. Alternatively, you may need to research how to remove the infected file manually.

It bears repeating that it is extremely important to keep antivirus software up to date and configured to automatically download updates. It is equally important to keep the email scanner and resident scanner portions of the application turned on. Regular system scans are recommended, and these can be scheduled. You can also manually start a scan at any time.

Firewalls

A *firewall* is a security barrier that filters and controls the flow of information coming into and out of a private network. Firewalls protect systems from unauthorized access by filtering the information that comes through the Internet connection into your LAN or computer system. If an incoming packet of information is flagged by the firewall filters, it is not allowed through. In this way, firewalls prevent dangerous network traffic from coming into the LAN.

The filters used by firewalls are simply sets of rules that define and control which type of traffic to allow and which type of traffic to block.

In an organization, a network administrator can set up and implement security rules on a firewall that control how employees connect to web sites, whether instant messaging applications are allowed, whether files are allowed to leave the company over the network and so on.

A firewall protects your network from malicious activity coming from outside your network, and provides a "door" through which people can communicate between a secured network (the LAN) and the open, unsecured Internet. A network firewall is placed between a LAN and the Internet.

A firewall can be a dedicated computer system, a specialized firewall appliance, or it can be implemented on a networking device such as a router. In a home or small office networking environment where a broadband router is used, a firewall is usually built into the broadband router.

Note: Firewalls keep private data private. They do not, however, encrypt data nor do they protect against viruses.

Desktop Firewalls

Firewalls can also be implemented through software. Also known as personal firewalls, desktop firewalls offer protection for an individual system instead of an entire network. Tools such as Norton 360 or AVG can detect and respond to attacks on a computer system.

Desktop firewalls offer many firewall features, such as inspection of all incoming transmissions for security threats. When a firewall is used in conjunction with antivirus software, a personal computer is secure, provided that the user updates these applications frequently.

Many operating systems include built-in (native) desktop firewall software. Windows, for example, includes Windows Firewall which is enabled by default. Mac OS X also ships with a built-in firewall, which you can enable from the Security & Privacy tab in System Settings.

Firewall Challenges

Firewalls can present challenges to network users. Sometimes firewall settings block access to particular web sites, or block streaming audio or video from coming into a network. If your corporate system is behind a firewall and you have difficulty connecting to specific Internet sites or services, you may need to contact a network administrator, who can then adjust the firewall configuration.

You may also learn, however, that the service or web site you want to access conflicts with your organization's security policy.

Monitoring Software

Most network administrators protect their networks through network monitoring software. These programs track and record network activity such as user logons, server performance and network traffic conditions. If logon events are tracked, then any time you log on to a network system, that activity is recorded in a server log. If a hacker logs on using your account, and manages to damage the network, the electronic trail may lead to you. If you suspect that your account has been compromised, contact the network administrator immediately so you can change your user name and password.

In some organizations, administrators take monitoring to a whole other level by installing PC surveillance software. Software of this type records all PC activity, allowing the administrator to capture your keystrokes, view screenshots, and see your email, instant message conversations, and web activity.

Remember that computers in your school or workplace are not your private property; accordingly, any activity you perform on those computers may not be private.

Security is an especially important component of remote access because communication across a public network (such as the Internet) is vulnerable to interception or eavesdropping. For this reason, remote access methods must provide for authentication and encryption. *Authentication* is the process of confirming the identity of a user or computer system. *Encryption* is the process of converting data into an unreadable form of text, which then requires a decryption key in order to be read.

In the past, remote access was provided through remote access servers, modems and dedicated phone lines. In most modern networks, however, access is obtained using a virtual private network (VPN) connection.

A VPN is an encrypted connection between two computers. VPNs allow secure, private communications across long distances using the Internet as the pathway for communication instead of using a dedicated private line.

VPNs make it possible for telecommuters and traveling/remote employees to establish a secure connection to the company network from outside the company premises. VPNs also make it possible for a company with several satellite offices to establish secure connections between all their locations.

Using VPN

Telecommuters, remote employees, and traveling employees use VPN to connect to their company networks from the outside.

In order for a network to support VPN connections, a VPN server must be set up to receive incoming connections. Any user who wants to make a VPN connection from a remote location (for example, from home or from a hotel room) must install and then launch VPN client software to open a connection with the VPN server.

Users must log on using a valid user name and password, just as if they were logging on to the network from inside the corporate office.

Backup and Restore

Objective 1-4.1, 1-4.2, 1-4.3

A computing device is useful only if the data it contains is valid and accessible. An easy way to protect data is to schedule regular backups. A *backup* is a duplicate copy of a program, a disk, or data, made either for archiving purposes or for safeguarding files from loss if the active copy is damaged or destroyed.

Backups should be written on a storage medium other than the source of the backup. That is, if you are backing up your hard drive, do not create the backup on the same hard drive. Instead, choose a location such as a different internal hard drive, an external hard drive, a flash drive, CD or DVD, or a network location (such as a network server hard disk) or a cloud location (such as OneDrive).

Keeping a current backup of all your important files is essential to ensuring that your data can be recovered in the event of a failure or loss. Windows includes built-in features that make it easy and convenient to back up both system data and your personal files.

Backing Up Your Personal Files

The operating system, drivers, personalization settings, apps and other software can be re-installed on a computer fairly easily should they become damaged or accidentally deleted. Your personal files on the other hand cannot be easily replaced or re-created.

Your personal files are your documents, your photos, videos, downloads and so on. Think of how long it took you to create and refine your Office files. Think of the old photos you may have scanned and saved on your disk, or the new wedding or graduation day videos you might have transferred to and even edited on your computer. Would it be easy to replace these if something happened to your hard drive?

Your personal files are the most important items to back up on your computer. You have choices on how you want to back up your personal files, including:

Copying files to cloud storage – this is as easy as dragging important files to your local OneDrive, Drive, Dropbox or iCloud folder. You have already learned how to back up files using cloud storage.

Using File History in Windows 10 – this feature configures Windows 10 to automatically create an hourly backup of your personal files whenever the destination media (for example, an external hard drive or a flash drive) is connected to the PC.

Using Windows Backup and Restore – this is a feature from Windows 7 that configures Windows to automatically create a weekly backup of all important files on the computer; this includes your personal files *and* the files saved in the default Windows folders (these are operating system files, settings, registry entries and so on) used by the operating system. Backup and Restore requires significant storage space.

File History

The File History feature is the main backup tool in Windows 10 for backing up your personal files. Additionally, it automatically stores a version history of your files, allowing you to restore previous versions of a file if needed.

To use File History, configure it once, and keep the selected backup media connected. To configure the feature, connect an external drive, open the **Settings** app and then click **Update & security** to open the Update & Security window. In the left pane of the window, click **Backup**.

Click **Add a drive**, then select an external drive in the Select a drive window. The Automatically back up my files option will appear and will be automatically turned on. Windows will back up your files to the drive whenever you connect it to your computer.

Click **More options** to view the Backup Options page.

Use the settings on this page to control how often to backup up, and how often to keep backup files. You can create a backup immediately by clicking the **Back up now** button, and you can specify which folders under your user profile to include in the backup. By default, these folders include: Desktop, Documents, Downloads, Music, Pictures, Videos and more. You can add or exclude folders as required.

Windows Backup and Restore

You can use Windows Backup and Restore to back up the entire system or only the files and folders you select. You can allow Windows to choose what to back up or you can select the individual folders, libraries and drives that you want to back up. By default, backups are created on a regular schedule. You can change the schedule, and you can create a backup manually at any time. Once you set up Windows Backup, Windows keeps track of the files and folders that are new or modified and adds them to your backup (assuming that your specified backup storage media is connected to the system at the time of the scheduled backup).

If you have never used Windows Backup before, you need to set it up first by following the steps in the wizard. Open the Control Panel and navigate to **System and Security**, click **Backup and Restore (Windows 7)** page, then click **Set up backup**.

Select the destination for the backup file, then click **Next**. By default, Windows will back up data saved in libraries, on the Desktop, and in default Windows folders. Windows will also create a system image, which can be used to restore your computer if it stops working. Click **Next** if you want to accept the default settings, or click **Let me choose** to specify custom settings.

You are given an opportunity to review the current backup settings.

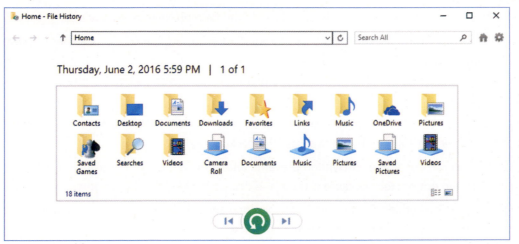

Click **Change schedule** if you want to adjust the backup schedule. By default, Windows runs a backup every Sunday at 7:00 PM. However, you can configure Windows to run a daily, weekly, or monthly backup. You can also specify not to schedule any further backups.

Click **Save settings and run backup** to create a backup.

Restoring Personal Files

If you accidentally delete a file that you need, or if one of your files becomes corrupted, you can easily restore it to your hard drive from the saved backup media.

- If you backed up using OneDrive, simply copy the required files or folders from the OneDrive folder and paste them to your hard drive using File Explorer.

- If you backed up using File History, open the **Settings** app, click **Update & security**, click **Backup** in the left pane, click **More options**, scroll to the bottom of the window and click **Restore files from a current backup**. Select the files or folders you want, then click the green button to restore them to your computer.

- If you backed up using Backup and Restore, open the Control Panel and navigate to **System and Security**, click **Backup and Restore (Windows 7)** page, then click the **Restore my files** button to open the Restore Files window. Use the Browse for files and Browse for folders buttons to select the specific files and folders you want to restore.

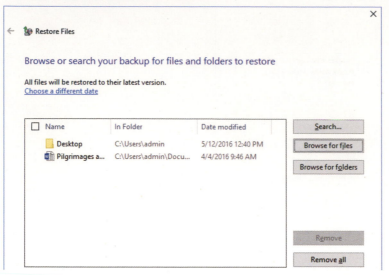

When you have selected all the files and folders you want to restore, click **Next**. Specify whether you want to restore the files to their original location or to a different location, then click **Restore**. When the restoration is complete, click **Finish**.

Secure Backups

As an individual user, you may not give much thought to backing up. You have complete control over how often you back up your files, or whether you even back them up at all. However, the people responsible for protecting an organization's data must adhere to well-defined (and usually quite stringent) backup policies and procedures.

Businesses which handle other peoples' personal information (for example, financial information or medical information) are required by law to maintain and secure backups for a requisite number of years. That is, the data must remain accessible, and it must be protected from unauthorized access.

Maintaining secure backups requires compliance with at least the following rules:

- The backups should be redundant. That is, there should be more than one copy of any given backup.

- At least one copy of the backup should be stored off-site. Storing backups in another physical location ensures that if disaster (such as an earthquake or a fire) strikes and a company's computers are destroyed along with any backups that are stored on the premises, there is still a copy of the backup data that is safe.

- Off-site storage locations must be secure. That is, only authorized personnel (those with a key or a passcode) should be able to physically access the backup media.

- Backups should be encrypted. Encryption prevents unauthorized users from using any information they manage to intercept or steal, because without the decryption key, the data is unreadable.

- Backups should be verified. This means that someone should check the backup media to be sure that the information copied to it is accessible and complete.

There are many government regulations pertaining to protecting people's private information. Companies take these regulations very seriously.

Backing Up PC System Files and Settings

System files are vital to the function of the operating system, and they can become corrupt over time. Additionally, system settings can become damaged or misconfigured as software, updates, drivers, and apps are installed. System file corruption or misconfiguration can lead to problems using your computer. For example, some applications may stop working, or the system might start freezing up, or some hardware may cease to function. In some cases, you may not be able to boot up at all.

Windows includes several built-in tools you can use to back up system files. You can use the backup to recover damaged files or to reverse misconfigurations. These tools include:

- system restore points
- system image files

Even if you are not experienced enough to use these advanced tools to recover or repair your computer on your own, system file backups are an invaluable tool in the hands of a technical specialist who can use them to restore your system for you.

System Restore Points

A *restore point* is a saved snapshot of your computer's Windows system files, program files, and Windows registry settings at a specific point in time. User files are not included in a restore point. Restore points are named and stored by their creation date.

System Restore is a protection feature built into Windows; however, it must be enabled before any restore points can be created. To ensure that this protection feature is enabled on your Windows 10 system:

1. Click in the taskbar search box, then type: restore.

2. Click **Create a restore point** in the Start menu to open the System Protection tab in the System Properties dialog box.

3. Click your hard drive in the Available Drives list box. If *On* displays in the Protection column, then the feature is enabled.

4. If protection is turned off for your hard drive, click **Configure**.

5. Click Turn on system protection.

6. Drag the Max Usage slider to about the 5% point (between the first two tick marks on the scale). This reserves a portion of the hard disk for storage of restore points.

7.   Click **Apply**, then click **OK**.

8.   Click **OK** once more to close the System Properties dialog box.

When it is enabled, System Restore automatically creates restore points on your system once per week, and before major system events, such as installing a program or a device driver, or installing operating system updates.

You can also manually create a restore point at any time. To manually create a restore point:

1.   Click in the taskbar search box, then type: restore.

2.   Click **Create a restore point** in the Start menu to open the System Protection tab in the System Properties dialog box.

3.   Click **Create**.

4.   Type a name for the restore point, then click **Create**.

5.   When the message that a restore point was successfully created appears, click **Close**, then click **OK**.

When you restore from a restore point, System Restore restores the system files, program files, and registry settings from the restore point to your computer. This effectively "rolls back" your system to a previous state. This is useful when unexpected problems occur. For example, after an update, you may discover that you can't launch certain programs, or maybe when you try to access the Internet your system freezes. If you use System Restore and select a restore point that was created before you installed the update, this can restore your system files to the previous state before any problem occurred.

You may want to ask a technical specialist to guide you through rolling back your system to a restore point. However, the steps are:

1.   Click in the taskbar search box, then type: restore.

2.   Click **Create a restore point** in the Start menu to open the System Protection tab in the System Properties dialog box.

3.   Click **System Restore**, then click **Next** to display a list of saved restore points. The most recently created restore points appear at the top of the list. You can select the **Show more restore points** check box to view older restore points.

4.   Select the restore point you want to roll back to, then click **Next**.

5.   Click **Finish** and follow the prompts that appear.

System Image / Repair Disc

A *system image* is an exact image of a hard drive; it includes Windows and your system settings, programs, and files. You can use a system image to restore the contents of your computer (to the state it was in when you created the image) if your hard drive or computer ever stops working. When you restore your computer from a system image, it is a complete restoration; you cannot choose individual items to restore, and all your current programs, system settings and files are replaced.

When you create a backup using Windows Backup and Restore, Windows creates a system image. When the image is created, you are given the option to create a repair disc, which you can use to boot your computer and begin the process of re-creating your system from an image.

You can also create a system image at any time by following these steps:

1. Connect an external hard drive or other removable media with a large storage capacity.

2. Click in the taskbar search box, then type: backup.

3. Click **Backup and Restore (Windows 7) Control panel** in the Start menu to open the Backup and Restore (Windows 7) page in the Control Panel.

4. Click the **Create a system image** link.

5. Select the media on which to create the image, then click **Next**.

6. Confirm the settings, then click **Start backup**.

A technical specialist can guide you through the process of recovering your system from an image file; or you can provide the image file media to the specialist if he or she will be making repairs.

Backing Up Your Mobile Data

It is always a good idea to back up your personal data (such as contacts, saved text messages, and photos) on your mobile devices. You can use a USB cable and copy the data to your PC (this is the old school method), or you can use the phone's built-in backup utilities and associated cloud storage. You can also turn on automatic backup so that your data is continually backed up.

Android

Android phones are connected to a Google account and Google can automate and streamline the backup process.

1. Go to **Settings**, **Personal**, **Backup and reset**.

2. Turn on both **Back up my data** and **Automatic restore**.

3. Ensure that your backup account is set to your Gmail account.

Turning these options on ensures that your personal data (including application data, Wi-Fi passwords, bookmarks and other settings) are always backed up and can easily be restored.

iPhone/iOS

Devices running iOS (including iPhones, iPads and iPod touch devices) can be backed up using iCloud or iTunes. iCloud stores backups in the cloud, while iTunes stores backups on your Mac or PC.

To make a backup using iCloud:

1. Connect to a Wi-Fi network.

2. Tap **Settings**, **iCloud**, **Backup**.

3. Make sure iCloud Backup is turned on.

4. Tap **Back Up Now**.

To make a backup using iTunes:

1. Open iTunes and connect your device to your computer.

2. Save content that you downloaded from the iTunes Store or App Store by clicking **File**, **Devices**, **Transfer Purchases**.

3. To create your backup, click **Back Up Now**.

Using Factory Reset Options for PC

When you use a factory reset option on your device, you are resetting the device to the state it was in when it came out of the factory – clean, new, ready to be set up. Sometimes, you may want to reset a device because it is running slowly or improperly and you just want to start over, from scratch. Other times, you will want to reset a device that you are getting ready to donate or gift to another person.

Always create a backup of your personal files before resetting your device.

Windows 10 Refresh and Reset

The Refresh and Reset options (available in Windows 8 and later) enable you to restore the Windows operating system to a default configuration without having to reinstall the operating system from a DVD or USB drive.

- **Refreshing a PC** gives you a fresh installation of Windows without deleting your personal files (pictures, documents, videos, and so on), your personalization settings, or apps that you installed from the Windows store. Applications that you installed from installation media or from the Internet will be removed however. If you are experiencing problems with your computer (for example, the computer freezes or applications will not load), performing a refresh may resolve the issue.

- **Resetting a PC** gives you a fresh installation of Windows and preserves nothing. It is just like formatting the hard disk and starting over with a fresh installation of the operating system. All your personal files, personalization settings, apps and applications will be removed, and your PC settings will be changed back to their defaults. Use the Reset option to set your computer back to its factory default state. This option also allows you to fully clean the drive, which is considered best practice if you want to donate the PC because it makes it difficult for other people to recover the files you have removed.

To refresh or reset your Windows 10 PC:

1. Click **Start**, **Settings**, **Update & security**.
2. In the left panel, click **Recovery**, then under Reset this PC, click **Get started**.
3. In the Choose an option box, select either **Keep my files** or **Remove everything**.

Resetting Mobile Devices

Mobile devices include a factory reset feature that restores the device to the state it was in when it left the factory. Resetting removes your personal files, any apps that you installed, and any customizations you may have added, such as personal accounts, ringtones, screen savers, network passwords, and so on.

Resetting your phone or tablet may be necessary for troubleshooting purposes; although most people use this option only when they are planning to donate or gift their mobile device. Remember that if you use a GSM mobile device, the installed SIM card includes your personal account information. Always remove the SIM card before donating or giving your phone to someone else.

Always back up your personal files before resetting.

Android

Depending on the version of Android you are using, you may find that in addition to an option for performing a factory data reset, you can use options for resetting only the phone settings (for example, ringtones or Do Not Disturb settings); or for resetting only the network settings (such as those for Wi-Fi, Bluetooth and mobile data).

To restore your Android device to its factory settings.

1.   Go to **Settings**, **Personal**, **Backup and reset**.

2.   Tap **Factory data reset**.

3.   Tap **Reset Phone**.

If your smartphone or tablet has expandable storage, the menu may ask if you'd like to wipe the external memory card, which is not really necessary since you can pop the card out of the slot.

iPhone/iOS

In iOS 7 and up, a security feature called Activation Lock requires the Apple ID used to set up the phone initially in order to reset it. If you do not disable Activation Lock, the next person who gets your iPhone won't be able to use it. You can disable Activation Lock by turning off iCloud/Find My iPhone.

To turn off iCloud/Find My iPhone:

1.   Go to **Settings**.

2.   Tap **iCloud**.

3.   Scroll to the bottom of the screen and tap **Sign Out**. Enter your Apple ID /iCloud password if prompted.

To restore your iOS device to its factory settings:

1.   Go to **Settings**.

2.   Tap **General**.

3.   Tap **Reset**.

4.   Tap **Erase All Content and Settings** and enter your passcode if prompted.

5.   Tap **Erase** to proceed.

Note: Industry experts recommend that you encrypt your phone's (or tablet's) data before resetting if you plan to sell or give your phone away. Encrypting the data before resetting ensures any personal data left behind will be unusable, even for people with advanced technical know-how.

Troubleshooting

Objective 1-3.13

Troubleshooting is a systematic approach to solving a problem. Essentially, it is an organized process of trial and error. You may need to try several different approaches before you can narrow down and find a solution, and generally, you use a process of elimination. This means you make a list of things that could be causing the problem and then test them out one by one to eliminate them as the cause.

Here are some general troubleshooting tips:

*   Write down your steps. This will help you remember exactly what you've done and prevent you from testing the same possible causes again.

– Are you close enough to the Wi-Fi hotspot? WLAN devices have a limited range, especially if they are using older WLAN standards such as 802.11b or 802.11g.

Don't be discouraged if troubleshooting takes a while. It is a process, and the more practice you get, the better you will become.

Lesson Summary

In this lesson, you learned about the need for computer security, how to identify risks and how to combat them. You also learned how to back up and restore files, and to reset devices, and you learned about the basics of troubleshooting. You should now be able to:

☑ explain the need for security

☑ describe how to keep your user name and password safe

☑ describe the risks presented by viruses, worms, Trojans, and malware

☑ describe the risks associated with network connections

☑ protect your information when using public computers

☑ describe the risks presented by social engineering and phishing

☑ describe methods for protecting against risks

☑ explain how and why to back up and restore your data and your settings

☑ explain how to reset personal devices to their factory settings

☑ describe basic troubleshooting techniques

☑ understand basic troubleshooting techniques

Review Questions

1. Which of the following passwords is the most secure?
   a. NeXt-Chg9917A
   c. Nextchg9917
   b. PaSW0rd
   d. pA$$word003

2. How do you access the Lock command using the Start menu?
   a. Click the Start button, click your user account name and then click Lock.
   b. Click Start, click Power, and then click Lock.
   c. Click Start, click Shutdown and then click Lock.
   d. You can only access the Lock command from the Power Options page in the Control Panel.

3. Eduardo's computer started to display strange error messages, and then everything in his Documents folder was erased. Eduardo was probably the victim of a:
   a. Virus
   b. System misconfiguration
   c. Spyware application
   d. Phishing exploit

4. A hacker can gain remote access to your computer through:
   a. A Trojan
   c. A virus
   b. A worm
   d. Adware

5. Which software application automatically downloads advertisements?
   a. Adware
   b. Spyware
   c. Desktop firewall
   d. Monitoring software

6. Which of the following is not dangerous but can be used to store a user name and password?
   a. Cookie
   b. Spyware
   c. Adware
   d. Trojan

7. Claudia is connecting to a Wi-Fi network at the airport. How, should she identify this Wi-Fi network to her operating system?
   a. As a Public network.
   b. As a Work network.
   c. As a Home network.
   d. As a Private network.

8. When using a public computer, what else should you do aside from logging out of your online accounts?
   a. Clear caches and cookies.
   b. Restart the computer.
   c. Turn the computer power off.
   d. Lock the system.

9. What do you call the practice of tricking people into giving you unauthorized access to a building or to a computer system?
   a. Social engineering
   b. Hacking
   c. Spyware
   d. Phishing

10. Which of the following can you use to remove viruses from your computer?
    a. Antivirus software
    b. A desktop firewall
    c. Network monitoring software
    d. A hardware firewall

11. Which of the following prevents potentially dangerous network traffic from coming into the LAN?
    a. A firewall
    b. Antivirus software
    c. A browser cache
    d. A modem

12. Which of the following is designed to track and record network activities?
    a. Monitoring software
    b. Firewalls
    c. Login accounts
    d. Backup software

13. Which protocol indicates you are on a secure web site for e-commerce transactions?
    a. HTTPS
    b. HTTP
    c. FTP
    d. SMTP

14. Katarina is traveling and must connect securely to her company's network in order to retrieve several sensitive documents. How should she make this connection?
    a. Use VPN.
    b. Use a Wi-Fi hot spot.
    c. Use her web browser.
    d. Use her web browser and type in https as the protocol.

19. Close the **About Me – Google Docs** tab. Your Drive window should resemble the one shown in the following figure.

20. Close the Drive tab, sign out of Gmail, then close your browser.

Local Apps

Objective 2-6.1, 2-6.2

In contrast to web apps, local apps are installed on a device and run directly on that device. As such, they are designed to run on specific devices, and are written for specific operating systems such as iOS, Mac OS X, Windows, or Android.

While you can use apps on a desktop PC (discussed in Computing Fundamentals), most people interact with apps on their tablets and smart phones. These mobile apps are specifically designed to run on hand held devices with small touch screen interfaces. They optimize the appearance of displayed data even on the small screen, and they are often capable of synchronizing files between devices (such as a smart phone and a desktop system).

Most mobile devices are sold with several apps included as pre-installed software. For example, most smart phones already include a web browser, email client, calendar, mapping program, and an app for buying music or other media. They also include an app that takes you to the device's app store, where you can obtain more apps.

App Stores

An app store is a digital platform for distributing software. A user accesses the app store and can browse the available titles, select an app, and then download the app.

Because apps that run on devices are platform-specific, different platforms utilize different app stores:

App Store Name	Platform	Notes and Devices
Google Play Store (or simply, Play Store)	Android	The Play Store is operated by Google. Android phones and Google TV devices include access to the Play Store, and many also include access to the Amazon Appstore as well.
App Store	iOS	The App Store is operated by Apple. Apps can be downloaded directly to iOS devices such as iPhone, iPod Touch and iPad tablet. On your desktop, you can access apps via iTunes.

LINE – use this app to log into
images, video and audio, and cc

Skype – use this app to log in
conduct free phone calls and vic

Pages – this is a word processir
iOS operating systems.

Office Mobile – these are mobi
and PowerPoint documents on y
(Microsoft ID) in order to sign ir

Word – this mobile app brings
Microsoft ID to use the basic fea
365 subscription (which is not fr

Content Apps

Content apps aggregate (group
whenever you launch the app. T
accounts, and track your online

A few examples include:

CNN – brings news headlines, a

Fox News – also brings news he

Google – displays local weather

New York Times – brings cor
subscription app.

WikiPedia Mobile – use this ap
Android, iOS, Windows, and Fire

iTunesU – use this app to acces
also use this app to access free

Creativity Apps

Creativity apps are those that al
category, and depending on yo
tools categories.

A few examples include:

Afterlight – this is an image ed
edit images with this photo edi

Windows Store	Windows	This app store is operated by Microsoft. You can get apps for your Surface Pro or Windows 10 (or Windows 8.0/8.1) desktop here.
Appstore for Android (via Amazon)	Android	This is an app store for Android devices, operated by Amazon.com. Amazon devices, such as the Kindle Fire include access to the Amazon Appstore (instead of access to Google Play). BlackBerry 10.3 devices also include access.
BlackBerry World	BlackBerry	This is an app store for BlackBerry devices.

In most cases, the app for accessing your default app store will be pre-installed on your device.

Accounts and Access

Many apps are tied to accounts you have created for particular services. If you want to use the Facebook app, you need an associated Facebook account. If you want to use a Microsoft Office app, you need to have a Microsoft account to use the basic features; if you want to use all the features of the app, you need an Office 365 subscription.

As you install an app, you will be prompted to enter any requisite account information. Thereafter, you can simply tap the app icon and be automatically logged in to your account.

Additionally, many apps require access to various settings and services on your device in order to provide full performance. In most cases, the apps will "ask" for access when you install them or when you start using them. Typical areas of access include:

- contacts list
- location
- phone
- SMS
- photos and media files
- camera
- microphone
- Wi-Fi connection
- device ID
- storage
- calendar

Browsing an App Store

An app store is organized like many online stores – top picks or featured items may be presented on the first page; however, you can usually tap an option that will allow you to browse by category.

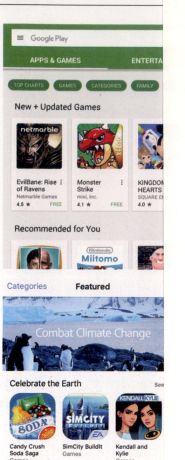

Apps may be categorized b...
operating system each will...
appear in more than one cat...

App genres are loosely grou...

Productivity/Communica...

Productivity apps are progra...
other files, or you can use the...

The following are just a few e...

Gmail – use this app to log...
network notifications, and wh...

Google Hangouts – use this...
service that lets you participa...
other items from your accou...

Draw Something – this app is a game in which players take turns drawing a picture to represent the guess-word for his/her partner to guess. Correct guesses earn one to three coins. Coins can be used to purchase more shades of color for creating drawings, or to purchase "bombs", which can be used to skip advertisements between rounds of play. The free version includes ads; the standard version allows a player to obtain bombs in exchange for watching advertisements, and a "pro" version was developed for iPad which offers unlimited bombs.

Smart Tools – this app lets you use your smart phone as various types of tools, such as a level, a flashlight, a ruler, magnetic field detector, and so on.

Social Media Apps

Social media (or social networking) sites are web sites you can join to connect with people and share pictures, video, or text about yourself, your interests, your thoughts and so on.

Examples of social media apps include:

Facebook – use this app to log in to your Facebook account and view your page and other people's pages, to post comments, view notifications, and so on.

Twitter – use this app to log into your Twitter account. You use Twitter to send and read short 140-character messages called "*tweets*". Registered users can read and post tweets, and unregistered users can only read them.

Instagram - Instagram is a social networking app designed for sharing photos and videos from a smartphone. Everyone who creates an account has a profile and a news feed, and when you post a photo or video, it will be displayed on your profile. People who follow you will see your posts in their own newsfeeds, just as you will see the posts of people you choose to follow.

Audio Apps

Audio apps facilitate the streaming and playing of audio content on your device. Some apps play stored content, while others enable you to *stream* audio content.

When you stream an audio file, your device receives a constant flow of data from the source location and can begin to play back the file almost immediately. (In contrast, when you download a file, you make a copy of it and store it on your device. You can download audio and video files and then play them back later, after the copying process is complete. Downloading, however, can take a long time depending on your bandwidth and on the size of the file.) Streaming an audio file is like listening to the radio; it does not store a copy of the file on your device.

Example audio apps include:

Audible – provides spoken audio entertainment through digital audiobooks, radio, and TV programs and audio versions of magazines and newspapers. The app is free, although you will have to pay for content.

iTunes Music – use this app to access Apple's streaming music catalog and stream songs to your device. This is a paid subscription app.

Pandora – use this app to stream "radio station style" music from Pandora's servers. You create "custom radio stations" by selecting genres of music, artists, albums and even specific songs. This app has free and premium paid subscriptions versions. The free versions include ads.

Spotify – use this app to stream music from a library of over 20,000 songs. There are free and subscription-based versions of the app, and both include a radio feature that creates a random playlist of songs chosen based on specified genres and decades. The free version includes ads. Some artists do not allow their songs to be offered through Spotify.

Video Apps

Use video apps to stream video content on your device. Many of the video apps described here can be used on a wide variety of devices, including desktop PCs, tablets, phones, game consoles, and Internet-enabled televisions (smart TVs).

Be aware that streaming video over 3G or 4G/LTE networks can use up your monthly cellular data plan allowance very quickly. It is recommended that you use Wi-Fi if you want to stream video – especially high definition video.

Example video apps include:

Hulu – use this app to stream TV shows, clips, movies and other streaming media from Hulu.com. There are a limited number of free shows you can stream, and there are two subscription levels (limited commercials and no commercials) that provide access to all the available content for a monthly fee. Hulu is offered only to users in Japan, the United States and its overseas territories.

Netflix – use this app to stream movies and TV shows. Although it started as a DVD rental company, Netflix also offers Internet video-streaming service to users in over 40 countries. Netflix also offers original television shows, and releases all episodes at once. There are three subscription plans:

- the basic plan allows you to watch Netflix on one screen at a time in standard definition video quality.
- The middle plan allows you to watch on two screens at a time and high definition is available.
- The premium plan allows you to watch on up to four screens at a time and both high and ultra-high definition are available (assuming you have sufficient Internet bandwidth).

UStream.tv – use this app to watch and broadcast live video from your iPhone, iPad or Android phone. You can use UStream to broadcast on 3G, 4G/LTE and Wi-Fi networks. A wide variety of membership plans are available. The basic plan is free, and professional broadcasting plans can cost up to $999USD/month.

WatchESPN – use this app to watch live games and studio shows with 24/7 access to ESPN, ESPN2, ESPN3, ESPNU, and other ESPN-related networks. The app is free and runs on Android and iOS; it also runs on Windows and Mac OS X. You must have a subscription to ESPN with a participating video provider or affiliated TV/Internet service provider.

YouTube – use this app to view, rate, share, upload and comment on videos on the YouTube web site, which is a video sharing web site. You can subscribe to various YouTube channels and view content for free. You can also pay a subscription fee for YouTube Red, which gives you advertising-free access to videos. The app lets you browse recommendations, see the latest from your favorite channels and look up videos you have liked and watched previously, all from within the app.

Searching in the App Store

In addition to browsing the categories, you can type the name of a specific app in the Search bar and search for it. The app store will display the best matches.

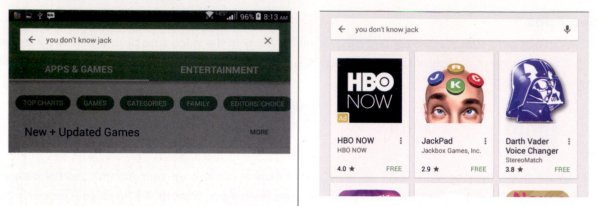

As you view the items in the app store, you will notice that many apps are free, but for some, there is a charge.

The price is usually displayed in the vicinity of the rating.

Obtaining an App

Obtaining an app is a matter of finding the one you want and tapping it to install it.

Open the app store on your device, and browse the categories, or if you know the name of the particular app you want, search for it using the Search bar.

When the app appears in the list, tap it to open its detail page.

Notice that you can view the average rating, the number of downloads, and possibly see a list of similar apps. In some cases, you can tap a link to read more about the app.

Click **Install** to download and install the app. When the installation is complete, the app will display an Open button.

Tap **Open** to launch the app.

Some apps require you to accept certain terms and conditions.

Some apps will ask for permission to access particular features before they open for the first time.

Once you have accepted the terms and granted appropriate permissions, the app will run.

Paid Apps

The procedure for installing a paid app is essentially the same as installing a free app, except that you must also enter payment information.

Instead of an Install button, the app's detail page displays a price button. Tap the price and follow the screen prompt.

You will be prompted to enter payment information or enter a code that can be redeemed to complete your purchase.

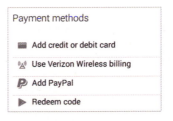

The options that display will vary depending on your device

In-App Purchases

In-app purchases are purchases made from within a mobile app. Many free apps include options for in-app purchases. Typically, you would make an in-app purchase in order to access special content or unlock certain features, or to turn off advertisements, or obtain virtual money or special powers in a game. When you make an in-app purchase, the purchasing process is completed directly from within the app and it may be as quick and easy as tapping an icon, depending on how you have configured your device.

You can configure settings on your mobile device that make in-app purchase streamlined or force you to enter a password. If you want the process to be automatic, you must make sure that your payment information is up to date.

However, if you configure your device to ask for a password, it is much less likely that you will be surprised by accidental or unwanted purchases.

Authenticating Purchases

Requiring authentication for all purchases requires that you enter a password any and every time you (or someone else using your device) begin to make an in-app purchase.

On Android devices, you can protect against accidental or unwanted purchases by turning on Authentication:

1. Open the **Google Play Store** app.

2. Touch the menu icon, then tap **Settings**.

3. Touch **Require authentication** for purchases.

4. Choose a setting

5. Follow the on-screen instructions (for example, you may be asked to enter your Google password), then click **OK**.

To protect against accidental or unwanted in-app purchases on your iPhone, you can add restrictions to protect your iTunes Store account:

1. Go to **Settings** > **General** > **Restrictions**.

2. Tap **Enable Restrictions**.

3. Enter a Restrictions passcode that you'll remember and confirm your passcode. You should choose a passcode that's different from the passcode you use to unlock your device.

   After you tap Enable Restrictions, you'll see what's allowed on your device. To prevent only in-app purchases, turn off In-App Purchases.

If you want to disable purchasing completely, turn off iTunes Store, iBooks Store, Installing Apps, and In-App Purchases.

Deleting an App

If you do not want to use an app any longer, you can uninstall it from your device.

To delete an app on an Android device:

1. Open the **Google Play Store** app.

2. Touch the menu icon, then tap **My apps & games**.

3. On the Installed tab, touch any app labeled "Installed" to open the options.

4. Tap **Uninstall** to remove it, and confirm the deletion if prompted.

5. Close the Google Play Store app.

To uninstall an app on an iPhone or iPad:

1. Start your device and go to the Home screen.

2. Find the icon for the app you want to delete.

3. Press and hold the icon until all of the phone's icons begin to jiggle. This causes each icon to display a small "x" at the upper-left corner. (Apps that come pre-installed on iPhone or iPad cannot be deleted, and will not display the x.).

4. Tap the x for the app you want to remove, and confirm that you want to delete the app and its data.

Recovering a Deleted App

If you accidentally delete an app, or if you delete it on purpose and then change your mind, you can recover the app without having to pay for it again.

On Android:

1. Open the **Play Store**.

2. On the Play Store home page, click the **Menu** button.

3. Tap **My apps & games**. This displays a list of apps in two tabs – the Installed tab, and the All tab.

4. Tap the **All** tab and view the list of apps. Apps that are currently installed will display either the word "Installed" or the word "Update." Apps that you have deleted will display either the word "Free" or the word "Purchased."

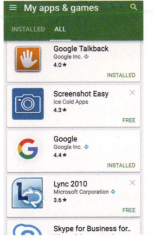

5. To recover an app, tap it in the list, then click the **Install** button to re-install it on your device.

On iOS:

1. Open the App Store.

2. Tap **Updates** from the menu at the bottom.

3. Tap **Purchased**. This displays a list of apps in two tabs – the All tab and the Not on This iPhone tab.

4. Tap the **Not on This iPhone** tab and view the list of apps.

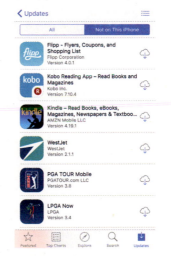

5. Find the app that you want to recover, then tap on the cloud icon to reinstall it.

Note that you can also search for the app on the App Store and download and install it again. When you download an app that you have already paid for, you will not be charged again.

Exercise 8-2: Working with mobile apps

In this exercise, you will browse an app store, install, launch, and then delete an app on your mobile device.

Note: This exercise assumes that you have a mobile device and sufficient rights to install free apps.

1. On your mobile device, access the Home screen.

2. Tap **Apps** if necessary, then access your device's default app store. List a few of the apps that appear at the top of the screen.

3. Describe how the apps are organized.

4. Find and tap a button that will allow you to view apps by category. Are there several categories available? Are your surprised by how many there are?

5. At the top of the screen, click in the Search box and type: dictionary, then tap the **Search** button. Are there many dictionary apps available for your device? Are there more than simple dictionaries listed?

6. Tap one of the free apps to view its detail page. How many times has the app been downloaded? What other information about the app can you see?

7. Install the free app and give it access to some of your device's features. How long does it take to download the app?

8. When the Open button displays, tap it to launch the app.

9. Spend a little time in the app. (If the app includes in-app purchases, be careful to avoid making any accidental purchases.) Does the app include advertising?

10. Evaluate the app: Is it easy to use? Is it useful?

11. Close the app (by tapping its Close button) and return to the Home screen. Did the app add its icon to your Home screen?

12. Use the steps appropriate for your device in the Deleting an App section of this lesson to uninstall the newly added app.

Limitations

Objective 2-6.3

Apps and application software can bring the power to get things done right to your fingertips. They enable you to create and work with a wide variety of documents and files on various devices and from various locations.

However, it is important to remember that apps and applications are designed for specific hardware and specific operating systems. Accordingly, you may not be able to find a specific app in your app store. For example, even though the Amazon Kindle Fire runs the Android operating system, there is not (as of the time of this writing) an app for the Chrome web browser that is supported on the Kindle. Instead, Kindle offers its own web browser named Silk.

If you cannot find a specific app, you can usually find comparable ones – most app stores group similar apps near one another.

In cases where an app is available only for specific versions of a mobile operating system, you may be able to upgrade the operating system on your device if upgrades are available, and then install the desired app.

Keep in mind also that an installed app must work with the hardware on your device. You may install a full-featured photo editing app on your phone, but if your phone has a low-quality camera, your photos will only be as good as the hardware allows.

Lesson Summary

In this lesson, you learned about the wide variety of options you have when choosing apps and applications. You should now be able to:

☑ describe the difference between apps and applications

☑ identify various types of application software and the tasks for which they are suited

☑ understand and use web apps

☑ use an app store to browse and find apps

☑ install, delete and recover apps

☑ describe the strengths and weaknesses of apps and applications

Review Questions

1. Which type of program is designed to be used on touch screen devices such as a tablet?

   a. Application programs   b. Apps

2. What is a productivity program dedicated to?

   a. Producing information

   b. Keeping track of files or folders

   c. Recording the amount of time you spend online

   d. Tracking items you search for

3. What do some users refer to web apps as?

   a. Shareware   c. Software as a Service

   b. Add-ware   d. Freeware

4. Which term properly describes a web app that will run in a browser on any computing device regardless of the operating system being used?

   a. Compatible   c. Productivity programs

   b. Platform-independent d. Cloud based

5. What is a digital platform for distributing software called?

   a. Downloading   c. App store

   b. E-commerce   d. Vendor Cart

6. What do you need to have before you can use the Facebook app?

   a. Facebook account   c. Apple account

   b. Microsoft account   d. Google account

7. Which of the following is an example of a productivity/communication app?
   a. Twitter
   c. CNN
   b. Skype
   d. iTunes

8. What kind of app groups news and information, presenting them on the device when you launch the app?
   a. Productivity/Communication
   c. Audio
   b. Social Media
   d. Content

9. What type of app is the Smart Tools app?
   a. Content
   c. Creativity
   b. Productivity/Communication
   d. Social Media

10. Which program best represents what you can do on a social media or social networking site?
    a. Netflix
    c. Instagram
    b. Google
    d. iTunes

11. What is it called when your device receives a constant flow of data from a source location and then plays the file instantly?
    a. Downloading
    c. Uploading
    b. Streaming
    d. Flowing

12. Which of the following apps can stream video to your device?
    a. Hulu
    c. iTunes
    b. Spotify
    d. Facebook

13. Which option should you use when you want to obtain an app?
    a. Install
    b. Open

14. How can you access special content or unlock certain features in an app?
    a. Make an in-app purchase.
    b. Buy the full version of the app in the app store.
    c. Download a cheat sheet from another user.
    d. Purchase the special content from the vendor's web site.

15. Lucy wants to put the Hoop-de-Doo app on her BlackBerry, but she cannot find it in the BlackBerry World app store. What is the most likely reason for this?
    a. Lucy has not finished paying for her BlackBerry phone.
    b. Lucy does not have a Hoop-de-Doo account.
    c. The app is not compatible with the BlackBerry operating system.
    d. Lucy has required authentication for all her in-app purchases.

Lesson 9: Using Microsoft Word

Lesson Objectives

This lesson introduces how to use a desktop application, specifically Microsoft Word, to create simple documents. You will also be introduced to common features you will find in other desktop applications. Upon completion of this lesson, you will be able to:

- ☐ start and exit Microsoft Word
- ☐ identify some common screen elements
- ☐ create, save, and open documents
- ☐ change view options for documents
- ☐ insert, select, modify, and format text
- ☐ manipulate text using common features
- ☐ use the ruler to create, modify or delete tab settings
- ☐ change margins, paper size, or the orientation

- ☐ insert or remove page breaks
- ☐ insert or remove page numbers
- ☐ apply column formats
- ☐ use find and replace
- ☐ print and preview documents
- ☐ insert pictures or multimedia files
- ☐ work with tables
- ☐ track changes made in documents

Identifying Common Features

Every computing device follows specific standards for how an app or application works; this is often set by the operating system installed on the device. For instance, every touch-screen device allows you to use a finger and tap to access the program or a feature such as playing a song. It also enables you to use your index finger and the thumb to "pinch" in or out to zoom in or out on the screen. An Apple device such as the MacBook displays icons at the top left corner of the program window to minimize, maximize, restore down, or close a program. A Windows device also has icons to minimize, maximize, restore down, or close a program; the difference is that these icons are located at the top right corner of the program window.

You will find as you begin using various devices (whether they are mobile or desktop models), that there are a number of common elements on the screen and that there are common methods for performing specific tasks. Many of these common elements appear in the same location on the screen; for example, the first two tabs of the ribbon in any Microsoft Office program are the File and Home tabs. Other tabs in the ribbon are program-specific.

Among application programs, and often within the operating system as well, you can use common methods to perform actions such as copying, moving, and pasting items, selecting items, navigating the interface, formatting or enhancing the look of text, and printing. Additionally, the same keyboard shortcuts are assigned by default in many programs for accessing these common features. For instance, press CTRL+C to copy a selection or press CTRL+A to select all items in the document.

Key Fact: You can also click the ⊞ (**Save**) button on the Quick Access toolbar; or press CTRL+S to quickly save the document.

To save an existing document with a different name, use **Save As** in the **File** tab.

The first time you save a document, the Backstage view opens with the Save As tab selected. The first panel displays the available locations for saving your document (these locations are associated with your Microsoft or network account).

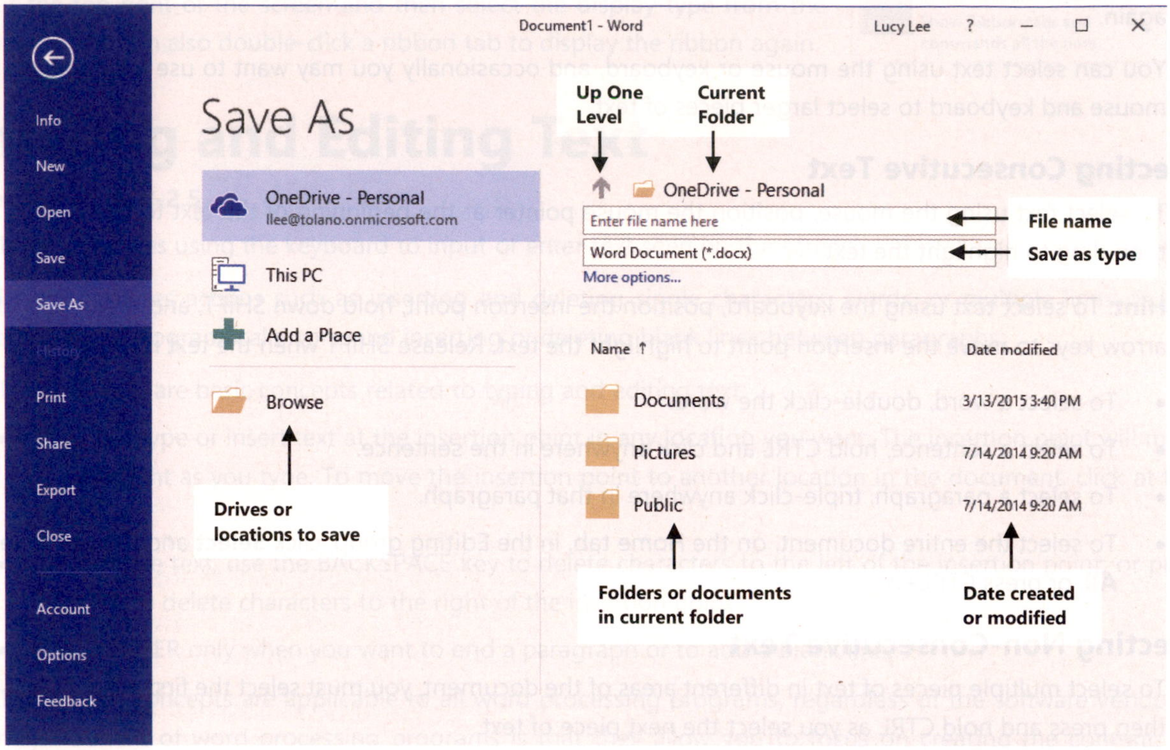

The second panel provides you options regarding the file name and file type. It will also display a list of commonly-accessed folders (for example, Documents, or Pictures). These folders vary based on the location currently selected in the first panel. For instance, the first screen in the following images displays what appears if you are using OneDrive, the online storage location provided by Microsoft; the second image displays folders available in the Documents folder on the local drive.

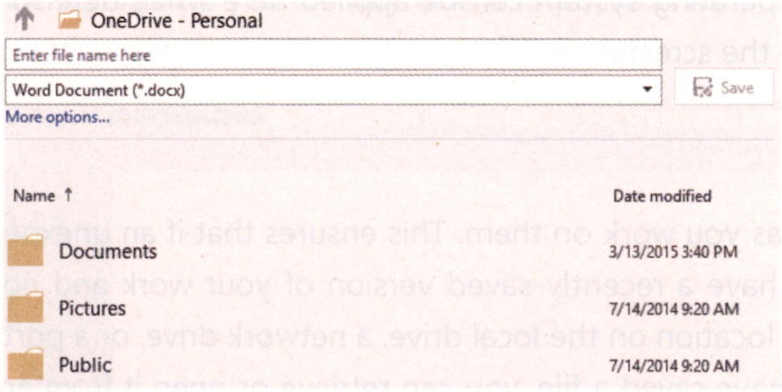

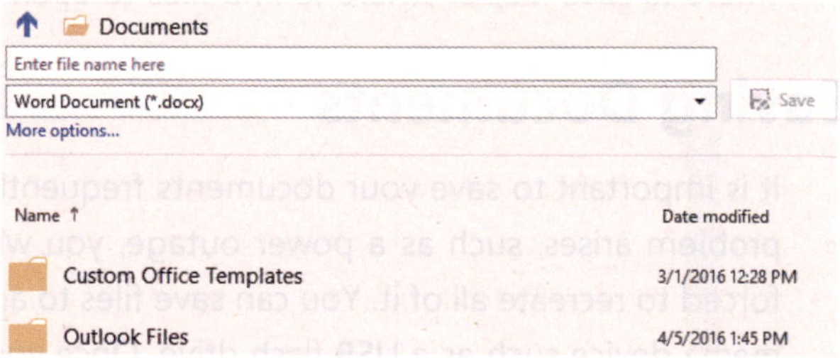

Notice how the location is clearly identified at the top of the second panel, thereby giving you the option to click the arrow before the location name if you want to move to another location. You can also click **More options** (below the file type) to open the Save As dialog box, from which you can navigate to any location.

Click **Save** to save the document.

How often you save a document depends on how much work you put into it. If you make a large number of changes, save the document frequently as you work to preserve your changes. If you see a message from Word prompting you to save a document, this means Word recognizes something has changed in the document since it was last saved. If you're not sure whether you should save the document again, err on the side of caution and save it with a different name than the original.

Understanding Word and File Types

By default, Word automatically assigns a *.docx* extension to the end of the file name; however, you can save a Word document in other file formats.

Word, like most word processing applications, can handle several document types. This allows you to create a file in one program and save it to a format readable by other programs. For example, if you create a file in Word and need to share the file with someone who does not have Word, but has an application that supports any of these listed file types, you can save your document to the type you have in common and then successfully share the file.

File types commonly associated with word processing programs include:

- Word Document (.docx) – this is the file type associated with Microsoft Word 2007 and later. This is the default format for Word 2016.

- Word Document (.doc) – this is the file type associated with Microsoft Word versions prior to 2007. Many word processing programs can open files with a .doc extension.

- Plain Text (.txt) – a text file that can be read on any operating system. This format does not include formatting of any kind, nor does it include tables or images.

- Rich Text Format (.rtf) – a text file that preserves font and paragraph formatting and can include embedded images.

- Portable Document Format (.pdf) – a file format developed by Adobe Systems that allows you to view documents (with formatting and images) on any operating system.
- Publisher Document File (.pub) – the default file format used in Microsoft Publisher. This type of file includes layout information and can include formatting, graphics, hyperlinks, charts and other types of objects.

To save a Word document as a different file type, click the arrow for the Save as type field (the field below the file name field) to display a list of available file formats.

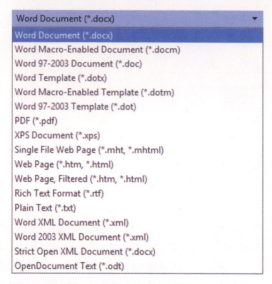

Starting a New Document

Each time you start Word, the Backstage view appears where you can easily create a new blank document, choose from a variety of built-in templates that will help you lay out particular types of documents (such as invitations, meeting agendas, or business memos), or open an existing document.

- To create a new blank document, in Backstage, click **New** and then click **Blank document** from the list of documents.

- To choose from the variety of pre-designed templates for a new document, click one of the templates displayed, and click **Create**.

Each time you create a new document, a document number will automatically appear in the title bar. For example, if you have three new Word documents open and you create another new one, Word will assign it the number "4" and the title bar will display "Document4." Document numbering resets back to Document1 each time you start a new session of Word. Use this generic name as a reminder that you have not yet saved the file with a descriptive and memorable name.

Closing a Document

Once you have finished editing a document, close the document to clear the screen and memory; this enables you to start or open another document without old documents cluttering up your screen.

To close a document, click the **File** tab and then **Close**.

To close the Word application, click ❌ (**Close**).

Opening a Document

Once a file is saved, you can open it from wherever it is located; the document is presented on the screen for further processing. You can open as many documents as needed; only the amount of available memory on your system limits the number of documents you can have open simultaneously.

Use one of the following methods to open a document:

- Click the **File** tab, click **Open**, and then click the file name from the list of Recent documents; or

- click the **File** tab, click **Open**, click the location where the file or its folder is located and click **Browse** to select the file using the Open dialog box.

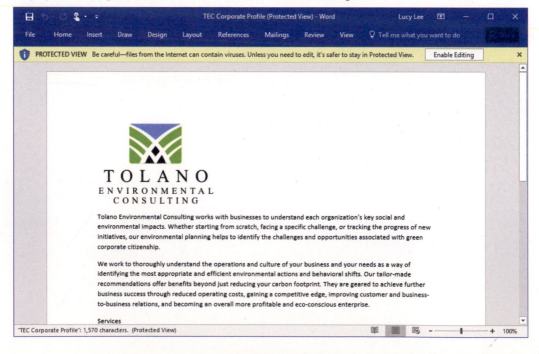

Key Fact: You can also press CTRL+O or CTRL+F12 and then navigate to where the file is located. This can be used with all Office applications.

Read-only Mode and Protected View

The Read only attribute can help prevent others from making changes to a document. There are two methods you can use to apply this attribute to a document from within Word.

Any time you open a document that comes to your computer over the Internet (for example, as an email attachment), Word opens the document in Protected View. Protected View automatically applies the read-only attribute to the file until you specify otherwise, thereby protecting you from content that may potentially contain viruses, malware, or other items that can be harmful to your computer.

You can identify a file that is in Protected View the moment you open it. When the file is opened, Word displays a message below the ribbon similar to the following:

You can click Enable Editing to open the document for editing, or you can choose to keep working in Protected View to protect your computer or to ensure that you do not inadvertently make changes to the file while you are viewing it.

A file opened in Protected View is in read-only mode; you will not be able to do anything other than read the file until you click **Enable Editing**. When you view the properties for this file in Backstage, the following screen displays:

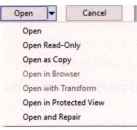

Notice that Word reminds you that you are still in Protected View. You can then choose to view more information about this mode, or choose another action.

You can manually open a file in Protected View using an option in the Open dialog box. Click **File** and **Open**, then click **Browse** to open the Open dialog box. Navigate to the file, click it to select it, then click the arrow for the Open button and click **Open in Protected View**.

Notice that you can also choose to open the file in read-only format if you do not want to inadvertently make changes to the document. If you select this option, Word will prompt you to save the file with a different name, thereby keeping the original file intact.

Opening or Saving with the Read-Only Option

The Read-only option can be applied to a document when you open it or when you save it.

To open a document as read-only, display the Open dialog box, select the file to open, then click the arrow for the Open button, then choose the Open Read-Only command.

To save a document with the read-only feature, use a method to save the document that will display the Save as dialog box. Then click the arrow next to the Tools command and click General Options.

Once you click the **Read-only recommended** option, you can click **OK** and then click **Save**. Anyone who opens this document is then notified that the file is read only and can only be saved with a different name than the original.

14. Click **File** and click **Save As**. Ensure **This PC** is selected and then click the **Word** folder if necessary.

15. In the file name field, adjust the file name to *Global Warming Blog (old Word) – Student,* click the arrow for the Save as type field and click **Word 97-2003 Document**. Click **Save**.

Microsoft Word Compatibility Checker	?	×

The following features in this document are not supported by earlier versions of Word. These features may be lost or degraded when you save this document in an earlier file format. Click Continue to save the document. To keep all of your features, click Cancel, and then save the file in one of the new file formats.

Summary	Occurrences
Content controls will be converted to static content.	2
Help	

☑ Check compatibility when saving documents

[Continue]   [Cancel]

16. Click **Continue** to have Word maintain the compatibility check when saving the file.

    Notice how the title bar in Word reflects the compatible file format:

    Global Warming (old Word) - Student [Compatibility Mode] - Word

Suppose you have been asked to save this file in a format that can be inserted into a web design program such as Adobe Dreamweaver or given to someone who may need the text to be compatible with the HTML language used for web pages.

17. Click **File**, click **Save As**, change the file name to *Global Warming Blog (web) – Student*, then click the arrow for the Save as type field. Scroll in the list and click **Web Page (*.htm, *.html)** and click **Save**. Notice that the file retains its formatting: the heading is bold and in a large font; there is a horizontal rule across the page, and then your blog post paragraph is displayed underneath.

Suppose now that you have been asked to save this file again as a plain text file so that if there are problems with the HTML code created by Word, the web master can import text from the plain text file. Plain text files do not include any formatting.

18. Click **File**, click **Save As**, change the name of the file to *Global Warming Blog (plain) – Student*, and then click the arrow for the Save as type field. Scroll in the list and click **Plain Text (*.txt)** and click **Save**.

File Conversion - Global Warming Blog - Student.txt	?	×

Warning: Saving as a text file will cause all formatting, pictures, and objects in your file to be lost.

Text encoding:
◉ Windows (Default)   ○ MS-DOS   ○ Other encoding:

	Wang Taiwan
	Western European (DOS)
	Western European (IA5)
	Western European (ISO)
	Western European (Mac)
	Western European (Windows)

Options:
☐ Insert line breaks
End lines with: CR / LF ▼
☐ Allow character substitution

Preview:

Global Warming

A lot of people have been talking about this topic for years now – some claim global warming is happening and increasing significantly every year, while others claim it is a huge scam. How many of us truly know what global warming is and what is really changing in the world?

[OK]   [Cancel]

19. Click **OK** to allow Word to convert the file to plain text.

Now try working with basic file management tools.

20. Click the **Close** button at the top right corner of the current document window and click Don't Save if prompted to save the changes.

The document should no longer be visible on the screen.

21. Using the Windows taskbar, point at the Word icon to display the preview windows for each document. Move to the one with the new blank document and click the **Close** button in the preview window to close this document.

22. Click inside the first blog document, then press CTRL+W to close the document.

The Word application window remains open with no open documents.

The screen should now display with a grey background (depending on your color scheme).

23. Click the **File** tab, then click **Open** to display the Open tab of the Backstage view.

The list in the right pane shows the Word documents you recently worked on under the Today title. If there are any other recently used documents on this computer, they will display below the list of documents for today also.

24. Click **My First Blog - Student**.

This document opens and displays on the screen.

25. Click the **File** tab and click **Open**.

Global Warming Blog (old Word) - Student
Desktop » 7500-Student-Files » Word

Global Warming Blog - Student
Desktop » 7500-Student-Files » Word

Global Warming Blog (plain) - Student
Desktop » 7500-Student-Files » Word

Global Warming Blog (web) - Student
Desktop » 7500-Student-Files » Word

Notice that there are four documents listed for the Global Warming Blog files; also notice the icon at the left of the file that identifies the file format of the document.

26. Click the **Global Warming Blog (old Word)** file with the outlined Word icon – this is the document you saved in Word 97-2003 format. **Click Register Later**, if necessary.

27. Press CTRL+O, and in the Recent list for Today, click the **Global Warming Blog (web)** file with the Internet Explorer icon at the left (this should be the HTML version). If prompted with the message to register on a blog, click **Register Later** to continue.

This file will appear similar to the Word version. However, an HTML file saved in Word may not always render perfectly in a web design program or inside a web browser. This is why a web designer may ask you for the file in plain text so he/she can format the page from scratch. Let's look at this page in a web browser.

28. In the taskbar, click the **File Explorer** icon, navigate to the Word folder in the 7500-Student-Files folder, then double-click the HTML version of this document to open it a web browser. Does it look exactly the same as it does in Word or can you see subtle differences? The more complex the formatting, the more opportunities there are for unexpected results in the web browser.

29. In the taskbar, point at the Word icon and click inside any one of the open documents to return to the Word window.

30. Press CTRL+O, and in the Recent list for Today, click the **Global Warming Blog (plain)** file with horizontal lines, but no application icon. (This is the plain text file.)

31. When prompted, click **OK** to allow Word to convert the file to plain text. Notice that plain text includes no formatting, and no graphic elements.

```
Global Warming


A lot of people have been talking about this topic for
years now – some claim global warming is happening and
increasing significantly every year, while others claim
it is a huge scam. How many of us truly know what global
warming is and what is really changing in the world?
```

Now try opening a file created by someone else.

32. Press CTRL+O, click **This PC**, and click the path that shows where the student data files are located at the top of the list.

33. In the Open dialog box, click **Newsletter A01**, then click **Open**.

34. On the Windows taskbar, point at the Word icon and click the **My First Blog – Student** preview window to switch to this document.

35. Click **File**, click **Save As** and then click **More Options**. Click the arrow next to the **Tools** command and then click General Options.

36. Click **Read-only recommended** and click **OK**. Click **Save**.

37. Close the open Word documents, but leave the application window open.

38. Open the *My First Blog – Student* document. Word alerts you that the author has suggested that you open it in read-only mode.

39. Click **Yes** to open the document in read-only mode.

40. Close all documents without saving.

41. Close the web browser and close the File Explorer window.

Manipulating Text

Objective 2-1.1, 2-1.7, 2-1.8, 2-1.11

Editing is the process of adding, deleting, or changing text. In many cases, you will select text before you edit it. Be careful when making changes to selected text. The moment you press a key or click an option, all the selected text is affected.

Customizing the View

On occasion you may need to change the view to see more or less of the document before you can select the piece of text. You can adjust how a document displays by selecting the appropriate option using the **View** tab.

Read Mode – Useful for reading a document, as pages are adapted to the size of your monitor for easy reading. A series of buttons you can use in Read mode appears across the top of the screen. This view displays automatically when you are viewing a Word file sent as an attachment in email.

Print Layout – Displays file contents as if you sent the document to the printer, and this is the only view in which the vertical ruler displays.

Web Layout – Adjusts text and other elements, such as pictures, to show how the document will look as a Web page.

Outline – Collapses a document to display headings to assist you in organizing content flow.

Draft – Displays the document to the full width of the screen with only the horizontal ruler visible.

To switch between the commonly used views, click one of the view buttons at the lower right corner of the status bar.

Adjusting the Zoom

The ability to enlarge the text display can be very useful when you are working with a small font size, whereas the ability to reduce the zoom display is useful when you are working with landscape or horizontal orientation.

To adjust the zoom display, click an option from the zoom area on the status bar.

Click the **Zoom level** button to open the Zoom dialog box if you want to choose a specific zoom percentage or the number of pages to show.

You can set the zoom percentage anywhere from 10% to 500%, or you can have Word automatically adjust the magnification to view the entire width of the page of text on screen. When changing the view, the position of the insertion point will determine the zoom area.

Keep in mind that the Zoom feature controls only the screen display. The amount of text that displays when you change the zoom percentage is based on the display settings and size of your monitor. Changing the magnification level has no effect on the size of the text or images when it is printed.

Using Undo

Any time you perform an action and then need to reverse the action (such as adding, deleting, or formatting text) on the Quick Access toolbar, click 🔄 (**Undo**) to undo the last action or command performed.

Key Fact: You can also press CTRL+Z to undo the last action. This works in all Office applications.

You can also click the arrow for the **Undo** button to display a list of the last 100 consecutive actions performed. You can undo sequential actions only. For example, in the illustration at the right, to undo the Estimated Sales 2017 text, you must also undo the two actions before this action.

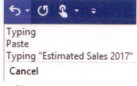

The Undo command cannot be used to reverse certain actions, such as saving a file or printing a file. Generally, the Undo feature cannot be used on any commands accessed through the File tab.

Using Repeat or Redo

If you change your mind after undoing an action, you can redo the action by clicking the 🔁 (**Redo**) button on the Quick Access toolbar. This key will appear in color once there is an action to undo or redo.

If you want Word to repeat the last action, on the Quick Access toolbar click 🔄 (**Repeat**). You can repeat this action anywhere in the document simply by clicking in the next location and clicking **Repeat**. For instance, you changed the spacing for a paragraph and would like to use the same spacing on other paragraphs on page 2. You can repeat the spacing change action as many times as you need until you perform a different action.

Key Fact: You can also press CTRL+Y to redo the last action, or press F4 to repeat the last action. This works in all Office applications.

Using Cut, Copy, and Paste

Occasionally you may want to insert text into a document from another document, or from another location in the current document. Word uses the Clipboard to temporarily store any cut or copied items such as text or graphics. You can then paste these items into place wherever you choose. The main difference in using Cut and Copy is that the cut command actually removes the selection from its original spot and pastes or places it in a new location; using the Copy command makes a copy of the selection, leaving the original intact and pastes the copy in the new location.

- To cut or move an item, select the item first and then on the Home tab, in the Clipboard group, click ✂ Cut.

- To copy an item, first select the item and then on the Home tab, in the Clipboard group, click 📋 Copy.

- To paste an item, first place the insertion point where you want to paste the item and then on the Home tab, in the Clipboard group, click **Paste**.

Key Fact: You can also press CTRL+X to cut an item, CTRL+C to copy an item, or CTRL+V to paste the item. These keys are commonly used in other applications.

Once you paste an item, the (Ctrl) (**Paste Options**) button appears at the bottom right of the pasted item with choices for pasting the selected item. For example, you can specify to match the formatting in the destination area, keep the source formatting, or paste only text, if text and graphics were copied.

Using the Office Clipboard

While the traditional Windows Clipboard offers the ability to store only one item, Office offers the ability to store and retrieve up to 24 items. It also shows you the contents of the Clipboard, along with an icon representing the software program that was used to create each item.

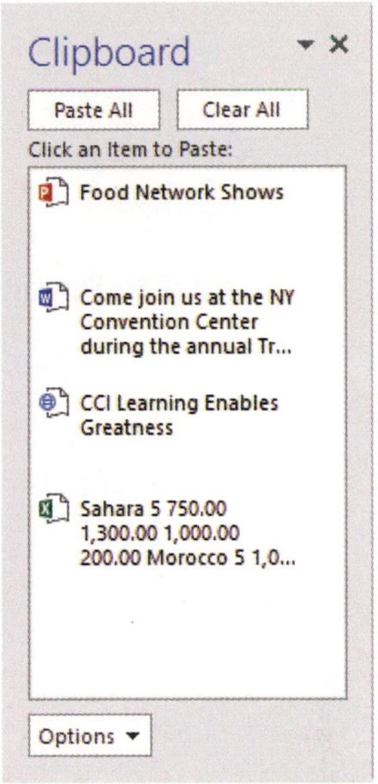

To display the Clipboard task pane, on the Home tab, in the Clipboard group, click the **Clipboard** dialog box launcher.

You can collect items from any programs (up to the maximum of 24 items) and then paste them into one or more documents. As you collect new items, previous items accumulated on the Clipboard will be replaced by the newer items.

To paste one item into the current location in the document, click that item on the Clipboard.

Point at an item on the Clipboard to display a drop-down arrow at the right of the item; click that arrow to display a menu: use **Delete** to delete only this item from the Clipboard; or use **Paste** to paste only this item into the current location.

Understanding Drag and Drop

Once text is selected, you can quickly move text by dragging it to the new location and then dropping or releasing the mouse button to place the text. As you drag selected text, the mouse cursor will display as ; use this as a reminder that you are dragging text.

Hint: It is recommended that you use drag and drop when you need to move text a small distance in the document.

Exercise 9-2: Basic Edits

In this exercise you will practice using the zoom buttons, apply different views, open a file in protected mode, and copy and paste text.

1. Click **File**, click **Open**, ensure **This PC** is selected in the first column and **Word** is selected in the Recent Folders. Click **TEC Employee List** to open this file.
2. Click the + button on the zoom bar at the lower right corner of the screen.

   The magnification level of the document content increases by 10%. Remember that changing the zoom affects only the display, not the actual size of the characters when the document is printed.
3. Click the + button two more times.
4. Click the **Zoom level** button to open the Zoom dialog box and then change the **Percent** to **75** and click **OK**.

5. Click the  (**Read Mode**) button and notice how the view now changes for you.

6. Click the **View** menu to see what options are available to you while in this view.

Edit Document

Navigation Pane

Show Comments

Column Width   ▶

Page Color   ▶

Layout   ▶

7. Click **Edit Document** to exit this view mode.

8. Close the document without saving it.

Now try opening a document that was sent previously as an attachment from the New York office. As it is an original file sent from Marketing, you want to protect it from any possible changes so you will open it using Protected View.

9. Click **File** and then click **Open** if necessary, the click **Browse** to open the Open dialog box.

10. From the student data files, select **TEC Corporate Profile** and click the arrow for **Open**. Then click **Open in Protected View**.

    The warning prompt should appear across the top of the document, indicating that this document is now in protected view, preventing any changes being made to the file.

11. Click **File** and read the information in Backstage, indicating the file has been protected from any changes until you enable editing.

12. Click the **Save** tab in the panel in the left. You cannot save the file because saving is disabled in Protected View.

Microsoft Word	✕
⚠ Saving is disabled in Protected View. If you trust the source of this file and would like to save, click Enable Saving.	
Enable Saving Cancel	

13. In the message box, click **Enable Saving** to save the document.

    Notice that the warning prompt about the protected view mode no longer appears.

14. Click **File** and click **Close**.

In this part of the exercise, you will copy information from one document and paste it into a new document.

15. Press CTRL+N to create a new blank document. Type: `Estimated Sales 2017` and press ENTER.

16. Click **File** and then click **Open**. Navigate to the student data files location, select **Sales Figures 2016** and click **Open**.

17. Move the cursor to the beginning of the table, starting with the text *Popular Tours*.

18. Click and drag to highlight the figures in the entire table and then on the Home tab, in the Clipboard group, click **Copy**.

19. Switch to the new document and in the blank line below the title, on the Home tab, in the Clipboard group, click **Paste**.

    The table of figures has been copied from one document to another.

20. On the Quick Access toolbar, click the **Undo** button.

    The pasted item is cleared, giving you the option to redo the paste (that is, to reverse the last action).

21. On the Home tab, in the Clipboard group, click **Paste** once more.

    The information is pasted into the document again, and in fact, you could paste this information into other areas of the same document or to another document, as needed.

22. Save the new document in the 7500-Student-Files\Word folder as: `Estimated Sales 2017 - Student` and then close it.

23. Close all other documents without saving.

Applying Formatting

Objective 2-2.1, 2-2.3, 2-2.5

Formatting refers to any process that alters the appearance or position of text or other objects in the document. Word provides a number of formatting options that can be applied within a document for all types of objects; accordingly, be careful with the number of formatting options you apply, considering who your audience is and how they will view the message in the document. For example, if you apply the All Caps, Bold, Italic, and Superscript formats to a sentence, it can be very distracting and difficult to read.

- You can apply formatting to text as you type it or after you have typed it. It can be easier and faster to wait until all the text in your document has been typed and edited before you format it. You need only remember that you must select the existing text before you can apply formatting to it.

- You can turn most formatting features on and off by clicking the appropriate button on the ribbon or Mini toolbar. When a feature is active, it appears in a different color from the other buttons. An arrow beside a button indicates that you can select additional options for the feature.

- When you want to remove all formatting from selected text, on the Home tab, in the Font group, click (**Clear Formatting**).

Enhancing Text Characters

Character formatting refers to any feature that changes the appearance of characters on the screen and in print. You can control the following aspects of character formatting:

Font – Describes the typeface of characters on the screen and in print such as `Courier New` or *Bradley*.

Font Size – Refers to the height of the characters (as characters get taller, they also grow wider.)

Character Formatting – Refers to the special stylized variations applied to plain characters to make them stand out from other text. They include bold, italics, and various kinds of underlines.

Effects – Apply special effects to the text, such as ~~strikethrough~~, superscript or subscript, shadow, SMALL CAPS, and so on.

There are several ways to apply formatting to selected text characters:

- The quickest method is to click the appropriate formatting button from the Font group on the Home tab.

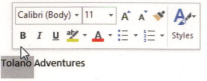

- As you select text for formatting, you will see the Mini toolbar appear; it contains buttons for applying specific, common features for formatting characters and paragraphs.

Enhancing Paragraphs

Word provides a number of tools that allow you to change an entire paragraph to best suit the message in your document. Many of the following items will affect the amount of vertical white space between lines of text and paragraphs. Several of these tools can also assist you in maintaining consistency in order to produce a professional-looking document.

Aligning Text

Alignment refers to the way the left and right edges of a paragraph line up horizontally on the page. You can easily change the alignment in your document using one of the following four options in the Paragraph group on the Home tab

Align Left – Aligns text to the left margin with a ragged or uneven edge on the right side of the text.

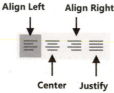

Center – Aligns text between the left and right margins to an imaginary line down the middle of the page.

Align Right – Aligns text to the right margin with a ragged or uneven edge on the left side of the text.

Justify – Aligns text so the left and right edges of the text are flush with the margins and each line of text is evenly spaced out between the margins, except for the last line of each paragraph.

Changing Line Spacing

Line spacing refers to the amount of space between lines of typed text, measured from the baseline of one line to the baseline of the next. Word automatically adjusts the amount of space between lines according to the size of the characters being used. However, you can also specify that line spacing be set to an exact measurement.

It's important to note that a precise line spacing setting will not adjust to accommodate larger text if the font size is changed. It's also important to note that, if you decrease line spacing too much, the lines of text may overwrite each other, or the text may not display.

To set or change the line spacing, on the Home tab, in the Paragraph group, click [icon] (**Line and Paragraph Spacing**).

1.0
1.15
1.5
2.0
2.5
3.0
Line Spacing Options...
Add Space Before Paragraph
Remove Space After Paragraph

Setting Paragraph Spacing

Paragraph spacing refers to the amount of space between paragraphs of text. Although it is possible to create extra space between paragraphs by pressing ENTER to insert blank lines, most published documents are set to insert a specific amount of space between paragraphs. This enables you to set spacing slightly smaller than a full line, which then reduces the amount of white space on a page and ensures consistency throughout a document.

To set or change the paragraph spacing, click the **Layout** tab, in the Paragraph group, set the spacing as required:

Spacing
Before: 0 pt
After: 8 pt

Exercise 9-3: Basic Formatting

In this exercise, you will apply basic formatting features in a document.

1. Click **File**, click **Open**, ensure **This PC** is selected as the location, and open the **Word** folder. Double-click the **Budget Memo** file.

2. Double-click the word **To** in the first line and then click **Bold** in the Font group of the Home tab.

    Hint: If the Mini toolbar appears when you select the text, click the **Bold** button in the toolbar.

3. Select the entire Re: line of text and click **Bold** once more.

4. In the second paragraph starting with In planning ..., select the **3%** text. On the Home tab, in the Font group, click the down arrow for the Font color and click **Green** in the Standard Colors row.

5. With the text still selected, press CTRL+B to add bold to the text.

6. Select the four paragraphs of the memo and then on the Home tab, in the Paragraph group, click the down arrow for Line Spacing. Click **1.0**.

    Notice the line spacing has reduced while the spacing between the paragraphs remains unchanged.

7. With the four paragraphs still selected, click the **Layout** tab and in the Paragraph group, click the increment button for After and change this to **12pt**. This increases the spacing between paragraphs.

8. Save this document as Budget Memo – Student and then close it.

Understanding Tab Settings

Setting tabs or tab stops is similar to aligning text; the difference is that setting tabs allows you to align information at specific intervals across the page so that text is lined up in columns.

Use appropriate tab alignment characters to match the type of data that will be entered. For instance, you can use a right tab to line up whole integer numbers, but would probably want to use a decimal tab to line up values with decimal places.

Click in the Tab Selector box to choose the alignment type; a ScreenTip appears defining each symbol and how it will align your tabbed columns:

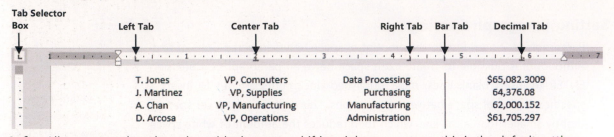

Left – Aligns text at the tab setting with characters shifting right as you type; this is the default setting.

Center – Centers text along an imaginary line down from the tab setting, with characters shifting evenly to the left and right as you type.

Right – Aligns all text along the right edge of the tab setting with characters shifting left as you type.

Bar – Displays a small vertical line as a separator between the previous and next column of information.

Decimal – Aligns to the left of the decimal point until you type the decimal point, then text shifts to the right of the decimal point.

In order to use tabs for aligning text, you need to do two things:

1. Define the position of the tab "stops" on the page.

2. Use the TAB key when entering text.

To insert a tab setting, select an alignment type from the Tab Selector box, then click on the horizontal ruler at the measurement for this tab stop. Once all tab stops are set on the ruler, begin typing the text for the report.

Pressing the TAB key tells Word to "move the insertion point to the text tab stop position on this line". You can then continue entering text (how the text flows at the new position will depend on the type of tab being used). Pressing TAB again will move the insertion point to the position of the next tab stop on the line, and so on. When you have entered the desired text at the last of your tab stop positions on the line, press ENTER to start a new paragraph. Press TAB to move to the position of your first tab stop in the next paragraph, and so on.

When you need to edit a tab setting that is currently applied to existing text, be sure to select the text first; otherwise, the revised tab setting is applied only to the current line. For example, to adjust a tab setting for a list of 10 names, select the 10 lines of text and then drag the tab character to its new location on the ruler.

Consider the following tips regarding setting tabs:

- Click the Tab Selector box until the desired tab alignment character displays and then click in the ruler where the tab stop is to be placed.

- The items in the Tab Selector box cycle through each time you click the box; if you go pass the alignment option you want, click until the desired character appears.

- When placing a tab stop on the ruler, position the pointer close to the measurement mark in the bottom half of the ruler. A vertical dash line will appear to verify the tab stop as you click in the ruler to set the tab stop.

- To remove a tab stop, click the tab character on the ruler and drag it up or down off the ruler.

Key Fact: To clear all the current tabs at once press CTRL+Q.

- To adjust the position of a tab stop, click the tab character on the ruler and drag it to the new position.

Exercise 9-4: Coffee Sales

In this exercise you will create a simple sales report by setting tabs on the ruler.

1. Create a new document and save it as Coffee Sales – Student.

2. Click the **View** tab, and in the Show group, check that the ruler is on; if it is off, click the option.

3. Type: Coffee Sales as the title and press ENTER.

4. At the far left of the ruler, click the Tab Selector until you see the Right Tab alignment character appear. Then click at **2.5"**, **3.5"**, **4.5"**, and **5.5"**.

5. Press TAB and type: Q1. Press TAB, type: Q2, press TAB, type: Q3, press TAB and type: Q4. Press ENTER.

6. Type: Arabica and press TAB. Type: 4558, press TAB, type: 4905, press TAB, type: 4201, press TAB, type: 4013 and press ENTER.

7. Type: Espresso and press TAB. Type: 2895, press TAB, type: 3595, press TAB, type: 2572, press TAB, type: 2218 and press ENTER.

8. Save and close this document.

Formatting the Document

Objective 2-2.2, 2-2.5

There are several options you can use to alter the way pages are laid out for different types of documents. Options include, for example, setting the margins to print differently for odd and even pages or changing the paper size in order to print an envelope. These options can be quickly selected from the **Layout** tab.

Changing the Paper Size

The default paper size is determined by the Language and Regional settings for your system (the following example is set for English US which uses 8½" by 11" or standard Letter size in this region); you can change this for any document using the Layout tab. To change the paper size for a document, on the Layout tab, in the Page Setup group, click **Size** and then select the required size from the list.

Changing the Orientation

Orientation refers to the way the document will print on the page. **Portrait** refers to a vertical orientation, while **Landscape** refers to a horizontal orientation. To change the orientation for a document, on the Layout tab, in the Page Setup group, click **Orientation**, then select an option.

Changing Margins

Margins determine the amount of space between the edge of the paper and the area where the text is printed. You can adjust the margin settings for the entire document or for specific parts of the document.

The boundaries for the top and bottom margins are easy to see; they appear as the divider line between the lighter (inside margins) and darker (outside margins) shades on the ruler. When you position the mouse pointer at the margin point on the vertical and horizontal rulers, a ScreenTip appears similar to those shown at the right.

The margin boundaries for the left and right margins appear on the top ruler, although the indent markers may obscure the left margin markers. You can access the left margin marker by pointing precisely between the Left Indent and First Line Indent markers. You can access the right margin marker by pointing above the Right Indent marker.

- To change your margins, on the Layout tab, in the Page Setup group, click **Margins**; or

- to adjust the margins using the ruler, point the mouse pointer at the margin and, when the appropriate arrow appears, drag to the measurement you want for the margin.

Adding Page Numbers

You can add page numbers to a document at any time. Page numbers can be inserted at any position on the page, though they are usually placed in the header or footer. To insert page numbers into your document, on the Insert tab, in the Header & Footer group, click **Page Number**.

Top of Page – Displays possible positions from a gallery of top-of-page numbering options.

Bottom of Page – Displays possible positions from a gallery of bottom-of-page numbering options.

Page Margins – Displays possible positions from a gallery of margin numbering options.

Current Position – Displays numbering options (page number only, page # of #, and so on) to apply to the current page number location.

Format Page Numbers – Displays various numbering styles (1, 2, 3; i, ii, iii), as well as the option to begin numbering at a digit other than the number 1.

Applying Columns

Word allows you to set up newspaper-style columns wherein text from the bottom of one column flows to the top of the next; this makes it an ideal layout for documents such as newsletters and reports. The number of columns you create depends on factors such as paper size and orientation, font size, and document layout (for example, for print or the Web), as well as the column width and margins you choose.

You can apply columns to text before or after you type. You may find it easier to type and edit the text first, and then apply multiple columns formatting.

To create columns, on the Layout tab, in the Page Setup group, click **Columns**.

If you want to end the flow of text at the bottom of one column, insert a column break and force text to the top of the next column. To insert a column break, press CTRL+SHIFT+ENTER.

Note that when you change the column layout of a document, the entire document changes unless you specify otherwise. To change the column layout for only a portion of the document, select that portion of text and make the appropriate column layout change. Word automatically inserts the appropriate breaks for this selection.

Exercise 9-5: Recipe

In this exercise, you will change some settings for a document that improve the readability of the recipes.

1. Open the *Recipe* file and save as `Recipe - Student`.

2. Click the **Layout** tab and in the Page Setup group, click **Orientation** and then click **Landscape**.

3. In the Page Setup group, click **Columns** and then click **Two**.

4. Select the **Quick and Easy Recipes** title and in the Page Setup group, click **Columns** and click **One**.

   The main title should now be on a separate line and its single column spans across the width of the document.

5. Click at the beginning of Recipe #15 and press CTRL+SHIFT+ENTER to insert a column break.

Quick and Easy Recipes

Recipe #11

Easy Chicken Pot Pie

1 ½ cups cooked chicken, cut into ¼" pieces
1 ½ cups frozen mixed vegetables
2 cans Cream of Mushroom soup
2 cans Pillsbury® Biscuits
Salt and pepper for taste

Mix first three ingredients in large bowl and add pinches of salt and pepper for taste. Spread mixture in large baking dish. Open and separate biscuits and then line top of mixture. Don't worry if you don't cover the entire surface as the biscuits will spread a bit as they bake.

Place in 350°F oven for approximately 30-45 minutes, depending on how hot your oven gets.

Remove and let cool for 15 minutes to set. Serve with salad.

Recipe #15

Easy Cheese and Broccoli Casserole

1.5 lbs chicken meat (either white or dark)
1 head of broccoli, cut into bite-sized pieces
1 can cream of mushroom soup
1 can cream of chicken soup
1 package shredded cheddar (or your preference) cheese

In a small pan, steam chicken meat to quickly cook them (they do not need to be totally cooked). Then slice cooked meat into small bite-size pieces.

In another smaller bowl, pour contents of both soup cans and stir to break up the pieces.

In a 9"x14" casserole pan, layer the bottom of the casserole dish with the chicken and broccoli pieces. Then pour the soup mixture over top, blending the soup into areas around the chicken and broccoli. Sprinkle enough cheese to preference as top layer.

Bake in 350°F oven for approximately 30 minutes (or until cheese begins to brown and harden). Remove and let cool. Serve with rice or noodles.

Notice the recipe titles now line up at the top of each column.

6. Select the main title, click the **Home** tab and in the Font group, click **Bold**. Click the down arrow for the Font Size and click **16**. In the Paragraph group, click **Center**.

7. Select the **Recipe #11** text. Apply bold and change the font size to **14pt**. Repeat this step for the Recipe #15 text.

8. Bold the title of Recipe #11, change the font size to **12pt** and change the font color to **blue**.

9. Bold the title of Recipe #15, change the font size to **12pt** and change the font color to **green**.

10. Click the **Insert** tab and in the Header & Footer group, click **Page Number**. Click **Bottom of Page** and then click **Circle**.

11. On the Design tab of the Header & Footer Tools ribbon, click **Close Header and Footer**.

12. Save and close the document.

Preparing the Document for Printing

Objective 2-1.3, 2-1.5, 2-2.6, 2-2.7

Before distributing your document to others, always take a moment to look over the document to correct any spelling, grammatical, or contextual errors, and to remove any repetitive text. This helps to ensure your document represents you and your company/school in a professional manner.

Proofing the Document

Word provides tools to automate proofing and also displays visual hints if it encounters an item that should be reviewed.

contrat   Red wavy lines indicate the word is not recognized in either the current or custom Word dictionary.

there   Blue wavy lines indicate grammatical or structural errors or a potential contextual error.

The Spelling and Grammar feature provides options to help you check for spelling and grammatical errors, such as the ability to create custom dictionaries for special terms you may use in your work. The spelling portion checks for incorrect spelling, duplicate words, and occurrences of incorrect capitalization. The grammar portion detects sentences with grammatical errors or weak writing style, based on widely accepted standards in the language (English only) overall as well as some regional variations (such as American versus British English).

In Word, the Spelling and Grammar feature works in the background to check for mistakes as you type. This enables you to correct mistakes immediately. However, you can still run a spelling and grammar check when you are finished creating the document.

To run a Spelling and Grammar check, on the Review tab, in the Proofing group, click **Spelling & Grammar**.

Key Fact: You can also press F7 to begin a spell check of the entire document. This works in all Office applications.

Spelling   ▾ ✕

Washinton

[Ignore] [Ignore All] [Add]

Washington

[Change] [Change All]

Washington 🔊
Word currently does not have a dictionary installed for English (United States). To see definitions:
Get a Dictionary

English (United States) ▾

Grammar   ▾ ✕

In

[Ignore]

in

[Change]

Capitalization in Titles
Articles and short prepositions and conjunctions should be in lower case within titles. The first word in a title is always capitalized.

• Instead of: Steinbeck published Once there Was a War in 1958.
• Consider: Steinbeck published Once There Was a War in 1958.

• Instead of: Of Mice And Men is a novel by John Steinbeck.
• Consider: Of Mice and Men is a novel by John Steinbeck.

▾

When Word finds the first misspelled word in the document, it displays the item in the Spelling and Grammar pane at the top. You click an option to specify how you want to proceed:

Ignore – Ignores this occurrence of this spelling but continues to search for other occurrences of this spelling.

Ignore All – Ignores all occurrences of this spelling; this might apply to a person's name or some technical jargon.

Add – Adds this spelling to your custom dictionary. In addition to providing a regular dictionary, Word allows you to build a custom dictionary so that it will not identify as misspelled words names, jargon, slang, or regional spellings you use often.

Suggestions – Displays a list of alternatives for the misspelled word. If the correct word is in the list, click it and then click **Change**, or **Change All**, or double-click the word to change it immediately.

Change – Changes this occurrence with the selected word in the suggestions box.

Change All – Changes all words with this spelling with the selected word in the suggestions box.

Near the bottom of the pane is a definition of the word, if applicable, and a list of words that can be used in place of this word. This is helpful if you find yourself repeating the word several times on a page. The types of words that appear will depend on the type of word, (that is, if it is a noun, verb or adjective). If you have sound available on your device, you can also click the speaker icon to hear the pronunciation of the word.

Grammatical or contextual errors appear in the Grammar pane as the grammar checker encounters them. Grammatical errors occur when Word has detected a structural error in the text such as too many spaces, incorrect or missing punctuation, incorrect verb tense, or passive versus active voice in the sentence.

Contextual error refers to words that have the same sound but different spellings and meanings depending on the context. Some words that often give rise to contextual errors include:

• there (refers to a place), their (possessive form), or they're (contraction for they are)

• its (possessive form) and it's (contraction for it is)

- where (refers to a location), ware (goods or services), and wear (attire or clothing)
- write (use a tool to scribe ideas) and right (direction or suitability)
- allot (to distribute) and a lot (quantity)

Contextual errors, as with spelling or grammar errors, appear in at the top of the Spelling and Grammar pane.

Suggestions – Provides a list of suggestions as to how to fix this error.

Ignore – Ignores this occurrence but continues to find other occurrences of the same grammatical error.

Change – Changes the error identified in the top box with the highlighted option in the Suggestions box.

In the lower half of the pane you will see an explanation as to why the text was marked as an error; the text in this box changes to reflect the grammatical error identified.

Finding and Replacing Items

You can use the Find feature to locate occurrences of specific words, phrases, symbols, codes, formatting, or any combination of these items in your document. You might use the Find feature as a quick way to find a word you think you may have misspelled or to refer back to a particular piece of information. Once you've found what you're looking for, you can replace it, check for other occurrences, or continue working with your document.

To activate the Find feature, press CTRL+F to display the Navigation pane.

With the Navigation pane, you need only enter the text you want to find in the Search field and press ENTER, or click 🔍 (**Search for more things**) to have Word search your document. Word lists any matches it finds in the Navigation pane as summaries where you can see some of the text around the found occurrence to determine if this is an item you want to view or change. When you click a result in the list, Word moves the insertion point to that document location so you can make a change, if needed. If there are a large number of results, use the ▲ ▼ buttons to scroll up and down in the list to find the item you want to review.

Each time you activate the Find feature within any given Word session, Word will display the last search criteria entered. When you exit Word, all the boxes in the Find and Replace dialog box will clear.

To immediately clear the search field, click the ✕ (**Stop searching**) button.

Replacing Items

To activate the Replace feature, on the Home tab, in the Editing group, click **Replace**.

Key Fact: You can also press CTRL+H to open the Find and Replace dialog box.

If you searched for an item prior to activating Replace, the search criteria displays in the Find what field. You can then enter what the replacement text should be in the Replace with field.

More – Display other options that can be applied to narrow the search.

Replace – Replace this one occurrence.

Replace All – Replace all occurrences.

Find Next – Find the next occurrence to determine whether it should be replaced.

Cancel – Cancel or close this feature.

Printing the Document

The Print feature enables you to preview the document as it will appear when printed. This gives you an opportunity to review the document before you print or distribute it to discover if there are problems with the appearance or layout. You can also use some of the print options to adjust or change the margins or orientation, or display one or more pages at a time prior to printing.

To preview or print a document, click the **File** tab and click **Print**.

Key Fact: Press CTRL+P to display the print options in Backstage. This works for all Office applications.

Use the options in the first panel to control what prints, how it will print, and where it will print.

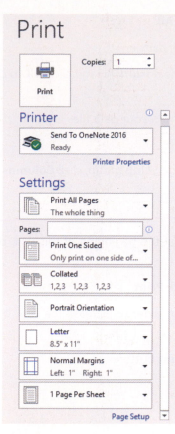

Print

Print – Print the document with the settings currently shown.

Copies – Enables you to specify the number of copies to be printed.

Printer – Select a printer from the list of installed printers. Use the **Printer Properties** link to choose options for how the output is printed, such as single- or double-sided, or black-and-white or color. Some options in the properties for your printer may be available in specific print options.

Settings – Select how much of the document or which specific pages or items to print.

– Alternatively, use the Pages: [_____] ⓘ field to enter specific pages to print:

- #   Print from one page to another, inclusive (for example 5-7)

#,#,#   Print only the following pages (for example 3,7,10)

- #   Print from page 1 to a specific page (for example 1-6)

-   Print from a specific page to the end of the document (for example 13-)

Print Sides – Specify whether to print on one or both sides of each sheet of paper.

Collated – If printing multiple copies, choose how each page is printed, for example complete copies of the full document, or copies of each page individually (which must then be collated into full documents).

Orientation – Choose which orientation should be used for printing this document.

Paper Size – Choose the paper size to use for printing this document.

Margins – Choose the margins to apply when printing this document.

Pages per Sheet – Select the number of pages to print per sheet.

Use the options at the bottom of the second panel to move among pages in the document, to adjust the zoom level, or to zoom into the page.

◀ 1 of 1 ▶   54% — ⎯⏐⎯⏐⎯ + ⊡

Exercise 9-6: Newsletter

In this exercise, you will look at different options to proof and review the document prior to sending it to print.

1. Open the *Newsletter A01* and save it as `Newsletter A01 - Student`.

2. Press F7 to spell check the entire document.

3. Read the information in the Grammar pane to see what Microsoft considers to be wrong in the document. Then click **Change**.

4. Read the description of the next error and click **Change**.

5. Click **OK** when prompted that the spell check is complete.

6. Press CTRL+F to display the Navigation pane. Type: vendor in the search field and press ENTER.

   There should be two results highlighted in yellow for you to peruse, as needed.

7. Close the Navigation pane and press CTRL+H to display the Find and Replace dialog box.

8. Click in the **Replace with** field, type: partner and then click **Replace All**.

   You have now replaced the two occurrences of vendor with the word, partner.

9. Click **Yes** if prompted to continue searching from the beginning of the document, and click **OK** to close the message box. Then close the Find and Replace dialog box.

10. Save and close this document and then open the *TEC Employee List* from your data files location.

    This document has multiple pages consisting of one column of data.

11. Press CTRL+A to select all the text. Click the **Layout** tab and in the Page Setup group, click **Columns** and then click **Three**.

12. Select the title of the report and change this to one column only.

13. Move to the bottom of column three where the Sydney title is and at the beginning of this text, press CTRL+SHIFT+ENTER to force it to the top of the next page.

14. Save the file as TEC Employee List – Student, click **File** and then click **Print**.

15. At the far right bottom of the screen, click the + button on the zoom slider to increase the view of the document. Then click the arrow at the left of the page number to return to Page 1.

16. Click **Print All Pages**. Click **Print Current Page** and then click the **Print** button.

17. Save and close the document.

Working with Pictures

Objective 2-7.1, 2-7.2

You can add pictures to any document from sources such as digital photographs, graphics files, scanned images, or you can go online to find pictures on the Office.com site. Word provides the facility to insert picture files in a wide variety of file formats; some commonly used formats are Windows Metafile (*.wmf), JPEG File Interchangeable format (*.jpg, *jpeg), Portable Network Graphics (*.png), Windows Bitmap (*.bmp), or Graphics Interchange format (*.gif).

To insert a picture, position the mouse pointer in the document where you want the picture to be placed, and then on the Insert tab, in the Illustrations group, click **Picture**.

Word displays a dialog box which you use to select the picture file, similar to opening a text file. Navigate to where the picture file is located, select it and then insert it into the document.

You can also search online for pictures; position the mouse pointer where you want the graphic to be placed, and then on the Insert tab, in the Illustrations group, click **Online Pictures**.

Once you enter the search criteria, you can click the ⌕ or press ENTER to begin the search.

The number and variety of pictures that appear will vary. By default, the search results are images covered under the Creative Commons license. If you want to view as many pictures as possible that match the search criteria, click the down arrow at the right of the CC Only field and click **All Images**.

Note: It is your responsibility to ensure you are not violating copyright laws when you insert images returned in the search results page.

You can point at an image to show some properties about the picture, specifically where this picture is located and who may own the picture, as seen in the following:

To insert the image, click the checkbox at the top left of the image and then click **Insert**.

If there is more than one image on the search results page that you would like to insert into the document, click each image you want to use. The images will be inserted into the current cursor location, and can then be moved to other parts of the document.

You can also narrow the search by choosing one of the links below the search field if you have specific requirements such as the size of the image.

Size ▾   Type ▾   Color ▾

To search for another category of pictures, delete the text in the search field and enter the new search criteria.

Fun Fact: You can insert pictures using both these methods in all Office applications.

Manipulating Objects

Any picture you insert into a document will appear with eight handles when it is selected in the document, as shown in the following image. *Handles* are the small circles or squares that appear around the perimeter of the picture; they confirm that the object has been selected and that you can now make changes to it. These handles may vary in appearance but always appear around the selected picture.

You can insert pictures into a document as *inline objects* (the default setting) or as *floating objects*.

- An inline object acts as a text character in a paragraph.
- A floating object can be placed anywhere (it floats) in the document.

Regardless of which way you insert a picture initially, you will be able to switch from inline to floating or vice versa, using the Wrap Text feature from the Format tab of the Picture Tools ribbon.

Fun Fact: You must select a picture (display its handles), before you can manipulate it in any Office application.

Moving a Picture

The drag-and-drop method is the easiest way to move a picture. However, take note of whether the picture is inline or floating before you try to move it, as this determines how and where you can move the picture:

- If it is an inline object, the mouse pointer displays as when you drag it.
- If it is a floating object, the mouse pointer displays as and when you drag the picture, it changes to .

Sizing a Picture

When you insert a picture into a document, it appears at its original size, or the largest size that the page will accommodate. You can resize or *scale* the picture to any proportions you want. You use the same methods to size a picture whether it is inline or floating.

You can use the handles to size a picture:

- Vertically, by dragging the middle horizontal handle at the top or bottom edge in or out.
- Horizontally, by dragging the middle vertical handle at the left or right edge in or out.
- On two adjacent sides at once, by dragging one of the corner handles in or out.

If you want to ensure that your resized picture remains in proportion, press SHIFT before you drag the appropriate handle.

Wrapping Text Around a Picture

Wrapping styles affect the way the text flows around pictures and change the way pictures are positioned in relation to the surrounding text.

By default, the picture wrapping style is *In Line with Text*, which places the inline graphic at the insertion point on a line of text in the document. The graphic then moves with the text, as if it were a text character.

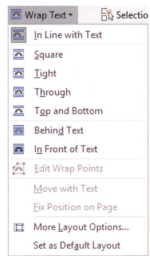

Changing the wrapping style enables the picture to "float" or be positioned anywhere in the document.

To change the text wrapping style for a picture object, select the picture and then on the Format tab of Picture Tools, in the Arrange group, click **Wrap Text** to choose the appropriate text wrapping style.

Each text wrapping style provides a different effect for the picture and the text in the document. Use the previews to see which text wrap style is suitable for the picture and the document. You can also use a combination of these methods to achieve the desired effect.

Cropping a Picture

Cropping refers to the ability to "cut off" certain portions of the picture. Using this feature, you can crop pictures horizontally (at the top or bottom) or vertically (at the sides); for more precise cropping, you must use a dedicated graphics program.

- To crop the top or bottom of the picture, drag the top or bottom crop handle when you see ▤.
- To crop the left or right side of the picture, drag the left or right crop handle when you see ▤.
- To adjust two adjacent sides of a picture, drag one of the corner crop handles when you see ⌐.

Note: The mouse cursor displays the appropriate direction based on the side you are cropping.

Exercise 9-7: Newsletter with Pictures

In this exercise, you will add pictures to a document and then manipulate the graphics. This exercise uses pictures available from CC web sites. The number and types of pictures will vary based on changes made by web sites; focus should be on the task such as sizing, moving, or cropping.

1. Open the *Newsletter A01* file and save it as `Newsletter A01 with pictures - Student`.
2. Delete the **New Office** text below the What's New heading.
3. Click the **Insert** tab and in the Illustrations group, click **Online Pictures**.
4. Click in the search field, type: announcements and press ENTER.
5. Scroll through the pictures and the click the checkbox for the picture similar to the following:

6. Click **Insert** to insert the picture into the document. With the picture selected, click the top right handle and drag inward to make the picture approximately 1" in height.
7. Under Picture Tools, click the **Format** tab in the Arrange group, click **Wrap Text** and click **Square**.
8. Position the mouse cursor anywhere inside the picture and drag it so that the top of the paragraph aligns with the top of the picture, as shown here:

What's New

...e services ... more tours! We are now in Seattle and will be having an open house on 16th. Andrew McSweeney is moving from our UK office to manage the Tolano Adventures division, and Jennifer Wilson will be managing the Tolano Environmental Consulting division. Come out and welcome them to the new location and the beautiful state of Washington!

With more resources on the West Coast, we will be able to offer more service and faster communications with customers and new vendors. We are also exploring new opportunities and services we can offer with the focus to the Pacific / Asian coast lines.

9. Ensure the picture is still selected, and then on the Format tab, in the Size group, click **Crop**.
10. Using the crop handles around the picture, try to crop out as much of the white space around the picture as possible, similar to the figure shown below, then click outside the image.

What's New

∾ More se
⚓ 16th. An
∾ division
Come o

With more resources on the

11. At the end of the With more resources ... paragraph, press ENTER to create a blank line.

12. Click in this blank line, then click the **Insert** tab, and in the Illustrations group, click **Pictures**.

13. Navigate to the Word folder in the student data files, if not there already, and then double-click the **balloons** picture.

    The picture should fill the width of the page. If you were actually creating this newsletter, you would continue to add or modify pictures. For the purpose of this exercise, you will stop working on this document.

14. Save and close the document.

Using Tables

Objective 2-2.5, 2-2.9

Use the Table feature to arrange columns of text and numbers, group paragraphs side by side, or create forms. The following figure shows a table.

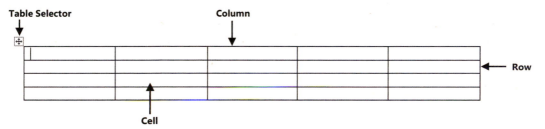

When working with a table, you are working with cells within the table (the intersection between a column and a row). You can create a table before or after you type the text.

You can enter text, numbers or graphics into each cell. Text longer than the width of the cell will automatically wrap to the next line in the same cell.

Use the ⊞ (**Table Selector**) to select the entire table; it appears at the top left corner of a table when your cursor is in or near the table.

Once you create a table, the Table Tools ribbon appears providing further options for the design or layout of the table. The Insertion point must be somewhere in the table before this ribbon displays.

Inserting a Table

To insert a table, use one of the following methods:

- On the Insert tab, in the Tables group, click **Table**.

15. What keyboard shortcut can you use to create a column break?
    a. CTRL+ENTER
    b. SHIFT+ENTER
    c. CTRL+ALT+ENTER
    d. CTRL+SHIFT+ENTER

16. Which option displays the Navigation pane to find an item?
    a. CTRL+D   c. CTRL+H
    b. CTRL+F   d. CTRL+N

17. How can you recognize a spelling error in a Word file?
    a. The noted error appears with a green wavy line.
    b. The noted error appears with a blue wavy line.
    c. The noted error appears with a purple wavy line.
    d. The noted error appears with a red wavy line.

18. Which keyboard shortcut displays the Print options in the Backstage view for all Office applications?
    a. CTRL+A   c. CTRL+P
    b. CTRL+R   d. CTRL+V

19. How can you identify that an image or object has been selected for manipulation?
    a. It displays handles around its perimeter.
    b. It displays in a darker shadow.
    c. A circular handle appears across the top of the image or object.
    d. A four-headed arrow appears when you point the cursor at the image/object.

20. How can you crop a picture in Word?
    a. Horizontally only.
    b. Vertically only.
    c. Horizontally and vertically.
    d. You cannot crop a picture in Word.

21. What is the intersection of a row and a column in a table called?
    a. Text box   c. Box
    b. Cell   d. Active cell

22. How can you select an entire table quickly?
    a. Click the Tab Selector.   c. Press CTRL+A.
    b. Click in the Selection Bar.   d. Click the Table Selector.

23. How would you turn off the Track Changes feature when you are finished with the feature?
    a. Click the Track Changes button again.
    b. Press ESC.
    c. Press ENTER.
    d. Click Accept All Changes.

Lesson 10: Using Microsoft Excel

Lesson Objectives

This lesson introduces you to how to use a spreadsheet application to create simple reports such as budgets, or cash flows. Upon completion of this lesson, you should be able to:

- □ understand basic terminology or concepts for spreadsheets
- □ create a new blank worksheet or use a template to create a new worksheet
- □ enter or edit data in a worksheet
- □ open, close or save workbooks
- □ select cells for a variety of purposes
- □ copy and move data

- □ change the column width or row height
- □ create simple formulas and use common built-in functions
- □ format the data in a worksheet to enhance it
- □ work with charts
- □ sort or filter information in a worksheet
- □ work with tables
- □ preview and print a report

Looking at the Excel Screen

Objective 2-3.1, 2-3.6

As with any Office application, when you first start the program, you see the Backstage view:

You can select a template for creating a new workbook, or click the Open Other Workbooks link to access the Open tab in the Backstage view. As you work in Excel, recently used files will display in the left pane of the startup screen. A new, blank workbook is shown in the following figure.

Name Box – Look here for the address of the active cell. For example, if the Name box displays A21, this indicates the active cell is where column A and row 21 intersect.

Insert Function – Open a dialog box that will help you choose and insert a built-in function.

Formula Bar – View the contents of the active cell. Under certain circumstances, you can use this bar to create or edit entries in the worksheet.

Select All – Click to select all the cells in the worksheet.

Active Cell – Indicates the current cell with the thick border around the cell.

Column Headings – The sequential letters at the top of each column enable you to identify columns.

Row Headings – The sequential numbers on the left side of each row enable you to identify rows.

Tab Scrolling – Use these arrows to navigate between the worksheets in the workbook.

Sheet Tab – The name of the current or active worksheet on screen.

Scroll Bars – Use these to move horizontally or vertically within the current or active worksheet.

Worksheets are used whenever you need a report or document that tracks numerical information. Typical reports include budgets, cash flow analysis reports, revenue and expense reports, financial reports, an inventory analysis, or a document tracking data such as employee vacation time or student grades.

Understanding Basic Terminology

- An Excel file is called a *workbook* and a workbook contains one or more individual worksheets. For instance, a file named AM 2015 Figures could contain a worksheet that shows a summary of the company's revenue and expenses, another worksheet with quarterly summaries, and a worksheet that shows business expenses, and so on.

- A *worksheet* contains rows numbered from 1 to 1,048,576, and columns assigned with letters or letter combinations from A to Z, then AA to ZZ, then AAA to AZZ, and so on up to XFD.

- A *cell* is the intersection of a row and a column and can contain one single value (text or number), or formula. For instance, cell B5 is the "box" that you will find when you follow down column B to row 5.

   - Each cell has its own *address*, or a reference you can use to find it within a worksheet.

   - The *active cell* is the cell currently displayed with a thick border, such as cell A1 in the previous picture.

Entering Data in the Worksheet

You should always try to organize the information on a worksheet in a way that will be clear to you and to anyone else who may be using or analyzing the content. Include appropriate labels and descriptions in your reports so your audience understands what they are viewing.

You can insert three types of data into worksheet cells:

Labels – Text entries appear in the cells exactly as you enter them; default to left align.

Values – Numeric values; default to right aligned.

Formulas – Composed of cell references, arithmetic operators, and functions (calculation commands) that perform operations on data.

Entering Text or Labels

To enter information, click a cell to select it and then type the entry. Use the BACKSPACE key or DELETE key to correct any input errors. When you finish typing, press ENTER to move to the next cell below, or press TAB to move to the next cell to the right. You can also click another cell or press any arrow key to accept the input in the current cell.

The following image is an example of how to organize your data so that you can clearly see its purpose:

◢	A	B	C	D	E	F
1	ABC Company					
2		Q1	Q2	Q3	Q4	Total
3	Region 1	541,000.00	275,000.00	280,000.00	310,000.00	$ 1,406,000
4	Region 2	125,000.00	127,000.00	122,000.00	126,000.00	$ 500,000
5	Region 3	96,000.00	100,000.00	102,000.00	205,000.00	$ 503,000
6	Total	$ 762,000	$ 502,000	$ 504,000	$ 641,000	$ 2,409,000

When entering information, consider the following:

- You can enter or edit data directly in the active cell, or use the Formula bar for long data entries.

- Labels can be up to 32,767 characters long.

- If a label is longer than the width of the cell, it will display past the column border as long as the adjoining cell to the right is empty. Entries in adjoining cells cut off the display at the column border. The long text label may not be visible, but it is still completely contained in the cell in which it was entered.

- You can easily change the appearance and alignment of any entry in any cell.

- The maximum length of formula contents is 8,192 characters.

Entering Numbers or Dates

Numbers are constant values such as dollars and percentages; by default, they align to the right side of a cell. If you enter characters other than numbers, Excel treats the entire entry as a label. Excel displays values with no formatting, allowing you to format them yourself.

When entering dates, you can enter them in a numeric form such as 2-26-05 or as text, Month day, year). When entering dates, note the following:

- The default format of the date value is m-d-yy, although you can change this using the Region and Language settings in the Control Panel.

- The date value does not have to be the full day, month, and year. It can be just the day and month (formatted mmm-dd), or the month and year (formatted mmm-yyyy).

Moving Around the Worksheet

You can move around the cells of a worksheet using the following methods:

Scroll Bars – Click the arrow buttons at either end of a scroll bar to move one row or column at a time. Click and drag the scroll box to display another location in the worksheet.

LEFT, **RIGHT**, **UP**, or **DOWN** – Press a direction key to move one cell at a time.

HOME – Moves to column A in the current row.

CTRL+HOME – Moves to cell A1.

CTRL+END – Moves to the last cell with data in your report.

CTRL+G or **F5** – Displays the Go To dialog box which you can use to move quickly to a cell address.

You can also use the horizontal or vertical scroll bar to move to other areas of the worksheet. As you begin to work with multiple worksheets, you can use the arrows at the far left below the worksheet to navigate to these sheets; alternatively, you can click the sheet tab for the sheet you want to view.

Managing Workbooks

Objective 2-3.11, 2-3.12

Basic file management tasks, such as saving a file, opening a file, creating a new file, or closing a file are similar across all applications in the Office suite.

Creating a New Blank Workbook

When you start Excel, the Backstage view appears and you can choose to create a new workbook or open an existing one. If you create a new blank workbook, it is automatically named Book1. Each time you create a new workbook during the same session, Excel will number it sequentially as Book2, Book3, and so on. When you exit Excel and start a new session later, the numbering begins at 1.

To create a new blank workbook in Backstage, click **New**, and double-click **Blank workbook**.

Key Fact: You can also press CTRL+N to create a new blank workbook, or a new blank document type in any Office application.

Creating a New Workbook from a Template

To create a new workbook using a template, click the **File** tab, and click **New**.

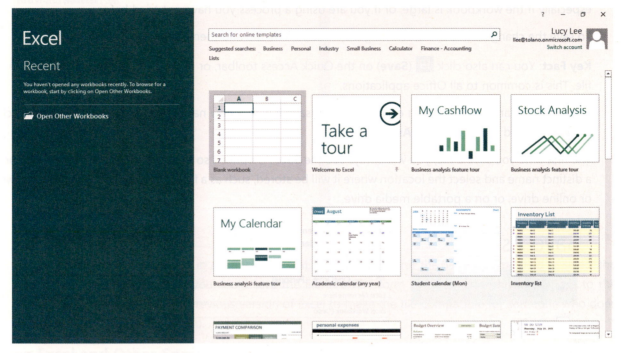

Click a template to open a larger view of the template contents.

Click **Create** to create a new workbook based on the selected template. Alternatively, click the arrow at either side of the template to view other templates in the list on either side of this template. To exit the preview, click the ✕ at the top right corner of the preview window.

Each new workbook you create using a template displays the name of the template plus a number (for example, Working budget1) as a reminder that this is a new file that should be saved with a different name, preferably one that describes the type of data in the workbook.

As you learned in a previous lesson, all applications in the Office suite automatically open files received over the Internet in Protected Mode. You should understand that Protected Mode and Read-Only mode work the same in Excel as they do in Word.

Closing Workbooks

When you are finished working with the current workbook, save the changes and then close the workbook to protect it from accidental changes. Closing files also frees up system resources for other files. When you close a workbook, Excel displays any other open workbooks or a blank background screen if no workbooks are open.

To close a workbook, click the **File** tab and click **Close**.

Key Fact: You can also press CTRL+W or CTRL+F4 to close the workbook, or click the **Close** button to shut down the application. These work in any Office application.

Exercise 10-1: Create New

In this exercise you will create new workbooks and enter data in one of them. You will also save some of the new files for future use.

1. Start Microsoft Excel, if necessary. Click **Blank workbook** to create a new workbook.

    Excel displays the new blank workbook that contains a blank worksheet.

2. Press CTRL+N to quickly create another new blank workbook.

    This new workbook should show Book2 in the title bar (the number may vary depending on how many times you pressed the shortcut key). Notice that the active cell is A1 – it should be highlighted with a darker border around it and both column A and row 1 change color because these contain the cell that is currently active. As you click in different cells, the column heading and row number will change color accordingly.

3. In cell **A1** of Book2, type: `<Your Name> - Bank Reconciliation` and press ENTER.

    The cursor should now be in cell A2 (you are still in column A but now in row 2).

4. Type: `Date` and press TAB to go to cell **B2**.

5. Type: `Item` and press TAB to move to cell **C2**. Type: `Cash In`.

6. Press TAB to move to cell **D2**, type: `Cash Out`, press TAB to go to E2, type: `Balance`, and press ENTER.

    This time the cursor is in cell A3.

7. Press TAB to go to cell **B3**, type: `Cash in Bank`, press TAB to move to cell **C3**, type: `525` and press ENTER.

8. In cell **A4**, type: `Jan 1` and press TAB. Continue entering the information as shown:

	A	B	C	D	E
1	Lucy Lee - Bank Reconciliation				
2	Date	Item	Cash In	Cash Out	Balance
3		Cash in Ba	525		
4	1-Jan	Payday	1000		
5	5-Jan	Mortgage		500	
6	10-Jan	Gas		48.5	
7	12-Jan	Visa		235.67	

9. On the Quick Access Toolbar, click **Save**.

10. Click **This PC** in the middle pane and click the arrow at the left of Documents. Navigate to the *Excel* folder in the student data files, then in the file name field, type: Bank Reconciliation - Student (use your name or initials in place of "Student") and click **Save**.

11. Click in cell **B1** and type in **today's date** using the mmm dd, yyyy format, for example, May 11, 2016 and press ENTER.

    You should notice the title text has been cut off by the date. This is an example of why you want to watch where you are entering data and how it affects areas in the report.

12. Save the workbook again.

Now create a new workbook using a template.

13. Click the **File** tab and then click **New**.

14. Scroll in the list and then click **Simple monthly budget**. Click **Create**.

    Notice how Excel created a new copy of this file for you using a similar name (Simple monthly budget1) to remind you of which template you used. If you were planning to use this form, you could click each field to enter the appropriate information. For the purpose of this demonstration, you will just save it.

15. Press CTRL+S to save this file. Click **This PC** and navigate to the **Excel** folder in the student data files.

16. Click in the filename field, type: Simple monthly budget - Student and press ENTER.

17. Press CTRL+N to create a new blank workbook.

    You now have at least four workbooks open (the number will depend on the number of times you created a blank workbook or a new document from a template).

18. Point at the Excel icon on the Windows taskbar and you should have at least four preview windows displayed.

19. Click the **Bank Reconciliation - Student** file.

    This file is now the active workbook on the screen.

20. Point at the Excel icon and then click the blank workbook created in step 17.

21. Close this workbook by pressing CTRL+W.

22. Then press CTRL+W to close all other workbooks.

Now try opening a file.

23. Click **File** and then click **Open**.

    There should be at least two files in the list of files most recently accessed.

24. Click **Bank Reconciliation – Student** from the list.

25. Press CTRL+O and click **Simple monthly budget – Student**.

26. Click **File**, click **Open**, and click **This PC**. Ensure you are viewing the contents of the **Excel** folder, then click **Tour Prices** to open this file.

Now save this file in another format so you can send it to someone who is using an earlier version of Excel.

27. Click **File**, click **Save As**. Click the arrow for the **Save as type** field and then click **Excel 97-2003 Workbook (*.xls)**. Click **Save**.

Using the Office Clipboard

You can cut or copy more than one cell range, and keep up to 24 cell ranges in the Office Clipboard at one time. You can then paste any or all these items in any sequence. When you cut or copy the 25th item, the first one in the list will disappear, making room for this new entry.

Activate the commands for cut, copy, and paste using the Home tab, in the Clipboard group, or with the keyboard shortcuts. Display the Office Clipboard at any time by clicking the **Clipboard** dialog box launcher in the Clipboard group of the Home tab.

As with all Office applications, the Office Clipboard can contain cut or copied items from any application, including a non-Office application.

Paste All – Paste all items in the same order they were collected into the current location on the worksheet.

Clear All – Clear the Office Clipboard of all entries.

Options – Set how the Office Clipboard works.

Changing the Column Widths

You can adjust column widths to display more characters. When a text entry in a cell is longer than the width of the column, Excel displays the text by overflowing the entry into the cells to the right, if they are empty. If the cell to the right contains information, the text is truncated or "cut off" at the column boundary.

2	Date	Item	Cash In
3		Cash in Ba	525
4	1-Jan	Payday	1000

If the width is not wide enough to display all the digits of a numeric or date value, Excel displays # symbols. If you increase the width of the column sufficiently, the value will be shown in standard format using any assigned cell formatting.

▲	A	B	C	D	E	F
1	**2015-2016 Packages**					
2						
3		**Tour Prices Breakdown (Average based on 4-day Trip)**				
4	**Travel Item**	**Group**	**Tour**	**Flight**	**Hotel**	**Misc.**
5	Perth Camel Train	20	1,000.00	800.00	500.00	
6	Queensland Camel Camp	10	900.00	800.00	550.00	100.0
7	Sahara	5	750.00	#######	#######	200.0
8	Morocco	5	1,000.00	#######	#######	150.0
9	Uluru	5	600.00	900.00	600.00	300.0
10	Dubai	8	400.00	#######	600.00	250.0
11	Minqin County	20	500.00	#######	750.00	300.0

Column widths can be set between zero and 255 characters. When you change a column width, the stored contents of the cells do not change, only the number of the characters displayed.

To change the width of a column, on the Home tab, in the Cells group, click **Format**, and then **Column Width**.

Type a value in the Column width box and click **OK** or press ENTER.

Hint: You can also point the mouse pointer on the line at the right edge of the column header to be adjusted, and when you see ✛, click and drag to the required width for the column.

Adjusting the Row Height

When you need to adjust the row height so the row is smaller or larger than others in the worksheet, on the Home tab, in the Cells group, click **Format**, and then **Row Height**.

Row Height	?	×
Row height:	15	
OK		Cancel

Type a value in the Row height box and click **OK** or press ENTER.

Hint: You can also point at the bottom edge of the row header to be adjusted, and when you see ✛, click and drag to the height required.

Manipulating Rows, Columns, or Cells

Insert new rows, columns, or cells when you need to add information or separate parts of the worksheet. Delete rows, columns, or cells of data that you do not need in the worksheet.

Inserting Rows, Columns, or Cells

You can insert a new row above the current row, and a new column to the left of the current column. You can insert one or more rows or columns at the same time.

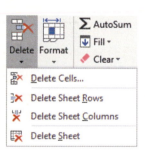

You can also insert cells in specific areas of the worksheet; use caution when activating this option as it can alter the structure of your worksheet. On the Home tab, in the Cells group, click the arrow for **Insert** to select the item to be inserted.

Be careful using these commands as they affect the entire worksheet and may affect areas of the worksheet you are not viewing on the screen. For example, if you want to insert a row but only have one cell in the row selected, click the arrow for the Insert command to insert the row; do not click the Insert command on its own as Excel will insert a cell in the current cursor location only for that one column.

Hint: Click the row heading or column heading where you want to insert a new row or column. Then press CTRL++ on the Numeric Keypad.

Deleting Rows, Columns, or Cells

You can delete one or several rows or columns, or shift cells over in place of deleted cells. Deleting the contents of a cell affects only the contents, not the structure of the worksheet. Deleting a cell affects the structure of the worksheet. On the Home tab, in the Cells group, click the arrow for **Delete** to select the item to be deleted.

Hint: Click the row heading or column heading where you want to delete. Then press CTRL+− on the Numeric Keypad.

Be careful when deleting entire rows or columns to ensure you do not accidentally delete valuable data not currently displayed on the screen.

Exercise 10-2: Bank Reconciliation

In this exercise you will complete a workbook by adding similar entries into cells of a worksheet as well as adjust the column widths to make the report comprehensive.

1.   Click **File**, click **Open**, and click the **Bank Reconciliation - Student** file to open it.

2.   Click **File**, click **Save As**, and in the File name field, type: Bank Reconciliation adjusted - Student as the new name and then click **Save**.

3.   Click **B1** and press DELETE. Then on the Quick Access Toolbar, click **Undo**.

     The date should be back in the report.

4.   On the Quick Access Toolbar, click **Redo** to remove the date again.

5.   On the Home tab, in the Clipboard group, click the **Clipboard** dialog box launcher button.

6.   Select cells **B4** and **C4** which contain the payday information. Then on the Home tab, in the Clipboard group, click **Copy**.

     Notice how the Office Clipboard now shows an entry for the contents of this cell range. You should also notice the marquee around cells B4 and C4, reminding you this is the original source for the copy action.

7.   Click in cell **B8** and then click the entry in the Clipboard.

◢	A	B	C	D	E
1	Lucy Lee - Bank Reconciliation				
2	Date	Item	Cash In	Cash Out	Balance
3		Cash in Ba	525		
4	1-Jan	Payday	1000		
5	5-Jan	Mortgage		500	
6	10-Jan	Gas		48.5	
7	12-Jan	Visa		235.67	
8		Payday	1000		
9			(Ctrl) ▾		

     You have just successfully copied and pasted an entry from one cell range to another (the marquee no longer appears around the original source).

8.   Click in cell **A8**, type: Jan 15 and press ENTER.

9.   In cell **A9**, type: Gas, press TAB twice, type: 53.45 and press ENTER. The information has been entered into the wrong cells.

10. Select cells **A9** to **C9**, and press CTRL+X to cut the information.

11. Click in cell **B9**, and press CTRL+V to paste this entry into this location.

12. Click the ✕ on the Office Clipboard. Then save the workbook.

Now try adjusting the worksheet to improve the readability of the report.

13. Place the cursor between the column heading for **B** and **C**. You should see the ↔ icon appear between the column headers.

14. Click and drag to the right to increase the size of column **B**.

     Notice as you drag that Excel displays a small ScreenTip indicating the width of the column, such as 12.14.

15. Release the mouse when you see the **12.71** or **13.00** measurement.

Now insert a blank row to place some room between the title of the report and the column headings.

16. Click the **row 2 heading**. On the Home tab, in the Cells group, click **Insert**.

     Excel automatically inserted a row as a result of selecting the entire row before selecting the command; Excel can recognize what or where you want to apply a feature.

17. Save the workbook.

Creating Simple Formulas

Objective 2-3.5

A formula is a calculation using numbers (or other data) in a cell or from other cells. It can be as simple as a single cell or it can be as complex as required in a large worksheet of one workbook that may be linked to other workbooks. Using a formula to calculate values enables you to focus on the data and allow Excel to automatically recalculate the results if the data changes.

To begin a formula in any cell, you must enter = (equals symbol). Depending on the formula, this is usually followed by a cell address, a mathematical operand, and then another cell address, as seen in the following:

=B3*F16

- You can enter a cell address into a formula by typing it directly into the cell, or by clicking on the cells to be included.

- The cell into which you enter a formula will display the result of the formula; the formula itself will be visible in the Formula bar.

Excel calculates formulas in "natural order": exponents first, then multiplication and division, and then addition and subtraction. This order can be altered by inserting parentheses or brackets around portions of the formula; Excel will calculate the portions inside parentheses before calculating the other items in the formula.

The following symbols are used in Excel to represent standard mathematical operators:

*	Multiplication	+	Addition
/	Division	-	Subtraction

Cells containing formulas can be copied to other cells. If these formulas contain cell references, Excel will automatically adjust the cell references when you paste the formulas into a new location.

Using Common Built-In Functions

Excel provides over 300 built-in functions for mathematical and data operations. Functions accept numbers, values, and cell references as *arguments* within parentheses, following this format:

=FUNCTION(numbers or values or cell references)

Some common functions you will use include:

=**SUM** – Calculates the sum of the values in the range of specified cells.

=**AVERAGE** – Calculates an average of the values in the specified cells (totals the range and divides the total by the number of entries).

=**MIN** – Displays the minimum value in the range of specified cells.

=**MAX** – Displays the maximum value in the range of specified cells.

=**COUNT** – Counts the number of values within the specified range.

Cell ranges in a function should be indicated as follows:

<first cell address>:<last cell address>   E4:G6

You can specify a range by typing the cell reference directly or by using the "point-to" method, where you use the mouse to click and drag to select the cell range. The latter method allows you to visually identify the cell range, which reduces the chance that you will enter incorrect cell references.

Be sure to verify that you have selected the correct cell range for the function. If there is even one blank cell between cells, the range may not include all cells.

Using Absolute and Relative Addresses

Most formulas entered into an Excel worksheet refer to cell addresses which are *relative*. If you copy a formula with a relative cell address and paste it to another cell, Excel will automatically adjust the cell references in the pasted cell to reflect the new location. For example, suppose you have a formula that adds three rows together within one column; you can copy this formula to another column to add the same three rows in the new column. The cell addresses used in the formula are relative to the column in which you place the formula.

An *absolute* cell address refers to an exact or fixed location on the worksheet.

To change a relative cell address to an absolute (fixed) cell address in a formula or function:

- Type a dollar sign before the row number and/or column letter; or
- press F4 once you enter the cell address.

Exercise 10-3: Bank Reconciliation Formulas

In this exercise, you will enter a few simple formulas using math operators.

1. Ensure the *Bank Reconciliation adjusted – Student* file is open and save it as Bank Reconciliation with formulas - Student.

2. Click in cell **E4**. Type: =C4 and press ENTER.

   You successfully entered a simple formula into cell F4 that inserts the contents of cell C4 as the starting formula.

3. In cell **E5**, type: =C5+E4 and press ENTER.

   Excel now displays the total of the starting balance plus the amount of the new cash.

4. Click in cell **C4** and type: 725. Press ENTER.

   Notice how the formula updates to accommodate the new value. You can see how using a formula saves you the time of having to change the data if you had entered it manually.

5. Click in cell **E6** and type: = to start the formula. Click cell **E5**, type: - (dash or minus sign), click cell **D6** and press ENTER.

	A	B	C	D	E
1	Lucy Lee - Bank Reconciliation				
2					
3	Date	Item	Cash In	Cash Out	Balance
4		Cash in Bank	725		725
5	1-Jan	Payday	1000		1725
6	5-Jan	Mortgage		500	1225
7	10-Jan	Gas		48.5	
8	12-Jan	Visa		235.67	

Notice how this time you clicked the cells for the formula instead of typing the cell addresses manually.

6. Click cell **E6** and press CTRL+C. Then select cells **E7:E8** and press ENTER.

	A	B	C	D	E
1	Lucy Lee - Bank Reconciliation				
2					
3	Date	Item	Cash In	Cash Out	Balance
4		Cash in Bank	725		725
5	1-Jan	Payday	1000		1725
6	5-Jan	Mortgage		500	1225
7	10-Jan	Gas		48.5	1176.5
8	12-Jan	Visa		235.67	940.83
9	15-Jan	Payday	1000		

Excel has copied the formula in cell E6 and adjusted the cell addresses for the next two rows. This is an example of relative cell referencing.

7. In cell **E9**, type: =E8+C9 and press ENTER.

If you were to continue with the report, you would continue to enter data to indicate the cash going into and out of the bank account, inserting formulas as applicable to calculate the changes.

8. Save and close the report.

Now try using functions in a worksheet to show totals for the pricing set on tours for the upcoming year.

9. Open the *Tour Prices* file and save as Tour Prices - Student.

10. Click the column heading for Column C, drag across to Column G, then release the mouse button. Columns C through G are now selected.

11. In the Home tab, in the Cells group, click Format, then click Column Width to open the Column Width dialog box. Type: 11 and then press ENTER to change the width of the selected columns to 11.

12. Click in cell **G5**. Then on the Home tab, in the Editing group, click **AutoSum**.

	A	B	C	D	E	F	G	H	I
1	**2015-2016 Packages**								
2									
3		**Tour Prices Breakdown (Average based on 4-day Trip)**							
4	**Travel Item**	**Group**	**Tour**	**Flight**	**Hotel**	**Misc.**	**Total Cost**		
5	Perth Camel Train	20	1,000.00	800.00	500.00		=SUM(B5:F5)		
6	Queensland Camel Camp	10	900.00	800.00	550.00	100.00	SUM(number1, [number2], ...)		
7	Sahara	5	750.00	1,300.00	1,000.00	200.00			

Excel now identifies the cells you may want to sum or total. If these are correct, you need only accept the suggested cell range. If you need to change the range of cells, click to select the cells you want to be included in the formula.

13. Press ENTER to accept the formula in this cell and move the cursor to the next cell below.

You will now insert formulas to total the remaining tours.

14. Click in cell **G5** again and then on the Home tab, in the Clipboard group, click **Copy**. Excel copies the formula to the clipboard.

15. Click cell **G6** and drag down to cell **G15**. Press ENTER.

	A	B	C	D	E	F	G
1	**2015-2016 Packages**						
2							
3		Tour Prices Breakdown (Average based on 4-day Trip)					
4	**Travel Item**	**Group**	**Tour**	**Flight**	**Hotel**	**Misc.**	**Total Cost**
5	Perth Camel Train	20	1,000.00	800.00	500.00		$ 2,320.00
6	Queensland Camel Camp	10	900.00	800.00	550.00	100.00	$ 2,360.00
7	Sahara	5	750.00	1,300.00	1,000.00	200.00	$ 3,255.00
8	Morocco	5	1,000.00	1,200.00	1,000.00	150.00	$ 3,355.00
9	Uluru	5	600.00	900.00	600.00	300.00	$ 2,405.00
10	Dubai	8	400.00	1,500.00	600.00	250.00	$ 2,758.00
11	Minqin County	20	500.00	1,200.00	750.00	300.00	$ 2,770.00
12	Westwood Cemetery	25	50.00	250.00	800.00	200.00	$ 1,325.00
13	Forest Lawns	10	50.00	250.00	800.00	200.00	$ 1,310.00
14	Whatley House	10	50.00	300.00	500.00	300.00	$ 1,160.00
15	Edinburgh Castle	20	50.00	1,200.00	700.00	350.00	$ 2,320.00

Excel pastes the formula into the remaining cells.

16. Click cell **G6** to see how the formula appears.

    You should notice that the cell references for the AutoSum range have adjusted to reflect the total for this row instead. That is, the range is B6:F6 for row 6, but it will be B7:F7 for row 7 and so on.

17. Save the worksheet.

Suppose there is now a possibility that you may have to raise the tour prices by 25% to cover varying exchange rates.

18. Click cell **A20**, type: Exchange Rate as the label and press TAB. In cell **B20**, type: 1.25 as the rate and press ENTER.

19. Click cell **I5**. Type: = and then click cell **G5**.

20. Type: * to insert a multiplication operator and then click cell **B20**. Press ENTER to accept the formula.

21. Copy the results of this cell down to the cell **I15**.

c.	Total Cost		
	$ 2,320.00	$2,900.00	
00.00	$ 2,360.00	$ -	
00.00	$ 3,255.00	$ -	
50.00	$ 3,355.00	$ -	
00.00	$ 2,405.00	$ -	
50.00	$ 2,758.00	$ -	
00.00	$ 2,770.00	$ -	
00.00	$ 1,325.00	$ -	
00.00	$ 1,310.00	$ -	
00.00	$ 1,160.00	$ -	
50.00	$ 2,320.00	$ -	

You should notice that the remaining cells have no results in them from the copying of the original formula. This is because Excel uses relative cell addressing by default. What we need to do is set the appropriate cell in the original formula to be static or absolute so the new rate will be calculated correctly in the remaining cells.

22. Click in cell **I5** and then click in the Formula bar to activate the Edit mode. With the cursor at the end of the **B20** cell address reference, press F4.

> =G5*B20|

23. Press ENTER to accept this change.

    You have specified that cell B20 is an absolute cell address. Neither the row nor the column will be adjusted as you copy and paste.

24. Copy this formula down to cell **I15**.

$2,900.00
$2,950.00
$4,068.75
$4,193.75
$3,006.25
$3,447.50
$3,462.50
$1,656.25
$1,637.50
$1,450.00
$2,900.00

25. Click in several of the cells to look at the formula, and notice how the first cell changed to recognize the value but the cell with the Exchange Rate stayed constant.

26. Save and close the workbook.

What Does Formatting Mean?

Objective 2-3.9, 2-3.10

Formatting refers to changing the appearance of data to draw attention to parts of the worksheet, or to make the data easier to read. Formatting does not affect any underlying values.

- You can format a cell or range of cells at any time, either before or after you enter the data.
- A cell remains formatted until you clear the format or reformat the cell.
- When you enter new data in the cell, Excel will display it in the existing format.
- When you copy or fill a cell, you copy its format along with the cell contents.

To apply formatting, on the Home tab, click the command to apply formatting from the appropriate group.

Excel provides other methods to access formatting options such as keyboard shortcuts or the Mini toolbar; the following demonstrates the most commonly used method to access these formatting options.

Hint: You can also press CTRL+1 to display the Format Cells dialog box for further options on formatting various elements of the worksheet.

Even though you only entered the row total for the first row, Excel has automatically inserted them for the rest of the rows, except the Total row. This demonstrates one of the advantages of identifying this range of cells as a table.

12. Click cell **F5**.

You can see that the formula used for this sum total is specifically used for tables.

Now insert the Total Row calculation for this new column.

13. Select cell **F16**, click its drop-down arrow, and select **Sum**.

14. Save the workbook.

Now add a new row at the bottom of the table.

15. Select cell **F15** and press TAB.

Notice that Excel automatically shifts the Total row down by one row and that the formula in cell **F15** is copied down to this new row.

16. In cell **A16**, type: December 2016 as the new value and press TAB. Then enter the following values into the remaining cells of the row:

B16	8969
C16	7375
D16	7
E16	1

Notice also that the statistical formulas in row 17 (these were all Sum but you may have selected Average or other formulas instead) automatically updated even though the new data were added at the bottom of the list.

Now add a new column between the Complaints and Total columns.

17. Select cell **F8**, then on the Home tab, in the Cells group, click the arrow for **Insert**, and click **Insert Table Columns to the Left**.

18. Click cell **F4** and type: Other. Then enter the following values into the remaining cells of the column:

F5	500	F11	200
F6	300	F12	480
F7	250	F13	100
F8	450	F14	200
F9	400	F15	150
F10	220	F16	300

19. Select cell **F17**, click the drop-down arrow and click **Sum**.

By adding a column to the table, you must ensure that the Total column at the far right includes this new column.

20. Click cell **G6**, and note the formula in the Formula bar. Press F2, delete the table cell reference [Complaints], and replace it with: [Other]. Then press ENTER.

> =SUM(CallVolume[@[Sales Inquiries]:[Other]])

Notice how Excel automatically updates the total in G17 once you change the field headings that are included in the table.

If no longer needed, a column (or row) can be easily removed from a table.

21. Click any cell in the range D4 to D17, then on the Home tab, in the Cells group, click the arrow for **Delete**, and click **Delete Table Columns**.

4	Month	Sales Inquiries	Service Inquiries	Complaints	Other	Total
5	Jan-16	8947	4799	26	500	14272
6	Feb-16	3643	5658	14	300	9615
7	Mar-16	5861	9739	7	250	15857
8	Apr-16	3741	4429	25	450	8645
9	May-16	4537	5420	19	400	10376
10	Jun-16	3146	1417	12	220	4795
11	Jul-16	2533	7811	6	200	10550
12	Aug-16	7209	2188	15	480	9892
13	Sep-16	1082	8718	24	100	9924
14	Oct-16	2748	8002	14	200	10964
15	Nov-16	5617	5000	7	150	10774
16	Dec-16	8969	7375	1	300	16645
17	**Total**	58033	70556	170	3550	132309

Now try adding another row of data to the table using a different method.

22. Enter the following values:

A18	January 2017
B18	7000
C18	4000
D18	20
E18	200

23. Ensure that cell F17 is **not** the active cell, then position the cursor at the bottom right corner of cell **F17** so that the cursor changes to a ↘.

24. Click and drag the resize handle down to row **18**.

Hint: If the Total row is not activated for this table, the new row would have been automatically added to the table.

4	Month	Sales Inquiries	Service Inquiries	Complaints	Other	Total
5	Jan-16	8947	4799	26	500	14272
6	Feb-16	3643	5658	14	300	9615
7	Mar-16	5861	9739	7	250	15857
8	Apr-16	3741	4429	25	450	8645
9	May-16	4537	5420	19	400	10376
10	Jun-16	3146	1417	12	220	4795
11	Jul-16	2533	7811	6	200	10550
12	Aug-16	7209	2188	15	480	9892
13	Sep-16	1082	8718	24	100	9924
14	Oct-16	2748	8002	14	200	10964
15	Nov-16	5617	5000	7	150	10774
16	Dec-16	8969	7375	1	300	16645
17	Jan-17	7000	4000	20	200	11220
18	**Total**	65033	74556	190	3750	143529

Relational Database Management Systems (RDBMS)

A database application, on the other hand, is designed to handle complex relationships between various items of data, and is correctly referred to as a *relational database management system (RDBMS)*.

Many relational database applications are available on the market. Oracle, SQL Server, MySQL, PostgreSQL, Sybase, IBM DB2, and Microsoft Access are just a few. These programs offer various features and interfaces, but all of them access stored data in a standard manner – through Structured Query Language (SQL).

Structured Query Language (SQL)

Structured Query Language (SQL) is the standard language used to create and work with databases. Once a database has been created, SQL is also used to retrieve and manipulate the data. Any interaction among a user, program and database takes place through the use of SQL.

Even though various RDBMS applications provide their own user interface, SQL is used (often behind the scenes) to create and manage both the database elements themselves and their data.

Connectivity Standards and APIs

Generally speaking, a database is not portable from one RDBMS to another, but different RDBMS can inter-operate using one of the following application programming interface standards:

- **Open Database Connectivity (ODBC)** – a standard programming interface for accessing a number of different databases, including Access, DB2, SQL Server, and MySQL.

- **Java Database Connectivity (JDBC)** – a standard programming interface for accessing Oracle databases, which run on the Java platform.

An *application programming interface (API)* is a set of programming building blocks that specify how software components should interact. There are APIs for operating systems, applications, and web sites.

These interfaces make it possible to connect databases to web pages. Web designers can then use server-side programming languages to build web pages on the fly based on current database content. (You will learn more about this shortly.)

Multiple, Related Tables

Unlike spreadsheet databases which store all the information in a single table, relational databases store data in multiple tables which are related to one another.

Let's consider a database that tracks activities for a gardening supply company. There might be a table that contains customer information, a table that contains order information, a table that contains detail information for each order and a table that contains product information.

Because the data stored in each table is related to data in the other tables of the database, a complete set of information can be retrieved. For example, you could retrieve the complete information for a particular order, as shown in the following figure.

Order Number	First Name	Last Name	Order Date	OrderStatus:
1	Helen	Anderson	2/19/2015	Not Shipped

Item ⌄	Qty ⌄	Description ⌄	Price ⌄	LineTotal ⌄
1	1	Fieldstone stepper garden path	175.5	$175.50
2	2	Garden Hose Vinyl 50 FT	15.25	$30.50
3	2	Rosemary seed, organic	3.68	$7.36
*				

This complete set of information is extracted from the Customers, Orders, OrderItems and InventoryItems tables, as shown in the following figure:

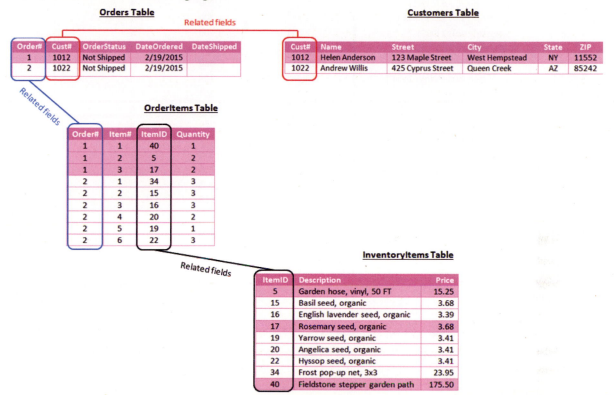

The shaded rows in the figure show that Order #1 was placed by Helen Anderson (Customer #1012) on 2/19/2015. The order includes three line items: one for a garden hose (item #5), one for some rosemary seed (item #17) and one for fieldstones for a garden path (item #40).

Note that each table in the database stores data about a specific type of thing. For example, the Customers table stores information only about customers; it does not include information about orders or inventory. In database terms, the specific type of thing for which data is stored is called an entity. Usually, there is a table for each entity represented in the database.

Database Tables

Objective 2-4.3, 2-4.4

In a database, data is stored in tables.

The data in a table is organized into a series of rows and columns. The following figure shows a portion of a typical Access database table containing product information for items sold by a garden supply shop.

ItemID ▾	Description ▾	UnitPrice ▾	QuantityInStock ▾	VendorID ▾	Click to Add ▾
1	Potting soil 6 Quarts	4.25	1,200	4	
2	Potting soil 12 Quarts	8.25	1,200	4	
3	Potting soil 2 CUFT	12.50	1,200	4	
4	Potting soil 3.8 CUFT	30.25	1,200	4	
5	Garden Hose Vinyl 50 FT	15.25	680	6	
6	Garden Hose Vinyl 100 FT	30.98	127	6	
7	Garden Hose Vinyl 25 FT	9.98	254	6	
8	Garden Hose Rubber 50 FT	23.99	95	6	
9	Garden Hose Rubber 25 FT	15.75	50	6	
10	Garden Hose Rubber 100 FT	42.45	107	6	
11	Watermelon seed, organic	3.10	8,250	1	
12	Red pear seed, organic	3.10	6,750	1	
13	Shelling peas seed, organic	3.10	825	1	
14	Artichoke seed, organic	3.10	738	1	

Field   Record

In a database:

- Each row in a table can be referred to as a *row* or a *record*. In the table shown in the preceding figure, each record contains information about a different products sold by a garden supply shop.

- Each column in a table can be referred to as a *column*, a *field*, or an *attribute*. Each field contains a different type of information, such as item number, description, unit price and so on for each product.

Table Metadata

In a spreadsheet, you can create a table simply by opening a blank workbook and typing. In fact, you can enter any type of text or value into any cell at will. A database table, however, is a different animal.

The structure of a database table must be explicitly defined before you can enter any data. A table's structural definition includes items such as:

- The name of the table – each table within a database must have a unique name

- The name of each field (column) in the table

- The data type of each field (column)

   - The data type determines what type of data the field can contain. Each field can contain only one type of data. If the field is designed to accept text data, only text can be added to the field. If you enter a number into a text field, that number is treated as text (which means that you cannot perform any calculations on such numbers.) If you define a field to accept numeric data, you cannot enter text into that field.

- The size of each field (column)

    - The size determines the range of numeric or date values that can be entered, or determines the maximum number of characters that can be entered in a text field.

The following figure show two views of the same table in Microsoft Access – the left portion shows the defined structure of the table, and the right portion shows the data stored in the defined table structure.

Without this clearly defined structure, the data itself is simply a collection of items presented out of context and without relation to other things. A database table's defined structure helps the user to make sense out of the data, and to understand what the data is.

Because the defined structure of the database table describes the data it holds, the structure is considered metadata. Metadata is simply data that describes other data.

Note: You may have worked with metadata before. Computer files have metadata associated with them in the form of file properties, which you can use to locate a specific document, or a particular image, or a specific version of a program. If you have ever viewed a file's properties in Windows, or added tags to an image on a social media site, you have worked with metadata.

Table metadata (that is, table structure) can be represented by a simple layout called a table schema, which lists the name of the table and the names of each field in the table. Database designers create table schemas while they are planning a database.

Products
ItemID
Description
UnitPrice
QuantityInStock
VendorID

Products
ItemID
Description
UnitPrice
QuantityInStock
VendorID

Once tables are created, many database products can render table schemas to give the database designer an overview of the tables in the database. The following schema is generated in Microsoft Access.

Primary Key

A *primary key* is a field (or a combination of fields) that uniquely identifies each record stored in a table. No two records in a table may be exact duplicates; however, two records may have identical data, other than the primary key.

The primary key, therefore, must be unique and it cannot contain a null value. In a database, null is equivalent to "unknown." *Null* is not the same thing as zero (0).

Assigning a primary key prevents the entry of any record that contains duplicate or null values in the primary key field. When you add a record to a table for which a primary key has been assigned, the RDBMS checks to make sure you have included a value in the primary key field and that the value you entered does not already exist in the primary key field of any other record in the table. When you sketch a table schema, you can indicate the primary key by adding the notation "(PK)" to the right of the field name or by underlining the primary key field. Microsoft Access uses a key icon to the left of the field name to denote a primary key.

Note: A primary key that is comprised of a combination of fields is called a composite key.

The following figure shows schemas for two tables. The Products table has a single field primary key (the ItemID field), and the OrderItems table has a composite primary key (the OrderID field + the LineItem field).

Selecting a Primary Key

Selecting a primary key can be a challenge. Many times a simple numerical value that increments automatically (for example, an "ID" field) is added to a table to serve as the primary key. However, sometimes a table already includes a field that is a natural choice for use as a primary key. For example, in a table that tracked book sales, an ISBN field would be a good choice.

A primary key should:

- be a value that will never change
- be a value that is extremely unlikely to be null

Good choices for primary keys include unique identifiers issued by an organization (such as an Employee ID number or a Student ID number), or an ID field.

Poor choices for primary keys include people's names (as these are likely to be duplicated, and they sometimes change), and Social Security numbers (not everyone has one, and businesses do not like to store them because of the potential liability if they are lost or stolen).

Consider the table shown in the following figure:

Fname	Lname	Suffix	Address	City	State	ZIP
Carl	Henderson		1517 White Plains Road	Bronx	NY	10451
Dennis	Henderson		55 E Delta	Mesa	AZ	85213
Edward	Henderson	Jr.	28974 E Patagonia	El Paso	TX	79901
Mary	Halloran		97 W. Washington	Olympia	WA	98505
Dennis	Henderson		1021 NE 40th Street	Lincoln	NE	68506

Notice that there are two entries for a person named Dennis Henderson. If you looked only at the Fname and Lname fields, the records appear to be duplicates. However, if you look at these fields and the Address field, you can see that the records are not duplicates. It would be possible to use the combination Fname+Lname+Address as a *composite primary key*.

It would also be possible to use the ZIP field as a primary key because right now each entry for a ZIP code is unique.

Neither of these is really a good solution. If we used the ZIP field as a primary key, we would be unable to add a record for another person living in the same ZIP code as any person already listed in the table. Using the combination Fname+Lname+Address field is not a good solution either because people move, and the primary key for a person who relocates would change.

A better solution for this table would be to add an ID field, as shown in the following figure:

ID ▾	Fname ▾	Lname ▾	Suffix ▾	Address ▾	City ▾	State ▾	ZIP ▾	Click to Add ▾
1	Carl	Henderson		1517 White Plains Road	Bronx	NY	10451	
2	Dennis	Henderson		55 E Delta	Mesa	AZ	85213	
3	Edward	Henderson	Jr.	28974 E Patagonia	El Paso	TX	79901	
4	Mary	Halloran		97 W. Washington	Olympia	WA	98505	
5	Dennis	Henderson		1021 NE 40th Street	Lincoln	NE	68506	
*	(New)							

Revised Table B

When you use an ID field as a primary key, you can manually enter the ID number, or you can elect to have the RDBMS create ID numbers automatically. In Microsoft Access you can create ID numbers automatically by setting the ID field's data type property to AutoNumber. A field with an AutoNumber data type is automatically updated with a unique sequential number whenever a record is added to the table. The value in an AutoNumber field cannot be deleted or changed.

Exercise 11-1: Selecting a Key

In this exercise, you will examine table schemas and select an appropriate primary key for each table.

1. What would be a good primary key for the Students table? _____

Students
FirstName
MiddleName
LastName
Address
City
State
ZIP
SocialSecurityNum
StudentID
Grade

2. What would be a good primary key for the Movies table? _____

Movies
Title
Director
Year
Length
MovieID
Producer

Table Relationships – Foreign Keys

The data in a relational database is stored in multiple tables, so naturally, there needs to be a way to bring the data from those separate tables together in a meaningful way. This is accomplished through the defining of table relationships.

Table relationships are defined through the creation and association of foreign keys. A *foreign key* is a column (or combination of columns) in a table that references the primary key in another table. For example, consider the simple scenario of customers and orders. Suppose we have a Customers table, and an Orders table as shown in the following figure:

Customers
CustomerID (PK)
FirstName
LastName
Street
City
State
ZIP
Phone

A one-to-many relationship exists naturally between customers and orders. One customer may place zero, one, or many orders; but an order can be placed by only one customer.

The way the tables are configured right now, there is no way to keep track of which customer places an order. We want to be able to trace an order back to the customer who placed it.

Orders
OrderID
OrderStatus
DateOrdered
DateShipped

The best way to keep track of which customer places an order is to create a field that is common in both tables.

In the Orders table, this common field will become a foreign key when we create a relationship between the tables.

Orders
OrderID
CustomerID *(fk)*
OrderStatus
DateOrdered
DateShipped

Here we see a revised design of the Orders table: it now includes a field named CustomerID. This is the common field – it exists in both tables.

In the Customers table, the CustomerID field is the primary key (denoted by (PK) in the diagram. In the Orders table, the CustomerID field will become the foreign key when a relationship is created between the two tables. The foreign key is denoted by (fk) in the diagram.

Customers
CustomerID (PK)
FirstName
LastName
Street
City
State
ZIP
Phone

Once the common field is added to the Orders table, you can create a relationship between the two tables.

In Access, you can open a special window called the Relationships window and drag the primary key field from the Customers table onto the common field in the Orders table and Access will create the relationship.

Behind the scenes, SQL adds a constraint that will not allow you to add a record to the Orders table if the value in the foreign key field does not match a value in the primary key field of a record in the Customers table.

It is as this point that the CustomerID field in the Orders table becomes a foreign key.

Orders
OrderID
CustomerID *(fk)*
OrderStatus
DateOrdered
DateShipped

That is, when you create a record for a new order, the value that you enter in the CustomerID field in the Orders table must reference a record that already exists in the Customers table.

You cannot create an order for a customer who does not exist.

The following figure shows the data in the Customers table and the Orders table. In the Customers table, the CustomerID field is the primary key and it uniquely identifies each customer; however, in the Orders table, the CustomerID field is a foreign key and is used to refer to a specific customer in the Customers table. Note that the primary key to which a foreign key maps is also known as a *parent* key.

Primary Key (parent key)

Customers

CustomerID	FirstName	LastName	Street	City
1012	Helen	Anderson	123 Maple Street	West Hempst
1022	Andrew	Willis	425 Cyprus Street	Queen Creek
1030	Alice	Goldman	78 West Elm	Mesa
1034	Robert	Meyers	29 River Street	Mesa
1035	Anna	Billings	516 E Chessman Ave	Wantaugh
1042	Sarah	Armstrong	256 W Delaware Ave	Island Park
1044	Melissa	Sharon	1517 Hillsdale Lane	Flagstaff

Foreign Key (child

Orders

OrderID	CustomerID	OrderStatus	DateOrder
1	1012	Not Shipped	2/19/
2	1022	Not Shipped	1/24/
3	1030	Not Shipped	3/17/
4	1034	Not Shipped	5/13/
5	1035	Not Shipped	7/20/
6	1042	Not Shipped	9/19/

The line drawn between the two tables represents the relationship between the two tables. Note that the line is drawn connecting the common fields. Often, the common fields have the same field name, but that is not a requirement. However, common fields must have the same data type.

When you create relationships between tables, you can view and work with data stored in multiple tables. For example, you can view customer and order information contained in two different tables to see which customer placed a particular order. The related tables shown in the figure indicate that in order 1, customer number 1012, Helen Anderson, placed an order on February 19th.

Relationship Types

There are three types of relationships that can be established between tables:

One-to-One	A relationship in which each record in Table A can have only one matching record in Table B, and vice versa. This type of relationship is not very common.
One-to-Many	A relationship in which a record in Table A can have many matching records in Table B, but a record in Table B has only one matching record in Table A. The relationship is established between the primary key in Table A and the foreign key in Table B.
Many-to-Many	A relationship in which one record in Table A or Table B can be related to many matching records in the other table. For example, suppose a database contains data about students and classes. Each student can be enrolled in several classes, and each class can have many students. This is a many-to-many relationship. Relational databases cannot directly handle many-to-many relationships, and these must be replaced by multiple one-to-many relationships.

Database Metadata (Database Schema)

Earlier, you examined table metadata. However, there is also metadata for the entire database – the database schema.

The *database schema* represents a logical view of the entire database. It defines how the data is organized and how the tables within the database are related to one another.

You can represent relationships in a database schema by drawing lines between the key fields in the related tables. The primary key of each table should be denoted either by an underlined field name or a representative icon.

You represent the "one" side of a one-to-many relationship by drawing a 1 beside the parent key, and you represent the "many" side of a one-to-many relationship by drawing an infinity symbol (∞) beside the foreign key.

The following figure shows a schema (generated in Microsoft Access) for a database with four tables.

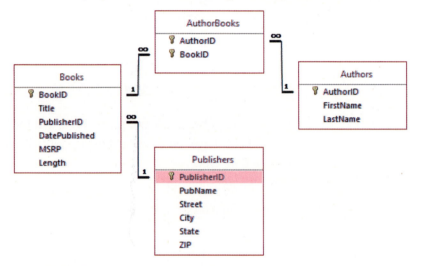

The database schema in the preceding figure describes the following relationships:

- There is a one-to-many relationship between the Publishers table and the Books table (based on the PublisherID field).

- There is a one-to-many relationship between the Books table and the AuthorBooks table (based on the BookID field).

- There is a one-to-many relationship between the Authors table and the AuthorBooks table (based on the AuthorID field).

Notice that the AuthorBooks table is related to both the Books table and the Authors table. These two one-to-many relationships support the many-to-many relationship between books and authors: one author can write many books, and a book can have many (that is, more than one) authors.

Exercise 11-2: Reading Schemas

In this exercise, you will examine a database schema and answer a series of questions about the database it describes.

Consider the following database schema:

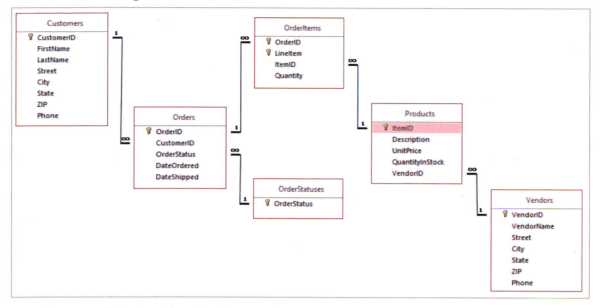

1. What type of relationship exists between the Customers table and the Orders table?

    _____

2. What type of relationship exists between the Orders table and the Products table?

    _____

3. What is the foreign key in the Products table?

    _____

4. Which table has a composite primary key?

    _____

5. What are the two foreign keys in the Orders table? _____ and _____

Database Queries

Objective 2-4.3

You use queries to view specific data in one or more database tables. A query asks a question of a table, such as "Which customers live in Arizona?" and selects records from the table which answer the question. The selected records are displayed in a result set.

To change the magnification for the presentation, use one of the following:

- On the far right of the status bar, click the button on either side of the zoom slider bar to zoom in or out by 10% at a time; or

— |——————|———— +

- click the 100% (**Zoom Level**) button to select a specific size or zoom percentage; or

| Zoom | ? | X |

Zoom to

- ◉ Fit   Percent: [72% ⬍]
- ○ 400%
- ○ 200%
- ○ 100%
- ○ 66%
- ○ 50%
- ○ 33%

[OK]   [Cancel]

- click the ⊞ (**Fit slide to current window**) button to quickly maximize the size of the slide on the screen from its previous zoom percentage.

Exercise 12-1: Travel

In this exercise you will create new presentations, open existing presentations, make changes and then save the changes.

1. Start Microsoft PowerPoint, if necessary. Then click **Blank Presentation** to create a new blank presentation.

2. In the Slide pane, click in the first placeholder and type: Travel has no age! and then press CTRL+ENTER to move to the sub-title placeholder.

   The text you just entered should appear in the placeholder for the main title of the presentation.

3. In the sub-title placeholder, type: Lucy Lee for the text, and then click anywhere away from the placeholder.

You will now enter text for the next few slides.

4. On the Home tab, in the Slides group, click **New Slide** to insert a new Title and Content slide.

5. Type: Agenda as the title of this slide. Press CTRL+ENTER and type the points for the agenda, as shown in the following:

   - Introduction
   - Picking a destination
   - Looking at all options
   - Going on my own or in a group
   - Using a Travel Consultant

6. Press ENTER after the last bullet point and then press TAB to tell PowerPoint you want to enter text at a sub-level for the last bullet point entered.

7. Type: Advantages and disadvantages and press ENTER.

   PowerPoint keeps you at the same level as this sub-text.

8. Type: Cost differences and press ENTER.

9. Press SHIFT+TAB to move up one level so the text for the upcoming bullet point is at the main level.

10. Type: Preparing for the Trip.

11. On the Quick Access toolbar, click  (**Save**). Click **This PC** as the location, navigate to the student data files location and then click the **PowerPoint** folder. Click in the file name field, type: Travel has no age - Student (insert your initials or name in place of "Student") and click **Save**.

Now create a new presentation using a template provided in PowerPoint.

12. Click the **File** tab and then click **New**. In the search field, type: certificates and press ENTER.

13. Click the **Certificate, Employee of the month (blue chain design)** and then click **Create**.

    If this template is not available, choose a certificate from the choices available on your system. It isn't important which certificate you use; the focus here is seeing how PowerPoint provides some pre-designed templates you can use to enter data as required.

You are now ready to save the file with a new name and make changes to the presentation.

14. Press CTRL+S to save the presentation. Click **This PC** as the location and then click or navigate to the **PowerPoint** folder. Type: Green Soles Certificate - Student as the new name and then click **Save**.

15. In the Slide pane, select the **Raffaella Bonaldi** text and type: Irma Greenwood.

16. Select the date and type in today's date. Save the certificate again.

Now look at the various ways you can close a presentation.

17. Press CTRL+N to create a new blank presentation.

18. Point at the PowerPoint icon on the Windows taskbar.

    You should have at least three preview windows, one for each open presentation (the number of windows may vary depending on how many presentations you have open or created during this exercise).

19. In the window with the blank presentation created in step 17, click the **Close** button.

When the border around a placeholder is a solid line, you are in *Select* mode and can affect the entire contents of the object. To activate Select mode quickly, position the mouse pointer on one of the borders of the placeholder, and then click when you see ⁺⊹ (mouse pointer with four-headed arrow).

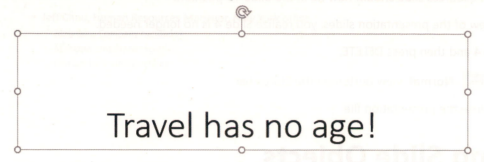

Travel has no age!

- To select multiple placeholders, click the first placeholder and press SHIFT or CTRL as you click to select other placeholders.

Manipulating Text

PowerPoint provides many ways to manipulate or edit selected text or placeholders, including inserting additional text or deleting existing text.

- To insert text, click in the placeholder to display the blinking insertion point and then move to where you want to enter the new text and start typing.

- To delete text, use BACKSPACE or DELETE.

Occasionally you may want to insert text into your presentation from another presentation, or from another location in the current presentation. Instead of retyping the information, you can use the Cut, Copy, and Paste commands.

- To cut or move an item, select the item first and then on the Home tab, in the Clipboard group, click ✂ Cut.

- To copy an item, first select the item and then on the Home tab, in the Clipboard group, click 🗐 Copy.

- To paste an item, first place the insertion point where you want to paste the item and then on the Home tab, in the Clipboard group, click **Paste**.

Key Fact: You can also press CTRL+X to cut an item, CTRL+C to copy an item, or CTRL+V to paste the item. These keys are commonly used in other applications.

PowerPoint uses the Clipboard to temporarily store any cut or copied items such as text or graphics, and you can paste wherever you choose. To display the Clipboard task pane, on the Home tab, in the Clipboard group, click the **Clipboard** dialog box launcher.

Checking the Spelling

The Spelling feature in PowerPoint provides various options when checking for spelling errors, including custom dictionaries for special terms.

The Spelling feature works in the background to check for spelling mistakes as you type. When PowerPoint detects a mistake, a wavy red line displays underneath the text. You can correct the mistakes immediately, or wait until you are finished creating the presentation.

PowerPoint also displays proofing icons at the left on the status bar to indicate when PowerPoint detects no errors (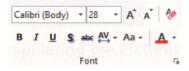) and when it detects a possible spelling error ( ).

To perform a manual spell check on the entire presentation, press F7.

Note: Remember that performing a spell check assures only the accuracy of the spelling in your slides; you should still proofread your presentation to ensure you are using the correct words.

Formatting Text

Formatting refers to the process of changing the appearance and position of objects on a slide.

Font – Describes the typeface of characters on the screen and in print such as `Courier New` or *Bradley*.

Font Size – Refers to the height of the characters (as characters get taller, they also grow wider.)

Character Formatting – Refers to the special stylized variations applied to plain characters to make them stand out from other text. They include bold, italics, and various kinds of underlines.

Effects – Apply special effects to the text, such as ~~strikethrough~~, superscript or subscript, c h a r a c t e r   s p a c i n g, SMALL CAPS, and so on.

The Font group in the Home tab enables quick, easy access to commonly used character formatting options directly from the Ribbon:

The Mini toolbar provides similar access to commonly used formatting options, and provides a mixture of character and paragraph formatting buttons. This toolbar appears only when you select text; once you move the mouse pointer away from the selection, you will need to select the text again to display this toolbar.

Aligning Text

Each built-in slide layout aligns text according to defaults set for that layout. Occasionally, you may want to change text alignment. To change the alignment, on the Home tab, in the Paragraph group, click the appropriate alignment option.

Inserting Media Objects

One advantage of using presentations is the ability to include multimedia files such as videos, music, or links to Web pages that provide more information. To insert a media file, on the Insert tab, in the Media group, click **Video** or **Audio**.

Hint: you can also click the **Insert Video** icon in a slide layout that contains icons for content.

Once you insert the media file, a new ribbon (Video Tools or Audio Tools) appears with two tabs for you to manipulate the video or audio file.

Exercise 12-3: Destress Your Day

In this exercise, you will open a presentation to insert and modify some pictures on the slides. You will also apply some formatting options to the presentation.

1. Open **De-stress your Day** from the data files location, and save it as De-stress your Day – Student.

2. Click slide **2** in the Slide Thumbnails pane.

3. Click the **Insert** tab and in the Images group, click **Online Pictures**.

4. In the Bing search field, type: stress and press ENTER.

5. Scroll through the list of pictures and then click one of your choice.

6. Click **Insert** to add the picture to the slide. If a Design Ideas task pane appears at the right, close it.

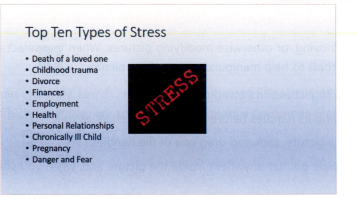

7. Point at one of the corner handles until you see the diagonal arrow, press SHIFT and then drag inwards to resize the picture to approximately 1.0" (2.5 cm) larger than its original size. (If your picture is big, drag inwards to make it a smaller.)

8. Point anywhere in the picture and then drag the picture to the right of the bullet list points.

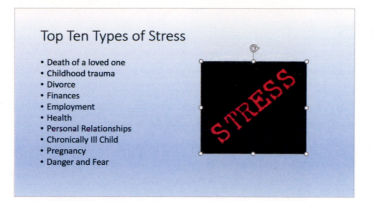

9. Make sure the picture is selected and on the **Format** tab, in the Size group, click the arrow for Crop and then click **Crop to Shape**.

10. In the Basic Shapes area, click **Plaque**.

11. Click slide **4**. On the Insert tab, in the Media group, click **Audio** and then click **Audio on My PC**. Navigate to the PowerPoint folder within the student data files and then insert the **Slowed_Breathing** file.

12. Close the Design Ideas pane if necessary. Drag the sound icon to the end of the Take deep breaths ... bullet point. Resize the icon so that it is approximately the same height as the text on this line.

13. With the sound icon still selected, click the **Format** tab on the Audio Tools ribbon and click **Color**. Click **Blue, Accent color 5 Dark** so the icon is noticeable but not obvious.

14. Save the presentation and then close it.

Animating Objects

Objective 2-5.4

You can animate objects and text to increase the effectiveness of your slide shows. You can also customize how the text, objects, and graphics enter (or become visible) when the slide displays, or how they exit (disappear from view). You can also use animation to emphasize objects on the slide.

To add animation, on the Animations tab, in the Animation group, click **More** to display the Animation Gallery. After applying an animation, you can choose how the animation will make its entrance or exit, and you can add special effects to add emphasis.

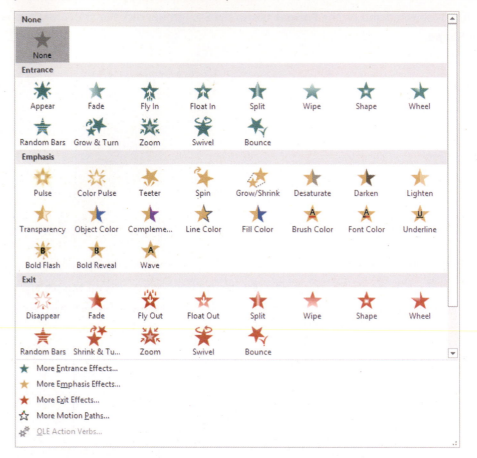

Once you choose an animation, you can set specific options for the animation using the **Timing** group:

Try to be consistent in the number and style of animation schemes used on the slides. Consider your audience and choose the speed and effects accordingly. Too many variations can be distracting. Remember that you may want to keep some elements, such as titles, static during the show to provide a focal point for your audience.

Customizing the Animation

You can adjust or customize how animation will occur during the presentation, as well as the speed and direction of animations, and the order in which text or objects appear on the slide. For instance, you may want the bullet points to appear one bullet at a time so your audience does not focus on the other text on your slide. You can also set an item to dim after it appears on the slide.

To customize the animation, on the Animations tab, in the Advanced Animation group, click **Animation Pane**. As you select each element to be animated, PowerPoint provides options that control when or how the element will appear.

Be sure to check the speed and timing of each animation, and play it to be sure it works well.

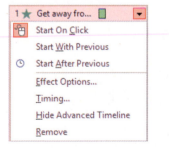

As you apply animation to elements on a slide, PowerPoint places numbered boxes on the slide to indicate the order in which the items will appear; the Animation Pane will also list the animations in numeric order.

You can rearrange the elements by using the ▲ or ▼ **Re-Order** arrows near the top of the pane; alternatively, you can drag an item to the required location. The numbers for the animations on the slide automatically reset themselves accordingly.

You can customize animation using the **Effect Options** commands for each animation type. The number or types of effects vary with the **Effect** command chosen. Be sure to test each animation prior to setting up for final presentation.

When you no longer want or need an animation, remove it from the Animation Pane list.

Animation options and effects vary from one animation to another. Use care when adding animation and effects; and always play or preview all the animations on your slides to be sure they appear in the proper order and that they remain visually appealing and are not overwhelming. Proper preview and preparation are important whether you animate all or only some of the elements on your slides.

Applying Slide Transitions

Slide transitions are special effects that you can apply as you move from one slide to the next during a slide show. Try to be consistent in the type of transitions you use between specific types of slides (such as bulleted lists or charts), as too much variation can distract your audience.

To apply a slide transition, on the Transitions tab, in the Transition to This Slide group, click **More** to display all transition styles in the gallery.

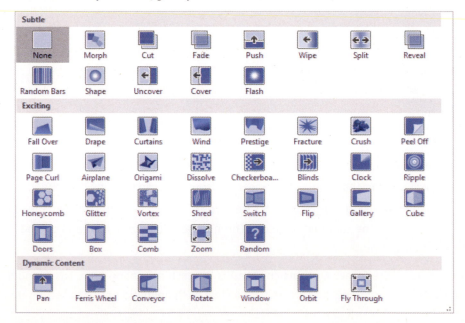

You can then point at a transition to preview it for the current slide. You can customize the transitions by adding sound or changing the speed. You can apply a transition to one slide only or to all the slides in the presentation.

You can use the options in the **Timing** group on the Transitions tab to apply the currently selected transition to all of the slides in the presentation.

You can also use the options here to specify how your slides should advance. For example, will a speaker present the show and click to advance to each new slide, or will the slices advance automatically after displaying for a specific amount of time such as for self-paced training purposes, or to capture the interest of viewers as they walk by your exhibition booth at a trade show.

Exercise 12-4: Exploring Seattle

In this exercise you will add a variety of animations and transitions to slides and individual objects.

1. Open the **Exploring Seattle Proposal** file and then save it as Exploring Seattle Proposal - Student.

2. Go to **slide 2** and review the contents on this slide.

3. Click the border for the content placeholder. Then click the **Animations** tab, and in the **Animation** gallery, click **Fly In** as the animation style.

4. Click the **Effect Options** button to the right of the gallery and click **From Left**.

5. On the Animations tab, in the Advanced Animation group, click **Animation Pane**.

6. In the Animation Pane, click the arrow for the **Content Placeholder** and click **Effect Options**. Click the **Text Animation** tab and then click the arrow for **Group text**.

This field determines how the bullet points appear on the slide and by which levels. We would like the bullet points to appear one line at a time, regardless of level so we need to choose the lowest level in the contents placeholder.

7. Click **By 4th Level Paragraphs** and then click **OK**.

The preview should confirm each bullet point flying in from the left one at a time.

8. On the slide, click the star graphic. On the Animations tab, in the Animation gallery, click **Fly In**. Click **Effect Options** and then click **From Left**.

The graphic should now fly in from the left during the preview. However, look at the numbers at the left of the contents placeholder. These numbers confirm the order the items will appear.

1. ○ Very successful in New York and London
2. ○ Set up for Seattle exclusively
3.   ○ Categorize by food type or location
4.   ○ Determine if there is a demand here also
5.   ○ Very popular tour in Canada
6.   10 ⭐ means popular place
7.   ○ Check tourism for stats on interests
8. ○ Contact restaurant owners
9.   ○ Special groups or tours

9. In the Animation Pane, click the expansion double arrow below the **Contents Placeholder** animation to expand the list of animations on the slide.

```
1 ★ Very successf... ▢
2 ★ Set up for Sea... ▢
3 ★ Categorize by... ▢
4 ★ Determine if t... ▢
5 ★ Very popular t... ▢
6 ★    means pop... ▢
7 ★ Check touris... ▢
8 ★ Contact resta... ▢
9 ★ Special group... ▢
   ≈
10 ★ Picture 2    ▢  ▼
```

10. Click the **Picture 2** item (if not already selected) and then click the **Up** re-order arrow near the top of the Animation Pane until it appears after the bullet point starting with *Very popular ...*

```
5 ★ Very popular t... ▢
6 ★ Picture 2    ▢    ▼
7 ★    means pop... ▢
8 ★ Check touris... ▢
```

As you watch the preview play, you should notice the star appears for the line appropriately but it still appears before the text. You want to change this to occur at the same time as the text.

11. In the Animation Pane, click the *means popular* text, then click the arrow for the *means popular* text and click **Start: With Previous**. Click item# **5** (Very popular ...) and then click **Play From** to watch the preview. Now the star comes in with the text.

Now change the entrance speed of the bulleted text content.

12. In the Animation Pane, click the **double arrow** to hide the individual parts of the Content Placeholder. Then click the arrow for the **Content Placeholder** and click **Timing**.

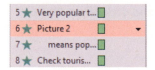

13. Click the arrow for **Duration** and then click **1 seconds (Fast)**. Click **OK**.

Note: Be sure to test the timing set for each slide; what you consider to be enough time may be too fast (or too slow) based on the amount of information on each slide.

14. Go back to slide 1. Click the **Transitions** tab and then in the Transition to This Slide gallery, click different transition styles. Then click **Push**. Click **Effect Options** and then click **From Top**.

15. Switch to Slide Sorter view. Click the star icon at the lower right corner below Slide 1 to view the transition applied to this slide.

16. Click the star icon for Slide 2 to view the animation.

You will now add transitions in Slide Sorter view.

17. Click **Slide 2**, then on the Transitions tab, in the Transition to This Slide gallery, click **Split**.

18. Click **Slide 3**, press and hold SHIFT, then click **Slide 7** to select all the remaining slides in the presentation, click the **Peel Off** transition to apply it to all selected slides. Set the duration to 1.5 seconds

19. Click **Slide 4** and change the transition to **Fracture**.

20. Double-click **Slide 1** to return to Normal view.

21. Close the Animation Pane. Then save and close the presentation when done.

Setting up Slide Shows

Objective 2-5.2

You can set up options for how the presentation will appear before or after you create your presentation. To set up options for your slide show, on the Slide Show tab, in the Set Up group, click **Set Up Slide Show**.

Use the options here to specify how you want to deliver your presentation, such as with a speaker, run on a computer at your booth, or in a window within a Web browser. You can also configure the presentation to support multiple monitors.

Viewing the Slide Show

To start a slide show, click ▭ (**Slide Show**) from the view buttons in the status bar.

The slide show displays in full screen mode. By default, at the end of the slide show, PowerPoint displays a black screen with the message "End of slide show, click to exit" at the top, indicating that the slide show has ended.

When running a slide show, you can set PowerPoint to advance the slides automatically at set time intervals, or you can advance the slides manually. To advance slides manually, click to move to the next slide or to display bullets points or objects on the slide.

To present a slideshow on another monitor or on a projector, you must consider both hardware components and software settings.

Hardware Considerations

Video Cables	Ensure you have the correct cable to connect from the video output port on your computer to the video input port on the second monitor or the projector or HD television. Most devices support VGA and either DVI or HDMI.
	If your devices do not have a port in common, or if both devices use the same technology but require different sized connectors be sure to bring an adapter so that you can adapt the video output to the receiving device.
Audio Cables	If your slide show includes embedded sound or video, you must ensure that the sound will be played back clearly and at a sufficient volume. If you are using an HDMI connection, and you are sending output to a projection device that includes speakers, such as an HD TV, then both picture and audio can be sent via the HDMI cable.
	If you are using a VGA cable, then you must send audio signals to the projection device separately using standard audio cables with connectors that will match the audio input ports on the projection device.
	If you are presenting your slide show on a projection device that does not include speakers, then you must ensure that your own device has sufficient sound output, or you can attach good quality speakers to your computer.
	If you will need to amplify your own voice as you deliver your presentation, you will need a microphone that can connect to an amplifier and speakers.

The following figures show an HDMI cable, a standard-to-mini HDMI adapter, and a standard audio cable with 3.5 mm connectors.

Note that when you connect your computer to an external display, the operating system will detect the additional hardware. You will need to specify to the operating system whether you want to mirror your desktop on the external display or extend your desktop across both displays. For details on configuring an external display, see Computing Fundamentals, Lesson 2, Connecting Peripherals.

Using Presenter View

To display a slideshow on another monitor or projection device, do one of the following:

- On the Slide Show tab, in the Set Up group, click **Set Up Slide Show**, then click the arrow for **Slide show monitor** and select the appropriate monitor, and click **OK**.

- on the Slide Show tab, in the Monitors group, click the arrow for **Monitor**, and select the appropriate monitor.

When you run the slide show, it will appear in full screen on another monitor (or projection device) while your primary monitor stays in PowerPoint mode.

If you turn on **Use Presenter View** with your secondary monitor, your primary monitor will change from PowerPoint display mode to the view shown in the following figure when you run the slide show:

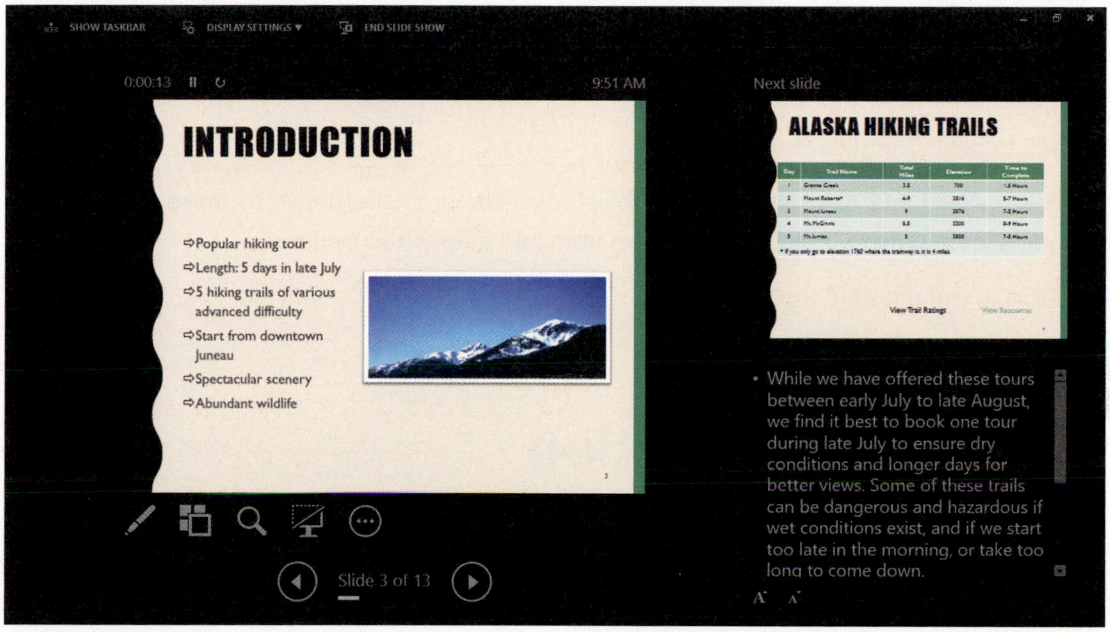

Notice the icons below the slide that you can use as the presenter rather than trying to find the icon at the lower right of the monitor that the audience is viewing. This view is very useful as it shows you the contents of the current slide as well as the contents of the next slide so you can see the flow of the presentation, or make adjustments as questions from the audience arise.

Another benefit of using this view is that you can see the speaker notes on the current slide and can adjust the font size of the notes using the buttons at the lower left.

To stop the slide show at any point, press ESC.

Exercise 12-5: Alaska Hiking

In this exercise, you will run a presentation as a slide show, review content and animation flow.

1. Open the **Alaska Hiking Tours** file and save it as Alaska Hiking Tours - Student.

First, ensure that you are not using Presenter view.

2. Click the **Slide Show** tab, then in the Monitors group, clear the **Use Presenter View** check box if necessary.

3. Press F5 to go into Slide Show view and then click to view the contents of several slides.

4. Point at the lower left corner to see the navigation tools and click the arrow buttons to move from one slide to another.

5. Click the ✐ **Pen** button and choose a pen style. You can use this tool to annotate your slides while you are presenting a slide show. Try to write or highlight something on the current slide, or move to another slide to use the pen.

6. When you are done viewing the slide show, press ESC to return to Normal view for PowerPoint. Note that you may need to press ESC twice and that you will be prompted to save or discard any screen annotations. Discard any annotations.

The presentation was originally set up to be delivered by a speaker. Suppose you are now asked to set up this presentation on the company Web site and allow people to view it on their own.

7. Click the **Slide Show** tab, and in the Set Up group, click **Set Up Slide Show**.

8. In the Show type area, click **Browsed by an individual (window)** and then click **OK**.

9. Press F5 to begin the slide show.

10. Use the Previous and Next arrows at the lower right corner of the screen to move from one slide to another. Click anywhere on the slide to move from one slide to the next slide.

11. Press ESC to exit the slide show view.

12. Save and close the presentation.

Sharing the Presentation

Objective 2-5.1

There are a number of ways to share a presentation, and the method you choose depends on what you want to share and who you want to share it with. Because sharing is a file management task, it is accomplished using either the Share tab or the Export tab in the Backstage view.

Using the Share Tab

Use the options on the Share tab to share your presentation as a whole.

From the Share tab, you can:

- Save your presentation to a cloud location and then provide access to others.

- Send your presentation as an email attachment.

  - You can attach your presentation as a presentation file, a PDF document, an XPS file (which can be viewed, but not edited, in an XPS viewer).

  - You can also elect to send the presentation as fax transmission over the Internet.

- Present your presentation online in a video conference using Skype for Business.

- Publish the presentation slides to your organization's SharePoint site or slide library.

- Send the presentation file as an attachment in an instant message.

Using the Export Tab

Use the options on the Export tab to generate presentation output in other file formats.

From the Export tab, you can:

- Create a PDF or XPS document. In contrast to simply dumping the output of the entire presentation into a PDF file that will be attached to an email (you do this on the Share tab), when you create a PDF/XPS from the Export tab, you can specify which slides to include, whether to include comments and ink markup, whether to include document properties, and whether to frame slides in the output.

- Save the presentation as an MP4 video file that can be played back on a variety of personal devices. You can burn the video to a disc, upload it to a web site, or email it as an attachment.

- Save the presentation and all the objects (fonts, videos, sounds, linked files) embedded within it into a package that can be burned onto a CD. A presentation package can be played back on most computers, even if PowerPoint is not installed.

- Create handouts in Word. Handouts include pictures of slides and text notes which are exported to a Word document. You can control the layout of the output, and you can opt to generate an outline of the presentation using the Outline only option.

- Change the file type of your presentation. You can save the presentation as:
  - One of several presentation file types (PowerPoint 97-2003 Presentation, PowerPoint Template, PowerPoint Show, or PowerPoint Picture Presentation).
  - A series of image files (PNG or JPEG) suitable for printing or displaying on a web site.
  - Another file type. Selecting this option opens the Save As dialog box, from which you can select an option in the Save as type drop-down list.

Note: Always remember to preview and proof your presentation before sharing.

Create Handouts in Word

Handouts are documents audience members can take with them after viewing a presentation. Because PowerPoint creates handouts in Word, you can edit and format them. To create handouts, click the **File** tab, click **Export**, and then click **Create Handouts**.

Click **Create Handouts** to view the options for creating the Word document.

You can select a layout, and specify how you want the slides inserted into the Word document. Select Paste to insert the slides themselves. If you select Paste link, then you would also need the original PowerPoint presentation in order to see the slides in the Word document. Once the handout document is created, the Word icon will flash in the Windows taskbar; you must save the Word file if you want to keep it.

Publishing the Presentation

If your organization or company uses SharePoint or another network storage system that provides a central location for employees or members to store and share files, you can publish your presentation slides.

When you publish slides, PowerPoint saves each slide as an individual file. PowerPoint automatically names each slide file with the presentation file name and a number, such as Exploring Seattle Proposal_004. This can be helpful when you need to find a particular slide. You can change the file name in the File Name column of the Publish Slides dialog box.

You can reuse published slides in multiple presentations; for example, you may want to reuse a slide with your company mission statement, organization structure, or contact information.

To publish a presentation, on the File tab, click **Share**. In the Share panel, click **Publish Slides** and then click the **Publish Slides** button.

Publish Slides

Publish slides to a slide library or a SharePoint site

- Store slides in a shared location for other people to use
- Track and review changes
- See the latest version
- Receive emails when changes are made

Publish
Slides

Within the Publish Slides dialog box, select the slides you want to publish and then specify a location for the slides to be stored. You can publish directly to a shared location, or publish to a local location and then move the published files to a shared location later.

Printing the Slides

You can print the slides in the presentation in various ways, such as one or more slides per page, as handouts, in a format that includes notes, grayscale, and so on. These methods can be selected using the print options.

Exercise 12-6: Exploring Seattle File Formats

In this exercise you will create handouts for a presentation and you will publish slides for upload to the company intranet. You will also export the file to different formats.

1. Open **Exploring Seattle Proposal** from the student data files.

2. Click the **File** tab, click **Export**, and click **Create PDF/XPS Document**. Then click **Create PDF/XPS**.

3. If necessary, click to turn on **Open file after publishing**. Ensure you are in the location of the student data files. Type: `PDF - Student` at the end of the file name and press ENTER. PowerPoint exports the presentation to a PDF and opens a PDF reader app on your system.

4. Scroll in the window that displays the PDF version and then close the window.

Now create an outline that can be used for a formal report.

5. Click **File**, click **Export**, and click **Create Handouts**. Then click **Create Handouts**.

6. Click **Outline only** and click **OK**.

7. Click the flashing **Word** icon on the taskbar.

Notice that although all the slide text is imported into the outline, the hierarchy of topics is not preserved. For example, *Exploring Seattle* and *Expanding the Restaurants Tour* are the title and sub-title text of the first slide, but there is no way to tell that in this version of the outline. Outlines exported to Word require some editing and formatting.

8. Click ▣ (**Save**) on the Quick Access toolbar. Click **This PC** and if necessary, navigate to the **PowerPoint** folder in the student data files location. Click in the file name and type: Exploring Seattle Proposal Outline - Student. Click **Save**. Then close Word.

Now try sharing a document as a PowerPoint show.

9. Click **File**, click **Export**, and click **Change File Type**. Click **PowerPoint Show** and then click **Save As**. Type: Show - Student at the end of the file name and press ENTER.

10. Close the show and exit PowerPoint, and then use File Explorer to navigate to the student data files location, then double-click **Exploring Seattle Proposal Show – Student** to launch the show.

Notice that the show runs independently of PowerPoint.

11. Click the mouse several times to move through the text on the first few slides, then press ESC to close the show.

12. Close the File Explorer window, and restart PowerPoint.

Now try creating a video of the presentation so the slide show can run on its own.

13. Re-open the **Exploring Seattle Proposal** presentation file.

14. Click **File**, click **Export**, click **Create a Video**.

15. Change the number of seconds spent on each slide to **3**. Then click **Create Video**.

16. Navigate to the PowerPoint folder in the student data location. Type: Video - Student at the end of the file name and click **Save**.

17. Once the video has been saved, start File Explorer and navigate to the student data location files for PowerPoint. Double-click **Exploring Seattle Proposal Video – Student**. When the video finishes, close the Movies & TV window.

Now try publishing the slides.

18. Return to PowerPoint, click **File**, click **Share**, click **Publish Slides**, and then click **Publish Slides**.

19. Click **Select All** and then click **Browse**. Navigate to the PowerPoint folder in the student data location and click **Select**.

20. Click **Publish**.

21. Minimize PowerPoint and use File Explorer to navigate to the PowerPoint folder in the student file location to view the various formats that you can use to share this presentation with others.

　　Exploring Seattle Proposal Outline - Student
　　Exploring Seattle Proposal PDF - Student
　　Exploring Seattle Proposal Show - Student
　　Exploring Seattle Proposal Video - Student
　　Exploring Seattle Proposal
　　Exploring Seattle Proposal_001
　　Exploring Seattle Proposal_002
　　Exploring Seattle Proposal_003
　　Exploring Seattle Proposal_004
　　Exploring Seattle Proposal_005
　　Exploring Seattle Proposal_006
　　Exploring Seattle Proposal_007

22. Close File Explorer.

Now look at various print options you can select to print a presentation file.

23. Maximize PowerPoint to the screen and click **slide 1**.

24. Click the **Notes** button on the status bar.

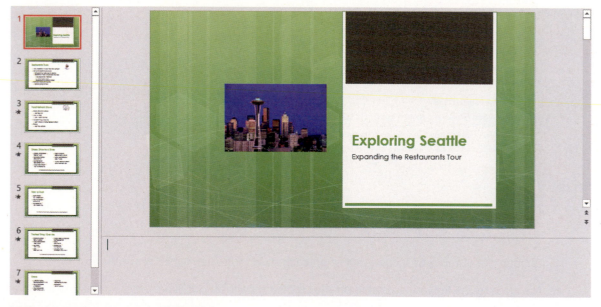

25. In the Notes Pane, type the following:

    The Restaurant Tour introduced last year was very popular with the few local
    restaurants chosen for the pilot. Feedback from customers indicated an interest
    to include some of the places mentioned on the Food Network and getting "group"
    rates and especially, seating.

26. Click **File** and then click **Print**.

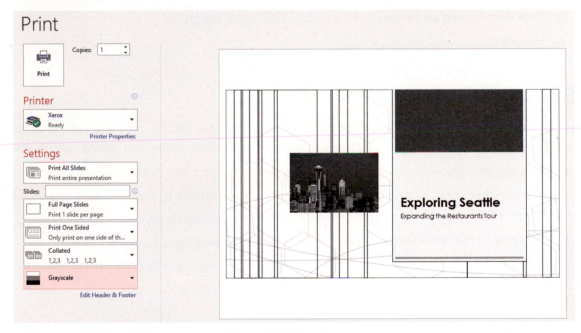

27. Click the **Color** print option and then click **Grayscale**.

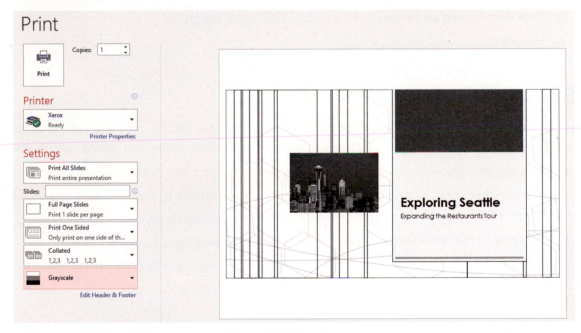

28. Click the **Full Page Slides** option and then click **Notes Pages**.

This print layout option is useful when you want to print a copy of the notes for review. In practical life, you would add more notes to the presentation than was required for this demonstration exercise.

29. Click Print to print all the slides of the presentation using this format.

30. Close the presentation without saving.

Lesson Summary

This lesson taught you how to use PowerPoint to create simple presentations, including adding slides, images, animation and transitions. You also learned how to share PowerPoint elements. You should now be able to:

☑ plan and design a presentation

☑ create, save, close, open, and switch between presentation files

☑ move around in a presentation

☑ change view displays

☑ insert, modify or delete slides

☑ change the layout or order of slides

☑ manipulate text or objects on slides

☑ insert pictures or multimedia objects on slides

☑ animate objects on the slides

☑ apply transitions to slides

☑ share presentations with others

☑ publish slides

Review Questions

1. A typical presentation contains what type of content in the first and second slides?

    a. Title and Introduction   c. Title and Contacts

    b. Title and Agenda   d. Title and Summary

2. Which view appears when you start PowerPoint?

    a. Backstage   c. Read

    b. Edit   d. Normal

3. When might you want to create a new presentation using a template?

    a. To use the slides in an existing presentation where you will simply change the text content where necessary.

    b. To use a predesigned presentation as a guide to what or how the content should be set up in the presentation.

    c. To save a copy of the colors and design used in a template that you can then use for your own requirements.

    d. To start a wizard that will guide you through the creation of a presentation one step at a time.

4. Which view displays the slides in a linear or grid manner?

    a. Normal   c. Slide Sorter

    b. Outline   d. Reading

5. Which slide layout is automatically inserted after a title slide layout?

    a. Title Only   c. Two Content

    b. Title and Content d. Comparison

6. Which option would you use to change the layout of a slide?

    a. New Slide   c. Layout

    b. Insert Slide d. Slide Layout

7. Which view would you use to rearrange the order of slides?

    a. Normal   c. Reading View

    b. Slide Sorter d. Slide Show

8. If you see a dashed line as the border of a text placeholder, which mode are you using?

    a. Edit mode   b. Select mode

9. Which key can you press to activate the spell checker tool for every slide in the presentation?

    a. F1   c. F7

    b. F5   d. F10

10. When searching for online pictures with Bing, what should you consider before clicking the All Images option?

    a. Whether to use actual photographs or clip art images if you are searching for a picture.

    b. The number of objects you can choose from a web search.

    c. Copyright, or who may own the object you want to use from the web search results.

    d. How fast your Internet connection is before activating any searches.

11. Before you can manipulate an image, what must you do first?

    a. You must have cited the source where you found this image.

    b. Ensure the image must be copyrighted to you or your company.

    c. Ensure the image must be a real photograph.

    d. You must select the picture.

12. On which tab would you find the command to include a video or audio file on a slide?

    a. Insert   c. Slide Show

    b. Design   d. View

13. What are the three types of animation effects you can apply to a slide object?

    a. Start, Continue, End

    b. Entrance, Emphasis, Exit

    c. Speed, Duration, Effect

    d. Speed, Timing, Effect

14. Which pane would you use to change or customize the animation of a slide object?

    a. Slide Thumbnails

    b. Notes

    c. Animation

    d. Effects

15. How do slide transitions differ from applying animations?

    a. Animations can be modified whereas transitions are preset features.

    b. Slide transitions affect the entire slide, regardless of the number of slide objects.

    c. You can only add three transitions on a slide but multiple animations for a slide object.

    d. There is no difference unless you use a theme in the presentation.

16. You will be delivering a presentation where an HD television has been set up to project the slides. What type of cable are you likely to need to plug to your computer to show the slides on this television?

    a. HD   c. HDMI

    b. Ethernet   d. Parallel

17. Which command would you use from the File tab if you wanted to turn the presentation into a video?

    a. Save As   c. Export

    b. Share   d. Publish

18. Why might you want to publish a presentation?

    a. To reuse the slides for another presentation.

    b. To save these slides to OneDrive.

    c. To restrict others from making changes to the slides.

    d. To use the slides in a format that can be viewed from a web page.

Lesson 13: Looking at the Internet

Lesson Objectives

In this lesson, you will learn about the nature of the Internet, and about the role and function of web browsers. Upon completion of this lesson, you should be able to:

- describe the nature of the Internet
- describe packets and how they make their way across the Internet
- differentiate between public and private networks
- specify a network location in Windows
- describe the function and characteristics of IP addresses
- understand the Domain Name System (DNS)
- describe domain types
- identify parts of a URL
- differentiate the Internet from the World Wide Web

- describe the role of HTML, CSS, and hyperlinks
- use a web browser
- describe different browsers
- work with browser settings
- describe browser functions and features
- use bookmarks/favorites
- handle pop-ups, cookies, and the browser cache
- understand browser extensions
- describe web site/web page standards

A Connected Community

As you have been making your way through this course, hopefully you have noticed the repeated theme of connectedness. When personal computers were brand new, they were strictly stand-alone devices. But we knew that connecting computers could be useful – and so we created networks. And then on a grand scale, we created the Internet.

At one time, data, phone and cellular networks were separate and distinct. But they are rapidly closing all the gaps and becoming one inter-connected network. Our personal devices – phones, tablets, TVs, and PCs – can connect from almost anywhere, and our world is becoming a connected community.

In this module, you will examine some of the technology that connects us, and consider the advantages, pitfalls, and responsibilities that come with living in a connected world.

Introducing the Internet

Objective 3-1.1

You use the Internet all the time – doing research, playing games, watching videos, or chatting with friends. You type in an address, or click a link, and pages of text, color, images and embedded audio and video files appear on the screen. Where does all the information come from? And how does it reach your computer?

The information you view in your browser comes to your computer through a series of networks. The Internet is a vast global network that functions in much the same way as your school or company network. Hierarchically, the Internet is comprised of many smaller networks which are connected together so that they can communicate and share information.

Backbone

At the core of the Internet is the backbone – a series of redundant, high-speed networks owned and operated by some of the largest long-distance voice carriers (for example, AT&T, Verizon, Sprint, or CenturyLink). Companies that operate networks on the backbone are called Tier 1 providers. Tier 1 provider networks connect with one another at Internet Exchange Points (IXPs) located along the backbone, and high-speed backbone routers keep network traffic moving.

Anyone who wants to access the Internet must ultimately connect to a Tier 1 provider network. Typically, this connection is supplied by a local Internet Service Provider (ISP), such as a cable or DSL company. These local ISPs negotiate with Tier 1 providers for Internet access. Individual consumers and businesses subscribe to their local ISPs (which in turn are connected to Tier 1 providers).

Hardware

Physically, the Internet is a collection of hardware. It consists of wires, routers, switches, microwave links, servers, and communication protocols. The hardware you use in your home LAN or in your school or office LAN is not much different than the hardware that forms the core of the Internet itself.

Packets

In any network, data that is exchanged from one computer to another travels across the network in a unit called a packet. A *packet* is a package of information. It contains address information for both the source computing device (the one that sends the packet) and its intended target or destination device. The addressing information is what makes it possible to deliver a packet from its source to its destination.

In addition to addressing information, a packet also contains a *data payload*. This data payload is the actual information that you want to send from one device to another. For example, a data payload may contain a request for a web page. If a packet is coming back to your computer from a web server, the data payload may contain part of the web page that you requested.

All data that is sent over a network – images, document files, web pages, audio and video files – must be broken down into packets before they can be transported across the network. The larger the file, the longer the process will take.

Routers

When you open a browser, type a URL in the Address bar, and press ENTER your computer breaks the request for a specific web page into packets and sends those packets out onto the network. Your home, school, or work router forwards those packets to your ISP, who forwards them onto the Internet. But how does your packet with the web page request travel across the Internet to get to the target web server?

Routers along the Internet read the addressing information and forward your packet accordingly. That is, your data packet passes from router to router along the Internet (and passes through several interconnecting networks along the way) until it reaches the network where the target web server resides. At the destination, the packets are reassembled into the original data transmission.

A router connects different networks to each other. A router also determines the best path for a transmission to take, and passes that transmission to the next router along the path.

You may be familiar with residential broadband routers, or even enterprise-level routers used in a company or school LAN. Routers all perform the same functions. However, high-speed Internet backbone routers must be powerful enough to handle the enormous amounts of data streaming through the backbone at speeds of gigabits-per-second.

Public Networks

Arguably, the most important thing you should understand about the Internet is that it is a public network. In fact, it is often referred to as "the public network." It is not centrally owned or controlled; it is available for anyone (with a valid IP address and an Internet connection) to access and use. For these reasons, no one can "police" the Internet to protect (or control, or monitor) the people who use it.

Think about all the people around the world who connect to the Internet every day. Any time you connect to the Internet, you can, potentially, connect to anyone else who is connected.

The great thing about the Internet is that any computer can exchange data, email, and programs with any other computer. And the bad thing about the Internet is that any computer can exchange data, email and programs (and also, unfortunately, viruses, Trojans and malware) with any other computer. Being connected can make any system vulnerable to unwanted activity such as eavesdropping or theft of personal information. For this reason, the Internet is also referred to as "the open network" or "the untrusted network."

In network diagrams, the Internet is represented by a cloud because its contents (and its participants) are unknown.

Private Networks

In contrast to the public, untrusted Internet, private networks are considered secure. All systems connected to a private network are trusted.

When you log on to a system that is inside your home, school, or corporate LAN, you have access to the resources connected to the LAN. Depending on your rights and permissions, you can likely access printers, email servers, and documents stored on network file shares. One of the benefits of maintaining a LAN is the ability to share resources.

Many organizations maintain intranets that allow their employees, partners, or students to access LAN resources from outside the LAN. An *intranet* is a private web site; you access it with your browser and you must log in using a valid user name and password. Once you are logged in, you can navigate the intranet web site to access the LAN resources that have been made available.

In Computing Fundamentals, you learned that you can gain access to a LAN from the outside using a Virtual Private Network (VPN) connection. An intranet and VPN serve the same general function – they allow access to the LAN from the outside for users with a valid user name and password.

Once you make a connection (that is, once you are "inside") your system is trusted just as if it were located physically within and connected directly to the LAN.

Specifying a Network Connection Type

The issue of trust becomes a serious one the moment you attach a network cable or join a WLAN. Network administrators use firewalls to keep potentially dangerous traffic out of the LAN. But who protects your system when you are connected to a public network at a public spot, such as at a hotel, or an airport, or a coffee shop?

The Windows operating system includes built-in mechanisms to help protect your system while you are connected to various networks. When you make a network connection for the first time, Windows asks what type of network you are connecting to (and you can change this setting for a connection at any time). You can choose:

Private – if you configure a connection as private, then your computer will automatically "discover" (that is, locate and identify) other computers, devices and content that is accessible on the network. More importantly, it also makes your PC discoverable and allows sharing of folders on your system. This is the appropriate setting for a connection to your or work (or school) network.

Public – if you configure a connection as public, Windows will not allow your PC to be discovered by other systems on the network, and sharing will be disabled. Use this setting for connections to public hotspots.

The connection type is displayed on the Network and Sharing Center page in the Control Panel.

View your basic network information	View your basic network information
View your active networks ———	View your active networks ———
Linksys22452_5Ghz Public network	**Linksys22452_5Ghz** Private network

The connection type is tied to the discoverability of your PC, which you access through the Settings app.

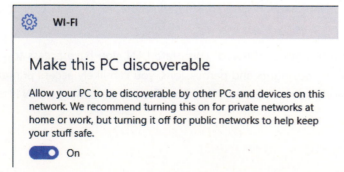

WI-FI

Make this PC discoverable

Allow your PC to be discoverable by other PCs and devices on this network. We recommend turning this on for private networks at home or work, but turning it off for public networks to help keep your stuff safe.

On

To configure a network connection as private:

1. Click **Start**, **Settings**, then click **Network & Internet**.

2. In the left pane, click either **Wi-Fi** or **Ethernet** (as appropriate) to display the current active connection(s).

3. Scroll down and click **Advanced options**.

4. Set the **Make this PC Discoverable** setting on.

Always choose the appropriate type of connection.

Exercise 13-1: Examining your connection type

In this exercise, you will examine your connection type settings.

1. Right-click your network connection icon in the taskbar, then click **Open Network and Sharing Center**.

2. Is your connection public or private? Is this setting what you expected? Why or why not?

3. Close the Control Panel.

Finding Computers on the Internet

Objective 3-1.1

In order for computers connected to a network to communicate with one another, they need to know how to locate each other. That is why each computer connected to a network must have a unique address.

You learned in Computing Fundamentals that this unique network address is called an IP address. When your computer breaks a message into packets and adds addressing information, that addressing information is an IP address.

IP Address Review

In IPv4, an IP address is represented by a grouping of four numbers (each between 0 and 255) separated by periods (or dots). This type of notation is called "dotted quad" notation.

For example, 66.235.120.127 is the IP address for the web server at Ask.com.

Anytime you visit the Ask.com web site, your computer exchanges packets of information with the Ask.com web server. Your computer uses the Ask.com web server's IP address in order to properly address the packets that it sends to the server. Once the addressed packets are sent out onto the Internet, routers guide the packets to the Ask.com web server. Because return address information (that is, your computer's IP address) is included in the packets, the Ask.com web server knows how to properly address the packets that it will return to your computer.

DNS

Have you ever typed an IP address into the address bar of your browser? Chances are you haven't.

Most people type a text-based web site address into the browser address bar. For example, you can visit the Ask.com web site by typing www.ask.com in the browser address bar. Your computer can discover the IP address of the Ask.com web server by querying (asking) a DNS server.

The *Domain Name System (DNS)* is a service that keeps track of the specific IP addresses of web servers around the Internet and maps those IP addresses to the text-based names we enter into the address bars of our browsers. These text-based names are called *domain names*.

DNS resolves text-based domain names into their IP addresses. For example, you can access the Ask.com web server at IP address 66.235.120.127 by typing: *www.ask.com* in your browser's address bar. In other words: 66.235.120.127 = www.ask.com.

Both the domain name and the IP address refer to the same resource, but the domain name is easier to remember. Without DNS, you would need to enter an IP address any time you wanted to access a resource on the Internet.

These mappings are stored in records in a DNS database. Every domain consists of DNS records. A *DNS record* is an entry in a DNS database. The network administrator will create one address record that maps the IP address to the domain name, and usually creates several records for aliases or nicknames that point back to the address record. If you enter an alias as a URL, for example "ask.com" or simply "ask," you can still navigate to the www.ask.com web server.

DNS Servers

The DNS service is made possible through DNS name servers, which are servers on the Internet whose sole function is to resolve domain names into their IP addresses. For example, when you enter a URL such as www.ccilearning.com into your browser's address bar, your computer contacts a domain name server to obtain the IP address related to this domain name. When your computer receives the IP address 160.153.73.246 from the domain name server, it can correctly address a web page request and send it to the web server. When the server responds, the CCI Learning Solutions site displays on the screen.

Note: If a DNS server is unreachable, you will not be able to navigate to a web site by entering its URL in the browser address bar. You can, however, still reach the site if you know its IP address.

Understanding Domain Names

Objective 3-1.1

A typical domain name consists of three labels separated by periods or dots.

www.ccilearning.com

Server Name | Registered Domain Name | Top-level Domain Name

Server Name	Identifies the name of the web server.
Registered Domain Name	Identifies the organization that owns the domain name. Each domain name is unique and is registered with the Internet Corporation for Assigned Names and Numbers (ICANN).
Top-level Domain	Identifies the category of the registered domain name.

Starting from the right, the domain name lists the most general category, then more specifically the company that owns the domain, and then the specific resource within the company that owns the domain. The domain name is like a road-map to a particular resource.

DNS Domain Levels

DNS is arranged into a hierarchy that consists of three levels:

- Root-level domain
- Top-level domains
- Second-level domains

The root-level domain is the top of the hierarchy and contains entries for each top-level domain.

Top-Level Domains (Generic Categories and Countries)

Top-level domains are the highest level domain names of the Internet. Every domain name ends with a top-level domain label.

There are two main groups of top-level domains:

- those that group domains into generic categories (commercial, educational, military, and so on), and
- country code top-level domains which are based on two-character codes signifying country abbreviations.

Generic Top-Level Domains

You can generally determine what type of information a web site contains (or what it is meant to do) simply by reading the generic top-level domain. The original seven generic top-level domains are:

.com	Represents commercial or company sites. Most web sites in this domain sell a service or product, usually through an online store or web page from which you can purchase items directly. The .com domain is considered a generic top-level domain and can be registered by anyone.
.net	Another type of commercial web site. It is generally hosted on a network managed by an Internet Service Provider (ISP).
.edu	Represents an education site created to share information about an academic institution, its curriculum, and other activities. This category may also be associated with research organizations.
.gov	Refers to a site associated with a local, regional, or national government. (Depending on the country, there may be additional levels included in the URL to identify specific areas such as states, municipalities, townships).
.int	Refers to international organizations.
.mil	Refers to military organizations.
.org	Identifies a site dedicated to a non-profit organization that may promote a specific cause such as foundations for heart attack and stroke prevention, or cancer for example.

Additional categories are added as the need arises. Examples include: .aero, .biz, .info, .jobs, .pro, and .travel.

Country Code Top-Level Domains

Other top-level domain names use a two-letter abbreviation and are meant to identify the country in which the web site is hosted; examples include:

au	Australia	**fr**	France	**jp**	Japan
br	Brazil	**il**	Israel	**mx**	Mexico
ca	Canada	**in**	India	**tw**	Tawain
cn	China	**it**	Italy	**uk**	United Kingdom
dk	Denmark				

Second-Level Domains

The second-level domains can be:

- a domain name registered by the company that owns it. *Amazon.com* and *Microsoft.com* are examples of second-level domains.

- categories of the top-level domain. For example, *.co.uk* indicates a commercial business within the United Kingdom, while *.police.uk* is used by UK police forces.

Subdomains

Additionally, second-level domains can be further divided into subdomains. For example, in the following URL: *support.xbox.com*

- **.com** is the top-level domain

- **.xbox** is the second-level domain

- **support** is a subdomain within the xbox second-level domain.

Understanding URLs

Objective 3-1.1

The text-based web site address you type into a browser address bar is called a *Uniform Resource Locator (URL)*. A URL is the global address of a resource on the World Wide Web. A URL consists of two basic parts: a protocol identifier and a domain name. These parts are separated by a colon : and two forward slashes / /.

Protocol identifier

http://www.ccilearning.com

Domain name

Protocol Identifier

Various protocols are used on the Internet to communicate with specific types of servers. The protocol used to request web pages from a web server is *HyperText Transfer Protocol (HTTP)*. Web servers also use HTTP to send web pages to the computers that request them.

Browsers assume that you want to use the http protocol when you enter a web site address. This allows you to simply type: "www.yahoo.com" instead of "http://www.yahoo.com." Some web browsers display the http:// protocol identifier in the address bar and others do not.

There's more than HTTP

Other protocols commonly used in URLs are:

HTTP Secure (HTTPS) – is a protocol used for secure web transactions, such as making purchases over the Internet. The HTTPS protocol allows you to use HTTP over a secure connection. In the past, these connections were secured by a protocol called Secure Sockets Layer (SSL). Today, Transport Layer Security (TLS) is the protocol used to secure the connection. However, TLS is often still referred to as "SSL" and HTTPS is often still referred to as "HTTP over SSL."

File Transfer Protocol (FTP) – used to transfer large files between a user's computer and a special type of server called an FTP server. If you want to use your web browser to access an FTP server to transfer a file, you must specify the ftp protocol in the URL; for example: ftp://aeneas.mit.edu.

Path and Filenames in URLs

Web servers (like any other PC) store files in directories on a hard drive. A URL can also include the path and filename of a specific document or web page stored on a server.

Consider the following URL: http://www.opera.com/browser/tutorials/mail/setup/#account-setup

- **#account-setup** is a web page
- **/browser/tutorials/mail/setup** is the path to the folder on the web server where the page is stored
- **"www"** is the name of the web server
- **opera.com** is the registered domain name of the company that owns the web server
- **.com** indicates that it is a commercial enterprise

What is the World Wide Web?

In our discussion of the Internet, we have made several references to the World Wide Web. While the Internet is a network comprised of hardware connections, the World Wide Web is a system of interlinked documents that are accessible on that network called the Internet.

There are countless millions of documents hosted on web servers – and if you can access a document by typing its address into a web browser, or by clicking a link that takes you to it, that document is part of the World Wide Web.

Documents hosted on web servers are generally referred to as web pages, and web pages usually contain links (called *hyperlinks*) to other pages located on web servers around the Internet. If you have ever visited a web site and clicked a link that took you to another web site (or to another page within the same web site), then you have used a hyperlink. These hyperlinks form the connections that make the World Wide Web possible – web pages around the world are connected to one another by hyperlinks.

What Exactly is a Web Page?

Objective 3-1.1

A web page is a file created with hypertext markup language (HTML). HTML is a special language that web page authors use to add text, hyperlinks, applications, video clips, sound and animation to web pages. A collection of related web pages is called a web site.

When web pages are designed properly, visitors can "point and click" to launch applications, navigate to specific areas of the web site, or visit related web sites – all within a web browser window.

HTML

HTML (the common name for Hypertext Markup Language) is a standardized language used to create web pages. The language is built using HTML elements, which consist of tags enclosed in angle brackets, as used in the "Hello World" HTML document shown in the following figure:

```
<!DOCTYPE html>
<html>
 <head>
  <title>My First Web Page</title>
 </head>
 <body>
  <p>Hello world!</p>
 </body>
</html>
```

Most HTML tags are written in pairs, such as <head> and </head>. The first tag in the pair is called the opening tag, and the second is called the closing tag. (Some tags, called empty elements, are not paired.)

Web browsers can read HTML files and render them into web pages. Browsers do not display the tags, but use them to determine how to represent the content of the page. You may have noticed from looking at the HTML example that the tags describe the structure of the page – there is a head section which can include styles or a web page title, and a body section that can include headings, bullet lists, and paragraphs of body text.

When you view the "Hello World" document in a browser, it appears as shown in the following figure:

HTML also allows images and objects to be embedded in web pages, and for pages to run scripts written in programming and scripting languages such as JavaScript and Perl.

CSS

Today's standard for web page design separates content/structure from presentation. The content and structure are defined in the HTML. Presentational attributes (that is, properties such as font colors, background styles, element alignment, and so on) are defined in *Cascading Style Sheets (CSS)*.

CSS allows web page authors to move presentational styling information into the head section of the HTML document (this is called internal CSS), or to a separate style sheet document (this is called external CSS) that is linked to the HTML document. The web browser reads the HTML document for content and structure, and looks to the style sheet for presentational information. The browser applies the styles defined in the style sheet to the HTML content as it renders the page.

The following figure shows the "Hello Word" document with a CSS paragraph style added to the head section. The opening and closing tags for the style are <style> and </style>.

```
<!DOCTYPE html>
<html>
 <head>
  <title>My First Web Page</title>
<style>
 P {
     font-size: 25px;
     text-align: center;
     color: red;
 }
 </style>
 </head>
 <body>
  <p>Hello world!</p>
 </body>
</html>
```

When you view the modified "Hello World" document in a browser, it appears as shown in the following figure. Notice that the browser applies the style and renders the page accordingly.

Hyperlinks

The World Wide Web is based on a collection of documents which are connected to one another through hyperlinks. You can click a hyperlink in a web page to move to another (connected) web page or to a particular section within the current web page. A hyperlink is a reference to data that is located somewhere other than the present location. A hyperlink can point to a whole document or to a specific element within a document.

Hyperlinks are HTML elements, and are embedded into web pages. Generally, a hyperlink consists of link text (which is the text or image that you click), and a target (which is the destination web page).

In HTML, links are defined with the <a> (anchor) tag and take the following form:

```
<a href= "url">link text</a>
```

The <a> tag is used to create an anchor to link from. The href attribute contains the address (URL) of the document to link to, and the link text is the text that will be displayed as the hyperlink. A sample hyperlink tag is as follows:

```
<a href="http://www.ccilearning.com">Visit CCI Learning</a>.
```

In the sample, "http://www.ccilearning.com" is the URL, and "Visit CCI Learning" is the link text.

Meet the Browser!

Web browsers (or simply, browsers) are software applications that enable users to easily access, view and navigate web pages on the Internet. Browsers allow you to interact with web sites and to experience the amazing rich media that is available on the World Wide Web.

You may be familiar with several browsers, such as Microsoft Edge, Microsoft Internet Explorer, Mozilla Firefox, Google Chrome, Apple Safari and Opera.

While a browser's primary function is to retrieve pages from a web server and display them on your screen, you should understand that browsers are complex software applications that provide a number of services, and they can be configured to suit your working style, and keep you safe while you are online.

Getting Where You Want to Go – The Address Bar

To visit a web page, you enter its URL into the browser address bar and press ENTER. The browser requests the page from the web server, and when it is received, the browser displays the page within the browser window. The address bar displays the URL of the page currently displayed in the browser window. If the web page includes a title, it is displayed in the window tab.

You can visit any web page by typing its URL into the address bar and pressing ENTER.

As you navigate to other pages within a web site (or as you visit pages on other web sites), the URL shown in the address field updates to show the address of the current page. Most browsers maintain a history of URLs that you can access from the address bar. Clicking a URL displayed in the address bar history list has the same effect as entering the URL directly into the address bar.

In addition to displaying the URL, the address bar often includes several buttons. The Internet Explorer address bar is shown here:

b https://www.bing.com/   🔎 ▾ 🔒 ↻

The Internet Explorer address bar includes the following buttons:

Search	You can search directly from the address bar, instead of first accessing a search engine page. Enter your search criteria in the address bar and then click the 🔍 (**Search**) button or press ENTER to view a list of web sites related to your search criteria.
Show Address	Click the ▾ (**Show Address**) button to display a history of the URLs of previously visited web sites.
Security report	Click the 🔒 (**Security report**) button to view digital certificates and encryption information. This button displays only when you are viewing a page over a secure protocol, such as https.
Refresh/Go	Click the ↻ (**Refresh**) button to re-display or refresh the contents of the current web page. The → (**Go to**) button displays in the address bar while you are typing in a web site address. You can click **Go to** instead of pressing ENTER to go to the site.
Stop	Click the ✕ (**Stop**) button to halt the downloading of information for a web page. The Stop button appears only while a page is loading.

Browser Scroll Bars

Browser windows (like other windows you may be used to seeing on a computer screen) support horizontal and vertical scroll bars that display when a window is too small to display all the contents of a web page. The following figure shows a browser window with a vertical scroll bar.

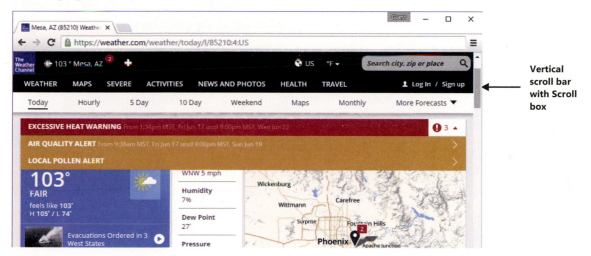

A scroll bar consists of three parts: an arrow button at each end of the bar, a scroll box, and the scroll area. The position of the scroll box within the scroll area provides an approximate gauge of where the information currently displayed in the window is in relation to the entire window's contents.

When you use a scroll bar to view different parts of the window, the action is called scrolling. Use one of the following methods to scroll a window:

- Click in the lighter shaded area above or below the scroll box to scroll up or down.
- Click the arrow at either end of the scroll bar to move up or down.
- Click and hold the mouse button on the arrow at either end to scroll the screen continuously in that direction.
- Drag the scroll box to a specific position in the scroll area to scroll to that location.

Studies have shown that most users do not mind scrolling vertically, but they have a strong dislike for scrolling horizontally. In response, web site designers create pages that use adjustable formats and layouts that respond automatically to changes in the size of the window. As a result, most web pages do not require horizontal scrolling, even though web browsers support horizontal scroll bars.

Standard Windows Control Buttons

Browser windows include the standard Minimize, Maximize/Restore and Close control buttons in the upper-right corner. The control buttons change the way a currently open window displays, as follows:

– (**Minimize**)	Temporarily closes the window, replacing it as a button on the taskbar. Click the button on the taskbar to open or restore the window.
▢ (**Maximize**)	Displays the window full screen.
⧉ (**Restore Down**)	Restores the window to the size it was before it was maximized.
✕ (**Close**)	Closes the window.

You can resize a browser window to any dimensions you as you would any other application window.

Browser Windows (Tabs)

Modern browsers allow for tabbed browsing. That is, you can view different web sites simultaneously – each in its own tab. Opening a new tab is the same as opening a new browser window. Browser tabs are similar to buttons in the Windows taskbar. You can open a separate web page in each tab, and switch between them by simply clicking on the tab. Only one tab can be the active tab at any given time.

Working with multiple open tabs allows you to compare information from different web sites, or copy and paste information from one web page into another.

To create a new tab, use one of the following methods:

* Click the **New tab** button; or
* press CTRL+T; or
* right-click the active tab and then click **New tab**; or
* if the Menu bar is displayed, click **File** and then click **New tab**.

In most browsers, when you open a new tab, the browser displays thumbnails of the sites you visit most often and/or thumbnails of top sites and suggested sites:

You can click a thumbnail to open that site in the active tab.

You can also right-click a tab and select **Duplicate tab** in the menu to open a new tab that displays the same web site. For example, if you are viewing the MSN web site, you could read one article in one tab, open a duplicate tab, and then click a link to view a different article on the MSN site in the other tab.

To view a link on a web page in another tab without leaving the current web page, right-click the link and then click **Open in new tab**. You can then view the contents of two different pages for the same web site.

To close a tab you no longer want to view, click the ✖ (**Close**) button on that tab. If you have multiple tabs open, you can right-click the active tab and specify to close the tab, or to close all the other open tabs.

Depending on the browser and how it has been configured, if you have multiple tabs open, and you click the **Close** button for the browser window, you may be prompted to specify whether you want to close only the current tab or close all the open tabs.

Hyperlinks in the Browser

In the web browser, hyperlinks often display as underlined or colored text. However, hyperlinks are not limited to text; pictures or icons or even specific areas on a graphic can be hyperlinks as well. When you view a web page in a web browser, hyperlinks behave in a specific manner. When you hover the mouse pointer over a hyperlink, the mouse pointer changes to a pointing hand 🖑 icon. When you click a hyperlink, you move to the web page that is designated as the target of that hyperlink. The web page may be part of the same web site, or may be a page on a different web site.

Some web pages contain links that are not readily visible on the screen until you position the mouse pointer over them, but once you see a 🖑, you know that you have found a hyperlink.

Sometimes hyperlinks are configured to open the target web page in the current browser window, while others open a new tab and then display the target web page within the new tab. Web developers also create hyperlinks that will download or copy files from a server onto your computer.

If you return to the anchor page after clicking a hyperlink, the hyperlink often displays in a different color, indicating that it has already been followed.

Popular Browsers

There are a wide variety of browsers freely available. Microsoft Edge, Microsoft Internet Explorer, Google Chrome, Mozilla Firefox, Opera, and Apple Safari are some of the most popular ones. The following images show each of these browsers. Note that although the browsers function in much the same way, a web page may appear a little different in each browser. This is because a browser's coding determines how it interprets the HTML code used to define a web page.

Microsoft Edge

Developed by Microsoft and released with Windows 10, Edge is Microsoft's newest browser interface. More streamlined than its predecessor, Edge features a reading view and minimalist command buttons. Edge's settings are tied in to the Windows 10 Settings app.

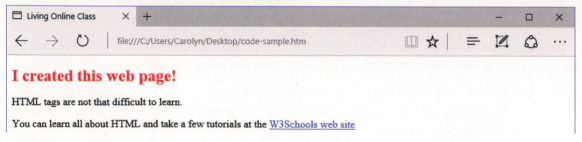

Microsoft Internet Explorer

Developed by Microsoft, Internet Explorer was one of the first graphical web browsers. It has been included with all versions of the Windows operating system since Windows 95. Microsoft Edge is configured as the default browser in Windows 10, but Internet Explorer is included as a Desktop app.

Mozilla Firefox

Firefox was originally developed by Mozilla Corporation and Mozilla Foundation in 2004. It is an open source web browser that is free to download.

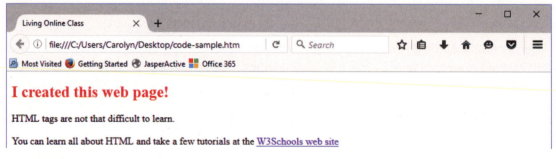

Google Chrome

Chrome was developed and released as a stable product in 2008. It was originally available as freeware although a large portion of its code was released in 2008 as an open source project called Chromium; newer releases of Chrome are based on this version. Note that in Chrome documentation, the address bar is referred to as the "omnibox."

Opera

Opera Software released its web browser as an individual product for download or as part of an Internet suite of products. It is one of the original web browsers introduced in 1994 and now is available for a number of computing devices, including several mobile devices.

Apple Safari

This web browser was originally designed for Apple computers and is the most commonly used one for any Apple computing device. Safari is also available in a Windows version.

Even though the appearance of each is slightly different from the others, all of them include the same features and capabilities.

Browsers and Page Rendering

A browser's job is to read the HTML code, interpret it, and then render the page in your window accordingly. However, not all browsers interpret HTML (and CSS styles) in the same way. Sometimes a web page may appear differently from one browser to the next. Additionally, not all browsers are coded to handle the latest HTML tags. For this reason, certain web page features (for example, floating images or Java) may not function in a particular browser. If you have trouble accessing a particular web site feature, using a different browser may solve the problem.

Additionally, keep in mind that browsers are updated fairly regularly and the default setting is to download and install updates automatically. Sometimes browser updates change the way certain tags are interpreted. You could be visiting a web site that you have used successfully many times in the past, and suddenly encounter a problem caused by a recent browser update. Web designers try to keep on top of issues such as these, and will often re-write certain areas of a web page to remedy a sudden issue. However, you can also try using a different browser.

Exercise 13-2: Using a web browser

This exercise assumes that you have downloaded and installed the Google Chrome web browser, as directed in Lesson 5 of Computing Fundamentals. If you prefer to use a different browser, adjust the steps as necessary. In this exercise, you will open a web browser, enter URLs, follow links, and open and close browser tabs.

1. Open the Google Chrome web browser.

2. In the address bar (or omnibox) type: `www.ccilearning.com` and press ENTER. The browser displays the CCI Learning web site.

3. Click in the address bar to select the current text, then type: `www.yahoo.com` and press ENTER. The browser displays the Yahoo.com web site.

4. Click the scroll box in the vertical scroll bar, then drag down to scroll the page vertically.

Now, open two more tabs.

5. Click **New tab** to open a new browser tab.

6. In the new tab, click in the address bar, type: `www.tolanoadventures.com` and press ENTER to visit the Tolano Adventures web site.

7. Press CTRL+T to open another new tab and type: `www.cnn.com` in the address bar and press ENTER.

8. Click the **Yahoo** tab. The Yahoo page is now the active tab.

9. Click the **Tolano Adventures** tab to make it the active tab.

10. Click the **CNN** tab and then click the **Close** button. You should now have only two tabs open: the Yahoo tab and the Tolano Adventures tab.

11. Click the **Yahoo** tab to make it active.

12. Scroll to the top of the page if necessary, then move the mouse cursor over the list of words that display along the left side of the window. The list begins with the words Mail, News, Sports, and so on.

    Notice that when you hover the mouse cursor over each word, it displays with an underline and the mouse pointer changes to a pointing hand icon identifying the current word as a hyperlink.

13. Click the link for **News** to open the Yahoo News page. Notice the links to various categories for news. There are also links to stories in the middle of the page.

14. Click another link to view one of the stories.

15. Click the Tolano Adventures tab to make it active.

16. Take a few moments to move the mouse cursor around the screen to see if you can find links on the page. The only links on the page are the words – Home, About Us, Services, and Contact Us – which provide navigation in the Tolano Adventures web site. Notice that these links do not appear with underlines, but the mouse pointer still changes when you hover over them. The appearance of links is left to the discretion of the web page author.

17. Position the mouse pointer on the Services link, and then click the link. You are now viewing a list of services that Tolano Adventures provides.

18. Move your cursor to point at the Biking/Cycling Tours link in the list and then click the hyperlink to move to this page to view its contents. As you click each hyperlink, the browser navigates to the web page specified as the target for that link.

19. Click the **Close** button to close the browser window, and specify to close all tabs if prompted.

Browser Navigation Tools

Browsers include navigation tools and features which make them easy to use. These include built-in navigation buttons, configurable settings, a home page, and various toolbars.

Back, Forward, and Refresh Buttons

Although web pages should provide their own navigation tools, every browser includes buttons that allow you to navigate among the sites you visit within any given browser session.

- The Back button moves back one page. The back button becomes active once you click a link or visit a different page by typing a URL in the address bar.

- The Forward button moves ahead one page. The forward button becomes active once you move back one page.

- The Refresh button reloads or re-displays a page. You may want to refresh a page if the content changes continuously, or if part of the page failed to load correctly.

The symbols used for these buttons are fairly universal. The following table illustrates how the buttons appear in various browsers.

Button	Internet Explorer	Edge	Firefox	Chrome	Opera	Safari
Back	←	←	←	←	<	◄
Forward	→	→	→	→	>	►
Refresh	↻	○	↻	↻	↻	↻

If a menu bar is available in the web browser, it can usually be displayed by pressing the ALT key. You can then use the View menu to go to a specific page or to refresh the screen. In general, the menu bar is hidden by default because the buttons enable you to navigate or access options faster.

Home Page and Start Page

A browser's start page is the page that displays by default when you open the browser. Each browser is configured with a default start page, but you usually can specify to show a blank page, or to show the new tab page, or to show the tabs from your last browser session at startup instead of the default start page. You can also specify a particular web page as your startup page.

Additionally, you can configure a browser Home page. The Home page is the page that displays whenever you click the Home button on the browser toolbar. That is, you can click the Home button to quickly return to the home page, no matter how many other web sites you have visited or how "deep" into a particular web site you have navigated.

In the not-too-distant past, most browsers displayed the Home button on the browser toolbar and automatically used the home page as the startup page. Today, it is less common to find a Home button displayed by default, although modern browsers still include one and allow you to configure a Home page and to configure the Home button to display. You can also specify to use your home page as your startup page. Some users consider a browser home page a "relic of the past," while others could not imagine using a browser without one.

The classic Home button generally looks like a house. The following figures show the Home button in Microsoft Edge, Microsoft Internet Explorer, Google Chrome, and Mozilla Firefox.

Microsoft Edge   Internet Explorer   Google Chrome   Mozilla Firefox

Note: Microsoft Edge, and Google Chrome do not display the Home button by default.

Settings

A browser includes numerous configurable settings that control not only its appearance, but its behavior. For example, you can configure your browser to block particular types of content, or to reject web site cookies, or to open multiple home pages each time you launch it.

In Microsoft Edge, you access the settings by clicking the ··· (**More**) button at the right end of the browser toolbar, and then clicking **Settings** in the menu. The Settings panel opens along the right side of the browser window.

SETTINGS	📌
Choose a theme	
Light ⌄	
Open with	
⦿ Start page	
○ New tab page	
○ Previous pages	
○ A specific page or pages	
Open new tabs with	
Top sites and suggested content ⌄	

In Google Chrome, you access the settings by clicking the ☰ (**Customize and control Google Chrome**) button at the right end of the browser toolbar, and then clicking **Settings**. The Chrome Settings page opens in a new browser tab.

In Internet Explorer, you access the settings by clicking the ⚙ (**Tools**) button, then clicking **Internet options** in the menu to open the Internet Options dialog box. You use the various tabs in the dialog box to configure Internet Explorer.

Setting a Home Page in Internet Explorer

To set your home page in Internet Explorer, click the **Tools** button, then click **Internet options** in the menu to open the Internet Options dialog box. Home page settings are located on the General tab.

In the Home page section of the General tab, you can:

- Click in the box and type the URL of the page you want to set as your home page, or

- click the **Use current** button to set the currently displayed page as the browser home page, or

- click the **Use default** button to reset the browser home page to its default setting, or

- click **Use new tab** to display a blank page as the home page.

Click the **Apply** button at the bottom of the dialog box to apply your settings, then click **OK** to close the dialog box. You can set multiple home pages by typing separate URLs on separate lines. When you set more than one page as the home page, each page opens in its own tab each time you open the browser, or click the Home button.

Setting a Home Page in Microsoft Edge

To set a home page in Microsoft Edge, click **More**, then click **Settings**. In the Open with section, click **A specific page or pages** to make the options available. By default, you can select MSN, Bing, or Custom. Click **Custom** to open a text box into which you can type the URL of the page you want to set as your home page.

SETTINGS   📌

Choose a theme

| Light   ⌄ |

Open with

○ Start page

○ New tab page

○ Previous pages

● A specific page or pages

| Custom   ⌄ |

| www.w3schools.com   ✕ | +

Open new tabs with

| Top sites and suggested content   ⌄ |

Favorites settings

[View favorites settings]

Clear browsing data

Enter the URL, then click the ⊞ (**Add**) button to add the URL as a home page. Click outside the Settings panel to close it.

Setting a Home Page in Google Chrome

To set a home page in Google Chrome, click **Customize and control Google Chrome**, then click **Settings**. In the Appearance section, click the **Show Home button** check box to enable the home page settings. To specify a home page other than the New Tab page, click the **Change** link to open the Home page dialog box.

Home page   ✕

● Use the New Tab page

○ Open this page: [📄   ]

[OK]   [Cancel]

Select **Open this page**, then type the URL of the page you want to set as your home page, and click **OK**.

Exercise 13-3: Navigating in a browser

In this exercise, you will use various navigation tools and you will configure browser settings.

1. Open the Microsoft Edge web browser.

2. Type: www.ccilearning.com and then press ENTER.

3. Click in the address bar to select the current text, type: www.google.com and then press ENTER.

4. Click the **Back** button to move back one page (to the CCI Learning page).

5. Click the **Forward** button to move forward one page to the Google page.

6. Close the Edge browser.

7. Open the Internet Explorer browser.

8. Click in the address bar, type: www.wikipedia.org, then press ENTER to move the Wikipedia page.

9. Click **Tools**, then click **Internet options** to open the Internet Options dialog box.

10. On the General tab, in the Home page section, click **Use current**. The text in the list box changes to the current URL (https://www.wikipedia.org/).

11. Click **Apply**, then click **OK**.

12. Press CTRL+T to open a new tab.

13. In the new tab, navigate to www.ccilearning.com.

14. In the new tab, click the **Home** button at the right end of the browser toolbar. The new tab now displays the browser home page – the Wikipedia page.

15. Click the **Close** button for the Internet Explorer window and click **Close all tabs** if prompted.

16. Restart Internet Explorer. The browser opens to the Wikipedia page.

17. Click **Tools**, **Internet options**, then in the Home page section, click **Use default** to return the browser to its original home page setting.

18. Click **Apply**, then click **OK**.

19. Click the **Home** button to navigate to the default home page.

20. Close Internet Explorer.

Set a home page in Chrome and make the Home button visible.

21. Open the Google Chrome browser.

22. Click **Customize and control Google Chrome**, then click **Settings** to view the Settings page.

23. In the Appearance section, click the **Show Home button** check box, then click the **Change** link.

24. In the Home page dialog box, click **Open this page**, click in the text box and type: www.w3schools.com. This specifies the W3 Schools web site as your browser home page. Click **OK** to close the dialog box and return to the Settings page.

25. In the browser toolbar, click the **Home** button. The W3 Schools web site displays.

26. Close the browser.

Browser Functions and Features

Objective 3-1.1

Browsers perform several functions. In addition to retrieving and displaying web pages, and handling addressing to allow users to navigate around the World Wide Web, browsers can play media files, upload and download content, search for information and bookmark web pages. In the following section, you will examine a few of the basic functions of a browser.

Uploading and Downloading

The terms uploading and downloading refer to the process of sending information from your computer to a server (uploading), and the process of receiving information from a server (downloading).

Many people think of downloading as the act of manually copying specific files, such as music files, application files, or document files, from a web site to their computers. While this is true, it is also true that every time you visit a web site, one or more pages from the web site are downloaded to your computer.

Most web pages include several pictures, and these pictures are not part of the page itself, but are stored separately on the web server. The web page contains placeholders where the pictures will be inserted when they are downloaded from the server. If pictures are excessively large in file size, they may take longer to display than the surrounding text. The same is true for multimedia elements such as audio or video files.

These elements are downloaded automatically, but separately, when your browser loads the web page, and these downloaded elements are stored on your hard drive in a special folder designed to hold temporary Internet files. Each browser includes a temporary Internet files folder for this purpose.

File Size and Connection Speed Considerations

In Computing Fundamentals, you learned that storage capacity and bandwidth (the speed of a network connection) are measured in thousands, millions, and billions of bits and bytes. The following tables are included for your review.

File size and storage capacity are measured in bits and bytes:

Measurement	Abbreviation	Equal to ...
Bit		A single binary digit
Byte	B	Eight bits
Kilobyte	KB	1,024 bytes (a thousand bytes)
Megabyte	MB	1,024 KB (a million bytes)
Gigabyte	GB	1,024 MB (a billion bytes)
Terabyte	TB	1,024 GB (a trillion bytes)
Petabyte	PB	1,024 GB (a quadrillion bytes)

Connection speed is measured in bits per second:

Measurement	Equal to ...
bps	Bits per second
Kbps	Thousand bits per second
Mbps	Million bits per second
Gbps	Billion bits per second

The speed of your Internet connection, and the file size of the elements on a web page directly affect your browsing experience. While image files can be large, audio files can be larger, and video files can be positively huge. Understanding relative file size and your connection speed enables you to formulate a realistic estimate of how long downloading a particular file may take.

The following table (from the Apple support page) compares estimated download times for downloading content from iTunes over a 5Mbps connection and a 1Mbps connection.

File	Approximate size	5Mbps	1Mbps
4-minute song	4MB	4-5 seconds	20-30 seconds
5-minute video	30MB	30-40 seconds	About 3 minutes
45-minute TV show	200MB	3-5 minutes	15-20 minutes
45-minute HDTV show	600MB	10-15 minutes	45 minutes – 1 hour
2-hour movie	1.0-1.5GB	18-24 minutes	1.5 – 2 hours
2-hour HD movie	3.0-4.5GB	30-70 minutes	4.5-6 hours

Advantages of Streaming

In Computing Fundamentals, you learned that streaming is the process of having a file delivered to your device in a constant and steady stream. Although you cannot save streamed content, you can see how streaming might be preferable to downloading when you want to watch high-definition movies and television shows; if you download the content, you may have to wait several hours before you can start viewing it, whereas if you stream the content, you can begin watching it immediately.

Searching from the Address Bar

While there are several well-known search engine sites on the Internet (you will learn how to use a search engine site later in this module), many modern browsers include a search box in the address bar, which allows you to search for information without first having to navigate to a search engine site.

Just click in the address bar and start typing. If you enter a complete URL, you will go directly to the web site. If you enter a search term or an incomplete address, a list of suggested search terms appears in a menu.

The following figures show address bar/omnibox search suggestions presented in Edge and Chrome.

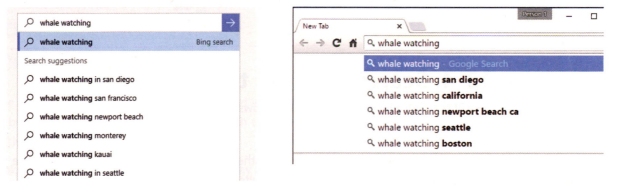

Click a suggested search term in the suggestion list to launch a search using the currently selected search engine.

Microsoft Edge, and Microsoft Internet Explorer, use Bing as the default search engine for searching from the address bar, while Google Chrome uses Google as its default search engine for searching from the omnibox. However, you can specify to use a different search engine.

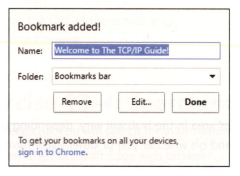

2. You can also specify where you want to save the bookmark. You can save it in the Favorites folder or in the Favorites bar. Click **Save** to save the bookmark.

Google Chrome

In Chrome, saved URLs are called bookmarks. Click ☆ (**Bookmark this page**) to bookmark the currently displayed page. Bookmarks are added to the Bookmarks bar by default. To toggle the display of the Bookmarks bar click **Customize and control Google Chrome**, point to **Bookmarks** and then click **Show bookmarks bar**.

| Apps | W3Schools Online We | CCI CCI Learning | Remote Web Access | Welcome to The TCP/ |

To bookmark a site in Chrome:

1. Click **Bookmark this page**. A panel opens, allowing you to name your bookmark (or to accept the name suggested by Chrome).

Bookmark added!

Name: Welcome to The TCP/IP Guide!

Folder: Bookmarks bar ▾

Remove   Edit...   Done

To get your bookmarks on all your devices, sign in to Chrome.

2. You can also specify where you want to save the bookmark. You can save it to the Bookmarks bar, to the built-in Other bookmarks folder, or to any bookmarks folder you may have created.

3. Click **Done** to save the bookmark.

Internet Explorer

In Internet Explorer, you access Favorites through the Favorites Center, which provides access to Favorites, the Newsfeed, and your browsing History. To open the Favorites Center, click ☆ (**View favorites, feeds, and history**) or press ALT+C.

The number of folders or web sites displayed in the Favorites pane will vary, depending on built-in bookmarks that came pre-configured with the browser, and on whether you or other users have already added bookmarks.

Links stored in the Favorites bar folder display as buttons when the Favorites bar toolbar is turned on.

Click a button in the Favorites Bar to access the site.

By default, new bookmarks are saved to the Favorites folder. You can also create your own folders for storing bookmark links to help keep your links organized. You can then organize your bookmarks into folders, move them, or delete them.

To bookmark a site in Internet Explorer:

- Click the **View favorites, feeds or history** button and then click **Add to favorites**, or

- press ALT+Z, and then click **Add to favorites**

Click the **Add** button in the Add a Favorite dialog box to add a bookmark for the current site to your Favorites. The dialog box provides options for specifying your own name for the bookmark link, for creating the link in a different folder (such as the Favorites bar folder), and for creating a new folder in which to save the link.

Once you add a web site bookmark to the Favorites list, you can access the site by clicking its bookmark in the Favorites list or clicking the bookmark in the Favorites bar if you saved the link to the Favorites bar.

Exercise 13-5: Adding Bookmarks/Favorites

In this exercise, you will add bookmarks and Favorites.

1. Open the Chrome web browser and navigate to www.ccilearning.com.

2. In the browser toolbar, click the **Bookmark this page** button. In the panel, ensure that Bookmarks bar displays in the Folder list box, then click **Done** to add the bookmark.

3. At the right end of the toolbar, click **Customize and control Google Chrome**, point to **Bookmarks**, then click **Show bookmarks bar** to turn on the display of the Bookmarks bar. Your new bookmark displays in the Bookmarks bar.

4. Navigate to www.w3schools.com (you can click the Home button to navigate to this site).

5. Click the **Bookmark this page** button, type: Web Lessons in the Name box, then click **Done**.

6. Navigate to www.howstuffworks.com.

7. Create a bookmark named How Stuff Works and add it to the Bookmarks bar.

8. Navigate to www.kayak.com, create a bookmark named Travel and add it to the Bookmarks bar.

9. Point at the bookmarks on the Bookmarks bar. Notice that as you point at each one, its name and URL display in a pop-up box.

10. In the Bookmarks bar, click **Web Lessons** to return to the W3 Schools web site.

11. In the Bookmarks bar, click **CCI Learning** to return to the CCI Learning web site.

12. Close the Chrome browser.

13. Open the Internet Explorer web browser.

14. Right-click the window title bar for Internet Explorer, then click **Favorites bar** to display the Favorites bar in the window.

15. Navigate to the sign in page for Microsoft at https://login.live.com.

16. Press ALT+C to open the Favorites Center, then click the drop-down arrow on the **Add to favorites** button, and click **Add to Favorites bar**. The bookmark is added.

17. In the toolbar, click the **Home** button to return to the browser home page.

18. On the Favorites bar, click the **Sign in to your Microsoft account** bookmark. You are taken to the sign in page.

19. Right-click the bookmark on the Favorites bar, then click **Rename**.

20. In the New name box, type: Microsoft Sign-In and press ENTER.

21. Close Internet Explorer.

Managing Bookmarks

Browsers include a management tool for working with bookmarks. In Internet Explorer, this is the Favorites Center; in Edge, it is the Hub; and in Chrome it is the Bookmarks Manager. These management centers allow you to create new bookmark folders, and to move and delete bookmarks. You can launch wizards that help you import bookmarks from other browsers. The Google Chrome Bookmark Manager is shown in the following figure:

Most bookmark management pages and panels work like the panes in File Explorer; you can drag and drop bookmarks, and right-click to open shortcut menus.

Deleting Bookmarks/Favorites

To remove a bookmark/Favorite, use one of the following methods:

- Right-click the bookmark on the Bookmarks bar or Favorites bar, then click **Delete** from the shortcut menu; or

- open a bookmark management page or panel, click a bookmark to select it, then press DELETE.

Exercise 13-6: Working with Bookmarks/Favorites

In this exercise, you will manage bookmarks and favorites.

1. Open the Internet Explorer browser, click the **View favorites, feeds, and history** button, click the drop-down arrow to the right of the **Add to favorites** button, then click **Import and export**.

2. Ensure that **Import from another browser** is selected in the Import/Export Settings screen, then click **Next**.

3. Select the check box for **Chrome**, click **Import**, then click **Finish**. Internet Explorer should now include the Microsoft Sign-In bookmark, and the four bookmarks you added to Chrome.

4. Open the Favorites Center, expand the Favorites Bar folder if necessary, then click **Travel** to move to the Kayak site. You can click a favorite in the Favorites Center or on the Favorites bar.

5. Minimize the Internet Explorer window.

6. Open the Microsoft Edge browser, then click the **Hub** button, then click the **Favorites settings** link.

7. Drag or click the **Show the favorites bar** slider to set it to the **On** position.

8. In the Import favorites section, select the check box for **Internet Explorer**, then click **Import**. Your bookmarks have now been imported into Edge.

9. Click outside the Hub to close it.

10. Test a few of the bookmarks by clicking them on the Favorites bar.

11. In the Edge browser, right-click the **Travel** bookmark in the Favorites bar, and click **Delete** to delete the bookmark.

12. Close the Edge browser.

13. Restore the Internet Explorer window, right-click **How Stuff Works** in the Favorites bar, then click **Delete** to delete the bookmark.

14. Close Internet Explorer.

15. Open the Google Chrome browser.

16. Click the **Customize and control Google Chrome** button, point to **Bookmarks**, then click **Bookmark manager** to open the Chrome bookmark manager.

17. If necessary, click the Bookmarks bar folder in the left pane. The four bookmarks display in the Organize pane on the right.

18. Drag the **CCI Learning** bookmark from the right pane into the *Other bookmarks* folder in the left pane. Notice that the Other bookmarks folder now displays at the right end of the browser toolbar.

19. In the Organize pane, click the drop-down arrow to the right of Organize and examine the available options.

20. In the Organize pane, right-click **Travel**, then click **Delete** to remove the bookmark.

21. In the Bookmark bar, click **Web Lessons** to move to the W3 Schools site.

22. In the Bookmark bar, click the **Other bookmarks** folder, then click **CCI Learning** to move to the CCI Learning web site.

23. In the Bookmark bar, click the **Other bookmarks** folder, then right-click **CCI Learning** and click **Delete** to remove the bookmark. The Other bookmarks folder no longer displays.

24. Close the Chrome browser.

Synchronizing Bookmarks

As you can probably imagine, your list of bookmarks/favorites builds up over time. The more you use bookmarks, the more you may come to rely on their convenience. You don't have to remember URLs – you simply click a button or favorite link and get where you want to go.

Suppose you do hours of research for a school project on your home computer, and plan to continue working on it during class time. Wouldn't it be convenient if you had access to the bookmarks/favorites on your home computer on the computer you were using in class?

Or suppose that you are doing research for your job on your office computer, and then come home and need to continue your work on your laptop. It would certainly be convenient to access the bookmarks/favorites you added to your work computer from your laptop.

That's where synchronizing bookmarks comes in handy. In fact, in most browsers, you can synchronize more than just your bookmarks – you can synchronize bookmarks, passwords, browser history, open tabs and more.

Chrome, Firefox, Safari, and Opera all offer built-in bookmark synchronization through free online accounts. Firefox uses the Firefox Sync account; Safari uses the iCloud account. Opera uses the Opera Link account, and in Chrome, you sign in using your Gmail account.

Once you have created an account, you sign in and specify which items you want to sync across your devices. When you use the browser on another device, simply sign in to your account, and all your bookmarks, history, and preferences, become available to you on that device.

In Windows 8.1 and above, synching across devices is built-in. When you sign in with a Microsoft account, your PC is connected to Microsoft servers online. This means that your personal settings and preferences are stored in OneDrive, and are synced to any PC that you sign in to.

- Your Start screen layout, chosen colors, themes, language preferences, browser history and favorites, and Windows Store app settings are synced between PCs.

- You can get to and share your photos, documents, and other files from OneDrive, Facebook, Flickr, and other services on all your PCs without signing in to each one.

You can specify which settings to sync, and you can turn off synching for specific settings. You can also turn off synching completely.

Browser Preferences and Settings

Objective 3-1.1

At the beginning of this lesson we spent some time discussing that the Internet is a public, and therefore, untrusted network. Accordingly, there are many tools at your disposal for keeping yourself protected while you are online. As you learned in Computing Fundamentals, firewalls protect a LAN from unwanted network traffic – such as hackers attempting to gain unauthorized access. Antivirus software protects your system from viruses, Trojans, and spyware.

However, your online activity can expose you to other dangers such as identity theft or theft of private/sensitive information. The best protection is to keep yourself educated and aware of potential dangers and to engage in safe computing. Fortunately, your browser contains several configurable settings that can help keep your private information private.

Handling Pop-ups

A pop-up is a small browser window that suddenly opens in front of the page you are viewing. Pop-ups contain command buttons or options that must be selected before you can continue with the current task. Pop-ups can remind a visitor to log on or to enter required information, but they are also used extensively for advertising on the web, and many users find them annoying because they remain open until you click an option or manually close them. Pop-ups can also be used for phishing (tricking users into sharing sensitive information) or for infecting a computer with malware if the user clicks on the pop-up.

To eliminate the need for interacting with pop-ups, browsers include built-in pop-up *blockers*. In most browsers, the pop-up blocker is enabled by default, and you can fine-tune the settings of the pop-up blocker so important messages (for example, log on screens, or session time-out warnings) are allowed to display.

To access pop-up blocker settings in Internet Explorer:

1. Click **Tools**, **Internet options** to open the Internet Options dialog box, then click the **Privacy** tab.

2. In the Pop-up Blocker section, select or clear the **Turn on Pop-up Blocker** check box, or click the **Settings** button to open the Pop-up Blocker Settings dialog box.

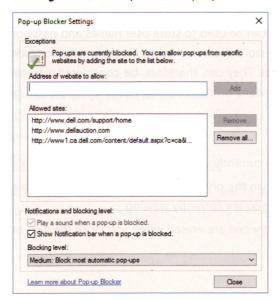

AutoFill/AutoComplete

AutoFill is a browser feature that can automatically fill out online forms with street addresses and credit card information. When a browser offers to remember your web site passwords, this is also part of the AutoFill feature. While it may be convenient, enabling AutoFill and storing sensitive information in any browser can put you at increased risk for identify theft if your system is compromised.

In Chrome you can configure these settings on the Advanced settings page, under the Password and forms heading. In Internet Explorer and Edge, this feature is called AutoComplete. In Internet Explorer you can access the settings on the Content tab of the Internet Options dialog box.

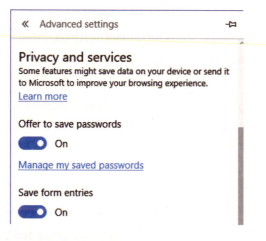

In Microsoft Edge, these settings can be accessed in the Advanced settings panel in the Privacy and services section.

Browser Cache

The browser cache is a folder on your hard drive that stores downloaded files (such as web pages, images, or fonts). The cache improves your browser's performance because it allows you to view previously accessed web pages without having to request them from the server again. For example, if you click a hyperlink on a web page, then click the browser's Back button, the browser can pull the previously viewed page from the cache.

Note: If you are viewing a page that includes dynamic content, such as the current status of an airline flight, and you notice that the information has not changed since you last viewed the page, your browser may be showing a cached page. To update the content, click F5 (Refresh) to force the browser to request a new updated page from the server.

When you enter a URL, your browser checks the cache to see if the page is already stored there. If the cache contains a recent version of the page, it will display the cached version instead of downloading the page from the web again. Loading cached pages is much faster than downloading them from a server.

When you enter information (such as your name, or address) into forms on web sites, that information is also stored in the browser cache. It is convenient to keep this information stored on your PC (the browser can complete much of the information the next time you need to enter it), but there are times when you will want to delete some or all of your information. For example, if you are using a public computer, you don't want to leave your personal information behind – this information is easily accessible to anyone who has physical access to the computer. To remove this information, you can clear the cache by deleting your browsing history.

Browsing History

Every browser includes a history function that stores the URLs of web sites you have visited in the browser's History folder.

The History folder stores the URLs of sites you have accessed within a defined period of time, and provides a convenient way to revisit web sites, especially if you cannot remember the exact URL. The following figures show the History folder in Google Chrome, Internet Explorer, and Microsoft Edge.

Google Chrome

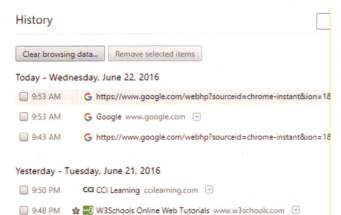

In Chrome, click **Customize and control Google Chrome**, point to **History**, then click **History**.

To go to a site, click a link in the list. You can also select the check box for a site and then click **Remove selected items** to remove the item from the History.

Internet Explorer

In Internet Explorer, click **View favorites, feeds, and history**, then click the **History** tab.

Click a date to expand it so that it displays the sites visited on that day. You can click a link to go to the site, expand a site to see the various pages you visited, or right-click a link and then click **Delete** to remove a given site from the History.

You can also display the View By Date drop-down list and specify to display the links by site, or most visited, or by order visited today.

Extending Browser Functionality

Objective 3-1.1

When the Internet was new, most web sites featured text and not much more. Over time, as technology, infrastructure and local processing power has increased, the World Wide Web has exploded into an arena filled with pictures, animations, audio, video, social and interactive activities.

When browsers were first designed, their focus was to help you read the text on web sites. Because web sites have changed and improved over time, special applications have been developed to help you extend the functionality of your browser so that you can enjoy the latest online features.

These browser extending technologies come in the form of plug-ins/add-ons, and in-browser apps.

Plug-ins/Add-ons

In order to present the interactive multimedia so abundant on the web, a browser may require applications that extend its usability. These applications are called plug-ins or add-ons. The terms plug-in and add-on are generally used loosely and mean essentially the same thing – they refer to applications that extend the abilities of the browser. These extension applications could be made by the company that made the browser, or by other companies or individuals.

In some circles, *plug-in* is the term to use when referring to third-party applications that will work on most popular browsers. Generally, these are full software applications that run in their own windows. Adobe Flash Player, Windows Media Player, Microsoft Silverlight, and Real Networks RealPlayer are examples of popular plug-ins. When you visit a web site and your browser encounters a file type that it cannot natively support, you may be prompted to download and install a plug-in/add-on so you can properly experience everything on the web page.

Plug-ins generally have a particular file type associated with them. For example, Windows Media Player can be used to play files that include the .wma (Windows media audio) and .wmv (Windows media video) file name extensions. The player also supports several video and audio file formats (such as .avi, .mpeg, .midi, .wav).

Add-on is the term to use when referring to browser-specific applications that generally modify the browser interface. For example, a Google Search toolbar, or a Firefox theme are examples of add-ons. Add-ons designed for use in a particular browser cannot be used in another browser; however, most are available in various versions. For example, there is a Google toolbar add-on for Firefox and for Internet Explorer.

Remember that the terms are used loosely and often interchangeably. To make things a little more confusing, within the various browsers themselves the terms add-ons, extensions, plug-ins and apps are all used to refer to these applications.

In-browser Apps

An in-browser app is a web-based type of browser extension – it is designed to extend the functionality of a browser by linking it to a web service. For example, the Pocket app (https://getpocket.com) is an app/service for managing a reading list of articles from the Internet. It is available for Firefox, Chrome, Internet Explorer, and Edge.

Sometimes we surf the web and find articles that spark our interest, but time constraints may prevent us from reading these articles immediately. If you have added Pocket to your browser, you can simply click the Add to Pocket button to save the article. You can even add tags.

Later, when you have time to read your saved articles, you can open your Pocket list and select the article(s) you want to view.

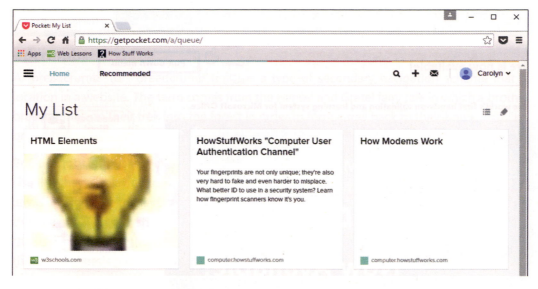

Web Standards

Objective 3-1.1, 3-2.1

In order to make web sites easy to use and navigate, and to provide a uniform surfing experience, web site designers and authors follow basic standard conventions that make the user comfortable when visiting a new site. These conventions include items such as a navigation bar, breadcrumbs, and standardized use of the mouse.

Additionally, most sites are structured in a standard fashion so that users know what to expect before they even visit.

Site Home Page

Typically, the first page you see when you access a web site is the top level page, called the *home page* or index page. The home page serves as the "starting point" for a web site. Usually, a home page contains links to all the other pages on the web site – allowing you to navigate to different areas. In a well-designed web site, each lower-level page includes a "home" link that will return you to the web site's home page with a single click. In many web sites, you can click the company logo to return to the site Home page.

Keep in mind that a web site home page is not the same as a browser home page. The browser home page is the web site that the browser displays automatically when you begin your browsing session. Each web site you visit has its own home page.

When you add a widget that pulls content from other sites (such as a stock ticker, or RSS feed widget), you should understand that you do not have control over the content, and you cannot modify the source of the content. The content is pre-determined and pre-published by the publisher/author/service provider of the widget.

"Standard" Pages

The layout and design of a web site is in the control of the web designer; however, there are a few standard pages that you may expect to see when you visit most commercial web sites. These include:

About Us	This page gives information about the company that owns the web site. Often this page includes contact information, links to social media pages, employment opportunities, and perhaps information about the company philosophy and its owners/directors.
Privacy Policy	Any site that collects personal information should provide a description of how they use your personal information.
Login page	Sites that allow access to secure areas (such as for the purpose of shopping online) usually provide a page for signing in to your account.
Online store	Sites that allow you to make purchases over the Internet host online stores. These may be subsections of the main web site, or may be entirely separate sites that you can access from the main site.

Using a Mouse on the Web

Most web sites treat mouse movements and clicks uniformly so that the user does not have to "learn" how to interact with each individual web site. The HTML5 standard makes it easy for web developers to capture and respond to various mouse events.

The following table describes how mouse actions are generally used in web pages:

Single click	Use a single click to follow a link, or click a button to perform an action.
Double-click	Many users double-click links even though a single click is all that is necessary. If you double-click within the web page text, you can select a word. Sometimes double-clicking can cause difficulty when using an online store – for example, double-clicking a "Place Order" button may result in a double order, depending on how the web page handles double-click events. In some online store web sites, a place order button is temporarily disabled immediately after a user clicks it; this allows time for the transaction to take place and to supply visual feedback to the user.
Delayed click or long press	Holding down the left mouse button on a link or clickable button generally has no result until you release the mouse button. On a touch screen device, however, a long press may open a shortcut menu, or it may select text and offer to copy the selection to the clipboard.
Pointing	When you hold the mouse pointer over some web elements (such as links in a navigation bar) you may be able to view the contents of a pull-down menu or the target of a hyperlink.
Mouse Over	A mouse over is a special effect that displays when you pass or point your mouse over a specific object on the screen. Popular mouse over effects are to change the appearance of a button or link, or to display a drop-down menu.

Drag and Drop | HTML5 supports drag and drop. That is, you can drag an object from one place on a web page and drop it into another location. This is useful for games, or online testing situations where you might need to match a phrase with its definition.

Exercise 13-7: Exploring a web site

In this exercise, you will explore the Nestlé company global web site.

1. Open the browser of your choice and navigate to www.nestle.com. If a message box appears suggesting that you visit the web site for Nestlé in your country to find coupons, recipes, and promotions, click **Close** to stay on the global site. If necessary, close the About cookies on this site message box.

2. In the navigation bar across the top of the home page, click **About us** to go to the About us page. Notice the left side navigation panel with links to various pages within the About us section of the web site.

3. In the left side navigation panel, click the **Quality and safety** link.

4. In the sub-menu that opens in the navigation panel, click **How we ensure food safety**. Notice the breadcrumb trail that displays just below the top navigation bar and just above the social media links.

5. In the breadcrumb trail (Home>About us>Quality and safety>How we ensure food safety), click **About us** to return to the About us page.

6. Near the top of the About us page, point at each of the social media icons. Notice that the URLs for Nestlé's social media pages display in screen tips near the bottom of the browser window.

7. Slowly drag your mouse across the links in the navigation bar. What effect is used to make the navigation links seem interactive?

8. Drag your mouse over the elongated rectangle buttons on the right side of the page. Are special effects added to these elements as well?

9. In the search box at the top of the page, type: cocoa processing then press ENTER. Notice that by default the search results page lists results only from this site, but that you can also search all Nestlé corporate sites.

10. In the search results page, click **Nestlé launches The Cocoa Plan** to view an article contained in the media section of the web site.

11. At the top of the page, click the Nestlé logo to return to the home page, and close the message box if necessary.

12. Scroll to the bottom of the home page, then click **Privacy** to open the privacy policy page. Scroll the page and take note of the three videos that answer different questions about the company privacy policy.

13. At the far right, click the **Feedback** button to open a form that you can fill out and submit. Companies often welcome feedback through their web sites.

14. Click the **Close** button (x) at the upper right corner of the feedback form.

15. Scroll to the bottom of the page, then click **Cookies** to open an informative page on how the web site uses cookies and other tracking technology.

16. In the navigation buttons at the right, click the **Contact Us** button to access the Contact Us page. Notice the links for job search, FAQs, consumer services and more.

17. Close your browser.

Lesson Summary

In this lesson, you learned about the nature of the Internet and about the role and function of web browsers. You should now be able to:

☑ describe the nature of the Internet

☑ describe packets and how they make their way across the Internet

☑ differentiate between public and private networks

☑ specify a network location in Windows

☑ describe the function and characteristics of IP addresses

☑ understand the Domain Name System (DNS)

☑ describe domain types

☑ identify parts of a URL

☑ differentiate the Internet from the World Wide Web

☑ describe the role of HTML, CSS, and hyperlinks

☑ use a web browser

☑ describe different web browsers

☑ work with browser settings

☑ describe browser functions and features

☑ use bookmarks/favorites

☑ handle pop-ups, cookies, and he browser cache

☑ understand browser extensions

☑ describe web site/web page standards

Review Questions

1. Your computer wants to send a request for a web page to the web server at CCI Learning.com. Which address information will your computer include in those packets?

   a. The web server's IP address.

   b. The web server's name.

   c. The street address where the web server is housed.

   d. The web server's domain name.

2. Which service enables users to access web sites by domain name instead of by IP address?

   a. DHCP   c. DSL

   b. DNS   d. CSS

3. Consider the following domain name: www.ccilearning.com. Which of the following is the top-level domain?

   a. www   c. com

   b. ccilearning   d. The entire name is the top-level domain.

4. What can you surmise from the following URL: https://bountifulbaskets.com.

   a. A user may be paying for a purchase.

   b. A user may be uploading a large file.

   c. A user may be downloading a large file.

   d. A user may be streaming a video.

5. Which of the following statements is accurate?
    a. HTML may be external or internal.
    b. CSS styling information should be added to the foot section of an HTML document.
    c. HTML and CSS allows web page designers to separate content/structure from presentation.
    d. All of these statements are true.

6. Which keyboard combination will open a new browser tab?
    a. CTRL+N   c. CTRL+W
    b. CTRL+T   d. CTRL+X

7. Which of the following is a web browser?
    a. Gmail   c. Google Docs
    b. Google Drive   d. Google Chrome

8. Which of the following data transfer speeds is the fastest?
    a. 30,000,000 bps   c. 300 Kbps
    b. 700 Mbps   d. 0.5 Gbps

9. Which of the following items would take the longest to download?
    a. A 50,000KB video.   c. A 0.5 GB video.
    b. A 60MB video.   d. There is no way to tell.

10. Ann visited a site last Tuesday which contained a meatloaf recipe that she really wants to try, but now she can't remember the URL. What should she do?
    a. Conduct a new search for meatloaf recipes and hope that she can find this one recipe again.
    b. Click the browser's Back button until she gets back to the page she wants.
    c. Click the browser's Refresh button.
    d. Look for the URL in the History folder.

11. Kevin was paying bills in his online banking site when he was timed out without warning. What might he need to do to prevent this from happening in the future?
    a. Adjust his pop-up blocker settings.
    b. Upgrade his browser.
    c. Switch to a different bank.
    d. Adjust the way his browser handles cookies.

12. Cookies are:
    a. text files   c. Trojans
    b. an example of malware   d. viruses

13. What is the purpose of a browser cache?
    a. To store keys that are used for encrypted transmissions.
    b. To improve browser performance.
    c. To store sensitive information.
    d. To upload information to a server.

14. What is the purpose of browser plug-ins and add-ons?
    a. To improve browser security.
    b. To encrypt wireless transmissions.
    c. To extend the functionality of a browser.
    d. To upload information to a server.

15. Which action is usually used to select an option in a web site menu?
    a. Single click   c. Mouse over
    b. Right-click   d. Double-click

Lesson 14: Managing Media Literacy

Lesson Objectives

This lesson teaches you how to use the information you may find online in a respectful and legal manner. Upon completion of this lesson, you should be able to:

☐ search for items on a specific web site

☐ search for items using search engines

☐ use tools to narrow the search criteria

☐ evaluate the validity of the information

☐ understand what copyright and fair use includes

☐ understand what intellectual property is

☐ recognize censorship or filtering

☐ understand what plagiarism is

Searching for Information

Objective 3-1.1

Millions of web servers worldwide are connected via the Internet. On average, each server hosts one thousand or more web pages.

No organization monitors the information on the Internet, which means you will find both good and questionable information there. Use your own discretion to determine what is appropriate viewing or what information is valid.

One of the main purposes of creating a web site is to share information with others. The design of the pages on a site will vary depending on the organization and the purpose of the business or service. Many sites include a search field somewhere along the top or along the left side of their web pages. You can use this search field to search the web site for specific information. Using the search field on a web page searches only that web site to which the page belongs; this is different from searching the entire Internet for information on a specific topic.

Additionally, different types of sites contain different types of information:

- Business web sites usually include pages that describe the company and its products or services, as well as areas for feedback or online purchases.

- Government web sites tend to include pages for each department, and additional pages with links to files or forms that you can download.

- Social networking sites such as Facebook or Twitter enable subscribers to share photographs, games and videos, chat online, or post simple messages.

- Blogs allow individuals to enter and share comments, experiences or information on pages devoted to specific topics.

- Wiki sites are used as sources of information and provide tools that enable individuals to add, edit or rearrange information on the site.

- Other sites allow individuals to upload multimedia items such as photographs, video, audio and podcasts. For example, YouTube includes both professional and amateur created videos.

- YouTube also welcomes uploads in the form of *podcasts* (audio files made available on the Internet for downloading. Often they are set up as discussions that can become episodic based on feedback). Anyone with an appropriate multimedia program can record audio, video, or both and save the files in a format that will be recognized as a podcast.

- News-related sites syndicate their breaking stories as RSS feeds, making current news available as it occurs (rather than at set times as on television, radio, or in print). Users can subscribe to one or more newsfeeds at no cost to get current news delivered to their desktop or mobile devices. RSS content can be viewed via a newsreader or RSS app.

- Sites designed to provide reference links can be found on individual web sites or set up as part of a search engine web site.

- Education web sites are available on the Internet; sites with an .edu domain are generally associated with an accredited school such as a university, high school, or college. These sites contain a wealth of information pertaining to curriculum planning, lesson plans, and may contain examples of reports or exams in addition to a list of resources for particular course types.

When searching for information, also consider using traditional sources such as the public library or a local university. Traditional sources like these still offer a wide variety of information in the form of periodicals, microfiche, reference books, and other types of publications that may not be available online.

All these methods to search for information are designed to provide you with alternatives when researching or acquiring knowledge on a specific topic. As you will see in forthcoming portions, you can search for items on a global basis or you can narrow the search to target a specific subject, in a specific context.

It is recommended that you compare the information you find on various sites to determine its accuracy before using the information in a report or project. In fact, in some cases, you may want to verify the information you find online with information you find in a more traditional source such as an encyclopedia or journal, especially if the topic is fact-based and easily verifiable.

One of the fastest ways to search for information is to use a search engine or search field on a particular web site. Any criteria you enter in a particular web site's search field will provide results from this web site only. This can make it much easier to search for information on a specific topic, service or item that is sold or provided by this company. The location of the search field will vary from site to site, although it is generally located near the top of the web page. For example, you can go to Microsoft's web site to find the information you want about the pricing structure and the applications included at each pricing level of Office 365.

Using Search Engine Technology

Objective 3-1.1

The purpose of any search engine is to provide links to information stored on other web sites. You come to a search engine site to pose a question; the search engine responds by displaying links with possible answers.

An Internet search engine has three basic tasks it can perform:

- search the Internet for pages that contain words relevant to the search criteria you enter
- build and maintain an index of key words
- display links to information that match the search criteria

A search engine web site specializes in making it easy to find information on any topic, located anywhere on the Internet. Some commonly used search engines at the time of this writing are Google, bing, Ask and Yahoo!.

Although the services provided by these companies vary, they all use similar technology. The search engine maintains a database of Internet URLs; each record in the database includes the URL, a short description, a title, keywords, and other site information. Users access the URL database via the search engine company's web site,

A search field on the search engine company's web site works in the same way as a search field on an organization's web site. The difference is that the search engine company's web site searches its database, compiles a list of records matching the keywords, and returns a list formatted as a web page.

Using Search Engines

To start a search, start your web browser, click in the Search field and enter your search criteria or *keywords*. The Search field may appear on the search engine's home page, or the web browser's home page.

Depending on the web browser, the options selected, and whether the keywords you enter are similar to any you have entered previously, a list of suggested search terms may appear as you begin to enter text in the search field.

craters	🔍
craters	
craters **of the moon**	
craters **and freighters**	
craters **definition**	
craters **on face**	
craters **of diamonds**	
craters **of the moon rv parks**	
craters **in tonsils**	

If one of these items matches what you want to find, you can:

- Click the item in the list, or
- use the DOWN or UP key to move to select the item, then press ENTER to accept the selection.

You can also simply finish typing your criteria and press ENTER or click the button to the right of the search field to begin the search. Sometimes, as you type your criteria, the search engine will insert suggested text into the search field as you type. You can press ENTER to accept the suggestion or continue typing. These features are part of a browser's *AutoComplete* option; a web browser can be set to remember all entries until and unless they are deleted.

When you click the Search button or press ENTER the search engine checks its database and displays the results.

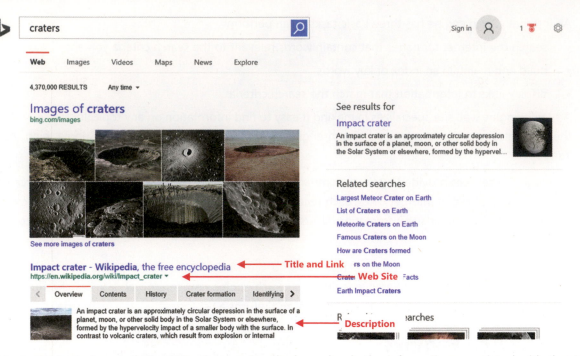

Most search engines rank the URLs they retrieve by how closely the information associated with that URL matches the keywords entered in the search field. Those that rank the highest are listed at the top of the search results.

Note: Sometimes web sites are written to include hidden keywords or tags simply for the purpose of making the site appear in a search results page. For this reason, some sites will appear in a list of results even though they do not seem to be related at all to the keywords or search criteria entered.

Typically, results number in the hundreds of thousands, or even millions.

Sometimes a search results page will include an area for related searches (as shown in the previous figure), and sometimes a search results page may feature excerpts from a particular web site in a panel on the right (as shown in the following figure).

Narrowing the Search Results

Chances are, you will not want to take the time to read through 100,000 results, much less click the links and check out the pages. Fortunately, you can use several methods to narrow your search results.

One easy way to narrow your search results is to indicate that you want the results to include only specific file types such as images, newsfeeds, or videos. For example, you could narrow the search to videos if you were looking for videos on how to fix a cell phone; or you could limit the results to image files if you want to find pictures of a famous 17th century painting, and so on.

You can do this by entering the search criteria and then clicking the link for the type of results you want to see. For instance, the following image shows a request for any videos on how to fix a cell phone:

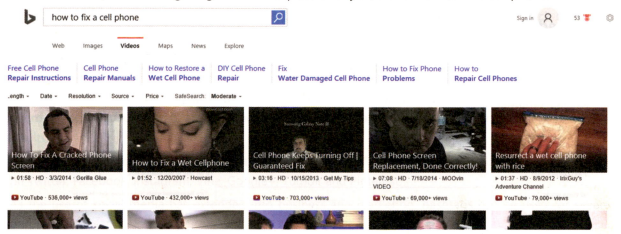

Using Boolean Operators

If you type in only one or two keywords, the search engine will look for all matches of either word, and that will return tens of thousands of matches, most of which may not be relevant! Being specific with your search criteria is highly useful.

- Choose more specific keywords; for example, typing *satellite images of great wall of china* is an effective way to narrow a search and produce better results than just typing *great wall of china*.

- Use keywords to find a specific item; for example, entering *lemon dessert recipes* will bring results for this topic, whereas *lemon recipes* will bring results for any type of recipe that uses lemons.

You can also use Boolean operators in your search criteria to narrow the search results. These operators include:

AND – Connect keywords with "AND" when you are searching for multiple terms in a single document; your search will include only documents that contain all your search terms. An example of this would be a search for pastries recipes AND lemon would display results for any pastry recipes that include lemon as part of the recipe.

OR – Search for documents that include one or another of your search terms, such as soccer leagues national OR international will produce a list of either national or international soccer leagues.

NOT – Use in conjunction with "AND" if you want to exclude certain results from your search; for instance, dwarf planets NOT Pluto would show results for information on dwarf planets that does not include Pluto.

NEAR – Use to look for terms in the same document that are within ten words of each other.

- How current is the web site?
    - Check when the site was last updated. It may be fine that a web site for a company that sells seasonal items hasn't been updated recently, but a reputable news site or travel agency should be updating their information at least daily. If they are not, you have reason to question the reliability or relevance of the information.

- If a web page offers facts and statistics, one way to determine their accuracy is by checking the author's and publisher's qualifications.
    - Who published this author's work and what is the relationship between the author and publisher?
    - Visit the About Us, Mission, Philosophy, Corporate Profile, and Background pages of the web site.
    - Follow any links to review additional information that assists in authenticating the author's credentials and the material presented. Links that are broken or lead to pages that are no longer available may call into question how up to date the information is.
    - Other links that appear legitimate may actually take you to a page or site that contains offensive content or sells another product or service. The webmaster or person in charge of the web site should be checking links occasionally to maintain the company's credibility and reliability.

- Use the URL as an indicator of whether the web site is affiliated with a recognized organization or institution as opposed to a group or individual without established credibility.
    - If a reputable organization reproduces information from other sources, it is more likely to ensure the information is faithful to the original than to be found altering material, either out of carelessness or a desire to support a certain viewpoint.

- The presence or absence of source references can help you assess the authenticity of material on the web. If a web site "quotes" information on a subject without providing the source of the information so you can check up on it, you have to wonder if the content has been altered or if it is being quoted out of context and without the original author's permission.
    - Be sure to research any articles listed to determine if they are factual; articles can be written for a variety of reasons, and are not necessarily based on facts.
    - A trustworthy article will also be referenced by other people or organizations on their web sites.

- If a site claims to offer technical expertise, check the source references if available.
    - Specific articles or reference papers do not need to be cited; but including a link to the source lends credibility to the web site.

- If you are viewing blog or wiki content, remember that authors need no qualifications to contribute.
    - Even though wiki content is reviewed by members of the public for accuracy, it is always wise to "comparison shop" and try to verify the information on more than one blog or wiki, as well as on related web sites.

- It is unlikely that you will come across information from any source that contains no bias of any type. However, reliable authors and web sites strive to inform their audience with accurate facts and statistics.
    - A bibliography or source list with links to other sites is a good indicator of the openness and objectivity of the information. Be sure to check a few of these links, even if available only in traditional paper format, and read the full articles to determine if the information here is fact or fiction.

- Look for depth of coverage of the topic, supported by other types of information.
    - Is the web site or author associated with other reputable organizations?
    - Do these organizations have credentials that support their ability to provide unbiased information?

- What types of sponsored advertisements or links appear on the site?

- Who owns the products or services being advertised on this web site?

- Many organizations offer accurate information on their web sites, but their agendas are well known to be biased and the information they provide is unbalanced. There is nothing wrong with stating an opinion as long as it is represented as such.

    - Any arguments should be supported with documentation; if the topic is controversial the presentation should provide viewpoints on both sides of the issue.

    - Check if the site offers an area called a *forum* where people can leave messages or posts. Read some of the posts to see if there is a balance of positive and negative comments, people offering facts versus opinions.

    - In general people sign up on forums that are of interest to them; however, it doesn't guarantee that everyone who posts is an expert in that field, having both factual experience and education to back up their comments.

- Check the tone of the message. Is the page factual and informative or does it seem more persuasive? If humor is used, do you find it effective or does the tone seem sarcastic or exaggerated?

- Is there advertising on the page, and if so how much? Do the ads seem independent of the content or are they selling similar or complementary products or services? Is this really a site that provides objective information, or is there a commercial bias?

    - Ads are usually an indicator that a vendor wants to attract your interest in their products, which means they have paid the organization in order to be able to advertise on this site. In some cases this may not influence you but it may also cause you to be more discriminating about doing business with this organization.

- How did you find the site? If a site has a good ranking in many search engines, this may indicate effort invested in the design and maintenance of the web site.

    - This is not necessarily a reliable indicator of information quality as some organizations pay to get good rankings.

- If you have any questions or doubts about the content on a web site, check to see if the author or publisher can be reached by phone, mail, or email and contact them directly with your concerns.

Exercise 14-3: Validating resources

In this exercise you will compare information on various sites and try to determine what information to include in a research project.

1. Open a web browser, if necessary.

2. In the search field, type: how good are tannins and then press ENTER.

    As you review the results, you should notice that the majority of results relate to specific food products while others may refer to reports about tannins in general.

3. Click one of the results for tannins in tea, and then take a few moments to review the contents on that page.

    What do you see on the page that may convince you of the article's accuracy? Or do you see things that make you doubtful? Can you tell when the page was written or last updated? Are there citations for photos, charts, or other images? Are there ads?

4. Go back to the main results page and click one of the Wikipedia links.

5. Take a few moments to review the contents and if possible, compare what you see here to what you saw on the previous site. Do you think one is more accurate than the other? Does one site give you more of the type of information you might be interested in? Which site would you consider to have more accurate facts?

There is no easy answer for determining which site might be more accurate or be more factual; this is where further research becomes important. In this particular case, the sites likely present similar facts and determining which is "better" is not an issue. But what would you do if one site says one thing, and another site says the opposite? Before finalizing any report where your Internet research has turned up conflicting "facts," always turn to a trusted resource such as a published book for more information and draw your conclusions after consulting the trusted resource.

Understanding Copyrights Issues

Objective 3-1.1

Information on the Internet is freely available for you to read, listen to, or otherwise enjoy. People create web sites for many reasons – to advertise, to educate, to entertain, to intellectually challenge. However, simply because information is presented on a web site which you can access freely, that does not imply that information is free for you to copy, use, distribute or present as your own.

Intellectual Property

Any created work or invention is considered to be the *intellectual property* of the person (or organization) who created it. Essentially, anything created by an individual or group on their own behalf is owned by that individual or group; anything created by an individual or group under contract to an organization belongs to the organization that paid the "fee for service."

Estimating the true value of intellectual property is not an easy or straight-forward task. For example, suppose ABC Company develops a training course on repairing an automobile device that converts voice to a text messages. How much is this intellectual property worth? Is it worth the cost of one book? The cost of enough books for an average Service department? The cost of conducting the training class itself? The cost of three years of classes? How do you factor in the time and money spent on creating ABC Company's particular style and method of instruction? Has the style and method evolved over several years of improving previous works?

As another example, consider that Peter has spent 10 years writing a musical. How do we calculate the value of this creative work? Do we factor in the software he used? Do we factor in years of musical training seminars that helped him refine his approach? Do we factor in the number of people who ask if they may stage and perform the opera?

The point is intellectual property is highly valuable, and it is often equally difficult to calculate the degree of loss or damage incurred by the individual or organization whose property was stolen. While it may seem like a small thing to "borrow" all or part of someone else's intellectual property, misusing it amounts to theft or *piracy*, and in some cases even industrial espionage.

Copyright

Copyright laws were created to protect intellectual property. *Copyright* refers to the protection of any material, published or unpublished, created by an individual or organization. This applies to books, music, videos, essays, white papers, pictures, software programs, web sites, and so on.

A copyright gives you ownership of your intellectual property. It can cover anything that you create – a painting, a photograph, a song or a book – if you created it, you own it. Copyright law grants you, and you alone, specific rights over your intellectual property. For example, you have the right to make and distribute copies of your work, perform or display your work publicly, or create additional works based on the original.

These are your rights alone. No one can make a copy of your painting, use your web site code on their web page, or perform a song written by you, unless you give your specific consent.

A copyright also gives you the exclusive right to sell your work. While it is difficult to determine the value of a work, the copyright guarantees that you and you alone have the opportunity to sell, lease or otherwise use your work in exchange for compensation.

As soon as an original work is fixed in a material form (a picture is painted, or a poem is printed, or a piece of code is saved to a disk), the work is protected by copyright. Generally, copyright protection begins from the date the work is created, applies for the entire lifetime of the author, and extends fifty years after the author's death.

When you have created an original work, it is advisable to put a copyright notice at the bottom. The notice includes the copyright symbol ©, followed by the date of creation, followed by your name. For example: Copyright © 2016 Nick Klassen. This is sufficient for asserting a copyright claim if someone violates your rights. For instance, if someone posts your song on their web site without your permission, you can make a claim and they will be forced to remove it.

However, if you want to be able to sue an offending party for monetary damages, then you should register your copyright with the copyright office in your region. For instance, to register a work with the U.S. Copyright Office, submit a completed application form, a nonrefundable filing fee, and a nonreturnable copy or copies of the work to be registered.

Copyrighted Material on Web Sites

Material presented on a web site is subject to the same copyright rules as information in any other media. As a rule, information is copyright-protected.

You can use copyrighted material only if the creator grants you the right to use it. Depending on the material, this could mean paying a royalty, or it could mean acknowledging the creator when you reproduce that content in your own work. It is your responsibility to determine what is required before using any part of an original work.

Fair Use

You are permitted to view the information published on a web site but restrictions apply to the way you use it. That is, you are limited to "fair use," which means that you can use portions of copyrighted information for the purpose of criticism or comment without seeking permission from the rights-holders. For example, if you are writing an essay on the results of a particular court case and want to comment on the judge's report, you can copy and paste the report from the web site with quotes and a reference. It does not matter whether your comments are positive or negative; the fair use principle protects you.

Copyright implicitly belongs to the owner of the web site or published material, even if no copyright symbol (©) or text appears on the product. The originator may have a patent on the product or technology, meaning that person has exclusive rights to make, use, or sell this product or technology. They may choose to license or grant you specific rights, but you cannot advertise the product or technology as your own. An example of this would be the Macintosh computer where Apple owns the patent for this computer and licenses information for the computer to programmers who want to create software for it.

If you wish to use information but are unsure about the copyright situation, send the web site owner an email asking for permission to use the information and describe how you intend to use it.

Some web sites allow you to use the information they provide as long as you quote it accurately and give them credit. However, you must be careful about this as the web site owner may not be the original creator of the information, and therefore does not have the legal right to grant permission.

The following is a list of sources you can research for more information on copyright or trademark laws, and what is applicable in your location:

http://whatiscopyright.org

http://www.copyright.gov (United States Copyright Office)

http://www.copyright.com (Copyright Clearance Center, Inc.)

http://www.tmexpress.com (Trademark Express)

http://fairuse.stanford.edu (Copyright and Fair Use at Stanford University Libraries)

http://strategis.gc.ca/sc_mrksv/cipo (Canadian Intellectual Property Office)

http://www.iipi.org (International Intellectual Property Institute)

http://www.wipo.int (World Intellectual Property Organization)

Legal Ramifications of Copyright Infringement

If you are found to be in violation of a copyright, you will receive a letter from legal sources asking you to remove the content if it is on your web site, or delete any files that you downloaded such as songs, movies, television shows, and so on. You may also find that the ISP has terminated all services for your account, and there is the possibility you may be sued for any damages and have to pay a monetary settlement to the copyright owner.

Licensing

Licensing occurs when you are given permission to use a particular product or service from a vendor. For example, Microsoft incorporates items considered to be part of a Creative Commons license with a note indicating your responsibility to respect the rights of others when you use an item from the Internet. The license agreement states that you will not resell these files or claim these as your own works.

When you purchase a software program, you are purchasing a license to install and use that program. Licenses come in a variety of forms, based on the number of computers that require this software to be installed.

Note: For more information on how to obtain or install software, please refer to Computing Fundamentals, Lesson 5.

Single Seat

- When you purchase a software program, you are purchasing a license to install and use that program on one computer only. The traditional method of purchasing software is to obtain the program on DVD with a booklet with instructions on how to install and use the program.
- You can also purchase and download software online. In such cases, you pay for the program, usually with a credit card, and then receive separate emails from the vendor confirming the purchase and providing a license number, often called the *product code* or *key code*.

Volume or Network

- An organization or company with a large number of users for a software program at various locations will usually purchase this type of license instead of individual copies.
- The number of systems onto which the software can be installed is determined by the terms of the volume license. This option is cost-effective as buying licenses "in bulk" is less expensive than purchasing individual licenses.
- This option is also cost-effective in reducing the amount of time a network administrator must spend installing the software on company systems because most volume licensed software can be installed from a central network location to remote computers throughout an organization. Network-based installation also eliminates the need to carry the software media around, thereby reducing the possibility of damage or loss.

Site

- This grants the purchaser permission to use the software on a network at a single location (site), with an unlimited number of end users. A site license usually allows you to copy and use the software on multiple computers at a single site.
- It is more expensive than purchasing a single copy but less expensive than purchasing a copy for each computer at the site. There may be a maximum specified number of simultaneous users.

Software as a Service (SaaS) or Application Service Provider (ASP)

- Software is sold as a service that enables you to access and use a software program from your system via a network, the organization intranet, or the Internet. You are required to log on to the appropriate network using a valid ID and password before you can access the software.
- Once a SaaS contract expires, you can no longer access that software until you renew the license. Managing the licenses is usually handled by a network administrator in an organization or by an ASP.

Shareware

- Shareware programs are usually available for you to try out for free for a limited amount of time. After the trial period, you can pay a nominal fee and continue using the program. In some instances, the trial version has limited capability, and once you pay the small fee, the restrictions are removed and you can access all the program features.

Freeware

- Freeware programs are available without charge and may also be shared with others at no charge. A potential drawback to using Shareware or Freeware is that support is often limited or non-existent and you are not automatically entitled to updates.

Bundling

- Software can also be "bundled" with a computer purchase. Some of these programs may require you to purchase a full version of the program or to register online before you have access to the program, while others may include the full version and require no further action on your part.

Open Source

- Programming code is made available to anyone; you can modify the program to suit your needs and also share your version with others; however, you are not permitted to charge anyone for it. The feature that distinguishes Open Source programs is that, by sharing the programming code as well as the program itself, users who like certain programs can build in new functions and also make them available to others.

Whichever way you obtain software, it is your responsibility to ensure you are observing the licensing rules. When you purchase licensed software, you will be notified by the vendor of any updates and you will be able to obtain them at no additional cost. If you use software without a valid license, you are violating the vendor's copyright and could be subject to legal action. A network administrator is aware of this responsibility and should take the necessary steps to ensure there are enough licenses for each computer in the organization. By accepting the *End User License Agreement (EULA)* at the time of installation, you further agree to abide by the rules for using the software on the computing device.

Piracy

Piracy is the unauthorized use or reproduction of someone else's work.

- If your friend buys and installs a software application and then gives the installation disk to you and you install it and use it on your computer that is piracy.

- If you download a song from a "sharing site" instead of purchasing it from the record label's online store, that is also piracy. The same is true for movies.

Piracy is considered a federal crime and can carry a penalty of up to ten years in prison.

Censorship and Filtering

As the Internet does not have a governing body that oversees the content placed online, there are many gray areas concerning what is considered good or bad material. This gives rise to debates over whether information should be censored or filtered with the intent to protect users from what may be considered offensive or dangerous information (such as how to make a bomb). Accordingly, many ISPs and organizations make use of different tools to help reduce certain types of information from being accessed.

- **Blockers and filters** - Software that enables you to control the type or amount of content that can be viewed; these are often used in academic or corporate organizations to limit or block access to specific information.

- **Blacklisting** – this is the act of putting a person (or a web site or domain) on a list that will deny them specific privileges or service. A network administrator can add certain sites or domains to a black list and any traffic from these sites will be blocked from entering the network; you can create a black list for your browser that blocks traffic from specific sites or domains. On a larger scale, ISPs can block traffic to and from specific sites and domains. They can also deny services to users who are blacklisted.

Arguably, the use of filters and blockers can be called *censorship*; however, one must also consider that an institution or organization has the right to enforce whatever guidelines it deems suitable concerning the use of their equipment and services. For instance, a company may filter Internet content coming into the network to prevent users from downloading software that has not been authorized; or a company can block access to Facebook to prevent employees from using Facebook while they are at work.

It is legal and appropriate for an organization to restrict access to specific sites to protect the reputation of the organization and avoid offending any customers or visitors to the organization's site. If you are using a computer that is owned by an organization, you are required to respect and adhere to the organization's computing policies, regardless of your personal preferences. Any questions or concerns about these policies can be directed to the network administrator.

While filters and blockers can prevent specific types of information from coming into a network (that is, these tools effect the people within the organization), these tools have no effect on the people outside the organization who share content that is considered questionable.

There is much disagreement concerning who should decide what constitutes offensive, dangerous, or exploitive information. For example, some web sites support a particular race or lifestyle and are often considered to be controversial or to promote "hate." The owners of these web sites are choosing to express their views through a medium that is available to anyone with Internet access, and in many countries, they are exercising their right of free expression. Unless a web site is deemed to have promoted an illegal action, the owners of the web site cannot be forced to shut down the site or to change their message.

The world consists of people from various cultures, beliefs, and lifestyles; what one person considers inappropriate or offensive may not be recognized in the same manner by another person. For example, some countries block their users from accessing any web sites outside their country because they feel this is best for their residents while other countries consider this an extreme form of censorship. Note that a governing body that has censored content for the entire country usually has control over all the Internet-connected computers in that country.

Another shortcoming associated with the use of filters and blocks is that sometimes users are able to hack into the blocker or filter software and change the configuration. Vendors of the filtering software must, therefore, constantly upgrade their product to protect against hacking.

Plagiarism

Plagiarism occurs when you use information created by another person and present it as if it were your own work, either word for word or with minor changes.

- The concept of plagiarism also applies to images. Many images that you find on the Internet are copyrighted. That means, the person who created the image (or took the photo) is its lawful owner, and you must obtain the owner's permission if you want to use the image in your own work.

- It is easy to find information on the Internet to use in your document, and just as easy for someone else to find it and recognize your use of it as plagiarism. There is also a wide availability of plagiarism detection tools that can be used to review files. Plagiarism is the same thing as theft. It does not matter that it is only a paragraph of text or a single picture; it is still stealing the original work of someone else.

- When using information from the Internet, always use it in its original form and cite the source material. This means, give credit to the person who wrote it. There are numerous places where you can find information on how to correctly insert citations or reference material in a document.

Failure to recognize and adhere to the laws surrounding plagiarism can lead to consequences such as a failure mark for a course, suspension or expulsion from the school, ruined academic reputation, or in the case of a business, legal action.

Exercise 14-4: Avoiding plagiarism

In this exercise you will examine information that should be cited.

Suppose you had to write a report based on a particular novel, *Lord of the Flies*. You need to also include reviews on the book made by publishers, users, and then your own opinion of the book.

1. Open a browser if necessary, and in the address bar, navigate to `www.barnesandnoble.com` and press ENTER.

2. In the search field, type: `lord of the flies` and press ENTER.

3. Click the version that has the cover of a large fly in golden tones, and a pair of glasses between the book title and the author name.

4. Scroll down the page until you see the Overview heading.

    Notice in this area you can read information about the plot of the book, as well as read rated reviews by others who have read the book (usually located below the description of the book). This information is very valuable as it meets the criteria for the report. However, do not take your information from only one source. Additionally, if you use one of the reviews from this web page, make sure you give credit to Barnes and Noble. Even though the review is by an individual, it is located on the Barnes and Noble web site. Fair Use allows you to include the review in your report, as long as you give credit to the store and cite the web site as the source of the information.

5. Navigate to `www.amazon.com`, type: `lord of the flies` in the search field there, and press ENTER.

6. From the results list, click the same edition of the book that you used previously.

7. Scroll down to see the reviews listed on this site.

    Again, if you were going to use any of these reviews, remember to give appropriate credit by indicating where you found the information.

8. Navigate to `www.bing.com`, in the search field type: `review of the lord of the flies book` and press ENTER.

You should now have a long list of various sites that contain reviews of this book. Accordingly, there are a number of sources available to you on the Internet to use when researching an item. Be careful of how you use the sources and ensure you do not copy a review word-for-word without providing credit to the author or web site; otherwise you have just plagiarized someone else's work.

Lesson Summary

This lesson taught you to you how to use the information you may find online in a respectful and legal manner. You should now be able to:

☑ search for items on a specific web site

☑ search for items using search engines

☑ use tools to narrow the search criteria

☑ evaluate the validity of the information

☑ understand what copyright and fair use includes

☑ understand what intellectual property is

☑ recognize censorship or filtering

☑ understand what plagiarism is

Review Questions

1. What kind of sites would contain comments or information on pages devoted to specific topics?
   a. Social networking
   b. Blogs
   c. Wikis
   d. News feeds

2. What is one of the fastest ways to search for an item on a specific web site?
   a. Use a search engine such as Google.com or Bing.com.
   b. Use the web browser search field.
   c. Use the search field on that specific web site.
   d. Use the search field from the Start menu.

3. What does the search engine maintain?
   a. Database of Internet URLs.
   b. Database with all the web pages in your country.
   c. Database with all the web pages on the Internet.
   d. Database of all the music files on the Internet.

4. How would you select an item that appears in a drop-down list while you are typing items into the search field?
   a. Press the F2 key to move to the item.
   b. Press the PGUP or PGDN key to move to the item.
   c. Double-click in the search field.
   d. Click the item in the list.
   e. Any of the previous.

5. Which Boolean statement would display results that will list golf courses where playoff tournaments occur but not include those played in Europe?
   a. golf courses OR playoffs NOT europe
   b. golf courses OR playoffs AND europe
   c. golf courses AND playoffs NOT europe
   d. golf courses AND playoffs OR europe

6. Which HTML object will help you find results for links to museums in Paris?
   a. museums image:paris
   b. museums anchor:paris
   c. paris anchor:museums
   d. museums links:paris

7. What is the benefit of using a hashtag to search for an item?
   a. Results will include postings made on social media sites.
   b. You limit the search to social media sites only.
   c. You can enter any text for the hashtag to find existing postings.
   d. The hashtag limits the search to items posted during the last week only.

8. Why should you compare different sites when researching information?
   a. To enable you to place the copyright © symbol at the bottom of your report.
   b. Comparing facts presented on different sites helps you determine their accuracy and validity.
   c. You need to show at least five resource locations in the bibliography.
   d. To check that each site was created in the same location.

9. Which of the following would not be considered as intellectual property and could be used by anyone without permission?
   a. Company logo
   b. Corporate Mission (print and online)
   c. Picture of a device created by a company
   d. Product created by a company
   e. Grocery list on a sticky note

10. If a company has numerous branches across the country as well as offices in other countries, what type of licensing should be obtained for the company computers?
    a. Site
    b. Network or volume
    c. Premium
    d. Open Source

11. What does blacklisting refer to?
    a. The act of deleting someone from your list of contacts.
    b. The act of adding a sender to your trash folder so you no longer see their messages.
    c. The act of putting someone on a list that will deny them specific privileges or service.
    d. The act of adding someone to your Safe Senders list.

12. When does plagiarism occur?
    a. When you log into a web site using someone else's account.
    b. When you copy someone else's work as your own and take credit for the work.
    c. When you sell your own work to someone else to use.
    d. When you sell your login ID and password to someone else.

Lesson 15: Digital Communication

Lesson Objectives

In this lesson, you will learn about various digital communications technologies. Upon completion of this lesson, you should be able to:

- [ ] explain the difference between real-time and delayed communications
- [ ] describe email and texting
- [ ] select the best communications tool for a given situation
- [ ] describe various phone calling technologies
- [ ] manage status and profile settings in Skype
- [ ] conduct group conversations in Skype
- [ ] describe how to conduct group conversations in Google Hangouts
- [ ] describe the benefits and function of online conferencing tools
- [ ] describe benefits and function of business collaboration tools
- [ ] describe distance learning technologies
- [ ] describe audio, video, and live streaming

Digital Communication Technologies

The Internet and widely available high speed broadband connections have made communicating with others quick, efficient, and affordable. As the traditional boundaries between the telephone network, cellular networks, and data networks are disappearing, we find that we have a wide variety of choices regarding the technologies and the devices we want to use in order to communicate.

In this lesson, we will examine various technologies for digital communication. You will notice that many of them overlap; different platforms and different applications are developed as the Internet evolves and as the required infrastructure is continuously put into place.

Real-Time (Synchronous) and Delayed (Asynchronous) Communications

Communication refers to any process that enables you to interact with others. Electronic communication is simply communication that involves using an electronic method such as email, instant/text messaging or electronic voice and video conferencing.

There are two essential time frames for communication: real-time and delayed. In *real-time* communication, information is sent and received instantly. A face-to-face conversation is an example of real-time communication. If Kelly and Marcie are having a face-to-face talk, then as soon as Kelly says something, Marcie hears it. Additionally, Marcie can respond immediately. And as soon as Marcie says something in reply, Kelly hears her reply. In digital communications, real-time exchanges are referred to as *synchronous*.

In *delayed* communication, there is a time delay between the sending and receiving of information. A mailed letter is an example of delayed communication. Kelly writes Marcie a letter. She puts the letter in an envelope, addresses and stamps the envelope and drops it off at the post office. In a few days, a letter carrier delivers Kelly's letter to Marcie's mailbox. When Marcie comes home from work, she checks the mail, brings it inside, and then opens and reads Kelly's letter. In digital communications, delayed exchanges are referred to as *asynchronous*.

Asynchronous Communications Tools

Objective 3-6.1, 3-6.2

The digital tools we will examine that provide asynchronous communications are email and text messaging. These tools are considered asynchronous because a delay is acceptable. That is, you can send a communication to your intended recipient regardless of your recipient's availability.

Electronic Mail (Email)

You have already spent some time sending and receiving email messages and sending files as email attachments. Email is a standard and popular method for exchanging business communications and personal messages when a response is not urgent.

You may spend your work day sitting at your desk sending and replying to email messages. You may also respond to messages as soon as they arrive, and you may receive replies as soon as you send messages out. In such a scenario, email correspondence occurs in real time; however, email is considered a delayed communication because a delay does not affect your ability to send or receive an email message.

Kelly can send an email message to Marcie whenever she likes. Marcie may be sitting at her desk, or Marcie may be at lunch, or Marcie may be on vacation in Europe. These factors do not affect Kelly's ability to send an email message to Marcie. And once Marcie becomes available, and she logs in to her email account, the messages that Kelly sent to her will be waiting in her Inbox.

It is convenient when Marcie is sitting at her desk waiting to receive and reply to Kelly's message; but it is not a requirement.

SMS Text Messages

You learned in Computing Fundamentals that SMS text messages are short messages (around 160 characters) sent over a cellular provider's network using the Short Message Service protocol. Text messaging is also considered a delayed communication. Kelly can text Marcie whether Marcie's phone is on or off. If Marcie's phone is turned off when Kelly sends her a text message, Marcie will receive the text message the next time she powers on her phone.

Using Text Messaging Effectively

Texting can be a good communications tool if you use it wisely.

Remember that even though texting "looks like" instant messaging, it is not necessarily real-time communication. You can send a text to a contact at any time; you have no way of knowing whether he or she is available when you send your text message. Your intended recipient may be unable to respond (perhaps they are driving, or in attendance at a meeting or a performance), or may be unaware that you have sent a text message. For example, the recipient's phone may be turned off, or the recipient may not have heard the alert sound of an incoming text, or may not have noticed the new text message icon on the cell phone.

You may receive an immediate response to a text message, but that is not guaranteed. If you require an immediate response, it may be better to place a phone call.

Always remember that if a situation is best resolved by speaking to someone directly, use the telephone or seek a face-to-face meeting.

When is a Text Appropriate?

If you can convey your message or question in relatively few words, a text is probably appropriate. If, on the other hand, it would require several screens of text to get your message across, email might be a better choice. Remember that several minutes of back and forth texting can be very disruptive for people who are trying to get their work done.

Remember also that, depending on the cell plan/data plan, people may be charged a fee for sending and receiving text messages, especially if they exceed a specific quota. Be considerate; ask about your recipient's preferred method of communication.

Audience consideration, however, is arguably the strongest determining factor:

* If your intended recipient is often away from the office, and seldom responds to email messages, text is probably appropriate. Some people who are negligent at answering email respond almost immediately to text messages.

* If your intended recipient is relatively inexperienced with technology, a phone call may be a better choice. Just because Grandmother owns a cell phone does not mean that she likes (or knows how) to text.

* If your intended recipient is visually impaired, or has trouble using his or her hands, a phone call might be much easier.

* On the other hand, if you need to communicate with someone who has a hard time hearing, a text might be the perfect solution to avoiding a frustrating conversation during which you might have to repeat yourself often, or speak at a volume louder than is normal or is comfortable for you.

To Text or Not to Text?

It is not always easy to determine when and when not to use text messaging. Here are a few guidelines:

* Use text if you must communicate, but are in a place or situation where speaking out loud would be inconsiderate or indiscreet.

* Avoid texting while driving. It is dangerous and against the law in many regions to text while driving. If you know that your intended recipient is on the road, refrain from sending SMS messages. Use email instead.

- Avoid sending and responding to texts if you are in a social setting, such as at the dinner table or involved in a conversation. Your "live" audience deserves your full attention. It is rude to ignore the people around you in order to engage in texting.

- Avoid sending text messages late at night. Many people react to a late-night text the same way they react to a late-night phone call; they fear it might be bad news. Think twice before sending – can your message wait until business hours tomorrow morning?

- Do not attempt send text messages while you are in an airplane that is taxiing, taking off, or landing.

Etiquette

Etiquette is a customary code of polite behavior (good manners) in society or among members of a particular profession or group. In matters relating to the Internet and electronic communication, etiquette is often referred to as *netiquette*. To observe netiquette, keep the following points in mind:

- If you are involved in text conversation with a group of people, consider the frequency of your messages. Do all members of the group need to receive all your texts? If not, start a new text to reply to an individual within the group instead of replying to the entire group.

- Remember that electronic modes of communication tend to be open to misinterpretation. Always remember that the recipient cannot see your face, and that it is very difficult to convey tone in a written message. For example, a sarcastic remark meant as a joke can easily hurt someone's feelings. Try to treat others in the same manner that you want to be treated, online or in person.

- Refrain from using all uppercase letters in your message as this is considered "shouting". Use shouting with utmost discretion.

- Do not use texting as a way of bullying or harassing someone in any manner.

- Refrain from using abbreviations and acronyms in business or school texts. Not everyone is familiar with these, and it can lead to misinterpretation or confusion.

- Refrain from using emoticons, which are symbols that attempt to convey to the recipient the sender's emotion, in business or school communications. They are considered unprofessional.

- Always try to respond to messages in a timely manner. Not all messages require an immediate response, but when a message contains a question or requires further action, be sure to send an appropriate reply.

- Always follow the rules and guidelines established by your school or organization (and local, regional and national laws if appropriate) regarding electronic communications.

Real-Time Communication Technologies

Objective 3-6.1

While asynchronous communication methods such as text and email provide you with a "history" of conversation threads and "proof" that certain communications were sent and received, sometimes there is just no substitute for real-time communications.

Remember that real-time communication is a live conversation. When you are engaged in a face-to-face conversation with another person, it is easy observe body language, facial expressions, and tone of voice. Each party can ask and answer questions as they arise. You can clarify points as you go, and "read" the other party to assess how well they understand what you are saying. You can also see whether they agree with you or not and adjust your communications as necessary to meet a need or bring the other person around to your point of view.

Technologies that provide real-time (or synchronous) communications include phone calls/conference calls, online meetings/video conferences (WebEx), and instant messaging.

Phone Calls

Phone calls are perhaps the finest example of a real-time communication technology at work. One of the better-known telephone company advertising slogans from the not-too-distant past was "Long Distance: the Next Best Thing to Being There." Another was "Reach Out and Touch Someone."

Phone calls are personal and give each participant the other party's full attention (or at least we hope so). Phone calls can be almost as effective and empowering as face-to-face communications. There are many situations in business and personal relations that require real-time, personal contact. Consider the following scenarios in which a phone call is probably the best means of communication to use (when a face to face meeting is not possible):

- **You are communicating with someone whom you do not know**. It can be intimidating to "converse" via email with someone whom you have never met.

- **You must convey a complicated idea**. Many people have a difficult time organizing complex concepts and ideas in writing. Sometimes you can compose a well-organized and coherent message, but the message becomes quite lengthy. Many people are immediately discouraged when they see large blocks of text staring at them, and they skim the message instead of reading it. This can lead to misunderstanding and frustration on both sides. If issues require further clarification, then messages must be sent back and forth perhaps several times. The possible added delay of email can make communications seem long and drawn out, and can make the entire process tiring and tedious.

- **You must discuss a sensitive topic**. Some matters are just not handled well through writing. Email and text can seem impersonal and cold. Voice, on the other hand, can convey a wealth of emotion – including support and understanding – when appropriate. Additionally, phone calls are private, while email, text, and chat could be seen or intercepted by people not involved in the discussion.

- **You require an immediate response**. Sometimes you need an answer right away. You can send an email and ask for an immediate reply, but how do you know whether the other party got your message? What if your recipient is on vacation or out sick? You have no way of knowing whether your inquiry/request is on anyone's "radar" so to speak.

- **You need to get a message to someone immediately**. Sometimes you need to send an urgent message and you need to be sure the other party has received it. For example, if you are on your way to a job interview and have to stop to fix a flat tire or to wait for an accident on the freeway to be cleared, it is a much better idea to call the person who is waiting to interview you than it is to send that person an email.

Phone Call Technologies

There are three basic technologies you can use to make phone calls. You can use:

Landline phones – when you place a call using a landline phone, voice signals are sent over the copper wires of the public switched telephone network. Incoming calls are free, but long-distance calling can become expensive.

Mobile phones – when you place a call using a mobile phone, voice signals are sent wirelessly over your cellular carrier's network. Most cellular plans offer unlimited calling, including long-distance calling, for a set monthly rate (international calls often incurs an extra charge).

VoIP phones – when you place a call using a VoIP phone, voice signals are sent as packets across the Internet.

Internet Phone Calls (VoIP)

Voice over Internet Protocol (VoIP) is a technology that allows you to make voice calls using a broadband Internet connection instead of a traditional telephone line. VoIP converts voice signals into small packets of digital data, adds addressing information to each packet, and then sends the packets across the Internet. This process should sound familiar to you – it is the same process used when your computer communicates with web servers or other computers over the Internet.

Because VoIP calls bypass the telephone network and use the Internet, VoIP calls are free (except for the fee you pay for Internet service). Many businesses use VoIP services because they are much less expensive than traditional telephone services, especially for long-distance calling.

Best of all, you can call landline phones and cell phones from your VoIP phone, and these types of phones can call you. Cellular networks, IP networks, and the telephone network connect to one another through specialized gateways. (A gateway is a network point that acts as an entrance into another network.)

Residential consumers can purchase VoIP phone service through their ISP (if the services are offered), or through a third party service provider such as Vonage. The provider will usually supply the required equipment.

Businesses may also purchase VoIP phone service through an Internet provider, or they may choose to implement their own VoIP solutions by modifying their existing data networks to support phone services.

Disadvantages

A disadvantage of using VoIP for phone calls is that calls are very sensitive to delay. If packets containing voice information take too long to traverse the Internet, the result is a conversation that sounds choppy or "broken." VoIP communications are also highly susceptible to echo and feedback, especially if one or more participants is using a speakerphone or laptop speakers as opposed to a headset.

Another major drawback to using VoIP is that it is dependent upon an Internet connection. If your Internet connection is not reliable, or is too slow, calls will have poor sound quality and may be dropped (that is, the connection can be lost). If your Internet connection goes down, you have no phone service.

Unlike landline phones, which will still function in the event of a power outage, VoIP service cannot function without electrical power. Even if your VoIP phone has a battery, your modem/router is dependent upon AC power. If your modem or router cannot function, your Internet connection goes down.

Conference Calling

A *conference call* is simply a call that involves three or more parties. Many business phones include a Conference button. Most consumer phones include a Flash button which you can use to create a conference call if a conference calling service is included in your phone plan.

Modern conference calling is not limited to audio only; almost all technologies that provide video calling support video conference calling.

You can participate in conference calls on landline, mobile, and VoIP phones.

WebEx

WebEx is a hosted service that you can use to conduct online meetings with anyone who has an Internet connection – including mobile users. Although only WebEx is described in this section, most online meetings occur in a similar fashion, regardless of the platform used to host the meeting.

An *online meeting* (sometimes called a web conference) is a meeting in which multiple participants can not only speak to each other, but also share visuals such as presentation files, documents, whiteboards, and even video. Within a meeting, different participants can "take control" and share files or progress through a presentation.

Participants can access an online meeting by clicking a link that they receive in an emailed meeting invitation. You can also be invited to an online meeting through an instant messaging application. WebEx software is delivered over the web as you need it; the first time you attend a meeting, the software will automatically install itself on your computer.

When you join an online meeting (depending on the platform being used to host the meeting) you have options on how to connect to audio. You can use your landline phone or a mobile phone (phone numbers for connecting are provided) or you can use VoIP via a headset connected to your computer.

Online meetings are often called *video conferences* because participants have the option to share the image and/or video via webcam. With WebEx you can speak with other participants and the image shown on your screen will change to show who is currently speaking.

WebEx also allows you to record online meetings, and to share or publish the recordings so that others can see what transpired during the meeting even if they were unable to attend.

WebEx services are provided by Cisco through various subscription or pay-per-use plans. You must have a subscription in order to host WebEx meetings, but anyone with a computer (or smart device) and an Internet connection can attend a meeting.

Web-conferencing equipment is expensive, demands high bandwidth and requires skilled IT staff. The advantages of using a hosted web-conferencing service include simple and easy administration, relatively low cost, and dedicated, professional support.

Skype – More than Just IM

Objective 3-6.1, 3-6.3

In Computing Fundamentals, you were introduced to Skype; you created a Skype account, downloaded and installed the Skype client, added a contact, exchanged messages with your contact, and shared files through Skype.

In this lesson, you will work with some of the group features of Skype, and you will examine aspects of Skype that communicate information about you – such as your profile information, your status, and your personal note. To begin, we will take a detailed look at the Skype interface. The following figure shows a sample instant messaging session in the Skype Desktop app.

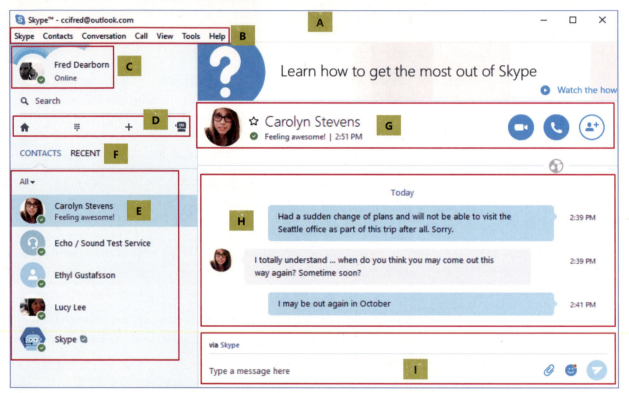

Note: Bots are applications that perform automated tasks using artificial intelligence. You can add Skype bots to your Contacts that will chat with you. Some assist with tasks and others provide entertainment.

A – Your Account	The account name you are using displays in the title bar. You can sign into Skype using a Skype name, a Microsoft account, or your Facebook sign-in details.
B – Menu Bar	Provides access to commands, including those for configuring settings.
C – Status Bar	Displays your screen name and current status (for example, Online, Away, Do Not Disturb, and so on). You can also add a personal note that your contacts can see.
D – Toolbar	Provides access to features such as Skype Home, an on-screen dial pad, a window for creating group conversations, and link to Skype bots which you can add to your Contacts.
E – Contacts List	Displays your contacts and an indicator of their current status.

F – Recent List	Lists recent conversations you have had.
G – Contact Summary	Displays the name, status, and note of the currently selected contact. Also provides buttons for turning an IM conversation into a video call or an audio call, and for creating a group conversation.
H – Conversation window	Displays the instant messaging conversation you are having.
I – Conversation box	Type your messages in the box, then press ENTER.

Because the consumer version of Skype is free, it may display advertising banners.

Adjusting Your Status

In Skype, your current status is indicated by a colored circle at the lower-right of your profile picture (or picture icon if you have not added a profile picture). Each of your contacts also has a status indicator next to their names in your contacts list.

By reading the status indicator of any contact, you can determine the best way to communicate with that contact. For example, if you see that your contact Kelly is offline, you can send an instant message to her with the knowledge that she will not see the message until the next time she signs in. If you really need to contact Kelly immediately, a phone call might be a better way to go.

If you roll your mouse over a contact's status icon, you can see extra information about their status. For example, if a contact is offline, you can see how long he or she has been offline, and whether the contact has set up call forwarding.

By default, Skype indicates that you are Online whenever you sign in. However, you can change your status at any time. In the menu bar, click **Skype**, point to **Online Status**, then click an option in the menu.

Online	This is your default status when you sign in. Your contacts can reach you via instant message or calling.
Away	Your contacts can see that you are signed in, but not necessarily at your computer. Instant messages are delivered immediately, and your contacts can still try to call you. You can configure Skype to automatically change your status to Away after you have been idle for a specified period of time.
Do Not Disturb	Your contacts can see that you are online, but that you do not want to be disturbed. They can still send you instant messages and call you, but you will not be alerted with sound notifications.
Invisible	You will appear to be offline, but you can still use Skype as usual. This is a good way to keep using Skype without "advertising" to your contacts that you are available.
Offline	Your status is automatically set to Offline when you are not signed into Skype. If you manually select this status, you cannot send instant messages or make or receive calls.

At the bottom of the Online Status menu, is the Set up Call forwarding option. You can set up call forwarding to forward Skype calls to a landline phone or a mobile phone. You must purchase Skype credit in order to set up call forwarding.

Once you set up call forwarding, you can set your status to Calls forwarded.

Managing Your Skype Profile

Your Skype profile, like any online profile, tells other people something about you.

Certain aspects of your Skype profile are public, some are visible only to you and your contacts, and some are private (not visible to anyone). For example, your email address is private; that means it is never displayed. However, people who already know your email address can use it to search for you.

The following figure shows the fields that comprise a Skype profile.

		Fred Dearborn	
	Accounts	ccifred@outlook.com Manage	Public
	Mood	Enter mood message	
	Mobile phone	+12065559997	Contacts
	Home phone	Add number	Contacts
	Office phone	+18005553321	Contacts
		˅ Hide full profile	
	Email	ccifred@outlook.com	Private
	Email	Add email address	Private
	Email	Add email address	Private
		˅ Hide full profile	
	Email	ccifred@outlook.com	Private
	Email	Add email address	Private
	Email	Add email address	Private
	Country/Region	United States ▾	Public
	Email	ccifred@outlook.com	Private
	Email	Add email address	Private
	Email	Add email address	Private
	Country/Region	United States ▾	Public
	State/Province	WA	Public
	Email	Add email address	Private
	Email	Add email address	Private
	Country/Region	United States ▾	Public
	State/Province	WA	Public
	City	Seattle	Public
	Time	10:56 AM My computer's ▾	Contacts ▾
	Website	Add homepage	Public
	Gender	Male ▾	Public
	Birth date	27 ▾ 3 ▾ Year ▾	Public
	Language	English ▾	Public
	Contacts	3	Contacts ▾
	About me	I check out radical vacation spots for Tolano Adventures!	Public

Change picture
Public ▾

You can set the field below your picture in your Skype profile to:

Public – everyone on Skype can see it.

Contacts only – only your contacts can see it.

Private – no one can see it.

You cannot change the setting for any of the fields that are grayed out.

Your contacts can view the profile information you have set to Public and the information you have set to Contacts. You may choose to share a lot of information, like Fred:

Contact profile	✕
☆ Fred Dearborn	
● Life is Great!	
11:27 AM Seattle, WA, United States	
Skype:	live:ccifred
Mobile:	+12065559997
Office:	+18005553321
	Add Number
About me	
I check out radical vacation spots for Tolano Adventures!	
Gender	
Male	
Language	
English	

Or you may choose to share very little, like Carolyn.

Contact profile	✕
☆ Carolyn Stevens	
● Feeling awesome!	
11:33 AM	
Skype:	live:cstevens1099
Office:	+18005553321
	Add Number

Or you may choose something in between.

Mood Messages

In Skype, your mood message can share a general idea, or can be customized to give a little more information on your current status. For example, perhaps you need to run to the post office. You can set your status to Away, and you can set your mood message to "Be back in 20 minutes" to let your contacts know that you do not anticipate being away for very long.

 ☆ Fred Dearborn
● At the Passport Office; back in an hour | 11:25 AM Seattle, WA, United States

Exercise 15-1: Managing your online status and profile

This exercise assumes that you created a Skype account, downloaded and installed the Skype Desktop client, and added at least one contact as directed in Computing Fundamentals, Lesson 5, Exercises 5-9 and 5-10. If you have not, please do so at this time.

In this exercise, you will work with your online status and your profile.

1. Start Skype and sign in.

2. Team up with a person sitting near you and decide who will be Student A and who will be Student B.

3. If necessary, add your teammate to your Skype contacts. (Refer to Lesson 5, Exercise 5-10 for step-by-step instructions, if you need to.)

Note that in order to demonstrate how alert sounds are affected by your status, you will be asked to click outside the Skype window many times during this exercise.

4. **Student A**: Click *Student B* in your Contacts list, then click in the message area, type a short message and press ENTER to send the instant message to Student B.

5. **Student B**: You should hear an alert when the message arrives. Click the **Recent** tab to see the new conversation with Student A.

6. **Student B**: Click the conversation in the Recent tab to open the conversation window with the message from Student A.

7. **Student B**: Click in the message area and type and send a response. Student A should not hear an alert because the Skype conversation window is open and active on his or her system.

8. **Student B**: Click **Skype**, **Online Status**, **Away** to change your status. Then click outside the Skype application window. (Restore the window if necessary so that you can click outside of it.)

9. **Student A**: Send another message to Student B.

10. **Student B**: Did you hear an alert when Student A sent you a message? Even if your status is set to Away, you will hear an alert if Skype is not the active window.

11. **Student B**: Change your status to **Do Not Disturb**. Skype displays a message box warning that you will not receive notifications.

12. **Student B**: Click **OK** to close the message box, then click outside the Skype window.

13. **Student A**: Send another message to Student B.

14. **Student B**: You did not hear an alert, but did you receive Student A's message? Messages still come through when your status is set to Do Not Disturb, but you will not hear notifications.

15. **Student B**: Set your status back to **Online**.

16. **Student A**: Click **Skype**, **Online Status**, **Invisible**, then click outside the Skype window.

17. **Student B**: Send a message to Student A.

18. **Student A**: Did you hear an alert when Student B sent you a message? Being invisible is like "lurking" online – you can "see and hear" everything, but no one can see you.

19. **Student A**: Set your status to **Offline**.

20. **Student B**: Send another message to Student A.

21. **Student A**: Did you receive Student B's message? When your status is set to offline, you will not receive messages that are sent to you.

22. **Student A**: Send a message to Student B.

23. **Student B**: Did you receive the message from Student A? Because Student A's status is set to *Offline*, he or she cannot send messages.

24. **Student A**: Set your status back to **Online**. Now you should receive the last message that Student B sent.

25. **Student B**: Now that Student A is back online, you should receive the message that Student A sent while he or she was offline.

Now, make some changes to your profile.

26. Click **Skype**, point to **Profile**, then click **Edit Your Profile** to open the profile management page.

27. Click the **Show full profile** link to expand the options displayed on the page. Notice that for most of these, you cannot change who sees the information. If you do not want everyone to see the information that would be listed in a Public field, do not enter information into that field.

28. Click the **Enter mood message** link to open the Mood field. Type a short phrase that summarizes your mood, then click the check mark that displays to the right of the field to accept the entry. Your teammate should be able to see your mood message almost immediately.

29. Click the **Home** button on the Skype toolbar.

Group Conversations

When you conduct a group conversation in Skype, anything you type and send is received by everyone in the group. Sometimes you may be having a conversation with a contact, and realize that you need to loop in another person. Other times, you may know that you need to converse with two or more people and you can start out as a group conversation.

To add a contact to a conversation already in progress, click the ⊕ (**Create new group**) button to open a window for adding contacts and turning your conversation into a group conversation.

Click the contact you want to add to the conversation. The name of contacts who will be added to the conversation appears in the box at the top of the window.

When you are finished adding contacts, click **Create group** to open a new group conversation window.

Notice that a group avatar 👥 now displays at the upper-left corner of the conversation window. Notice also that the previous portion of the conversation is not included in the new group conversation window.

Because you are now in a group conversation, the button at the far right 👤⁺ is now named *Add people*. You can click **Add people** to add more people into your group conversation.

If you want to save a group as a contact, right-click the group avatar, and click **Save Group in Your Contacts**.

Type a name for the group contact, then click **OK**.

To create a brand new group conversation to which you can add anyone you like, click ➕ (**Create a new conversation**) to open the window for adding contacts. Click the contacts you want to add to the group, then click the **Add** button to open a conversation window for the new group.

If you want to leave a group conversation, right-click the group avatar, then click **Leave Conversation**.

Click **Leave** to confirm. When a participant has left a conversation, the other participants are notified.

Today

Lucy Lee
I did - this morning.

Carolyn Stevens
Nothing yet here in Seattle

Carolyn Stevens has left
9:57 AM

Exercise 15-2: Conducting group conversations

In this exercise, you will participate in group conversations in Skype. Your teacher should divide the class into teams of four. Decide who will be Student A, Student B, Student C, and Student D.

Begin by clearing out your conversation history. This will make it easier to distinguish one conversation from another.

1.   Click **Tools**, then click **Options** to open the Skype Options page.

2. In the panel at the left, click **Privacy** to access the Privacy settings.

3. In the Allow IMs from section, click the **Clear history** button, then click **Delete** to confirm. Skype clears past conversations from your account.

4. Click **Save** to close the Skype Options page.

5. Ensure that everyone on your team is in your Contacts list. If not, add them now.

Start a conversation.

6. **Student A**: Send a message to Student B.

7. **Student B**: Click the **Recent** tab to see the new conversation, then click the conversation to open the conversation window.

8. **Student B**: Click in the message area and send a reply to Student A.

Change the conversation to a group conversation.

9. **Student A:** Click the **Create new group** icon at the upper right area of the conversation window, click Student C and Student D in the list of Contacts, then click **Create group**.

10. **Student A:** Click in the message area for the new group conversation window and send a message to everyone.

11. **Student B:** You should see a new group conversation listed in your Recent tab. The group conversation shows a group avatar instead of a contact icon or profile picture.

12. **Students C and D**: Click the **Recent** tab to see the new group conversation.

13. **Students B, C, and D**: Click the group conversation to open the conversation window.

14. **Everyone**: Take a few minutes to send messages to one another in the group conversation window.

Save the group as a contact.

15. **Student B**: Right-click the group avatar, click **Save Group in Your Contacts**, type: MyClassTeam, then press ENTER. Everyone should see a notification that Student B renamed the conversation to "MyClassTeam." Additionally, the new name should appear in the Recent tab.

16. **Student B**: Click the **Contacts** tab and scroll to the bottom of your Contacts to ensure that MyClassTeam has been saved as a contact. Group contacts appear at the bottom of the Contacts list. The group contact will be saved only in Student B's contacts list.

17. **Student D**: Right-click the group avatar, click **Leave Conversation**, then click **Leave** to confirm. A notification that Student D has left the conversation should appear in everyone's conversation window. Note that because Student D left the conversation, Student D is no longer saved in the *MyClassTeam* contact.

18. **Everyone**: Right-click the group avatar, click **Hide conversation**, and then click **OK** to hide the old conversation and keep the Skype interface uncluttered. (If you want to view hidden conversations, click View in the menu bar, then click Show Hidden Conversations.)

Checking Out Google Hangouts

In Computing Fundamentals, you used the Gmail chat feature from your Gmail Inbox. What you might not have realized is that Gmail chat is powered by Google Hangouts.

Google Hangouts is a communications platform that supports SMS, IM, group chat, VoIP calling, and video conferencing. Hangouts allows conversations between 2 or more users and can be accessed online through Gmail or the Hangouts website, through the Hangouts app, or through mobile apps for Android and iOS.

You can open a browser and navigate to https://hangouts.google.com and click the **Sign in** link, or you can sign into Gmail, then click the **Google apps** button, click **More**, and then click **Hangouts**. The Hangouts page is shown in the following figure.

Note: You can add an extension for the Chrome browser that lets you use Hangouts outside the browser window.

Your Gmail contacts are integrated into Hangouts and display in your Hangouts contact list. A green dot displays at the lower right of the contact icon for contacts who are currently signed in to Gmail. Click the icons in the vertical menu on the left to display contacts (the default view), conversations or phone calls. You can also click the **Menu** button (three horizontal lines) to open a menu of Hangouts options.

To start a conversation on Hangouts, click a contact to open a conversation window, type your message then press ENTER.

Notice the ▇◀ (**Video call**) icon at the upper left corner of the conversation window. You can turn a conversation into a video call with a click.

To add another participant, click ▇▲ (**Create a group Hangout**) to open a window of contacts you can add to the conversation. Select the contact to you want to add, then click **Create group**. A new conversation window opens, and any messages you send here will be sent to everyone in the group hangout.

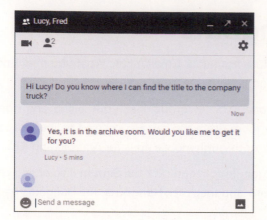

It is possible to add contacts who are not currently signed in to Gmail; however, they won't see the group conversation until they sign in.

To leave a group conversation, click the ⚙ (**Options**) button, click **Leave**, then confirm that you want to leave the conversation.

Online Conferencing

Objective 3-7.1

Because online conferencing uses the Internet to transfer voice and video signals, and because the Internet is a data network, online conferencing is well suited for exchanging digital files, sending instant messages, and sharing screens. For example, in an online conference call, you can pull up a YouTube video and play it in your browser and share your screen (and your audio) with everyone else on the call. You can even send the URL to everyone in an instant message while the video is playing.

Just about anything you can do on your computer or on the Internet on your own, you can do with others through online conferencing.

VoIP Conferencing

VoIP phone calls use the Internet to transfer voice packets between the phones used in a call or conference call. Any of the "phones" themselves can be a telephone handset, a conference room speaker box, a computer headset or PC speakers and a microphone.

The point is, you can use a computer to place and receive VoIP calls, including conference calls. In these scenarios, the computer is considered a software phone or "soft phone." You can use one of several applications – such as Skype or Google Hangouts – as an interface for your soft phone.

A powerful advantage to using your computer as a soft phone is the ability to transfer files and share screens during a call.

Using Skype for VoIP Calls

To begin an audio call on Skype, click the contact you want to call in the contacts pane, then click the 🔵 (**Call**) button. Skype displays the profile picture of the other party on your screen for the duration of the call.

You can click the ▤ (**Show contacts**) button to open the Contacts panel on the left side of the Skype call window. You can click the 🗩 (**Show IM**) button to open the Conversation window on the right side of the Skype call window, allowing you to send instant messages or files during a call.

You can use the buttons at the bottom of the screen to make adjustments and take actions during the call:

- Click 📷 (**Turn on video**) to toggle your video camera on or off.

- Click 🎤 (**Mute your microphone**) to mute or unmute your microphone.

- Click ➕ (**Add participants, send files and more**) to open a menu of options. You can send files on the call, send contact cards, share screens, add people to the call, or show the dial pad. When you send files or contact info, these are sent through the IM panel. The Show IM button on your recipient's screen will glow, indicating that there is information available.

- Click 📞 (**End call**) to leave the call.

Conference Calls

To conduct a conference call using Skype you can:

- Create a group conversation and then click the **Call** button; or

- add additional participants to a call that is already in progress.

To add participants to a call that is already in progress, click **Add participants, send files and more** to open a menu of options.

Send files...

Send Contacts...

Share screens...

Add people to this call...

Show dial pad

Click **Add people to this call**.

Click the participant you want to add, then click the **Add to call button**. The added participant's phone rings. If he or she answers, they are added to the call.

Screen Sharing

Screen sharing has many useful functions, including the ability to:

- deliver a presentation to the participants on your call,

- show a specific section of a document for which you need ideas or clarification,

- demonstrate how to accomplish a particular task on the computer, or within a specific application,

- demonstrate a problem or show an error message that you are receiving.

To share a screen during a Skype call, click **Add participants, send files and more**, then click **Share screens**.

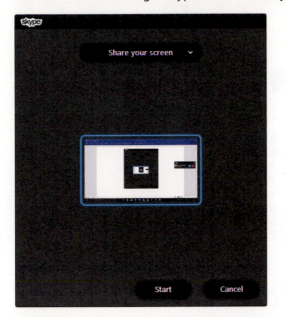

You can specify to share your entire screen (using the Share your screen option), or just the content that appears in a particular window (using the Share a window option). Make your selection using the drop-down arrow if necessary, then click **Start** to begin sharing.

Whatever displays on your screen (or in your selected window) appears in the other participants' Skype window. For example, if Fred decides to share a document in his Word application window, the other participants will see his Word document in their Skype windows, as shown in the following figure.

On your system (if you are the one sharing) all content that is visible to other participants appears inside a red border. The following figure shows Fred's Desktop. He has shared a window, and that shared window displays a red border.

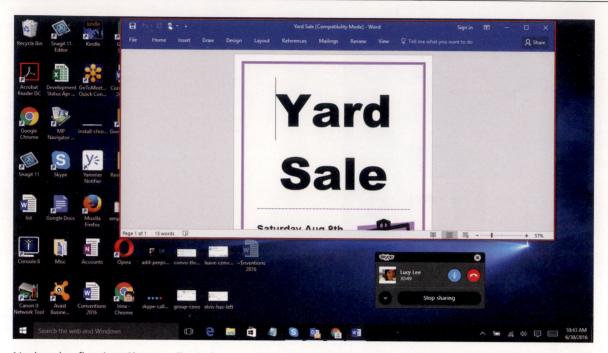

Notice the floating Skype call window in the previous figure. Fred can click **Stop sharing** in the floating window to stop sharing, or he can restore his own Skype window, click **Add participants, send files and more**, and then click **Stop sharing**.

Participants in a conference call can leave the call at any time by clicking the **End call** button. Leaving a conference call does not affect other participants who are still on the call. However, if the originator of a conference call ends the call, the call ends for everyone.

Exercise 15-3: Conferencing in Skype

A headset with a microphone is required for each student for this exercise. Each student should plug in his or her headset before beginning. You will work with your team from the previous exercise.

In this exercise, you will participate in a Skype phone conference. First, you will call one contact.

1. **Student A**: Click **Student B** in your Contacts list and click the **Call** button. If Student B has added any phone numbers to his or her profile, you will see a list of options. Click **Call Skype**.

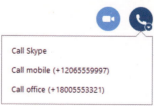

2. **Student B**: Click the green ![answer] (**Answer**) button to answer the call. Carry on a conversation for a moment or two.

3. **Student B**: Click **End call** to end the phone call.

Make a group call.

4. **Student B**: In your Contacts list, click the **MyClassTeam** contact, then in the message window click the 📞 (**Call group**) button. Skype rings for Student A and Student C.

5. **Students A and C**: Click **Answer** to join the call.

6. **Student B**: Click **Add participants, send files and more**, then click **Add people to this call**. In the list of contacts that opens, click Student D, then click **Add to call**.

7. **Student D**: Answer to join the call.

8. **Everyone**: Converse for a few minutes.

9. **Student C**: Click outside the Skype window, navigate to the *7500 Student Files/Digital Communication* folder, and open the **Castle Tour** presentation by double-clicking it.

10. **Student C**: Click the **Skype** button in the taskbar then click inside the Skype window.

11. **Student C**: Move your mouse in the Call window to make the controls appear, click **Add participants, send files and more**, then click **Share screens**. When the Share your screen box appears, click **Start**. You should now see your presentation on the screen, and a floating Skype call window. Everyone else should see your presentation in the call window.

12. **Student C**: Click a few of the slides in your presentation and get confirmation from your teammates that they can see each slide as you click it.

13. **Student C**: In the floating Skype call window, click **Stop sharing**. Everyone should now see the call window with icons for each of their teammates participating in the call.

14. **Student D**: Click **Add participants, send files and more**, then click **Send files**. Navigate to the *7500 Student Files/Digital Communication* folder, then double-click **Office on Demand** to send the file to your teammates.

15. **Students A, B, and C**: The Show IM icon in the lower-right corner of the call window should change color, indicating that an instant message has been received.

16. **Students A, B, and C**: Click the **Show IM** icon to open the IM pane and see the shared file.

17. **Students A, B, and C**: Click the document icon in the IM pane to download the file. If you are prompted to confirm that you want to accept the file, click **Accept**. The Save dialog box opens.

18. **Students A, B, and C**: In the Save dialog box, navigate to the Desktop, then click **Save**.

19. **Student B**: Click **End call** to terminate the conference call.

Video Conferencing

A video conference is a conference call that includes video. Aside from the obvious personal consumer appeal, video conferencing has many applications in business settings. Video conferences:

- **Can make employees from different locations feel more cohesive as a group**: When you recognize the faces of your colleagues, and can match those faces with voices, you feel as if you know them on a more personal level.

- **Can make everyone feel included**: If you and a small group of colleagues work in a satellite office, while the rest of the company works at headquarters, video conferencing for celebrations or recognition ceremonies can make everyone feel that they are part of the team.

- **Are ideal for demonstrating procedures**: A picture is worth a thousand words, but a live demonstration is even better. You can use video to demonstrate how to perform CPR, or how to reset a circuit in a breaker box, or how to use a particular option on a smart phone.

- **Bring a face-to-face quality to communications**: You are already familiar with the advantages of face-to-face communications, such as being able to read body language and facial expressions. Consider how advantageous it might be to interview prospective employees using video instead of flying them in for first-round interviews.

You can easily conduct videoconferences in Skype, Google Hangouts, and FaceTime.

Skype Video Conferencing

In Skype, you start a video conference by opening a conversation window and then clicking the **Video call** button. You can also turn an audio conference call into a video call by clicking the **Turn on video** button in the call window.

In a video conference, each participant's video displays in the call window. If a participant does not have a camera or elects not to turn on his or her camera, that participant's profile picture will display in the call window instead (just as it does in an audio call). The following figure shows a Skype video conference.

Video Conferencing in Google Hangouts

The first time you make a video call in Hangouts you may be prompted to allow Hangouts to use your computer's camera and microphone, and you must accept. Note that if you are using Internet Explorer, Firefox or Safari, (or if you are using an account that does not end in @gmail.com) you will need to download and install the latest version of the Hangouts plug-in before making video calls.

To make a video call from the Hangouts web page, click **VIDEO CALL** to start your video and open an invitation.

Invite people	✕
Sending invite as ccicarolyn@gmail.com	
Enter a name or email	
🔗 COPY LINK TO SHARE	INVITE

Type in the email address of the person you want to call. When Google recognizes the address as a valid email address, it displays it below the green line.

ccifreddie@gmail.com

✉ ccifreddie@gmail.com

Click the address to add it to the top of the Invite people dialog box.

The INVITE button becomes available. You can enter additional addresses as required. A video conference on Hangouts will support up to 10 users (including you). Click **INVITE** when you are ready to send the invitation(s).

If you receive an invitation, you can decline or answer in the panel on your Hangouts page, or in the chat roster in your Gmail page. (Hangouts is automatically turned on in Gmail.)

You can add people to a video call by clicking 🔲 in the video window to open an invitation. You can also click **Copy link to share** to copy a link to your clipboard. You can then paste the link into an email or chat window to share the video call information. Anyone in the Hangout can add more people after the video call starts, and anyone with a Google account can join a video call.

To share your screen during a Hangout video call, click the ⋮ (**Options**) button in the video window, click **Share screen**, specify to share your entire Desktop or your browser window, then click **Share**. To stop sharing, click **Stop** in the banner at the top of the screen, or click **Options**, **Stop Screenshare**.

To leave a Hangouts call, point to the bottom of the call window, then click the 🔴 (**End call**) icon.

Video Conferencing in FaceTime

FaceTime is a video chat application developed by Apple. FaceTime is supported on iPhone 4 or later, iPad 2 or later, iPad mini, and iPod touch 4th generation or later. It is also supported on Mac OS X 10.6.6 and later. The following image from the Apple Support web site (https://support.apple.com) shows a FaceTime video call in El Capitan:

FaceTime call options

Co-authoring Documents in SharePoint

Co-authoring is the simultaneous editing of a document by multiple authors. You can co-author documents in a SharePoint document library in Word, Excel, PowerPoint and OneNote, or in their online counterparts. For each product, the co-authoring functionality is very similar.

The following figure shows two co-workers, Carolyn Stevens and Philip Henderson, co-authoring an Excel workbook using Excel Online.

Notice that Carolyn can see precisely where Philip is editing the document. The blue border around cell A6 shows an icon with his name. Philip's name also appears beneath Carolyn's user name in the upper-right corner of the window.

If co-authors are signed in to Skype for Business at the time they are editing, they can communicate with one another. The following figure shows Carolyn co-editing a Word document with Philip. Carolyn is editing in her desktop version of Word, and Philip is using Word Online. Carolyn can click the share icon [👥2] to see who is editing. She can also click Philip's name to open an instant message window to send him an IM.

Long Island – 14 trails

Catskill Mountains – 44 trails

Authors editing this document

Carolyn Stevens

I think we s────── more trails in thes

Yes. definite   Philip Henders...

PAGE 1 OF 1   40 WORDS   👥2   ▯▯

Co-authoring is enabled in SharePoint libraries by default.

Skype for Business

In the workplace, Skype for Business is a communications and collaboration center; from here you can see which of your colleagues are available for communications, and you can launch into a communications session with one or more colleagues with one or two clicks.

From the Contacts panel you can you can start conversations with your co-workers, conduct online meetings, share screens, and more. The following figure shows the Contacts panel in the main Skype for Business window, and a conversation in a separate window.

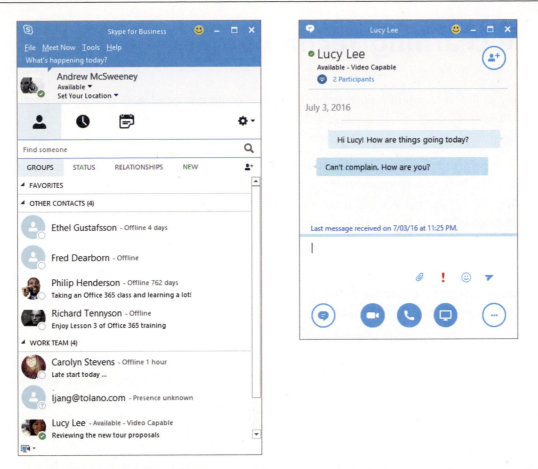

You can use the buttons at the bottom of the conversation window to send messages, attach files, insert emoticons, start a video call, start an audio call, share your screen, present files, or create and share a whiteboard or online poll that all participants can update.

Scheduling Online Meetings

Because Skype for Business is integrated with Microsoft Outlook, you can schedule and send invitations to online meetings from your Outlook Inbox. When it is time for the meeting, participants can click a link in the meeting invitation to join the online conference call.

One person organizes the meeting, and can designate particular people as presenters. During an online meeting, a presenter can share content and perform actions that control the flow of information.

Taking Control

Skype for Business allows participants to request and take control of a screen sharing session, allowing different people to present different portions of the meeting agenda, or various sections of a PowerPoint presentation. The ability to give or take control is also very helpful if you are having a computer issue and need help configuring your computer because you can give control to a member of the IT staff, who can configure your settings while you observe – even if that staff member is hundreds of miles away.

Recording Online Meetings

In addition to sharing content, presenters can capture the audio, video, instant messaging, application sharing, PowerPoint presentations, whiteboards and polling portions of an online meeting or group conversation.

Recordings can be published and made available for other people to view.

Distance Learning Technologies

Objective 3-6.4

The wide variety of digital communications technologies had made distance learning practical, affordable, and even fun. Lectures, assignments, assessments, communications and grades are managed through *Learning Management Systems* (LMS), and students "attend" class by logging in using a web browser.

Online classes can be asynchronous or synchronous in nature. In an asynchronous class, instructors provide material lists, lectures, tests, and assignments that can be accessed at any time (during an allotted time frame) that is convenient for the student. An "old-time" equivalent would be a mail correspondence course, where students mail their assignments to an instructor, and receive feedback in the mail.

Asynchronous classes are ideal for people who like to learn at their own pace, or for those who must juggle school with work and family obligations. Commonly-used features in asynchronous classes are:

Virtual libraries – these are repositories of documents, presentations, graphics, and audio and video files that you would have access to in order to read your assignments or perform research.

Email – this is how you interact with the teacher and with your peers in the class. You would receive materials, updates, reminders and assignments and assessments via email.

Discussion boards – you can post and respond to questions and share ideas, documents and links with your classmates.

Social networking – many LMS have social networking features such as blogs, wikis, and Facebook, Twitter, and YouTube integration built in.

Synchronous online classes occur in real time, and require students and instructors to be online at the same time. Lectures, discussions and presentations occur at a specific hour and all students must be online at that specific hour in order to participate.

Synchronous classes may be preferable for students who need to feel involved with their classmates. Commonly-used features in synchronous classes are:

Chat – synchronous chat rooms allow students to log in and interact with each other.

VoIP conference calls – you can dial in to a toll free number or log in to a website to participate in live lectures and discussions with your class. VoIP conferencing would be especially beneficial if you are learning to speak another language.

Video conferencing – you may join a video conference for occasions where you need to see demonstrations or need to observe certain happenings.

Live streaming – you may be able to stream live broadcasts of political speeches or concerts or live theater.

Streaming

Objective 3-8.1

Have you ever streamed audio from Audible, Pandora, or Spotify? Have you streamed video from Hulu, Netflix, or YouTube?

Streaming is included in this lesson about digital communication because businesses and individuals can create video or audio recordings of presentations, marketing pieces, product demonstrations, and so on, and make these recordings available as streaming media.

Throughout this course you have read about streaming and downloading. As you know, downloading a file requires time and storage space, while streaming a file allows you to listen/watch the content as soon as you begin the streaming process. The content is delivered to your device in a steady, consistent flow of data called a stream. *Audio streaming* involves audio only; video streaming can be video only or video with embedded audio.

When you stream audio or video media from a web site, a media server streams the content to you, and the content is played in a client media player application. If multiple people want to stream the same content, the media server sends a stream to each client. When you stream pre-recorded files such as these, you can pause, rewind, or fast-forward.

Some of the more popular websites that provide streaming services are Hulu, YouTube, Netflix, Pandora and Spotify.

You can also stream live content.

Live streaming is a little bit different than streaming pre-recorded files. Live streaming is the process of broadcasting real-time live audio/video footage as a video feed to an audience that accesses the stream over the Internet.

In live streaming, one file is sent out over the Internet, and multiple people can connect to the live feed and stream it to their devices. This makes it possible for people all over the world to view live events such as the World Cup, the Olympics, or a concert.

Connecting to a live stream is similar to tuning in to a television or radio broadcast, except that you connect to the Internet to receive the feed instead of using a television or radio antenna to receive the signals.

Business Applications

You can access an amazing array of content via live stream – sporting events, concerts, worship services, award ceremonies, debates and local town council meetings are just the tip of the iceberg. Low-cost services platforms like Livestream and no-cost services such as Google Hangouts on Air make it easy for businesses all over the world to stream live content, such as meetings, forums, and presentations.

Hangouts on Air is the video-recording/live streaming/.broadcasting tool that is free to anyone with a Google account. You can use Hangouts on Air to publicly broadcast Hangouts and stream them live on Google Plus and YouTube. The Hangout is automatically recorded and saved to your YouTube channel. From there you can edit it and share it even after it has been broadcast.

You can make a live streaming event private or public. A public event is search discoverable and is viewable by anyone. However, participants (those who can speak or present during the event) must be invited by the host. If you make your live streaming event private, you need to send the URL to people you want to invite as viewers.

A business or an individual can broadcast live video content using a camera and a computer. Viewers can play the content in a web browser, on an iOS or Android device, or through Roku or Apple TV.

Using chat, Twitter, or voice calls, viewers can interact with the broadcast host or with an assembled "panel" taking part in the broadcast, or with other viewers. In this respect, live streaming can perform the same functions as a video conference.

Lesson Summary

In this lesson, you learned about various digital communications technologies. You should now be able to:

☑ explain the difference between real-time and delayed communications

☑ describe email and texting

☑ select the best communications tool for a given situation

☑ describe various phone calling technologies

☑ manage status and profile settings in Skype

☑ conduct group conversations in Skype

☑ describe how to conduct group conversations in Google Hangouts

☑ describe the benefits and function of online conferencing tools

☑ describe benefits and function of business collaboration tools

☑ describe distance learning technologies

☑ describe audio, video, and live streaming

Review Questions

1. Which of the following is an example of asynchronous communication?

   a. A VoIP phone call.

   b. An email message.

   c. A landline phone call.

   d. A video conference.

2. Text messaging uses which protocol?

   a. Short Message Service

   b. Transmission Control Protocol

   c. Internet Protocol

   d. Dynamic Host Configuration Protocol

3. Which is an example of netiquette when sending a text message?

   a. Sending text at any time so others can be informed.

   b. Using emoticons in text to add interest to the message.

   c. Trying to respond to text messages on a timely basis.

   d. Using uppercase letters in the text message to express emotions.

4. Which of the following is an example of synchronous communication?

   a. A phone call.

   b. A blog post.

   c. A text message.

   d. A post on a discussion board.

5. Which of the following is true of VoIP phone calls?

   a. They require a mobile phone.

   b. They require a landline phone.

   c. They require an Internet connection.

   d. They use a cellular provider's network.

6. A conference call:

    a. requires a specialized handset.

    b. is limited to audio only.

    c. involves three or more parties.

    d. can be placed only on a landline phone.

7. Which of the following provides hosted WebEx service?

    a. Cisco   c. Skype

    b. Google   d. Chrome

8. Which Skype status makes you appear offline but allows you to use Skype as usual?

    a. Offline   c. Invisible

    b. Away   d. Do Not Disturb

9. Which of the following tasks can you perform while on a VoIP conference call?

    a. Share your screen with other users.

    b. Send files to other users.

    c. Add other participants to a call already in progress.

    d. You can perform all of these tasks while on a VoIP call.

10. Which of the following is true of video conferences?

    a. They can make remote employees feel included in company functions.

    b. They can make remote employees feel more cohesive as a group.

    c. They are a good tool for sharing visual demonstrations.

    d. All of these statements are true of video conferences.

11. Which of the following tools can you use to conduct video conferences?

    a. Skype

    b. Google Hangouts

    c. FaceTime

    d. You can use all of these tools to conduct video conferences.

12. Which of the following Office 365 tools provides for content management and co-authoring of documents?

    a. Outlook Web App (OWA)   c. Office Online

    b. SharePoint   d. Skype

13. Which of the following broadcasts live audio/video footage over the Internet?

    a. Downloading   c. Uploading

    b. Live streaming   d. Asynchronous communications

Lesson 16: Understanding Email, Contacts, and Calendaring

Lesson Objectives

This lesson teaches you what email programs are available and how email plays an important role in communicating with others. You will also learn to manage contacts and work with a calendar. Upon completion of this lesson, you should be able to:

- ☐ recognize various email programs
- ☐ understand how an email address is structured
- ☐ understand email etiquette
- ☐ create and send a new message to one or more recipients
- ☐ understand how to attach items to a message
- ☐ recognize when to reply, reply to all, or forward a message
- ☐ understand how to create a signature
- ☐ understand how to deal with spam or junk mail
- ☐ manage mail for deletion or archiving
- ☐ understand how to manage contacts
- ☐ understand how to create single and recurring events or appointments
- ☐ manage and share calendars

Working with Email

Objective 3-3.1

Before you can use email, you must have an email account. An email account can be provided by your ISP, provided by your school or organization, or provided by a web-based email provider such as Gmail, Live, Hotmail, iCloud, Zoho, or Yahoo!

You can choose a desktop application such as Outlook 2013 or Thunderbird 17. This means installing the application to the local drive on the computing device and configuring the account correctly so that you can send and receive messages. Desktop email clients are generally used with email accounts hosted by an ISP (although many ISPs offer a web-based interface for working with your email).

If your email account is from a web-based provider, you will log in to a web-based interface for working with your email account. All you need is a browser and an Internet connection. Updates to the email program for the browser environment are handled by the vendor and generally do not require any maintenance from you, whereas if you use a desktop application, you will be notified when updates are available and you will have to update your email client manually.

An email address is structured as follows:

jsmith@ccilearning.com   j.smith.909@myisp.uk.co

Mailbox **Name of** **Domain**   **Mailbox** **Name of** **Domain**
Name **Organization** **Category**   **Name** **Organization** **Category**

Mailbox Name

- Identifies a particular mailbox on an email server, and is based on company or ISP standards for email addresses.

- Some providers, especially web-based providers, allow you to create your own mailbox name, providing it is unique.

- The mailbox name is also considered the user name for the given account.

Name of Organization

- The middle part of an email address identifies the organization that owns the email server.

- This part of the address could be the full formal name of the organization, a shorter version of the company name, or a unique combination of words.

Domain Category

- Identifies the type of domain; for example, .com refers to a commercial organization while .uk refers to a country and the organization type, such as uk.co or uk.edu.

The *jsmith@ccilearning.com* address indicates that the address belongs to someone at a commercial company called CCI Learning. A fairly common company standard for mailbox names is to use your first initial followed by your last name. In the example email address, the user's first name begins with "J" and the user's last name is "Smith."

The *j.smith909@myisp.uk.co* email address suggests this address belongs to someone with the same first initial and last name as many other people; the number "909" helps to make this address unique. The account is with a company called My ISP, which is located in the United Kingdom.

Using an Email Program

Objective 3-3.1, 3-3.5,

Note: There are many email programs currently available; however, you will use only the web-based interface for Gmail in this lesson. Remember that the concepts remain the same regardless of the email program; the differences lie in where the commands and features are located in each program.

A popular web-based email program is Gmail, available through Google. No installation is required; all you need to do is create a Gmail account. You can quickly access Gmail by navigating to the Google web site and then clicking the **Gmail** link, usually shown on the top right corner.

A typical Gmail Inbox is shown in the following figure.

Labels   **Navigation Tools**   **Inbox Tabs**   **Account/App Options**

Settings

Inbox Tab Contents

Communication Options

Account/App Options

- At the far right of the Google search field, you will see the account currently logged in, the Google Apps icon, a bell icon indicating any notifications, and an icon to change your profile or switch to another account.

- The Google Apps icon displays a menu of other apps you can use, such as Calendar or Hangouts.

Navigation Tools

- This bar contains buttons to help you navigate or select items on the screen.

- The three buttons at the left pertain to the Inbox tab contents.

- The buttons at the right will help you move between messages.

   1–3 of 3   <   >

Settings

- Click the button with the gears icon to make changes to default settings in Gmail such as the adjusting the display mode, applying themes, or accessing account settings.

Display mode:
✓ Touch-enabled
Comfortable
Cozy
Compact

Configure inbox

Settings
Themes

Send feedback
Help

Labels

- Folders you can use to organize your messages to find on a later date. To see more, click the **More labels** command.

Inbox Tabs

- The Gmail Inbox is organized into three tabs called Primary, Social, and Promotions. Use these tabs to help organize your messages. Messages can be managed in the same manner regardless of which tab they appear on.

📥 Primary	👥 Social	🏷 Promotions	+

- Each tab displays the items you receive via email. Google attempts to categorize incoming messages for you.

Communication Options

- Use these icons when you want to communicate with someone else through Google Hangouts, either via phone or chat.

- Contacts will appear in the left panel below the labels and your login.

- Click the magnifying glass to view more details about a contact.

Creating New Messages

Sending an email message is similar to mailing a traditional letter. You write the body of the message, add address information and then send it. You must have an active email account before you can send or receive mail. To send mail, you must know the email address of each intended recipient. To send a message, follow these steps:

1. Create a new mail message.

2. Address the message to the recipient. Enter the email address for a Bcc or Cc recipient, as applicable.

3. Type the text for the subject, and then type the message, applying any formatting as required, such as bold text or indented paragraphs. If you need to email someone a file, attach it to the mail message.

4. Use the spell checker and proofread your message to eliminate spelling or grammatical errors.

5. Send the message.

Once you click the Send button, the message is sent to the email server for delivery. Gmail does not display an Outbox folder on a computing device such as a notebook; if you are using Gmail on an Android device, you will see an Outbox folder. Gmail will display a brief message confirming the action below the navigation bar. If there is a problem with delivering the message, Gmail will send an email indicating the error.

To create a new message in Gmail, in the left panel, click **Compose**.

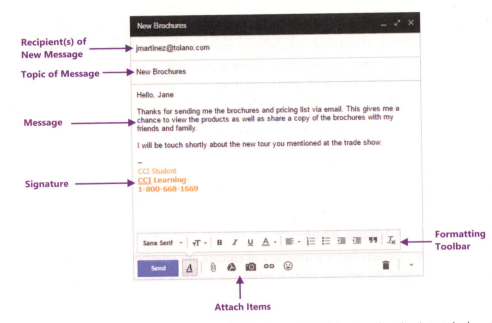

Once the new message window appears, type in the email addresses for the intended recipients or choose names from the list of contacts stored on your system. Regardless of the email program, the components of an email message are the same.

An email message includes:

- Recipient of New Message

  - You must enter at least one email address for an intended recipient.

  - You may send a message to several recipients by specifying more than one address.

  - The addressing lines are very important as they identify who will receive the email message:

    To – identifies the primary recipient(s) of the email.

    Cc or "carbon copy" – lists individuals who will also receive a copy of this email; when you list recipients in the Cc field, it is an indication that you are sending a copy of the message to them for information purposes only. That is, you do not expect a response from them.

    Bcc or "blind carbon copy" – lists individuals who will also receive a copy of this email. However, listing recipients in this field prevents anyone from seeing the email addresses. That is, no one else will know that the message was also sent to someone listed in the Bcc field.

- Subject line

  - A summarized single line of text to let the recipient know what the message is about.

  - Always enter something in the Subject line or the message could be flagged as junk by the mail server.

- Message pane

  - This is where you will enter the main text or body of the email message.

  - Most programs provide basic formatting options such as applying bold or italics, changing the font or the font size, and so on.

To display the header detail, open a message, click the down arrow for the Reply button at the far right of the open message, and in the drop-down menu, click **Show original**. The header information is listed in reverse chronological order; the data at the top is the most recent event, so if you want to trace the message from the sender, start at the bottom.

```
Delivered-To: student01cci@gmail.com
Received: by 10.202.170.215 with SMTP id t206csp269117oie;
        Tue, 2 Feb 2016 11:51:37 -0800 (PST)
X-Received: by 10.66.158.129 with SMTP id wu1mr50156616pab.146.1454442697177;
        Tue, 02 Feb 2016 11:51:37 -0800 (PST)
Return-Path: <3yAixVgwJDFk339JKL45EKXU7D19C.3FDJKL45EKRS3397D19C.3FD@calendar-server.bounces.google.com>
Received: from mail-pf0-x249.google.com (mail-pf0-x249.google.com. [2607:f8b0:400e:c00::249])
        by mx.google.com with ESMTPS id q28si2513968pfi.178.2016.02.02.11.51.37
        for <student01cci@gmail.com>
        (version=TLS1_2 cipher=ECDHE-RSA-AES128-GCM-SHA256 bits=128/128);
        Tue, 02 Feb 2016 11:51:37 -0800 (PST)
Received-SPF: pass (google.com: domain of 3yAixVgwJDFk339JKL45EKXU7D19C.3FDJKL45EKRS3397D19C.3FD@calendar·
Authentication-Results: mx.google.com;
        spf=pass (google.com: domain of 3yAixVgwJDFk339JKL45EKXU7D19C.3FDJKL45EKRS3397D19C.3FD@calendar-se:
        dkim=pass header.i=@google.com;
        dkim=pass header.i=@gmail.com;
        dmarc=pass (p=NONE dis=NONE) header.from=gmail.com
Received: by mail-pf0-x249.google.com with SMTP id n128so18996854pfn.1
        for <student01cci@gmail.com>; Tue, 02 Feb 2016 11:51:37 -0800 (PST)
DKIM-Signature: v=1; a=rsa-sha256; c=relaxed/relaxed;
        d=google.com; s=20120113;
        h=mime-version:reply-to:sender:auto-submitted:message-id:date:subject
         :from:to:content-type;
        bh=Pz19KdrdEwpZ8tJZ6BQt63d46/9HUjYeqADXqvipsK0=;
        b=ml66aZ0jfO2MwXikrDK+ZG8tX3m+b3bApnrtY3FJCE8X+YIiZiZTawNc3HyjCyjspb
         /mB6ulXnWPOd4+y6nYpIFoVWChwC0PJeNPhjL2umzsa0X5iq3EhDT1QD3hb7JXLKwKmx
         gPPiAMnUOK5rgQJGqGk08NiNKZOmU0IZ8Ry6snrrjPhtVXyyNpaK0Oz4P0xcXvqM77LD
         oIXGowbWKphT1QWL7zST2+JmpcD9x+BUwplcL7MZWV7kqvu98yJ/78aoTfBb43wbNQ/n
         z4iKNUxqjJX0TFFE0PWYqDL+FeONV1wFsNQ/WHGCpnwUA1bSnNJqckThQ3SC9LLe09px
         jXcA==
```

Organizing Messages

As you use your email account, your Inbox will begin to fill with messages and not all of them have the same urgency. Some messages require immediate response, some can wait, some require follow-up later, and some might just contain general information.

Selecting Message

Every message has a checkbox at the left that you can use to select that message for another action. To select multiple messages, click each message to which you want to apply an action. To select all messages, click the **Select** button above the Primary tab. You can also click the arrow for this button to display various types of messages to select.

Creating Folders

To keep yourself organized, you can set up folders and sub-folders for storing your messages.

To create a new folder, in the Folders List, click **More labels** and then click **Create new label**.

Enter the name for the new label and then press ENTER. The new label will then be listed near the bottom of the List.

If you want this new label to be nested below another label, click **Nest label under** and choose the label from the drop-down field below the command. Your new label is now a sub-label.

You can create as many new labels or nested labels as you need to manage your messages. You can also delete labels at any time.

Moving Messages

Once you have your labels in place, you can organize your messages by moving them under the appropriate label. To move messages, first select them, then use one of the following methods:

- Click the **Move to** button to move selected messages to the designated label; or.

Move to:

Personal
Personal/Miscellaneous
Social
Promotions
Updates
Forums

Spam
Trash

Create new
Manage labels

- drag the selected messages over the label where you want to move the messages.

▸ Personal
Move 2 conversations

Using Signatures

A signature is a block of text that is automatically added to the end of your messages whenever you create a new message. This saves you from having to enter your name and information or a product slogan each time you send a message. You can create as many signatures as required, but only one can be designated as the default signature. Enter text as appropriate for the purpose of the particular email account; for instance, if this is a business account, ensure your name, title, company name, and contact information are included so business customers know who you are and who you represent If this is a personal email account, you could use the nickname that most people know you by – that is, you can be informal in the signature.

To create a signature, from the top navigation bar, click the **Settings** button and then click **Settings**. Scroll down until you see the Signature area:

Signature:
(appended at the end of all outgoing messages)
Learn more

○ No signature
◉

Tahoma

☐ Insert this signature before quoted text in replies and remove the "--" line that precedes it.

Exercise 16-2: Working with messages

In this exercise, you will respond to some messages and organize messages in your Inbox.

1. Click **Compose** and address the message to the person at your right.

2. Type: Events List as the subject, and then type the following for the message body:

    Attached is the list of upcoming events for the rest of the year that we were interested in attending. Of course, we cannot attend all of the events so I need you to highlight the ones you most want to attend, and if possible, prioritize the events.

    That way, we can work on trying to get those tickets as soon as possible.

    Thanks!

3. Bold the word, prioritize and also change the color to **red RGB (255, 0, 0)**.

4. On the toolbar to the right of the **Send** button, click the **Attach files** button.

5. Navigate to the location where the student data files are located for this course. Then select the **Events List** document and click **Open** to attach it to the email message.

6. Send the message.

7. In your Inbox message list, click the *My First Message* email message to open it.

8. Click the **Reply** link and type: Yes, I agree. Gmail seems very easy to use, and I look forward to working in the Calendar. Send the message.

9. Click the **Back to Inbox** button, or click **Inbox** in the labels on the left

10. Click the **Birthday Surprise** message and then click **Forward**.

11. Type: nklassen@tolano.com in the To field. He will be the recipient of this message.

12. Type: For your information only as the body text and press ENTER. Then send the message.

13. Return to the Inbox and then open the *Events List* message.

14. Point at the preview of the attached file, then click **Download**.

    When you download files in the Chrome browser, a button with the downloaded file's name displays at the bottom of the bowser window when the download is complete. You can click the button to open the downloaded file. In other browsers, you may or may not be able to open the file from within the browser window. You can, however, access the file using File Explorer. The default location for downloaded files in Windows 10 is the Downloads folder (C:\Users\<user name>\Downloads).

15. Click the **Events List.docx** button to open and view the document.

16. Close Microsoft Word and then return to the Inbox.

17. Click **More labels** and then click **Create new label**.

18. Type: `Personal` and press ENTER.

    This label now appears at the left below the Drafts label.

19. Click **Create new label** once more, type: `Miscellaneous`, click **Nest label under**. Click the arrow to select **Personal**. Click **Create**.

    Notice the Personal label at the left now displays an arrow at the left of the label.

20. Click the arrow to display the contents of this label.

    > Drafts
    > ▾ Personal
    >   Miscellaneous

21. Click the checkbox at the left of the Events List and the Birthday Surprise messages.

22. Drag these messages over to Miscellaneous.

    Gmail should now display a message near the top of the window confirming that you have moved the messages.

Managing Spam

Spam refers to unsolicited mail; often spam messages promote products and services, or convey specific political/religious views. Spam mail is the same as junk mail. People or companies who send these types of messages are called *spammers*.

Spammers buy email address lists from companies that specialize in email marketing. It is natural for companies to want to market their products and "keep you informed." Reputable companies will ask for your email address and ask for permission to give your address to other companies who sell associated products and services. Companies must make their privacy policy available for viewing; the privacy policy must describe how your personal information may be used or shared. If you are visiting a web site and you are asked to create an account or sign up to receive a newsletter, check the privacy policy to see how your information may be used or shared. Creating an account, or providing your contact information is the same as giving your consent to share that information as outlined in the policy.

Most email programs include a filtering feature to block spam or other junk email. Many ISPs also run active spam filters on their mail servers to block the most common types of spam mail before they reach your email Inbox. You can also download and install a variety of programs to help block any spam messages that sneak by your ISP.

Note: If your screen shows the older Contact Manager interface, click the **Try Contacts preview** link.

Your "All contacts" list displays by default and includes two sets of people:

Frequently contacted – a list of everyone who has written to you or received a message from you

All contacts – a list of contacts that you added or edited yourself. This list is also updated when you sync your mobile device with the computer.

To add a contact manually:

1. Click the 🔴 (**Add new contact**) button. This opens a window for entering a contact name.

2. Type a name for the contact, then click **Create**. This opens the Edit contact window, which you can use to add contact information.

3. Enter the pertinent information, then click **Save**.

You can also add an email address to your Contacts list from an open message. Point at the email address and in the pop-up window that opens, click the **Add to contacts** link at the bottom left of the window

To search for a contact, enter the name in the Search for anyone field above the contacts.

Address Books

Although many people use the terms Contacts list and address book interchangeably, for purposes of distinction we will say that an *address book* is a central location where contact information for an entire organization is stored. Many businesses which use Microsoft Exchange, Exchange Online, or other locally managed email servers, provide a global address book that all employees may access. Address books such as these are created and maintained by the network administrator. The address book may include company-defined distribution groups as well as individual contact entries. In addition to using the global address book, employees can still maintain their own contact lists.

Organizations that use web-based email programs do not provide an address book for their employees; however, each employee can manage his or her own contact lists, and can share contact information with other users.

Most Desktop email programs also allow you to import contact lists created in programs. Generally, you would export your contacts from the original program to a .CSV or a vCard file, and then import the generated file into the new program. Some web-based programs include links for importing contacts from other web-based accounts.

In Gmail, you can import contacts from an exported file or from other web-based programs.

To import a contact list into your Gmail account, on the panel at the left, click **More** and then click **Import**. Make your selection, then follow the on-screen prompts.

📖 **Import contacts from other accounts**
YAHOO!   Yahoo Mail
o✉   Outlook.com
Aol.   AOL
✉   Other email provider
📖   CSV or vCard file
CANCEL

Exercise 16-3: Working with contacts

In this exercise you will work with the Contacts feature and add a new contact.

1. Click the **Gmail** link and then click **Contacts**.

    Because you have already used your Gmail account to send and receive messages, there are probably a few contacts that already appear in your frequently contacted list.

2. In the Frequently contacted area, click the email address (or name) of the person sitting at the right to open the Contact card.

3. Review the information on the contact. Then click the 🖊 (**Edit contact**) icon to edit information for the contact.

4. Click the **Add notes** link to open the field, and type: Gmail contact.

5. Click **Save**.

    The information now appears below the contact email address in the Contact card.

6. Click the **Back** arrow to return to the contacts list.

7. Click the **Add new contact** button at the lower right corner of the screen.

8. Type your name and click **Create**.

9. Click **Add an email** to open the field, and enter a personal email address.

10. Click **Add note** and type: new contact for practice. Then click **Save**.

11. Click **Back** to return to the contacts list.

    There should now be a contact in the All contacts list with your name.

12. Click the checkbox to the left of your name and a new toolbar will appear across the top of the screen.

13. Click the 🗑 button to indicate you want to delete this contact.

You can choose to simply delete the contact information at which point you could "restore" this information from the Trash folder. You can also choose to remove it from the contacts list.

14. Click **Remove from the "All contacts" list** option.

15. Ensure your contact is still selected, click 🗑 and then click **Delete**.

The contact no longer exists in the contacts lists.

Using the Gmail Calendar

Objective 3-4.1, 3-4.2, 3-4.3, 3-4.4

You can schedule various types of events such as appointments and meetings in the Calendar.

- An *appointment* is an activity that usually only involves you – such as a lunch date, a dental appointment, or a personal engagement. An appointment blocks the time in your calendar.

- A *meeting* is an appointment to which others are invited and may involve reserving resources such as rooms or audio-visual equipment.

Events that last an entire day or longer, such as an out of town conference or a birthday or anniversary do not block out time in your calendar.

When you schedule appointments, meetings or other activities which take less than a full day, the time in your calendar can be marked as free, tentative, busy or out of office. This is a very useful feature, especially if you want others to be able to see your availability. A colored bar indicating your availability will be displayed in your calendar.

To access the calendar in Gmail, click the **Google apps** icon at the top right corner of the screen, and then click **Calendar**.

Creating an Appointment

There are three methods you can use to enter an appointment, depending on how many details you want to enter when you create the appointment:

- To quickly create an appointment, click the arrow for the **Create** button to activate the Quick Add option:

- The second quick method is to click at the starting time for the appointment on the day of the appointment. Gmail then displays a window for you to fill in:

- To enter details when you create an appointment, click **Create** to see the New Message details screen (this is also the Edit screen), which allows you to name the appointment, select a date and time, enter notes, configure notifications, attach items, or even change the appointment into a meeting by adding guests. This is the same view you will see if you click an appointment on your calendar and click **Edit event**.

You can enter further details for the appointment as needed. Not all the options shown here are required for every appointment; in some cases, features such as attaching a file as reference for an appointment can be helpful.

Creating Recurring Appointments

If you have appointments that occur on a regular basis – say monthly or bi-weekly – you can set up a recurring appointment. Gmail will add additional occurrences of the appointment to your calendar on the appropriate dates. To create a recurring appointment, click the **Repeat** link in the Edit screen and Gmail will then display the dialog box shown in the following figure:

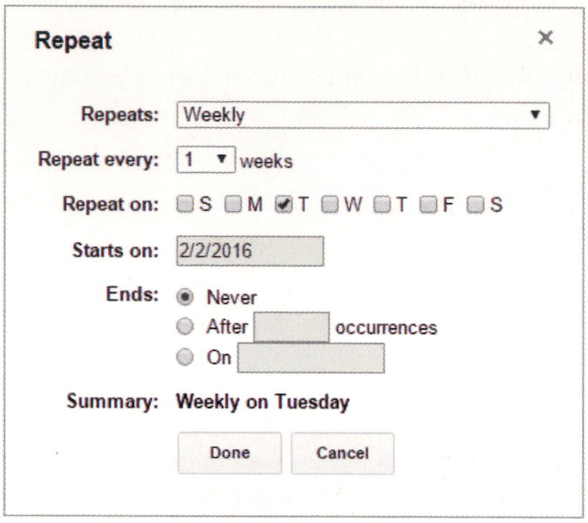

Once you have configured the settings for the recurring appointment and click **Done**, Gmail automatically adds the recurring appointment to your calendar. If you open any occurrence of a recurring appointment, Gmail displays the details for modification, as needed:

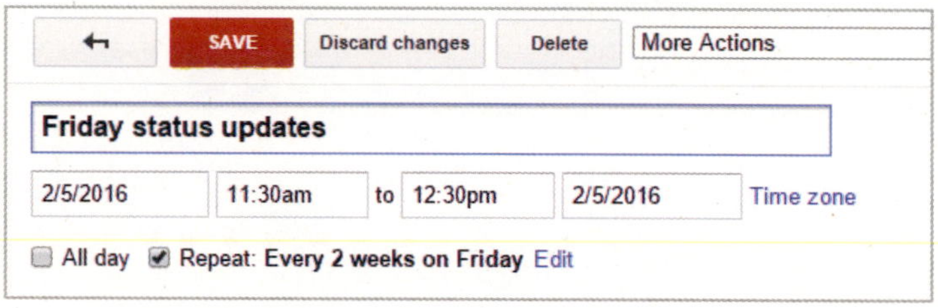

You can specify to save your changes to the open occurrence only (for example, you might need to change the meeting time for this one date only) or to all occurrences (for example, the location of the meeting is permanently changed).

You can also use the **Delete** button to delete a recurring event when it is no longer needed:

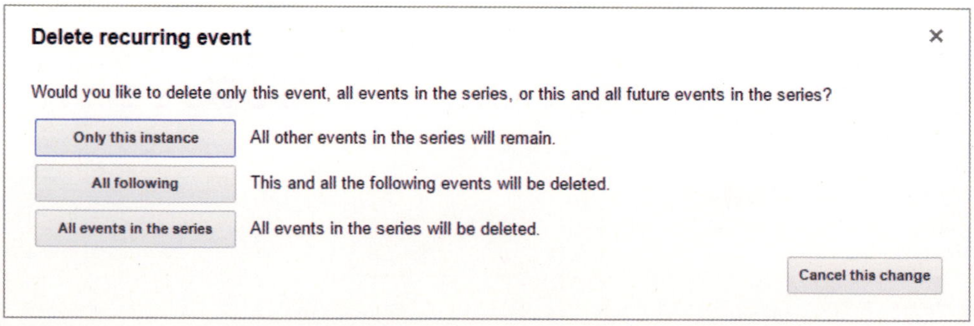

Notice how you can choose to delete this one instance of the meeting, delete all occurrences of this meeting from now on, or delete all occurrences (past, present, and future) of the meeting from the calendar.

Inviting Others to a Meeting

When you invite others to an appointment, the appointment becomes a meeting. To do this, open the Edit screen, click in the Add guests box, type the email address of an invitee and click **Add**. Repeat for each person you want to invite to the meeting.

Note that as you begin typing an email address, Google may show an address suggestion based on your contacts. If the suggested address is the correct one, you can click the suggested address to automatically add that person as an invitee.

Working with Multiple Calendars

In addition to updating your own calendar, you can share your calendar with others and request to view other people's calendars as well.

To share a calendar with someone, expand the My Calendars list and click the arrow to the right of your name to see a menu of options.

Click **Share this Calendar**.

To subscribe to one of these calendars, you need only select the appropriate calendar from the list. You can click **Preview** to see how the calendar appears:

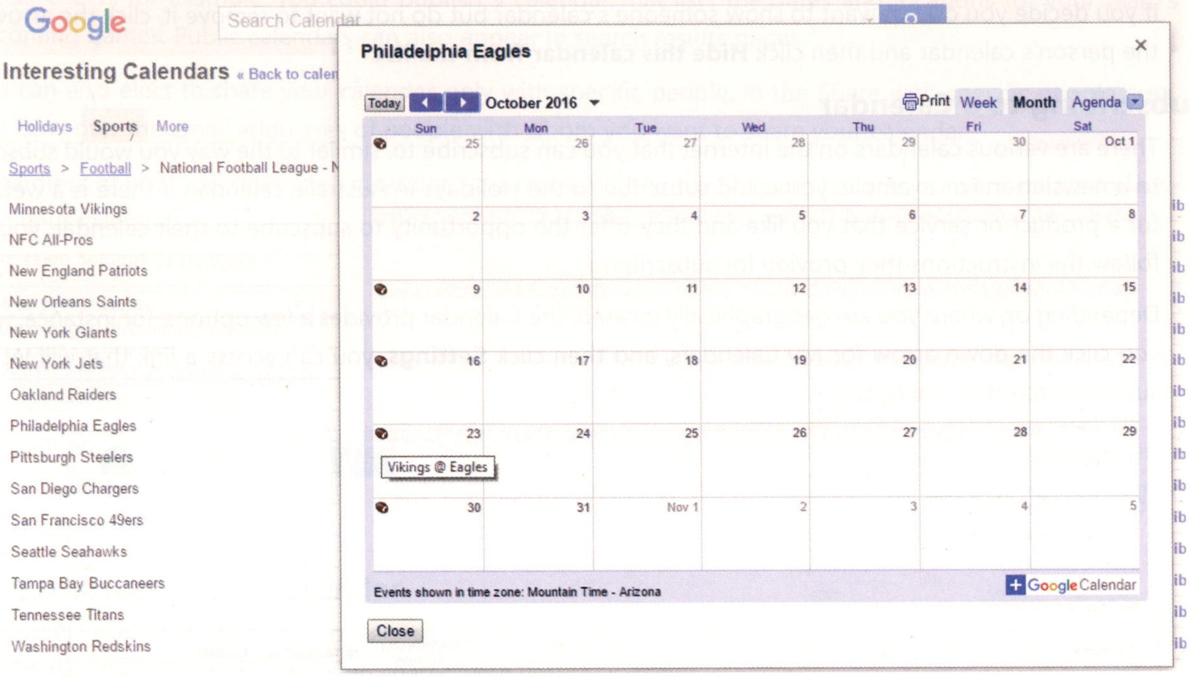

You can click **Subscribe** to automatically update your calendar.

In the More Tools area at the right of the screen, click a link to set up a different calendar:

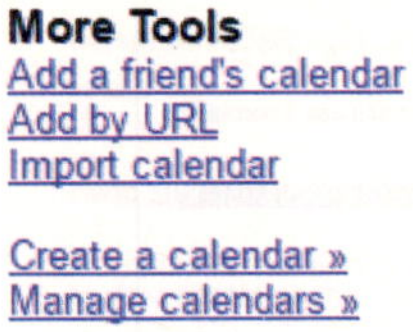

More Tools
Add a friend's calendar
Add by URL
Import calendar

Create a calendar »
Manage calendars »

Add a friend's calendar

- If you want to view or subscribe to a friend's calendar, you can send a request to that person; you will not gain access to the calendar until they have accepted your request.

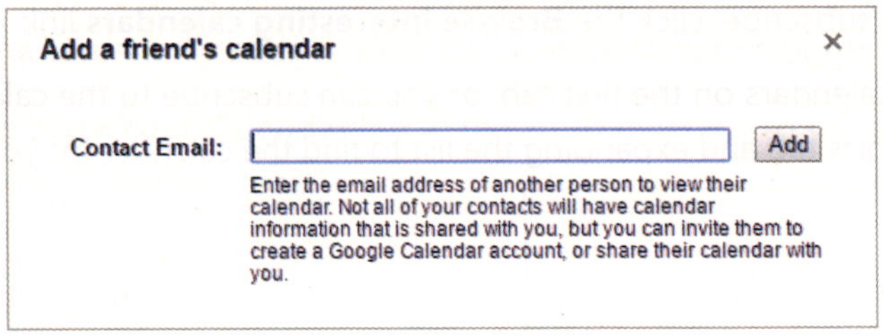

Add by URL

- If you know the web site address for a particular calendar, you can also enter it directly into this screen in order to view to the events on that calendar in your own calendar.

Add by URL   ✕

URL: [_____]

If you know the address to a calendar (in iCal format), you can
type in the address here.

☐ Make the calendar publicly accessible?

[Add Calendar | Cancel]

Import calendar

- If you have access to a calendar in another format that is compatible with the Google Calendar, use this option to select the file and import the events into your calendar.

Import calendar   ✕

File: [Choose File | No file chosen]

Choose the file that contains your events. Google Calendar can
import event information in iCal or CSV (MS Outlook)
format.Learn more

Calendar: [CCILearning Student ▼]

Choose the calendar where these events should be saved.

[Import | Cancel]

The Create a calendar and Manage calendars options on this screen are similar to the options for creating and managing calendar settings on the main calendar screen.

Exercise 16-4: Working with Calendar

In this exercise you will create some appointments in the calendar and then share the calendar with others in your class.

1. Click the **Google apps** icon and then click **Calendar**.

2. At the far right of the navigation bar, click the **Week** button if necessary to change the display of the calendar. Click **Month** to see how the view changes.

3. Click **Day** to see how this view appears.

   Notice how the views change to reflect the number of days you want to see; in fact, as you show fewer days on the screen, Calendar shows more details for each day, such as a bar with time intervals (an hour) to assist you in setting up new appointments.

4. Switch to the Week view again.

5. Click once in the time slot starting at **3:30pm** for the first Monday after today.

6. Type: Dental Cleaning as the subject name and then click **Edit event**.

7. Click in the **Description** area and type: Dr. Manuela Contigua, 206-999-8765.

8. Click **Save** to save this appointment

9. Click **Create** and in the appointment window, enter the following:
   Title: Status updates
   Start date: Next Thursday
   Start time: 9:30am
   End time: 11:00am

10. Click the **Repeat** option and ensure that **Weekly** is selected in the Repeats drop-down list. Set this appointment to repeat every **2 weeks** on Thursday and it should never end.

11. Click **Done** to save the recurrence settings.

12. Type: `3rd Floor Boardroom` for the location, and in the Description field, type: `Bi-weekly status updates for ongoing projects`.

13. Click in the field for Add guests and type the email address for the person at the right. Click **Add**. Also invite the person to the left.

14. Click **Save**. Then click **Send** to send the invitations to the guest.

    You have just created a recurring meeting and invited other people to attend the same meeting.

Now try sharing your calendar with someone else in the class. Check with your teacher as to who you will share the calendar with; alternatively, choose the person to your left.

15. Point at your calendar name under the My calendars heading, and click the arrow at the right. Click **Share this Calendar**.

16. Click the checkbox for **Make this calendar public**. Also click the **Share only my free/busy information (Hide details)** option. Then click **Save**.

    Your calendar is now available to anyone who may enter your name in the search field.

17. To reverse this, click the arrow at the right of your calendar name, click **Share this Calendar** and then uncheck the two options from step 13.

18. In the field below Person, in the Share with specific people section, enter the email address for your teacher, as applicable.

19. At the right of this field, click the arrow for the Permission Settings field and click **See only free/busy (hide details)**. Click **Add Person**.

    The person with whom you are sharing your calendar appears below your name. Only this person shares your calendar. Notice the trash can icon at the far right; you can click the trash can icon when you no longer want to share your calendar with this person.

20. Click **Save** to save your settings.

Ask a colleague to share his or her calendar.

21. In the main calendar screen, click in the field below Other Calendar, type the email address for the person at your right and press ENTER.

22. Leave the defaults as is and click **Send Invite**.

    You have just sent a request to your friend to share his/her calendar with you. Once your friend has accepted your request, their calendar appears in the Other calendars area. Any events in your friend's calendar will be visible in your calendar, but they will display in the same color as appears to the left of their calendar name.

Lesson Summary

This lesson taught you what email programs are available and how email plays an important role in communicating with others. You also learned to manage contacts and how to work with a calendar. You should now be able to:

☑ recognize various email programs

☑ understand how an email address is structured

☑ understand email etiquette

☑ create and send a new message to one or more recipients

☑ understand how to attach items in a message

☑ recognize when to reply, reply to all, or forward a message

☑ understand how to set up a signature

☑ understand how to deal with spam or junk mail

☑ manage mail for deletion or archiving

☑ understand how to manage contacts

☑ understand how to create single and recurring events or appointments

☑ manage and share calendars

Review Questions

1. In the following email address, which part is the name of the organization?

    bv_thorpe@mycable.com

    a. by_thorpe   c. .com

    b. mycable   d. mycable.com

2. From the main gmail.com window, how can you open an application such as the Calendar or Hangouts?
    a. Type the name of the application in the Search field.
    b. Click the Google Apps icon.
    c. Click the Google link at the top left.
    d. Click the Settings icon.

3. What is the purpose of the second toolbar in the New Message window?
    a. To help you format or enhance the look of selected text.
    b. To change where the message body will begin in the Message Pane.
    c. To enable you to attach items such as files or pictures with the message.
    d. To recognize when you are using the Cc or Bcc fields.

4. How can you use the Contacts List or Address Book when creating a new message?
    a. To identify whether your recipient is online.
    b. To insert the address of a contact as a recipient of the message.
    c. To blacklist a specific individual.
    d. To switch to the Contacts application to add new people.

5. Why should you always proof read your message even after completing a spell check?
    a. To find any errors where you might have used the wrong word (for example, their instead of there, or brakes instead of breaks).
    b. To ensure you are using the appropriate tone.
    c. To ensure that your message is clear.
    d. All of these are reasons for proofreading after running a spell check.

6. Why might you want to forward a message instead of simply replying to it?

    a. You want to move this message to another folder.

    b. You want to include this message in the calendar.

    c. Someone else could handle the request in the message better than you can.

    d. There is no difference between using forward versus replying to a message.

7. What is one criteria you should always consider when sending attachments?

    a. The size of your Sent Items folder.

    b. The size of your Inbox.

    c. The size of the attachment.

    d. The distance from your mail server to the recipient's mail server.

8. What can you do to reduce the possibility of receiving junk mail?

    a. Sign up for newsletters you are interested in from a web site.

    b. Refrain from replying to any messages you consider to be junk email.

    c. Use a business email when signing up for information from web sites.

    d. Have all email sent to your cellular phone as the central location for email.

9. What is an advantage of archiving your messages?

    a. It allows you to keep all your messages, but keeps your Inbox organized.

    b. It saves time by deleting all your messages at once.

    c. It moves older messages to another drive, such as a network drive.

    d. It copies all of your messages and stores the copies as threads.

10. If you want to invite someone to a meeting, where would you enter the recipient's name?

    a. In the Quick Add field

    b. In the New Message details screen

    c. In the field that opens when you right-click My calendar

    d. In the field that opens when you click Other calendars

11. How can you create a recurring appointment?

    a. Click Edit details for the appointment and then click Recurring.

    b. Click Edit event and then press CTRL+F to set the frequency pattern.

    c. Click Edit event for the appointment and then click Repeat.

    d. Copy the appointment and paste it every month in the calendar area.

12. How can you show or hide a shared calendar?

    a. Click the arrow for the person's calendar and then click the Hide option.

    b. The calendar automatically opens once you accept the request for sharing.

    c. Click Settings and then click to turn on or off the required calendar option.

    d. You cannot hide a shared calendar.

13. Which option would you use if you want to subscribe to a specific sports calendar?

    a. Add a friend's calendar

    b. Add a URL

    c. Browse interesting calendars

    d. Import calendar

Lesson 17: Your Life Online

Lesson Objectives

In this lesson, you will learn about your online identity and how to protect it. You will also learn about the adverse effects prolonged computing can have on your health. Upon completion of this lesson, you should be able to:

- ☐ describe the purpose of blogs, forums, and wikis
- ☐ understand the function of social media networks and how they work
- ☐ understand the difference between open and closed social networks
- ☐ describe how to use LinkedIn
- ☐ describe what constitutes your digital identity
- ☐ understand the importance of maintaining a good digital identity
- ☐ explain how to avoid cyber bullying
- ☐ understand the health risks that arise from prolonged computing

We Are Social Beings

By nature, humans are social beings – we need to share our ideas, express our opinions, and make connections with other people.

Some people are content with asking questions while others are happy to share what they know and to be recognized as a reliable source of information or advice. Before the digital age, you had to be published in a newspaper, magazine, or book to disseminate your knowledge, or opinions, or creative talents to the masses; but today there are numerous ways to share what you know with the public at large. (It is, of course, up to the public to decide whether to avail themselves of what you have shared.)

How Do We Share Information?

Objective 3-5.3

Almost as soon as personal computers became available, personal computer experts became available too. The 1980s and 1990s brought us scads of new software for the booming PC market, but not nearly as much software documentation or user manuals. Frustrated users had few places to turn to for help, and so they relied on other users – those who had a little more experience, or who (through trial and error) had discovered ways to make their new software programs do what they wanted them to do.

In those early days, you might have had to speak to someone in person or over the phone to get the guidance you needed. But when the Internet was emerging, computer bulletin board systems (BBS) made their entrance onto the scene. These were electronic message boards; users could log in and type messages to one another or post messages for public discussion. These were primitive, text-based communications over the Internet; but their popularity and their usefulness did not diminish. They simply evolved into the methods we use today for asking, sharing, and disseminating information.

Blogs

Blogs are online journals that include a communications element. Generally, the blog creator publishes or "posts" an article about a specific topic, and others can then post comments in response. Blogs can also include links to other peoples' blogs.

Blogs are a way of publishing your own work, and like any published author, the more readers you have, the more successful your blog is considered to be.

If you create and regularly update a blog, and if you can generate and maintain sufficient "traffic" (that is, people keep coming to read your posts), you can become recognized as an authority on your particular subject. If you include links to other peoples' blogs and they include links back to your blog (these links are called *trackbacks*), you further validate yourself as an authority on your subject matter.

To create a blog, you simply navigate to a blog site and create an account. Most sites include templates that enable you to start posting articles immediately. To post an article to your blog, you must sign in using the username and password you select when you create the account. You can also send a link to your blog to other users.

Below are several blog sites you can visit to create your own blog:

- Blogger   www.blogger.com
- WordPress   wordpress.com
- Tumblr   www.tumblr.com
- Xanga   www.xanga.com
- Weebly   www.weebly.com

Blogs can contain a lot of reliable information on a variety of subjects, and they are searchable.

Forums

Forums are online discussion sites (also called *discussion boards*) laid out in a question-and-answer format. People on a forum hold conversations in the form of posted messages. A forum is organized into categories, and each forum category is divided into topics or threads.

Under the topics, each discussion in a specific forum is listed. Click a category to view the topics, then click a topic to view the discussions.

If you join a forum, you can post a question and wait for knowledgeable users to respond.

Popular forums include:

- answers.microsoft.com – discussions about Microsoft products and Windows software.
- www.cnet.com/forums – forums on hardware, software, mobile devices and more.
- www.techrepublic.com/forums – a community of IT experts answer questions and share their knowledge.
- www.pctechbytes.com/forums – computer repair tips and instructions.
- www.w7forums.com – discussions, news and articles on installation, drivers, hardware and troubleshooting Windows 7.

Wikis

A wiki is a reference resource that is developed through the collaborative efforts of anyone who wants to contribute.

Wiki pages are hosted on a web server, and managed through wiki software which allows users to freely create and edit web page content using a web browser. The pages in a wiki are hyperlinked to one another.

Wikis are powerful because multiple people can – and usually do – collaborate on a single piece of content (let's call it an article). A single article could have one author or many authors. A wiki pools together the knowledge from its contributors to create the best possible collection of information.

Because wikis are hosted online, you use a search box to find information, and because the pages are linked, you can jump from any one article to several other articles. Editing and content creation occurs continuously, making it possible to find information on current topics. The efforts of the wiki community at large tends to ensure that articles are accurate (if there are points in question, these will often be marked on the page as needing citations or supporting evidence).

There are wikis devoted to entertainment, games, health, reference articles, travel, and more. There are even fandom wikis (created and maintained by the fan base of particular movies and television shows) and there are wikis about wikis. You can find information about almost any topic in a wiki article somewhere on the Web.

Social Media Networks

Objective 3-5.1

A *social media network* is a dedicated web site that enables users to communicate with one another. Users can post information, comment on other people's posts, upload pictures and videos, play games, send email messages or engage in online chat with one another.

You join a social media site to connect with people. Facebook, Twitter, LinkedIn, Pinterest, Tumblr, Instagram, Flickr and Vine are just a few examples of popular social media sites. The following figure shows pages from Facebook, Twitter and Tumblr.

You must create an account on a social media site before you can use it. Users who are under the age of thirteen may need a parent's permission to create an account.

When you join a site, you create a profile. A *profile* is a collection of information about you. It usually includes your name, your picture, a list of your interests and hobbies, and perhaps general information about where you live. Once you create a profile on a social media site, the site creates a page for you. You can then post pictures, video, or text about yourself on your page.

Building the Network

Once your page has been created, you then go about the task of inviting other people to connect with you (on your page) on this social media platform. Depending on the site you are using, these people may be called friends, or contacts, or connections; the terminology is not important. The important point is, these are the people who constitute your social network. A social network is a network of people – people you know, *and people who know people that you know*.

The power of a social networking is that your current friends can lead you to new friends.

Friends and Friend Requests

You invite people you know to be your "friends" on the site. Friends can see your page and your information. Anything you post on your page can be seen by all your friends, unless you take extra steps to share certain items with only selected friends.

You will probably also receive friend requests from other people who have their own pages on the site. A friend request is an invitation to become online friends. When you accept a friend request, you can then visit your friends' pages. And while you are there, you can see all of their friends, and send friend requests to these people as well.

Note: As a matter of personal safety, you should accept friend requests only from people you know. On some sites, you might consider asking a friend to introduce you to someone with whom you want to connect.

Why Do People Join Social Networks?

People join social media networks for a variety of reasons – to find old friends, or keep in touch with current friends, or to find new friends too. Some people join professional social media sites to expand their list of business contacts, to promote themselves, to advertise their particular skill sets, to look for job leads or to find people to fill open positions. Companies often create social media pages as a means of advertising upcoming events, to post job openings, and to promote brand awareness.

Often, social networks include blog, photo, message and chat features, and some people use social networking platforms as a way to collaborate with others.

Popular Social Media Networks

There are several types of social networks geared for specific purposes and for sharing different types of content. A few of the most popular are listed here:

- **Facebook** – designed to help people connect and stay connected, Facebook is perhaps the most popular social networking site in the world. The site is available in 17 languages and includes public features such as a classified ads board, groups, events, and personal web pages for each member.

- **LinkedIn** – a social network for professionals to post information about their job skills, interests, education and work history. Users can search for jobs, search for people with specific skills, and join groups devoted to specific professions.

- **Twitter** – an online microblogging network that allows members to broadcast short posts called "tweets." Registered users can post and read, while unregistered users can only read. To share a tweet that you like, you can re-tweet (repost) it to share with your followers.

- **Instagram** – a network for sharing photos and short (up to 60 seconds) videos. Users can also apply digital filters to their images.

- **Snapchat** – a mobile app that allows you to send pictures and videos called "snaps" to friends. However, the pictures and videos last for only a brief time, and then disappear shortly after being viewed. You can add snaps to your "story," which is a collection of your photos and videos which will last for 24 hours. You can also add captions, doodles, or a lens graphic over the top of a snap.

- **YouTube** – a video sharing network. Users can upload, view, rate, share and comment on videos. You can find video clips, TV clips, music videos, movie trailers and video blogs on YouTube. Most of the content is uploaded by individuals, but advertisers and media corporations also upload material there. Unregistered users can watch videos, and registered users can create their own channels and upload videos to those channels. Users can also subscribe to channels and receive notifications when new content has been added.

- **Vine** – a video sharing network that allows you to record and share videos that are up to 6 seconds long. Other users can like, comment or re-vine (which means they add someone else's video to their own timeline for their followers to see.

Open vs Closed Social Media Networks

Objective 3-5.2

The social media networks you are probably best acquainted with are open networks. That is, they are open to the general public; you simply need to create an account. Most require only a valid email address for sign-up and there is generally a minimum age requirement (for example, you must be 13 or older to open a Facebook account).

Enterprises and organizations, however, which often enforce policies that discourage the use of open social media networks while employees are at work, can benefit from implementing closed social networks.

A *closed social network* is a social network that is private and internal to a company or organization; in order to participate on a closed social network, you must have an account that is associated with your organization – usually you use your work email address to sign in.

Closed social networking services can be used for private communication and collaboration within a school or organization.

Advantages of Closed Networks

Closed social media networks allow businesses to harness and leverage the power of social networking. They include message boards, news feeds, shared file locations, search capability and more. They provide a central location for discussions, announcements, wikis, and file storage. Instead of emailing file attachments to each other, employees can access documents in a secure, central location for collaborative efforts.

Perhaps even more importantly, closed networks provide an opportunity and a platform for all employees to participate in company "happenings" and conversations. Previously, this privilege was limited to managers and executives. But now, long-time employees and new hires alike can immerse themselves in the culture of an organization, find documents and information on their own, and stay tuned in to what is going on company-wide.

The benefits to very large corporations can be profound. Pearson Education, for example, teamed with Jive Software to create *Neo* – a closed social network that connects over 30,000 employees in over 60 countries.

Yammer (which is integrated with Office 365) is a closed social network that provides a dedicated site where employees can share documents, collaborate on documents, follow colleagues/projects, and follow company-specific news feeds. Yammer also allows for the creation of groups, which allows you to join and participate in specific project teams or department teams. Mobile apps for Yammer allow you to stay connected wherever you are, and you can set up Desktop notifications so that you never miss an update. For file storage, Yammer is integrated with OneDrive for Business and SharePoint.

Slack is another widely used closed social media network. It is a cloud-based team collaboration tool that is designed to replace email as the preferred method of intra-company communication. Slack provides messaging, notification, and announcement services, supports team collaboration and integrated file storage with Google Drive. Closed social media networking allows employees to stay informed about things that are happening within the company, makes it very easy to disseminate information, and reduces Inbox clutter – instead of having to send an email announcement to all your employees, you can post an announcement to Yammer or Slack and everyone is notified. This makes users and IT departments happy.

Note: Facebook began as a closed network; its membership was originally limited to Harvard University students. Membership was later expanded first to other colleges in the Boston area, then to schools in the Ivy League, then to most universities in Canada and the United States, then to corporations, and then finally to the public.

Taking a Look at LinkedIn

Objective 3-5.1

LinkedIn is a social network of professional connections. You might think of it as an online resume or a job board, but it is so much more. The purpose of LinkedIn is to be visible, searchable, and findable. It is a platform on which you can get your name, talents, and abilities in front of people who are looking to hire or to contract.

On LinkedIn, people in your network are called *connections*. When your connections look at your profile, they can see your information, they can see how they are connected to you, and they can see whether you have any connections or other characteristics in common.

Your network is made up of 1st degree, 2nd degree, and 3rd degree connections, and members of any LinkedIn groups that you have joined.

- 1st degree – these are people you're directly connected to either because you have accepted their invitation to connect, or because they have accepted your invitation. You can contact them by sending a message on LinkedIn.

- 2nd degree – these are people who are connected to your 1st degree connections. You can send them an invitation to connect.

- 3rd degree – these are people who are connected to your 2nd degree connections.

Each person's degree of connectedness to you is represented by an icon that displays next to their name in search results pages and on their profiles. To see your 2nd degree connections, you can access one of your 1st degree connection's profiles, then view *their* contacts.

When you click the name of a 2nd degree connection, LinkedIn will show how you are connected.

You can also use an Advanced LinkedIn search and specify to show 2nd and 3rd degree connections.

Even if I remained a good friend, what would happen if someone hacked my email account and found your message? Now, the message is out of your hands and out of my hands, and the hacker can do with it what he likes. Maybe he will post it online for a laugh.

You should understand that anything you put into digital format and then send (or otherwise make available) to other people is out of your control forever. If it is something that might reflect poorly on your character, it could potentially be used as a weapon against you.

Be mindful of this whenever you send (or post) digital information.

Why Is Your Digital Identity Important?

Any time you post something online you are disseminating your message to the world – and, by extension – you are promoting your personal brand. Your personal brand distinguishes you from other people and creates an impression in the minds of potential customers or employers or admissions board panelists. It is a matter of perception.

Your girlfriend's parents may be Googling your name right now – and they are not the only ones.

Potential employers and school admissions boards also go online to see what they can find about potential employees or enrollees. They may have your resume (or transcript and application) and a long list of references in hand, but they will go online to get a fuller picture of who you are and whether you might be a good fit for their organization or university. In fact, current employers also keep an eye on the social media accounts of their employees. Be careful what you share.

Yes, they will check LinkedIn. But they will also check Facebook, Twitter, Google+, Instagram, YouTube and so on. These accounts can give them an idea of who you are as a person. What will they find? Will they find intelligent tweets about relief organizations and conservation efforts? Or will they find rantings against your college dean on your personal blog and a video of you tossing a lighted firecracker into your neighbor's mailbox on your YouTube channel?

What do you share on Facebook – thought-provoking articles or sexist jokes?

People will also look at which groups you participate in, and who you follow on Instagram and Twitter and the like. Do you follow volunteer organizations or political extremists? The people and groups you follow can speak volumes about your interests and beliefs.

Creating a Positive Online Identity

To ensure that Google shows people the information that you want them to see you need to put good information "out there" and refrain from sharing things that might reflect poorly on your character. To begin, you can take the following steps:

- Create and manage your LinkedIn account. Take the time to create a well-written professional profile.

- Manage your Facebook profile and remove any photos that do not show you in a professional light. It is fine to share information about your personal life on Facebook; but don't post anything that might be off-putting to a recruiter or potential employer.

- Create a Twitter account and use it to share information that others may find valuable, such as articles related to your business or industry, or upcoming volunteer events in your community.

- Create and post to a blog that shares positive and professional ideas.
- Before indiscriminately posting the first thing that pops into your mind, ask yourself these questions:
  - What am I sharing? Will it reflect positively or negatively on me?
  - How secure is it?
  - With whom am I sharing?
  - What kind of footprint does it leave behind?
- Never post (or send a communication) in anger. You may be justifiably angry, but consider whether you really want your digital "legacy" to include angry, hurtful communications. If necessary, write and send and angry email to yourself only. Look it over the next day, and then decide whether you still want to send it.

Personal Identity and Professional Identity

Some people prefer to maintain separate online identities – one for their personal pursuits and one that represents them professionally – while others believe a blended identity gives a better, fuller, more honest picture of the "real you."

Whichever way you decide to proceed, be mindful of the impression your online activities can leave in the minds of others.

Aliases

People who prefer to maintain both a personal and a professional online identity often use their real name for one identify and an alias for the other. For example, Carolyn Stevens who works for a fictitious company that specializes in adventure vacations might use might use "carolynstevens" for her personal profiles and "AdventurerCarolyn" for her professional ones.

In some profiles, such as gaming profiles, you are encouraged or even required to use an alias so that you are not personally identifiable by your gaming name.

People with common names – like John smith – are often forced to use aliases because all variations of their first and last names (john.smith, johnsmith, jsmith, j-smith, and so on) are already being used by someone else.

Managing Your Online Identity

It has been said that the best defense is a good offense. Take a proactive role in creating and maintaining a positive online identity. Be careful about what you share, and take the time to create and share material that shows you are intelligent, thoughtful, responsible.

Take the time to find articles about issues you care about and comment on them, and share them with others. If you have a personal blog, post to it regularly and keep your posts positive in nature. If your blog is about your profession, post articles that show others how to accomplish their goals or streamline a process. Share videos that show you participating in volunteer or community projects.

If you have fallen victim to bad judgment in the past, and there are videos, comments, or posts out there in cyberspace that attest to this bad judgment, remove what you can. Then put your efforts into filling cyberspace with positive contributions. The more "good stuff" you put out there, the deeper others will have to dig to find the bad stuff.

However, many people simply refused to buy a converter, and emergency legislation was drafted to allow some stations to continue broadcasting analog signals until September 1, 2015. The point is, if you refuse to change, you may be left behind.

We live in an exciting time of ground-breaking advancements, and it is important to approach new technology as a new opportunity rather than as an obstacle. Achieving digital literacy is important for everyone.

Audience Consideration

Even though new technology is available, not everyone is eager (or able) to jump onboard. This is important to remember if you market items to demographic groups that either cannot afford new technology or that include members who might be resistant to new technology.

In other words, consider your audience. If you want to market walk-in bathtubs or pre-paid funeral plans to people aged seventy and older, you should make sure that you advertise on the radio and on television and in printed media as well as advertising online. Additionally, make sure that you staff your company with live operators to receive incoming calls; it would be ill-advised to expect people in this age group to "apply online."

If you want to advertise up-coming community events or special services, it is fine to advertise on your web site or on Twitter. However, be sure to mail (or hand out) flyers to the community too, or you might pass over quite a few people who would have been interested. Just because the community theater director is a genius at advertising on social media, that does not mean the community at large will be trawling the Internet looking for announcements. Some people still need to see a flyer and hang it on their refrigerators!

Disengaging

While connectedness makes our world smaller and allows us to be aware of what is happening anywhere at almost any time, human beings also require time away from external stimuli. We need some time alone to simply "be" and to focus inward for a bit. That is, we require "down time" in order to maintain good mental health. It is unhealthy to be engaged 24/7.

Internet Addiction

Internet addiction is thought to be an impulse control disorder, similar to pathological gambling. While it is common for people to enjoy using the Internet to meet, socialize, and exchange ideas through chat rooms, social networking sites and online communities, some form an intense attachment to these activities and cannot pull themselves away. Some users spend endless hours online at the cost of damaging interpersonal relationships with the people in their lives.

The warning signs of internet addiction are:

- Thinking continually about previous online activity or anticipating the next online session.
- Using the Internet in increasing amounts of time in order to achieve satisfaction.
- Losing interest in other hobbies or pastimes.
- Being unsuccessful in trying to control, cut back or stop Internet use.
- Feeling restless, moody, depressed or irritable when attempting to cut down on Internet use.
- Spending more time online than originally intended.
- Suffering fatigue or experiencing a change in sleep habits.

- Risking significant relationships, job, educational or career opportunities because of Internet use.

- Lying to family members, therapists, or others about how much time you spend on the Internet.

- Using the Internet as a way to escape from problems or to relieve feelings of hopelessness, guilt, anxiety, or depression.

Physical symptoms can include: backache, headaches, weight gain or weight loss, disturbances in sleep, carpal tunnel syndrome and blurred or strained vision.

Internet addiction, like any other addiction, can cause personal, family, academic, financial and occupational problems. Family members feel cheated and even insignificant when you would rather spend time online with strangers than with them. If you lie about how much time you really spend online, then distrust enters your relationships.

In more extreme cases, Internet addicts may create online personas through which they pretend to be people other than themselves. Those at highest risk for creating these "secret lives" are those who suffer from low self-esteem or feelings of inadequacy. Inability to deal with these problems in "real life" lead to clinical problems of depression and anxiety.

Ergonomic Best Practices

Repetitive stress injuries (RSIs) become commonplace as users begin to work on their computers for long periods of time. RSIs are conditions that occur gradually over time and are caused by too many uninterrupted repetitions of an activity or motion, particularly if the activity or motion is unnatural or awkward. RSIs for computer users usually affect the hands, wrists and arms, but can also affect other joints such as the elbow or neck.

To combat RSIs, users can use ergonomically designed furniture and proper techniques for safely using the computer. *Ergonomics* is the science of designing equipment that maximizes safety and minimizes discomfort. Measures you can take to prevent RSIs when using your computer include:

- Sit in a chair that provides lower back support, armrests and adjustable height.

- Use an ergonomic keyboard, which allows your hands to rest in a more natural position when you type than a standard keyboard does.

- Tilt the monitor up about 10 degrees to prevent neck strain.

- Use a padded wrist support to support your wrists when you are not typing.

To prevent eyestrain or headaches, you can:

- Position your monitor from 24 to 30 inches away from your eyes.

- Adjust the monitor resolution so text and icons are large enough to see clearly.

- Ensure that the monitor does not flicker. The refresh rate should be at least 72 Hz.

- Avoid staring at the display screen for long periods of time.

If you work at a computer for several hours a day, keep ergonomics in mind. First and foremost, never work at the computer without taking regular breaks. Get up once every hour, stretch, and walk about to get the circulation going and to rest your eyes. The following are some other points to keep in mind when considering how to create and use a computer workstation.

- The work surface should be stable; everything on the work surface should be resting flat.

- The monitor and keyboard should be directly in front of you, not at an angle.

- The top of the monitor should be about 2 to 3 inches above your eyes. You should not need to tilt or crane your neck to view the contents of the screen.

- There should be no glare or reflection on the screen. Where possible, ensure you have natural light with blinds that enable you to reduce or block any glare or reflection. Alternatively, have a lamp with appropriate wattage that enables you to identify images clearly in a darker room.

- Ensure there is appropriate lighting to read the screen clearly at any time of day. There should be a light source directly above the monitor, whether it is fluorescent lighting or a desk lamp. Where possible, try to pick a light source that simulates natural light.

- Place any documents that you will be looking at as you type in a document holder in line with the monitor.

- When seated comfortably, position your arms so that your wrists are straight and flat, and your arms are close to your body.

- Keep your feet flat on the floor and your thighs and forearms parallel to the floor. If your feet do not reach the floor, use a foot rest. This will help with blood circulation as you sit for a period of time.

- The keyboard should be in a comfortable position so your arms are not straining to reach up or down to hit particular keys. This is also true for the mouse. Many users prefer to place the keyboard and mouse on a lower level than the level of the desk. Ensure the keyboard and mouse are close to you so you are not straining to reach them.

- When typing, try not to bend the wrists. Your wrists should be relatively parallel to the keyboard and if possible, use the entire arm to help with typing rather than just the fingers or the hand.

- If you feel strain on the wrist, arm or fingers when using the traditional mouse, try switching to a trackball, a larger mouse, or consider using a device that uses touch technology.

These guidelines also apply to notebook users, although an advantage of a notebook is the ability to take it with you anywhere, including the beach or in a vehicle. If you plan to put the notebook on your lap, ensure you are sitting appropriately as described in the guidelines, and where possible, use a tray or something sturdy to place the notebook on as you work. This will ensure a flat surface for the notebook as well as reduce the amount of heat generated by the notebook on your lap.

It is to your advantage to consider ergonomics when you work with a computing device for long stretches of time. Even with a portable device, think of how you are sitting and using the device as well as getting up periodically to stretch your muscles. Strains on your body can lead to more than just physical pain, but also lead to a reduction in mental alertness, low productivity, errors in your work, or absences from work or school from physical ailments.

Exercise 17-2: Assessing ergonomics

In this exercise, you will assess how you are positioned in front of the computer, and what you may want to correct in order to reduce the chance of personal injury.

1. Stand up and stretch your body, reaching high with your arms to stretch your back.

2. Take a look at the chair you were sitting in and note where the handles or levers are located. Find the one that adjusts the height of the chair and make the appropriate adjustments for yourself.

3. Look straight at the monitor and determine if it is at eye level. If possible, tilt the monitor so you can see it better without having to strain your neck.

4.   Pull the keyboard close enough to you so you are not stretching your arms or back to reach the keys.

5.   Repeat step 4 with the pointing device for your computer.

6.   Now work with someone in the class to review how you are positioned in front of the computer and determine whether there are things that could be adjusted to provide a better working environment.

Lesson Summary

In this lesson, you learned about your online identity and how to protect it. You also learned about the adverse effects prolonged computing can have on your health. You should now be able to:

☑ describe the purpose of blogs, forums, and wikis

☑ understand the function of social media networks and how they work

☑ understand the difference between open and closed social networks

☑ describe how to use LinkedIn

☑ describe what constitutes your digital identity

☑ understand the importance of maintaining a good digital identity

☑ explain how to avoid cyber bullying

☑ understand the health risks that arise from prolonged computing

Review Questions

1.   Shaun regularly writes articles on database theory and instructional pieces about using Microsoft SQL Server. Where does he most likely publish these?
     a.   On his blog.   c.   On Vine.
     b.   On Snapchat.   d.   On YouTube.

2.   Which social network features pictures and videos that disappear after they have been viewed?
     a.   Vine   c.   YouTube
     b.   Snapchat   d.   Facebook

3.   Which of the following is an example of a closed social media network?
     a.   Facebook   c.   Yammer
     b.   LinkedIn   d.   Twitter

4.   Which of the following social networks was created specifically for making and maintaining professional business connections?
     a.   Facebook   c.   Instagram
     b.   LinkedIn   d.   Twitter

5.   The collection of data about you that is available online is your:
     a.   Profile   c.   Blog
     b.   Digital identity   d.   Facebook post history

6. Helen posted a picture to Facebook and a week later she wanted to remove it. How can she be sure that it has been removed from the Internet?

    a. Deleting her post is sufficient; any posted picture can be removed from the Internet at any time.

    b. If she deletes the picture within one month of posting it, it will be permanently removed.

    c. She cannot be sure because reposts and sharing could keep it online indefinitely.

    d. She can call her ISP and request that the picture be removed.

7. Which is a good reason for using an alias online?

    a. To keep your personal and business identities separate.

    b. To remain anonymous while making rude comments on a co-worker's posts.

    c. To bully someone and keep them guessing about who it is.

    d. To enter a sweepstakes multiple times.

8. Which of the following is a good way to create a positive online identity?

    a. Share stories or articles about volunteer opportunities on social media.

    b. Comment intelligently and thoughtfully on other people's posts.

    c. Create a blog and post positive articles that reflect your character.

    d. All of these are good ways to create a positive online identity.

9. Which of the following is an example of cyber bullying?

    a. Sending a derogatory email to someone.

    b. Posting a compromising picture of someone on Facebook.

    c. Making unkind remarks about someone on social media.

    d. All of these.

10. Marissa tweeted for a week to advertise a mentoring project at the public library in which senior citizens were encouraged to mentor youth in specific job skills such as accounting, bookkeeping and filing. She also put this information on the library Facebook page. Although there is a large population of senior citizens within five blocks of the library, the turnout was disappointing. Which is a probable reason for the poor turnout?

    a. Senior citizens do not care about youth in their community.

    b. Seniors probably did not have transportation to the library.

    c. Seniors are not particularly active on Twitter and Facebook.

    d. All of these.

11. Which of the following is a sign of Internet addiction?

    a. Lying about how much time you spend online.

    b. Having a Facebook and a Twitter and an Instagram and a Vine account.

    c. Using an alias in one or more of your online accounts.

    d. Configuring your phone to alert you when someone messages you on Facebook.

IC3

CCI Learning

Internet and Computing Core Certification Guide
Global Standard 5

Using Windows 10 & Microsoft® Office 2016

Appendix A: Courseware Mapping

Appendix B: Glossary of Terms

Appendix C: Index

Courseware Mapping

Computing Fundamentals

		Objective Domain	Lesson
1		**Mobile devices**	
	1.1	Understand cellular phone concepts	3
	1.2	Be familiar with cellular-enabled tablets	3
	1.3	Be familiar with smart phone	2, 3, 5
	1.4	Understand the use of hard-wired phones	3
	1.5	Use of instant messaging	5
	1.6	Know how to configure notifications	6
2		**Hardware devices**	
	2.1	Types of Devices	2
	2.2	Know the impact of memory and storage on usage	2
	2.3	Know how to connect to different peripherals. Define types of connections; for example, 3.5 mil connections for an audio cable, VGA, HDMI, USB for most other things. Microphone port, Printers – wireless as well as USB, Cameras or audio can connect through Bluetooth or infrared connections.	2
	2.4	Understand the use of Ethernet ports.	2, 3
	2.5	Connect a device wireless network (Wi-Fi), Connecting a wireless printer, How to get a device onto Wi-Fi, How to enter password or passkey	3
	2.6	Understand power management and power settings, How to save battery time when using a laptop, Locate power settings and use them, Differentiate between sleep and hibernate.	1, 2
	2.7	Understand driver concepts as well as their device compatibility.	2
	2.8	Know platform implications and considerations, for example Mac, PC, Linux, iOS, Android, Firmware; define and describe SaaS applications that are delivered online.	2, 5
	2.9	Know platform compatibility, device limitations.	3, 4
	2.10	Know the difference between cellular, Wi-Fi, and wired networks; Define, in general, the difference among these types of networks; Implications of sending large files on cellular or streaming; Wi-Fi limitations by locations, wired networks you cannot move; Difference between an ISP provider and a cellular provider.	3
	2.11	Understand concepts regarding connecting to the internet; Organizations typically have both wired and wireless connections; For home use, one must purchase bandwidth and speed from an ISP that is non-cellular.	3
	2.12	Understand common hardware configurations; Laptop with multiple monitors, docking stations, CPU with a video card or some laptops have integrated video; Wireless keyboards, devices connected to a desktop and laptop.	2
	2.13	Implications for document usage.	2

		Objective Domain	Lesson
	2.14	Understand the pros and cons of touch screens vs non-touch screen devices; Limitations of input using a touch keyboard; Limitations of input using touch vs keyboard and mouse, such as fine selection points, efficiency of input, having multiple tabs open.	2
3	**Computer software and concepts**		
	3.1	Understand operating system versioning and update awareness; Implications of updates, understanding benefits and features of new updates.	1
	3.2	Know concepts surrounding applications vs. operating system vs. global settings; Global settings common to all operating systems; for example, password protection, power management configurations, screen resolution.	1
	3.3	Have a general understanding of operating systems and software settings.	1, 4
	3.4	Set software preferences; Understand basic software settings that a user can set; for example, changing frequency of AutoSave, changing a print setting, and changing settings in Microsoft Office using File/Options.	5
	3.5	Users and profiles; Basic concepts of users and profiles; for example, on a Windows PC, a family could use a computer and each user has a distinct account with a user profiles and own login and credentials; Understand that profiles are customizable.	1
	3.6	Know file structures and file/folder management.	4
	3.7	Document Management.	4
	3.8	Menu navigation.	1, 4
	3.9	Searching for files; Know where to go for files, use search options to find files; Use file search techniques such as WIN KEY and start typing; on a Mac Command + Spacebar; Understand that downloaded files go the Downloads folder.	4
	3.10	Rights and permissions (administrative rights); Understand that Admin-level rights exist and that you may not have permission to access all files in an organization; Describe why permissions are valuable in an organization.	4
	3.11	Define an IP address.	3
	3.12	Know how to install, uninstall, update, repair software; Software purchased on media might need to be reinstalled from the Internet.	5
	3.13	Troubleshooting.	7
4	**Backup and Restore**		
	4.1	Understand backing up concepts.	7
	4.2	Know how to back up and restore.	7
	4.3	Know how to complete a full system restore on a personal device; complete a full system restore/reset on a tablet and phone; define factory default setting; if a laptop, reformat a hard drive.	7
5	**File Sharing**		
	5.1	Understand file transfer options and characteristics.	4, 6

		Objective Domain	Lesson
6		**Cloud Computing**	
	6.1	Understand "cloud" concepts; Understand cloud storage vs. cloud access concepts; Define cloud storage and cloud access; Must have Internet access to get to cloud; Describe cloud storage of photos for different systems, such as iCloud.	6
	6.2	Know the benefits of using cloud storage; Safe storage, convenience.	6
	6.3	Access and use of the cloud.	6
	6.4	Web apps vs. local apps.	6
	6.5	Understand web app types.	5, 6
7		**Security**	
	7.1	Know credential management best practices	7
	7.2	Know the basic threats to security of computers, data, and identity	7
	7.3	Understand the implications of monitoring software (surveillance)	7
	7.4	Understand connecting to secured vs. unsecured network (wired and wireless)	7
	7.5	Know the use of and importance of anti-virus software	7
	7.6	Know the use of firewalls and basic settings	7
	7.7	Know e-commerce interactions and best practices	7
	7.8	Understand the basic definition and use of Virtual Private Networks (VPNs)	7

Key Applications

		Objective Domain	Lesson
1		**Common Application Features**	
	1.1	Know copy, cut, and paste keyboard equivalents	9, 10
	1.2	Understand the difference between plain text and HTML (text with markup)	9
	1.3	Know how to use spelling check	9, 12
	1.4	Know how to use reviewing features	9
	1.5	Know the find/replace feature	9
	1.6	Be able to select text or cells	9, 10, 12
	1.7	Be able to redo and undo	9, 10,
	1.8	Be able to drag and drop	9
	1.9	Know the read-only view	9
	1.10	Understand what a protected mode means	9
	1.11	Be able to use the zoom feature	9
2		**Word Processing Activities**	
	2.1	Perform basic formatting skills	9
	2.2	Adjust margins, page sizes, and page orientation	9
	2.3	Alter text and font styles	9

		Objective Domain	Lesson
	2.4	Create and save files	9
	2.5	Know page layout concepts	9
	2.6	Know how to print a word processing document	9
	2.7	Use and configure print views	9
	2.8	Use reviewing options within a word processing document	9
	2.9	Be able to use tables	9
	2.10	Understand which file types are compatible or editable with word processors	9
	2.11	Use word processing templates to increase productivity	9
3	**Spreadsheet Activities**		
	3.1	Understand common spreadsheet terms	10
	3.2	Be able to insert/delete rows and columns	10
	3.3	Be able to modify cell sizes	10
	3.4	Be able to filter and sort data	10
	3.5	Understand functions, formulas, and operators	10
	3.6	Be able to enter data in a spreadsheet	10
	3.7	Use and create spreadsheet charts	10
	3.8	Create spreadsheet tables	10
	3.9	Manipulate data within a spreadsheet	10
	3.10	Format data within spreadsheets	10
	3.11	Understand compatible spreadsheet file types. Examples include Csv, Xlsx, Tab delimited, etc.	10
	3.12	Be able to use spreadsheet templates to increase productivity	10
	3.13	Understand how a spreadsheet can be used as a simple database	10
4	**Databases**		
	4.1	Understand what data is	11
	4.2	Understand how websites utilize databases	11
	4.3	Know basic concepts of a relational database	11
	4.4	Know what metadata is	11
5	**Presentations**		
	5.1	Understand file types compatible with presentation software	12
	5.2	Understand how to connect to external/extended monitors to display presentation	12
	5.3	Be able to us presentation views and modes	12
	5.4	Know how to add animations, effects, and slide transitions	12
	5.5	Know how to create and organize slides	12
	5.6	Know how to design slides	12

	Objective Domain	Lesson
5.7	Identify presentation software options	12
6	**App Culture**	
6.1	Understand how to obtain apps	8
6.2	Identify different app genres	8
6.3	Understand strengths and limits of apps and applications	8
7	**Graphic Modification**	
7.1	Be able to import and insert images into documents	9, 12
7.2	Understand how to crop images	9, 12

Living Online

	Objective Domain	Lesson
1	**Internet (Navigation)**	
1.1	Understand what the Internet is	13, 14
2	**Common Functionality**	
2.1	Understand how to use common website navigation conventions	13
3	**Email Clients**	
3.1	Identify email applications	16
3.2	Understand contact management	16
4	**Calendaring**	
4.1	Know how to create events and appointments	16
4.2	Know how to share calendars	16
4.3	Know how to view multiple calendars; Multiple calendars can be connected in one view; show up in different colors in same user interface	16
4.4	Understand how to subscribe to calendars; A public calendar (like a municipal calendar) vs sharing your own calendar	16
5	**Social Media**	
5.1	Understand what a digital identity is (identity on social media); Concept of once you do something, it cannot be undone	17
5.2	Recognize the difference of internal (school/business) vs. open media sites; There are business and school social media sites, such as Neo and Yammer and Slack; Difference between an open social media site and a closed site; for example, Facebook started as a closed site (for students at a specific college), but is now an open site available to anyone who signs up for an account	17
5.3	Know what blogs, wikis, and forums are and how they are used	17
5.4	Know what cyber bullying is	17

	Objective Domain	Lesson
6	**Communications**	
	6.1	Know the best tool for the various situations and scenarios; Describe how different communication technologies (email, phone, text message) are suited for differing circumstances; for example, if you needed to get an urgent message to your boss, what technology is best? Describe which technology is likely to get the fastest and slowest response from the recipient	15
	6.2	Know how to use SMS texting; Describe appropriate use of SMS; for example, when communicating with your boss, maybe use text only if he or she is out of the office	15
	6.3	Know how to use chat platforms; Describe and demonstrate the use of Skype as a chat platform in business	15
	6.4	Understand options for and how to use distant/remote/individual learning technologies	15
7	**Online Conferencing**	
	7.1	Understand and identify online conference offerings	15
8	**Streaming**	
	8.1	Understand what streaming is and how it works with devices; Differentiate between streaming and downloading; Define live audio; Describe how you could stream the video of a live recording	15
9	**Digital Principles/Ethics/Skills/Citizenship**	
	9.1	Understand the necessity of coping with change in technology	17
	9.2	Understand Digital Wellness basics	17
	9.3	Understand an online identity management	17
	9.4	Know the difference between personal vs. professional identity	17

Glossary of Terms

AAOCC – acronym for: authentic, accuracy, objectivity, currency, and coverage, or the guidelines you can use to help evaluate information you find on the Internet.

Address – In a worksheet, a reference to a specific cell; in a network, a reference to a specific computer; on the World Wide Web, a reference to a specific web site.

Address Bar – In File Explorer, a field in which you can enter a path to a file or folder; in a browser it is the field in which you type a URL.

Address Book – Central location where contact information for an entire organization is stored.

Adware – Software that automatically displays or downloads advertisements.

Alias – An alternate (or false) name.

Alignment – The positioning of text or the contents of a cell; for example, left, right, or centered.

Antivirus Software – use to scan your computer for known viruses, and to eliminate any viruses that are discovered.

App Store – Digital platform for distributing software; different platforms utilize different app stores.

Apps – Small, light-weight programs you obtain from an app store; apps are generally designed to perform a single function.

Archive – A collection of files. Can refer to folders that have been compressed using a "zip" program, or to a collection of messages stored by an email program in an area separate from your Inbox.

Argument – A value that a function uses in order to perform a calculation.

Attachments – Files you include with a communication such as an email or a text message.

Authentication – The process of confirming the identity of a user or computer system.

AutoComplete – A feature that automatically completes a word you are typing.

Backup – A duplicate copy of a program, a disk, or data, made either for archiving purposes or for safeguarding files from loss if the active copy is damaged or destroyed.

Bandwidth – A measurement, expressed in bits per second (bps), of a network's capacity to move data from one location to another.

Bcc – Blind carbon copy; a field in the header of an email message. Other recipients of the message will not see who was named in the Bcc field.

Binary Digit (bit) – The smallest unit of data a computer can understand, represented by a zero (0) or a one (1).

Blacklisting – The act of putting a person (or a web site or domain) on a list that will deny them specific privileges or service.

Blockers/Filters – Special software that can be installed to control the type or amount of content that can be viewed on a computer.

Blog – An online journal that includes a communications element

Bluetooth – A wireless technology used to allow devices (such as computers and phones) to work with Bluetooth-enabled accessories.

Bookmark – a marked and stored location of an item such as a help topic or a particular web page on the Internet. You can click a bookmark to navigate directly to page on the Internet. Also known as Favorites.

Boolean Operators – Words or symbols you can use to narrow the results returned by a search

Breadcrumbs – In a website, a type of secondary navigation scheme that shows the user's current location; in File Explorer, the file path to the current location wherein each piece of text in the Address Bar is an active control.

Browser – A software application used to browse the World Wide Web.

Browser Home Page – Web page that displays whenever you click the Home button in the browser toolbar.

Byte – A group of eight bits used to represent one alphanumeric character.

Cache – Folders on a hard drive used by browsers to store downloaded files.

Cascading Style Sheets – Section of a web page (or a separate sheet attached to a web page) where presentational attributes (such as font colors, background styles, element alignment, and so on) are defined.

Cc – Carbon copy; a field in the header of any email message. Other recipients of the message will see who was named in this field.

Cell – Geographic area defined for communications services on a cellular network; also the intersection of a row and a column in a spreadsheet.

Censorship – The act of disallowing access to specific content through tools such as filters, blockers, or blacklists.

Check Box – An option in a dialog box used for selecting or activating items or features. If checked, the feature is activated. If unchecked, the feature has been turned off.

Closed Social Network – Social media network that is private and internal to a company or organization; you must use an account that is associated with your organization in order to participate.

Cloud Computing – Technology in which computing resources are delivered as a service over the Internet.

Columns – A feature that enables you to format the layout of your document into one, two, or three columns of text.

Conference Call – A call that involves three or more parties.

Contact – An entry in an email program containing information about a person or organization, including the name, address, telephone numbers, or other relevant information such as a picture, email address, IM address.

Contextual Tabs – Tabs that appear on the Ribbon only when appropriate

Control Panel – Area in Windows where you can access features to customize settings for devices on your system.

Cookie – A small text file placed on your computer by a Web site. Cookies store information about your preferences.

Copyright –Law that awards ownership of original works to the author or creator, whether the work is published or unpublished.

Criteria – Text or values you specify when conducting a search or query.

CRM – Customer Relationship Management; the practice of managing and analyzing interactions with customers in order to improve business relationships and increase customer retention.

Cyber Bullying – Bullying that utilizes online tools and environments; making online threats or posting hurtful comments are examples of cyber bullying.

Delete – To remove a selected item

Desktop – The screen background for Windows where windows, icons, and dialog boxes appear.

Device Driver – A program that enables the operating system to communicate with and control an installed hardware device.

Digital Footprints – A permanent record of the activities you have performed throughout your online life.

Digital/Online Identify – The collection of data about you that is available online; it includes your profile and your online activities (such as posts, shared pictures, uploaded videos, and so on).

Directory – The organization of files and folders on a disk.

Domain Name System (DNS) – A service that maps unique domain names to specific IP addresses.

Double-Click – The process of clicking the left (or primary) mouse button twice quickly.

Downloading – the process of copying a file (any type of file) from a server on the Internet to your device.

Drag – To point the mouse pointer at one corner of an area to select, and press and hold the left mouse button as you move or the mouse pointer to the opposite corner; when you release the mouse button the area is selected.

Drag and Drop – To move a selected item by pressing and holding the left mouse button as you move the mouse pointer to another location; when you release the mouse button, the selected item is deposited in the new location.

Email Address – The address assigned to you electronic Inbox; an email address includes your mailbox name followed by the @ symbol, followed by the name of the domain that hosts your account. A typical email address might be user@yourcompany.com

Encryption – the process of converting data into an unreadable form of text which then requires decryption key in order to be read. Files, folders or email messages can be encrypted so that unauthorized people cannot view or use the information.

Ergonomics – The science studying humans in a workplace environment and of designing equipment that maximizes safety, minimizes discomfort, and prevents workplace injuries

Ethernet – A network cabling protocol for transmitting data across a LAN; a wired connection to a LAN is called an Ethernet connection.

EULA – End User License Agreement; a license agreement you accept and agree to abide by when you install software.

Field – A data entry unit for holding a single piece of information; a category of information in a database table.

File Name Extension – A suffix added to the base name of a computer file; used to specify the format of a file and to identify which program(s) created and can open the file.

File Permissions – Rules that determine whether you can access a file and what you can do with it.

Firewall – A security barrier that filters and controls the flow of information coming into and out of a private network.

Firmware – Built-in programmable logic (software) that is embedded in a piece of hardware and controls how the device functions.

Floating Object – An object that can be placed in any position in a document because it "floats" above the text.

Folder – A container that stores files and other folders; also known as a directory or subdirectory.

Foreign Key – A column (or combination of columns) in a table the references the primary key in another table.

Formula – An expression which calculates a value; can be composed of values, cell references, arithmetic operators and functions.

Forum – An online discussion site where users post questions and answers to create conversations also called discussion boards.

Function – A pre-defined formula.

GUI – An acronym for Graphical User Interface; it provides menus and clickable buttons or icons to perform computing tasks. Windows is a GUI.

Hacker – A person who tries to gain unauthorized access to a computer system.

Handle – In social media accounts such as Twitter, a handle is the name by which you are recognized in the social network.

Handles – Small circles or squares that appear around the perimeter of a selected object.

Handouts – Documents that audience members can take with them after viewing a presentation.

Hardware – Physical components that comprise a computer or computing device.

Hashtag – A word or phrase preceded by a number sign or hash symbol (#); when you turn a word or phrase into a hashtag, it becomes a searchable link.

Header – Text or graphics that repeat at the top of every page. A header may include page numbers.

Hibernate – Power mode available only on laptops that stores open files and programs to disk and turns off the system. This mode draws no power.

Highlighted – Indicates that an object or text is selected and will be affected by the next action or command.

History – A function that stores and lists the URLs of web sites you visited.

Home Page – Top-level page of a web site (also called an Index page or a landing page).

Hosted Service – A service that is provided by a server located outside your own network.

HTTP – Hypertext Transfer Protocol; the protocol used to request and send web pages over the Internet.

Hyperlink – A reference to data that is located somewhere other than the present location; you click a hyperlink to jump to the targeted location.

Internet – A global network of computers. It is a large non-administered collection of computers that no one person or organization owns or is responsible for.

In-browser App – A web-based browser extension by linking to a web service.

Infrastructure – The underlying physical framework needed for the operation of a service or an enterprise; in networking, infrastructure is the hardware that supports high-speed communications and data transfer.

Inline Object – An object that acts as a text character in a paragraph.

Instant Messaging – A type of electronic communication that allows two or more participants to converse in real time by typing messages to one another

Intellectual Property – A work or invention that is the result of the creative effort of a company or individual; the creator has rights that restrict the use of his intellectual property by others

Interface – A point where two systems (or people, or networks, or devices) meet and exchange information.

Intranet – A private web site on your company's network; you must log in using a valid user name and password.

IP Address – Unique address that distinguishes one computer from another on a network; formatted as a series of four decimal numbers separated by periods (IPv4) or eight hexadecimal separated by colons (IPv6)

ISP – Internet Service Provider; a company that provides a connection to the Internet for a monthly fee

Keywords – Words that you enter in a search field as criteria for a search.

LAN – Local Area Network; a private network usually confined to one geographic location.

Legend – A box on a chart that explains the meaning of each line in a line chart, or bar in a bar chart.

Live Streaming – The process of broadcasting real-time live audio/video footage as a video feed to an audience that accesses the stream over the Internet.

LMS – Learning Management Systems; a software application designed to deliver electronic training courses, track student progress, and generate performance reports; an engine that powers eLearning.

Lock Screen – Screen that displays until the user performs the required gesture, or enters the correct information; a feature designed to keep unauthorized users from accessing your device.

Malware – Software that can harm a computer; usually refers specifically to spyware and adware

Margin – The white space or area from the edge of the paper to the text.

Microprocessor – Silicon chip that performs calculations and logical operations in the computer; also referred to as the Central Processing Unit (CPU) or simply as the processor.

Mini Toolbar – A contextual toolbar that appears only when you select text. As you move the mouse pointer over the toolbar, it becomes a functioning toolbar with commonly used text formatting options.

MMS – Multimedia Messaging Service; similar to SMS but provides a standard way to send messages that include multimedia content from one mobile device to another.

Mouse Pointer – An icon (usually an arrow) that follows the movement of the mouse (or other pointing device) on the screen

Name Box – This box displays the cell address of the active cell. It is located on the left below the toolbar.

Navigation Bar – A series of links (usually down the left side or across the top of the page) that provides access to various areas of a web site.

Netiquette – A customary code of good practices relating to electronic communications.

Network – A system for moving objects or information from one location to another.

Network Interface Card (NIC) – Hardware that must be installed on your computer before you can send or receive data between your computer and the network.

Network Share – A location on a server that is available over a network; used within the confines of a LAN.

OCR – Optical Character Recognition; functionality which allows a scanner to convert a scanned image into editable electronic text and save that editable text as a document.

Office Clipboard – A place to store data temporarily, pending retrieval.

Online Meeting – A meeting in which multiple participants can speak, share visuals, send files, and request and take control of material being presented.

Online Profile – A collection of information about you, including your user name, a picture, your hobbies and interests and so on.

Open-Source Software – Software for which the code base if freely available and modifiable; usually the software is distributed without charge.

Orientation – The direction of the paper for text flow; Portrait takes advantage of the length of the paper vertically whereas Landscape uses the length of the paper horizontally.

Packets – Small units of data that are transferred across a network; each packet includes address information for the source and destination device and a data payload.

Page Break – The division between two pages.

Password – A unique string of characters that must be provided before a logon or access is authorized.

Paste – The editing function of placing cut or copied data into a new location.

Path – The route you must follow to get to the location of a file on a disk.

Peripherals – Devices connected to a computer system by a cable or by using wireless technology.

Permissions – Rules associated with objects on a computer, such as files, folders and settings. Permissions – Determine whether you can access an object and what you can do with it.

Phishing – A the process of trying to gather sensitive information such as a password, or credit card details from an unsuspecting victim by pretending to be a trustworthy entity.

Piracy – the act of sharing or selling a copyrighted item without the owner's permission

Plagiarism – The act of passing off someone else's work or idea as your own without crediting the source.

Platform – Interface between an application (or app) and the operating system; the environment within which an application runs.

Plug-ins – Also known as Add-ons; small applications that extend the capabilities of web browsers.

Podcast – An audio or video file you can upload to play or broadcast from a media player or a Web site. Podcasts can also be broadcast in real time from your computer with a Webcam.

Pop-up Blocker – A utility in a browser that suppresses the display of pop-up windows.

Port – Socket into which you can connect peripheral devices to a computer.

Power Plan – A collection of hardware and system settings that manages how a computer utilizes power.

Primary Key – A field (or combination of fields) that uniquely identifies each record stored in a database table.

Private Browsing – An option that allows you to surf the web without saving any information about your browsing.

Program – A sequence of instructions that guides the computer through the performance of a specific task or sequence of tasks.

Proprietary Software – Software that is owned by an individual or a company, and sold as an executable file along with a license.

Protocol – A set of rules that enable devices to communicate with one another in an agreed-upon manner

Quick Access Toolbar – Located above the File tab and contains popular commands such as Save, Undo, and Redo. This toolbar can be customized for those commands you use frequently.

Radio Button – A selection that appears in a dialog box that allows a user to choose one item from a group of choices.

Range – A selection of cells in a worksheet.

Record – Information about a single item in a database table. A record contains fields (or columns) and each field contains a different piece of information about the item.

Recycle Bin – A temporary storage area for deleted files. Deleted files remain in the Recycle Bin until the deleted files are restored or the Recycle Bin is emptied.

Restore Point – A saved snapshot of your computer's Windows system files, program files, and Windows registry settings at a specific point in time.

Root Directory – The highest level of any directory on a disk; represented by the drive letter and a colon, followed by a backslash.

Row – A record in a database table or a numbered row (horizontal sequence of cells) in a worksheet.

Ruler – Located below the Ribbon in Word or PowerPoint; the ruler displays icons that allow you to perform functions such as changing margins, tabs and indents quickly.

SaaS – Software as a Service; a subscription service where you pay a monthly rate for access to software that is delivered over a network.

Save – The process of storing or copying the information stored in the memory to a disk.

Scanner – Device that converts a printed page or image into an electronic format

Screen Resolution – Refers to the degree of clarity with which text and images appear on screen.

Scroll Bars – Scroll bars automatically appear in a window if the contents are not entirely visible. A vertical or horizontal scroll bar may appear.

Search Box – A field in which you can enter criteria to search for help topics or file names that match what you type.

Search Engine – A service that maintains a database of Internet URLs and an index of key words; you use a search engine to find pages that contain information on text you specify as a criteria

Server – A computer designed to support other computers for business purposes; servers provide files and services to other systems on a network

Settings App – A Windows 10 app you can use to configure several system settings.

Sharing Link – A hyperlink you can send in the body of an email message that provides access to a file or folder stored in a cloud location.

Shortcut Keys – The commands activated by pressing the CTRL key with another key to perform a specific task, such as pressing CTRL+P will display the Print menu.

Shortcut Menu – The menu that appears when you click the right mouse button.

Signature – A block of text that appears at the bottom of an email that includes contact information on who sent the message.

Sleep – Power mode that leaves the computer on but puts it into a state that consumes less power. The display turns off, the fan stops, and work is put into memory.

Slide Layout – A blueprint or boiler plate for slides; each layout contains placeholders for various types of content

Slide Sorter – The view that displays multiple miniature slides on one screen; use this view to rearrange or sort your slides.

Smart Phones – Hand-held devices that combine the features of a standard cell phone with those of a personal computer.

SMS – Short Message Service; a protocol used by cellular providers to enable text messages to be sent from one mobile device to another.

Social Engineering – The practice of tricking users into giving out passwords or other types of access information.

Social Media Site – Web site where registered users connect with each other to build a social network in which they can share information, pictures, ideas, and opinions.

Software – Refers to any program that makes a computer run – including operating systems and application programs.

Spacing – Refers to the amount of white space between individual characters, words, lines or columns of text or objects.

Spam – Unsolicited electronic communications; often spam messages promote products and services, or convey specific political/religious views.

Speaker Notes – A PowerPoint feature that allows you to create notes on each slide in the presentation and then print these for your reference during the presentation.

Spelling & Grammar – A feature that checks the spelling and grammar in a document and usually provides a list of corrections for any error it finds.

Spyware – Software that is secretly placed on your system and gathers personal or private information without your consent or knowledge.

Status Bar – Located at the bottom of the screen. The status bar displays messages, cursor location, page number, section number, and whether specific features are active.

Streaming – The process of having a file delivered to your device in a constant and steady stream; the file is not stored on your computer.

Subfolder – A folder contained within another folder.

Symbol – A character that can be inserted into a document, either as a text character or for a bullet or numbering style.

System Image – An exact image of a hard drive; it includes Windows and the system settings, programs, and files. You can use a system image to restore the contents of your computer to the state it was in when you created the image.

Tab – Depending on the context used, it may refer to the TAB key on the keyboard, a page of options in a dialog box, a menu command on the Office 2016 Ribbon, or an option to display another page for further actions.

Table – A feature that enables you to create a grid layout for content consisting of columns and rows, similar to how a worksheet appears.

Task Pane – A window displayed at the side of the screen that appears when specific commands are activated such as the Office Clipboard

Taskbar – The area at the bottom of the screen that runs horizontally and contains the Start menu and other frequently used programs, folders or files.

Theme – A collection of coordinated appearance settings saved under a name; themes include font settings, color settings and text, border, and fill styles.

Touch Screen – An interface that allows you to touch or tap a screen to perform specific actions instead of using a mouse and keyboard.

Transition – Special effects that you can apply as you move from one slide to the next during a slide show

Trojan – A program designed to allow a hacker remote access to a target computer system.

Troubleshooting – A systematic approach to solving a problem; generally, the process of determining what may be causing an issue on the computer and then finding a resolution for the issue.

Undo – The feature that enables you to reverse the last action performed.

Upload – The process of sending data from your computer to a server

URL – Uniform Resource Locator; a global (text) address of a resource that is located on the World Wide Web. It consists of a protocol identifier and a domain name. Each URL is associated with a specific IP address. You enter a URL into a browser address bar to visit a web page.

User Name – A unique name associated with a particular computer or software account

User Profile – A collection of settings that make the computer look and function in a particular manner.

Video Conference – An online meeting in which participants share video via web cam.

Virtual – Term that refers to device that does not physically exist, but is made to appear and act as if it exists by software.

Virtual Personal Assistants – Voice-activated services that answer questions, make recommendations and perform actions on a device.

Virtual Private Network (VPN) – An encrypted connection between two computers that allows secure, private communications over long distances using the Internet.

Virus – A malicious program designed to take control of system operations, and damage or destroy data.

Voice Mail – A centralized system used in businesses for sending, storing, and retrieving audio messages.

VoIP – Voice over Internet Protocol; a technology that allows you to make voice calls using a broadband Internet connection instead of a traditional telephone line.

Web Apps – Applications that run on the World Wide Web instead of running directly on a device.

Web Servers – Servers that host or store a company's or an individual's web site.

WebEx – Hosted service that you can use to conduct online meetings with anyone who has an Internet connection.

Wide Area Network – A network that connects computers in multiple locations using communication lines owned by a public carrier; a WAN is a public network.

Widget – A small self-contained program you can add to a web site, blog or personalized web page. A widget brings external content into the web page.

Wireless Network (Wi-Fi) – A network that includes a wireless access point which supports wireless connections using one of 802.11 Wi-Fi standards

Word Wrap – A feature that moves text from the end of a line to the beginning of a new line as you type.

World Wide Web (WWW) – System of interlinked documents accessible on the Internet.

WYSIWYG – Refers to "What You See Is What You Get", a display mode that shows the document exactly as it will appear when you print it or when you view it in a web browser.

Index

=

=AVERAGE, 325
=COUNT, 325
=MAX, 325
=SUM, 325

2

2-in-1s, 50

A

AAOCC, 470
Absolute Addresses, 326
Account Options, 6
Account Types, 5
    Permissions, 6
Action Center, 14
    Quick Actions, 14
Active Cell, 312, 313
Add-ons, 450
Address Bar, 422
    Searching, 435
Address Book, 522
Address Books, 534
Ad-hoc, 85
Adware, 216
Aliases, 561
Aligning
    Text, 286
Alignment, 330
Android, 28
Animation, 392
    Animation Pane, 393
    Customization, 393
Animation Pane, 393
Antivirus Software, 220
API, 354
App Store
    Browsing, 251
App Stores, 159, 250
Apple Safari, 427
Application Programs, 2, 12
Application Service Provider, 477
Applications, 241
    Desktop publishing programs, 243
    Graphic design programs, 244
    Image editingprograms, 244
    Messaging, 165
    Presentation programs, 246
    Productivity progarms, 242
    Programs, 242
    Spreadsheet programs, 244
    Video editing programs, 246
    Web development programs, 245
    Word processing programs, 242
Appointment
    Recurring, 538

Appointments, 537
    Inviting others, 539
    Recurring, 538
Apps, 12, 50, 241, 450
    Audio, 254
    Buying, 257
    Cloud storage, 247
    Communication, 252
    Content, 253
    Deleting, 164, 258
    Limitations, 260
    Local, 250
    Non-SMS messaging, 167
    Obtaining, 163, 256
    Online, 247
    Productivity, 252
    Purchasing in-apps, 258
    Recovering deleted, 164, 259
    Settings, 17
    Social media, 254
    Stores, 250
    Video, 255
    Web, 247
Archiving, 533
Articles, 472
Asynchronous, 483
    Classes, 512
    Communications tools, 484
    Email, 484
    SMS text messages, 484
Attachments, 137, 528
    Opening, 529
Audio Apps, 254
Audio Ports, 62
Authentication, 226
AutoComplete, 446, 461
AutoFill, 446
AutoFilter, 339
Automatic Updating, 33
    Benefits and drawbacks, 35
    Windows 10, 34
Axes, 336
Axis titles, 336

B

Backbone, 412
    Tier 1 providers, 412
Backstage, 265, 372
Backstage view, 265
Backup, 226
    File History, 227
    Mobile data, 233
    PC system files and settings, 231
    Personal files, 226
    Refresh and Reset, 234
    Repair disc, 232
    Restoring personal files, 229
    Secure, 230

System image, 232
System restore points, 231
Using factor reset options, 234
Windows Backup and Restore, 228
Bandwidth, 40
Basic Cell Phone, 95
BlackBerry 10, 28
Blockers, 443, 478
Blogs, 548
Bluetooth, 66
Bookmarks, 437
    Deleting, 441
    Managing, 440
    Synchronizing, 442
Boolean Operators, 463
Borders, 330
Breadcrumbs, 453
Broadband, 74
    Cable, 75
    DSL, 75
    Fiber optic, 75
    Modems, 78
    Routers, 78
    Satellite Internet, 75
    Speeds, 76
    Testing the connection speed, 77
Broadband Cable, 75
Browser Features, 433
    Add-ons, 450
    Plug-ins, 450
Browser Functions, 433
Browser History
    Deleting, 448
Browser History, 447
Browser Navigation Tools, 429
Browser Preferences, 443
Browser Settings, 430
Browser Tabs, 424
Browsers, 422
    Address bar, 422
    Apple Safari, 427
    Apps, 450
    AutoComplete, 446
    AutoFill, 446
    Bookmarks, 437
    Cache, 446
    Downloading, 433
    Extending functionality, 450
    Features, 433
    Functions, 433
    Google Chrome, 426
    History folder, 447
    Hyperlinks, 425
    Microsoft Edge, 426
    Microsoft Internet Explorer, 426
    Mozilla Firefox, 426
    Opera, 427
    Page rendering, 427
    Popular, 425

Private browsing, 449
Scroll bars, 423
Setting a home page, 431
Streaming, 435
Uploading, 433
Using a mouse, 454
Windows Control Buttons, 424
Bullying, 562
Bundling, 477
Business Applications, 513
Byte, 39

C

C2R Installer, 150
Cache, 446
Caches, 218
Calendar, 536
Appointments, 537
Recurring appointment, 538
Calendars
Adding, 540
Multiple, 539
Subscribing, 541
Cascading Styles Sheets, 420
CD, 43
Cell, 313
Cell Address, 313
Cell Addresses
Absolute, 326
Relative, 326
Cell Services, 92
Contracts, 92
Obtaining, 92
Cells, 90
Deleting, 323
Inserting, 323
Network hub, 90
Cellular Carriers, 91
Types, 91
Cellular Devices, 94
Basic cell phone, 95
Cellular-enabled tablets, 95
Enabling Wi-Fi, 96
Mobile data, 96
Smart Phones, 95
Turning off data, 97
Cellular Generations, 91
Cellular Networks, 90
Carriers, 91
Generations, 91
Cellular Service
Different from Internet Service, 92
Cellular Services
Plan add-ons, 94
Plans, 94
Pre-paid, 93
Cellular-Enabled Tablets, 95
Censorship, 478
Central Processing Unit, 39
Certificate Authority, 225
Changing the view, 377

Character Formatting, 285, 387
Chart
Types, 334
Chart Layout, 336
Chart titles, 336
Chart Tools Ribbon, 334
Chart Types, 334
Charts, 333
Axes, 336
Axis titles, 336
Chart layouts, 336
Data labels, 336
Data table, 336
Error Bars, 336
Gridlines, 336
Legend, 336
Titles, 336
Chat, 167
Gmail, 167
Chromebooks, 49
Click-to-Run, 150
Client Systems, 179
Close
Documents, 273
Workbooks, 318
Close Button, 424
Cloud Accounts, 181
Managing, 182
Cloud Computing, 179
Accounts, 181
Applications, 206
Benefits, 180
Hosted service, 179
Cloud Storage
Dropbox, 204
iCloud, 202
Microsoft OneDrive, 192
Sharing, 189
Cloud-Based Applications, 206
Customer relationship management
software, 207
Learning management system, 206
Co-authoring Documents, 510
Code, 1
Collaboration Tools, 508
Office 365, 508
Colors, 331
Column Headings, 312
Column Width, 305
Column Widths, 322
Columns, 292
Breaking, 292
Deleting, 323
Inserting, 323
Common OS Features
Account Options, 6
Account Types, 5
Built-in power off procedures, 7
User accounts, 5
User profiles, 6
Communication Apps, 252

Communications
Friend requests, 550
Friends, 550
Compiling, 1
Compressing, 139
Computer Types, 44
2-in-1s, 50
Chromebooks, 49
Desktop, 45
Laptops, 47
Notebooks, 47
Servers, 44
Smart phones, 50
Tablets, 49
Computers and Your Health, 563
Audience consideration, 564
Coping with change, 563
Disengaging, 564
Computing Device
Inside components, 40
Conference Calling, 489
Conference Calls, 501
Conferencing
Calls, 501
Online, 500
VoIP, 500
Configuring, 156
Customizing toolbars, 156
Connectedness, 181
Connecting "Smart" Devices, 105
Connecting to the Internet
Private address, 79
Connection Speed, 434
Connections
Keyboards, 52
Troubleshooting, 237
Connectors, 59
Audio, 62
Infrared, 67
Network, 62
USB, 63
Video, 59
Contacts, 522, 533
Content Apps, 253
Content Management, 509
Contract Services, 92
Control Panel, 18
Categories, 19
Desktop display, 23
Password protection, 22
Power management, 22
Power plan settings, 56
Profile-specific settings, 23
Screen resolution, 21
Conversation, 525
Cookie, 216
cookies, 444
Cookies
Controlling, 445
Copyright, 475
Fair Use, 475

Licensing, 476
Sources of information, 476
Web sites, 475
Copyright Infringement, 388, 476
Copyrights, 474
Cortana, 12, 128
CPU. *See* Central Processing Unit
Cropping, 302
CSS, 420
Customer Relationship Management, 207
Customizing Toolbars, 156
Cut, Copy or Paste, 321
Cyber Bullying
What not to do, 563
What to do, 563
Cyberbullying, 562

D

Data, 353
Data Cap, 77
Data Labels, 336
Data Payload, 412
Data Table, 336
database, 353
Database
Attribute, 356
Column, 356
Composite primary keys, 358
Driven web pages, 366
Dynamic web pages, 366
Dynaset, 364
Field, 356
Foreign keys, 360
Forms, 364
Forms on the web, 368
Metadata, 362
Primary key, 357
Queries, 363
Queries on the web, 367
Record, 356
Relationship types, 361
Static pages, 366
Table metadata, 356
Table relationships, 360
Tables, 356
Web sites, 366
Where used, 366
Database Tables, 356
Databases
APIs, 354
Connectivity standards, 354
Data, 353
Multiple, related tables, 354
Relational database management systems, 354
Spreadsheet, 353
Structured Query Language, 354
Default Locations, 132
Defaults, 157
Delayed Communications, 484

Asynchronous, 484
Text messaging, 484
Deleting Apps, 164, 258
Desktop, 3
Cortana, 12
Customizing, 25
Navigating, 10
Search box, 12
Virtual, 14
Desktop apps, 12
Desktop Computers, 45
Common configurations, 46
Disadvantages, 46
Mac, 45
PC, 45
Used by, 46
Desktop Display, 23
Desktop Publishing, 243
Desktops
Virtual, 13
Device Drivers, 37
Dialog box launcher, 267
Dialog Boxes, 20
Digital Cameras, 66
Digital Certificate, 225
Digital Communication, 483
Digital Communications
Asynchronous, 484
Delayed, 484
Distance learning, 512
Real-time, 484
Streaming, 512
Synchronous, 484
Digital Footprints, 559
Digital Identify
Aliases, 561
Creating a positive online identify, 560
Important to remember, 560
Managing, 561
Online behavior, 562
Posting items, 559
Digital Identity, 559
Footprints, 559
Personal vs professional, 561
Digital Rights Management, 134
Digital Subscriber Line. *See* DSL
Directory, 105
File and folders, 112
Root, 105
Directory Structure, 103
Connected storage devices, 104
Drive letters, 103
Internal storage devices, 104
Mapped network locations, 104
Discussion Boards, 548
Disengaging, 564
Distance Learning, 512
DNS
Domain levels, 417
Second-level domains, 418

Top-level domains, 417
DNS Records, 416
DNS Servers, 416
Docking Station, 48
Domain Category, 518
Domain Levels, 417
Domain Name System, 416
DNS records, 416
Domain Name Systems
DNS servers, 416
Domain Names, 416
Downloading, 71, 76, 186, 433
Downloads Folder, 132
Downstream, 76
Draft, 281
Drag and Drop, 283
Drive Letters, 103
DRM. *See* Digital Rights Management
Dropbox, 204
DSL, 75
DVD, 43
Dynaset, 364

E

E-Commerce, 224
Be selective, 224
Exercise skepticism, 224
https, 224
Safe transactions, 224
Secured transactions, 224
Edit Mode, 385
Effects, 285, 387
Ehternet
Cables, 81
Electronic Mail, 484
Electronic Media, 134
Elevation Prompts, 151
Email, 484, 517
Address book, 522
Address structure, 518
Archiving, 533
Attachments, 528
Contacts, 522
Desktop application, 517
Domain category, 518
Gmail, 518
Junk, 532
Mailbox Name, 518
Organization Name, 518
Proofing, 522
Sending messages, 522
Signatures, 527
Spam, 531
Using, 518
Email Address, 518
Email Attachments, 137
Limitations, 138
Enabling Wi-Fi, 96
Encryption, 226
End User License Agreement, 3, 152, 478
Entering Data, 313

Dates, 314
Numbers, 314
Text, 313
Ergonomics, 565
Eyestrain, 565
Repetitive stress injuries, 565
Error Bars, 336
Ethernet, 62, 72, 78, 80
Network interface card, 81
Standards, 81
When to use, 82
Ethical Issues
Censhorship, 478
Copyright, 475
Fair use, 475
Intellectual Property, 474
Piracy, 478
Plagiarism, 479
Etiquette, 486
EULA. *See* End User License Agreement,
See End User License Agreement
Evaluating Information
Accuracy, 472
Advertising, 473
Affiliations, 472
Articles, 472
Bias, 472
Currentness, 472
Depth of coverage, 472
Forums, 473
Rankings, 473
Source references, 472
Sponsored links, 473
Tone, 473
Evaluating Information, 469
Excel
Absolute or Relative addresses, 326
Active cell, 312, 313
AutoFilter, 339
Basic terminology, 312
Cell, 313
Cell address, 313
Changing data, 320
Chart tools ribbon, 334
Chart types, 334
Charts, 333
Closing workbooks, 318
Column headings, 312
Column widths, 322
Common functions, 325
Creating a new blank workbook, 314
Creating a workbook from a
template, 315
Cut, copy or paste, 321
Deleting rows, columns or cells, 323
Entering data, 313
Filtering data, 339
Formatting, 329
Formula Bar, 312
Formulas, 313, 325
Insert Function, 312

Inserting rows, columns or cells, 323
Labels, 313
Moving around, 314
Name Box, 312
Office Clipboard, 322
Opening workbooks, 317
Previewing or printing workbooks,
348
Range of cells, 320
Row headings, 312
Row height, 323
Saving workbooks, 316
Scroll bars, 312
Sheet tab, 312
Tab scrolling, 312
Undo or Redo, 321
Values, 313
Workbook, 312
Worksheet, 313
External Drives, 43
Eyestrain, 565

F

Facebook, 551
Factory Reset Options, 234
Fair Use, 475
Favorites. *See* Bookmarks
Favorites center, 438
Favorites Center, 438
Fiber Optic, 75
Fiber Optic Service, 75
File
Permissions, 106
File Explorer, 107
Searching, 128
File History, 227
File Name Extensions, 119
File Size, 434
File Tab, 265
File Transfer Protocol, 419
File Types, 119
PowerPoint, 376
Files
Archived/compressed, 122
Audio, 119
Closing, 273
Compressing, 139
Copying, 125
Deleting, 130
Document, 120
Executable, 121
Extensions, 119
Graphics, 120
Identifying, 112
Moving, 126
Renaming, 127
Restoring, 130
Saving in Word, 269
Searching, 128
Selecting, 123
Types, 119

Video, 120
Windows 10, 122
Files Name Extensions
Viewing, 123
Windows 10, 122
Filtering, 339
AutoFilter, 339
Filters, 478
Finding
Computers on the Internet, 415
Finding Items, 295
FiOS, 75
Firewalls, 222
Challenges, 223
Desktop, 223
Firmware, 38
Flash Drives, 43
Flash Memory, 43
Folder
Permissions, 106
Folders, 103, 105
Changing the view, 116
Copying, 125
Creating, 112
Deleting, 130
Downloads, 132
Identifying, 112
Moving, 126
Options, 116
Pictures, 132, 133
Public, 135
Renaming, 113
Restoring, 130
Selecting, 123
Shared, 136
Shortcuts, 113
Subfolders, 105
Font, 285, 387
Font Size, 285, 387
Fonts, 330
Foreign Keys, 360
Formatting, 285, 329, 387
Aligning, 286
Aligning text, 387
Borders, 330
Cell Alignment, 330
Characters, 285, 387
Colors, 331
Decimal Digits, 330
Effects, 285, 387
Excel, 329
Font, 285, 387
Font Size, 285, 387
Fonts, 330
Keyboard shortcuts, 286
Numbers, 330
Patterns, 331
Sizes, 330
Tables, 304
Text, 387
Text characters, 285

7500-1 v1.00 © CCI Learning Solutions Inc.

Forms, 364, 368
Formula Bar, 312
Formulas, 325
    Creating, 325
    Mathematical operators, 325
Forum, 473
Forums, 548
Freeware, 477
Friend Requests, 550
FTP, 419
Functions, 325
    =AVERAGE, 325
    =COUNT, 325
    =MAX, 325
    =SUM, 325

G

Gateways, 78
Global Settings, 17, 21
Gmail, 518
    Address books, 534
    Calendar, 536
    Contacts, 533
Gmail Chat, 167
Gmail Screen, 518
Google Chrome, 426
Google Drive, 248
    Apps, 187
    Cloud storage, 183
    Content, 184, 193
    Mobile apps, 192
Google Hangouts, 499
Google Hangouts on Air, 513
Graphic Design, 244
Graphical User Interface, 2
Gridlines, 336
GUI. See Graphical User Interface

H

Hackers, 213
Handheld Device, 88
Handles, 300
Handouts, 402
Hard Disks, 42
Hardware, 1, 37, 412
    Device drivers, 37
    Firmware, 38
    Network infrastructure, 70
    Packets, 412
    Platform, 38
    Smart phone, 54
    Troubleshooting, 236
hashtag, 465
HDMI. See High-Definition Multimedia
    Interface
High-Definition Multimedia Interface, 59
Home Page, 429
    Setting, 431
    Site, 451
Home Screen, 30

App folder, 31
App screen, 31
App-shortcuts, 31
Dock, 31
Home screen indicator, 31
Notification icons, 31
Status bar, 31
Status icons, 31
Widget, 31
Host, 83
Hosted Service, 179
How much do I need?
    RAM, 41
    Storage, 42
HTML, 420, See hypertext markup
    language
    Hyperlinks, 421
    Tags, 420
HTTP. See Hypertext Transfer Protocol
    HTTP Secure (HTTPS), 419
https. See Hypertext Transfer Protocol
    Secure
Hyperlinks, 421
    Pointing hand, 425
HyperText Markup Language, 419
HyperText Transfer Protocol, 418
Hypertext Transfer Protocol Secure, 224

I

iCloud, 202
Illustrations
    Handles, 300
IM. See Instant Messaging
Image Editing, 244
In-Apps Purchases, 258
Index Page, 451
Infrastructure, 69, 86
Input Devices, 51
    Keyboards, 51
Insert Function, 312
Inserting
    Cells, 323
    Columns, 323
    Rows, 323
    Tables in Word, 303
Inserting Cells, 304
Inserting Columns, 304
Inserting Rows, 304
Instagram, 551
Installing, 150
Instant Messaging, 170
    Skype, 170
Intellectual Property, 474
Interface, 2
internet
    Routers, 413
Internet
    Backbone, 412
    Finding computers, 415
    Hardware, 412
    Home page, 451

HyperText Markup Language, 419
    Researching, 469
    Search engines, 460
    Searching, 459
    URL, 418
    Using a mouse, 454
    Web pages, 419
    Web standards, 451
    World Wide Web, 419
Internet Addiction, 564
Internet Connections, 70
    LAN, 78
Internet Protocol, 72
    Versions, 72
Internet Service, 74
    Choosing, 75
    Choosing a provider, 77
    Different from cellular service, 92
    Providers, 74
    Testing the connection speed, 77
    Upload or download speeds, 76
Internet Service Provider, 412, See ISP
Internetwork, 69
Intranet, 414
iOS, 28
IP. See Intellectual Property
IP Address, 415
IP Addresses, 72
    Connecting or finding, 72
    Important points, 80
    Public or Private, 79
    Unique, 79
IP Addressing
    DNS servers, 416
ISP, 74

J

Junk Mail, 532

K

Keyboard, 10
Keyboard / Dial Pad, 55
Keyboards, 51
    Connections, 52
    Virtual, 49, 51
Keywords, 461

L

Labels, 526
LAN, 71, 78
    Add shared printer, 83
    Wireless, 86
Landlines
    Advantages and Disadvantages, 98
Laptop Computers, 47
    Common configurations, 48
    Disadvantages, 47
Learning Management System, 206
Learning Management Systems, 512
Legend, 336

License
    Open source, 3
    Proprietary software, 2
Licenses, 476
Licensing, 476
    ASP, 477
    EULA, 478
    SAAS, 477
    Single seat, 477
    Site, 477
    Volume or Network, 477
Limitations of Apps, 260
Line Spacing, 286
LinkedIn, 551, 553
    Connections, 553
    Creating an account, 554
    Creating your profile, 554
    Inviting connections, 558
LinkedIn Profile, 554
Linux, 4
Livestream, 513
LMS. *See* Learning Management
    Systems, *See* Learning Management
    System
Local Apps, 250
Local Area Networks. *See* LAN
Local Location, 107
Lock Screen, 29
Locking, 215
Long Term Evolution. *See* LTE
Looking at the Screen
    View buttons, 266
LTE, 91

M

Mac OS, 4
Mailbox Full, 100
Mailbox Name, 518
Malware, 216
Mapping, 104
Margins, 289
    Boundaries, 290
    Setting, 290
Mathematical Operators, 325
Maximize Button, 424
Measuring
    Bandwidth, 40
    Capacity, 39
    Frequency, 39
Media, 390
Memory, 41
    Random Access Memory, 41
Merging Cells, 305
Message Headers, 525
Messages
    Address book, 522
    Archiving, 533
    Attachments, 528
    Conversation, 525
    Creating, 520
    Deleting, 533

Filtering, 531
Forward, 525
Headers, 525
Junk mail, 532
Labels, 526
Moving, 527
Proofing, 522
Reply, 524
Reply to all, 525
Sending, 520, 522
Signatures, 527
Spam, 531
Stop junk text, 532
Messaging
    Instant, 170
    Text, 166
Messaging Applications, 165
Metadata, 356, 362
Microphones, 62
Microprocessor, 39
Microsoft Account, 160
Microsoft Edge, 426
Microsoft Internet Explorer, 426
Microsoft Office
    Backstage, 265
Microsoft OneDrive, 192
Mini toolbar, 286
Mini Toolbar, 387
Minimize Button, 424
MMS. *See* Multimedia Message Service
Mobile
    Home screen, 30
    Lock screen, 29
    Power on / off, 29
    Resetting devices, 234
    Settings app, 32
    Virtual personal assistants, 32
Mobile Apps
    Google Drive, 192
    OneDrive, 202
Mobile Data, 96
    Backup, 233
    Enabling Wi-Fi, 96
    Turning off, 97
Mobile Notifications, 208
Mobile Operating Systems, 28
    Android, 28
    Blackberry, 28
    iOS, 28
    Touch screen, 28
    Windows Mobile, 28
Mobile Settings App, 32
Modems, 78
Monitoring, 223
Monitors, 60
    Second display device, 60
More Button, 267
Moving, 301
Moving Around
    Worksheets, 314
Mozilla Firefox, 426

Multimedia Messaging Service, 166
Multiple Calendars, 539
Multiple Displays, 61
Multiple, Related Tables, 354

N

Name Box, 312
Narrowing the Search
    AND, 463
    Boolean Operators, 463
    Hashtags, 464
    HTML Objects, 464
    NEAR, 463
    NOT, 463
    OR, 463
NAT. *See* Network Address Translation
Navigating
    Keyboard, 10
    Pointing device, 10
    Touch screen, 11
Navigation Bar, 453
    Breadcrumbs, 453
Netiquette, 486
Network
    Connecting to a network printer, 90
Network Address Translation, 80
Network Connection, 414
Network Connections, 217
    Mitigating risks, 217
    Wired, 217
    Wireless, 217
Network Coverage, 92
Network Hub, 90
Network Interface Card, 81
Network Printer, 89
    Connecting to, 90
Networks, 69
    Benefits, 70
    Cellular, 90
    Connections, 217
    Coverage, 92
    Ethernet, 80
    Infrastructure, 69
    Internetwork, 69
    IP addresses, 72
    LAN, 71
    NIC, 81
    Packets, 71
    Shared Printer, 83
    Sharing the Internet connection, 70
    Social Media, 549
    TCP/IP, 71
    Technology, 71
    WAN, 72
    Wireless LAN, 87
New
    Appointments, 537
    Documents, 272
    Messages, 520
    Presentations, 373
    Workbook from templates, 315

Workbooks, 314
New desktop, 14
NIC. *See* Network Interface Card
Non-SMS Messaging Apps, 167
Notebooks, 47
Notes Pane, 373
Notifications
    Configuring, 208
    Mobile, 208

O

Objects, 388
    Animating, 392
    Media, 390
    Online pictures, 388
    Pictures, 388
Obtaining Apps, 163, 256
OCR. *See* Optical Character Recognition
Office 365, 508
Office Clipboard, 283, 322
Office Online, 509
Office Suite, 509
OneDrive
    Mobile apps, 202
OneDrive for Business, 509
Online Behavior, 562
Online Conferencing, 500
Online Meeting, 489
Online Meetings, 511
Open
    Workbooks, 317
Open Source, 478
Opening
    Word documents, 273
Open-Source Software, 3
Opera, 427
Operating System, 1
    Automatic updating, 33
    Common features, 5
    Desktop, 3
    Linux, 4
    Mac OS, 4
    UNIX, 5
    Update categories, 33
    Updates, 33
    Versions or editions, 3
    Windows, 4
Operating Systems
    Desktop, 3
    Evolution, 2
    Mobile, 28
    Open Source, 2
    Proprietary, 2
    Purpose, 2
Optical Character Recognition, 132
Optical Discs and Drives, 43
    CDs, 43
    DVDs, 43
Orientation, 289
    Landscape, 289
    Portrait, 289

OS. *See* Operating System
Outline, 281
Outlook Web App (OWA), 508
Output Devices
    Peripherals, 59

P

Packets, 71, 412
    Data payload, 412
Page Numbers, 291
Page Rendering, 427
Page Setup, 289
    Margins, 289
    Orientation, 289
    Paper size, 289
Paper Size, 289
Paragraph Spacing, 287
Password Protection, 22
Passwords, 213
    Changing, 214
Paths, 105
Patterns, 331
Paying for Apps, 257
PBX, 98
Peripherals, 59
    Digital Cameras, 66
    Microphones, 62
    Monitors, 60
    Network, 62
    Ports, 59
    Printers, 64
    Speakers, 63
    USB, 63
    USB Flash Drives, 64
Permissions, 6, 106
    Local location, 107
    Network access, 106
    Remote location, 107
    Shared files or folders, 136
Personal Identity, 561
Phishing, 219
Phone Calls, 487
    Conference calling, 489
    Technologies, 488
    VoIP, 488
    WebEx, 489
Pictures, 298, 388
    Cropping, 302
    Manipulate, 389
    Manipulating, 300
    Moving, 301
    Sizing, 301
    Smart Phones, 133
    Wrapping Text, 301
Pictures Folder, 132, 133
Piracy, 478
Placeholder, 372
Placeholders, 373
    Edit mode, 385
    Select mode, 386
Plagiarism, 479

Platform, 38
Platforms, 148
Plug-ins, 450
Pointing Device, 10
Pointing Devices, 52
    Mouse, 52
    Stylus, 53
    Touch screens, 53
    Touchpad, 53
Pointing Hand, 425
Pop-up Blocker, 443
Pop-ups, 443
Ports, 59
    Audio, 59, 62
    Network, 59, 62
    USB, 59
    Video, 59
Power Management, 22
Power Off Procedures, 7
    Powering off a Windows computer, 7
    Starting a Windows computer, 7
Power On / Off, 29
Power Options, 8
    Hibernate, 8
    Restart, 8
    Shut down, 8
    Sleep, 8
Power Plan
    Settings, 56
Power Plans, 56
Powering Off a Windows Computer, 7
PowerPoint, 371
    Align text, 387
    Animation, 392
    Basic terminology, 373
    Closing a presentation, 376
    Customizing animation, 393
    Delete a slide, 382
    Edit screen, 372
    Entering Text, 375
    File formats, 376
    Format text, 387
    Handouts, 402
    Insert media, 390
    Insert online pictures, 388
    Insert pictures, 388
    Insert slides, 381
    Manipulate pictures, 389
    New presentations, 373
    Notes pane, 373
    Open a presentation, 377
    Placeholder, 372
    Placeholders, 373
    Planning your presentation, 374
    Presentation structure, 371
    Presenter view, 399
    Protected View, 377
    Publishing presentations, 402
    Rearrange slides, 383
    Saving a presentation, 375
    Select vs Edit mode, 385

Setting the slide show up, 397
Slide layouts, 382
Slide pane, 373
Slide thumbnails, 375
Slide transitions, 394
Slides tab, 372
Spell Checking, 387
Split bar, 373
Text objects, 386
Pre-Paid Services, 93
Presentation Structure, 371
Presentations, 246
Previewing, 348
Primary Key, 357
Selecting, 358
Primary Keys
Composite, 358
Print Layout, 281
Printing, 348
Documents, 296
Print options, 348
Private Branch Exchange. *See* PBX
Private Browsing, 449
Private IP Address, 79
Private Networks, 413
Productivity Apps, 252
Productivity Progra XE
"Applications:Productivity progarms"
ms, 242
Profile, 6
Profile Settings, 17
Profile-Specific Settings, 23
Programs, 1
Application, 2
Apps, 12
Code, 1
Compiling, 1
Operating system, 1
Proofing, 522
Proprietary Software, 2
Protected View, 274, 377
Protecting Yourself, 220
Antivirus software, 220
Authentication, 226
Avoiding viruses, 221
Encryption, 226
Firewalls, 222
Removing viruses, 222
Protocol
https, 224
Protocol Identifier, 418
Protocols, 71
Identifier, 418
Providers
Cellular, 90
Public Computers, 217
Public IP Address, 79
Viewing, 80
Publishing Presentations, 402

Q

Queries, 363, 367
Criteria, 364
On the web, 367
Quick Access Toolbar, 265, 266

R

RAM. *See* Random Access Memory
Random Access Memory, 41
How much do I need?, 41
Range, 320
RDBMS. *See* Relational Database
Management Systems
Read Mode, 281
Read-only, 274
Real-Time Communication
Technologies, 486
Real-time Communications, 484
Classes, 512
Phone calls, 487
Synchronous, 484
Recovering Apps, 164, 259
Recurring Appointments, 538
Recycle Bin, 130
Recyle Bin
Emptying, 131
Redo, 321
Refresh and Reset, 234
Registration, 152
Reinstalling, 155
Relationship Types, 361
Relative Addresses, 326
Remote Location, 107
Removable Media, 135
Repair Disc, 232
Repairing Software, 154
Repeat, 282
Repetitive Stress Injuries, 565
Replacing Items, 295
Researching, 469
Resetting Mobile Devices, 234
Restore, 226, 229
Restore Down Button, 424
Ribbon, 265, 266
Chart Tools, 334
Displaying dialog boxes or task
panes, 267
Gallery lists, 267
Groups, 267
More button, 267
Table Tools, 303
Tabs, 267
Risks, 215
Adware, 216
Cookies, 216
Malware, 216
Network connections, 217
Public computers, 217
Social engineering, 218
Spyware, 216

Viruses, 215
Worms, 215
Root Directory, 105
Routers, 78, 413
Row Headings, 312
Row Height, 305, 323
Rows
Deleting, 323
Inserting, 323

S

Satellite Internet, 75
Save
Workbooks, 316
Saving
Documents, 269
Presentations, 375
Scanners, 132
Schemas, 362
Database, 362
Screen Elements
Accessing commands and features,
266
File tab, 265
Quick Access toolbar, 265
Ribbon, 265
Ribbon, 266
ScreenTips, 266
Status Bar, 266
Title Bar, 265
Zoom Slider, 266
Screen Resolution, 21
Screen Sharing, 502
ScreenTips, 266
Scroll Bars, 312, 423
SD Cards. *See* Secure Digital Cards
Search Box, 12
Search Engine Technology, 460
Search Engines, 460
Boolean Operators, 463
HTML Objects, 464
Keywords, 461
Technology, 460
Searching, 128, 459
AAOCC, 470
AutoComplete, 461
Boolean Operators, 463
Cortana, 128
File Explorer, 128
HTML Objects, 464
Purpose or type, 459
Researching information, 469
Social media, 464
Traditional sources, 460
Windows search box, 128
Searching in a Browser, 435
Second Display Device, 60
Secure Digital Cards, 43
Secured Transactions, 224
Security, 213
Keeping your account safe, 214

Locking the system, 215
Passwords, 213
Risks, 215
Virtual private networks, 225
Select Mode, 385, 386
Selecting, 269, 320
Cells, 320
Consecutive text, 269
Server Systems, 179
Servers, 44
Common configurations, 45
Used by, 45
Service Providers, 74
Settings
Control Panel, 18
Global, 17
Profile, 17
Settings App, 17
Shared Printer, 83
Connecting to, 85
Disconnecting, 85
SharePoint, 508, 509
Co-authoring documents, 510
Content management, 509
Shareware, 477
Sharing
Cloud files, 189
Electronic media, 134
On a network, 137
Pictures, 134
Via email, 137
Sharing Files, 135
Pictures, 133
Sharing Information, 547
Blogs, 548
Forums, 548
Tracking changes, 307
Wikis, 549
Sheet Tab, 312
Short Message Service, 166
Sidebar
Action Center, 14
Signatures, 527
SIM. See Subscriber Identity Module
Single Seat License, 477
Site Home Page, 451
Site License, 477
Sizes, 330
Sizing, 301
Skype, 170, 490
Adding contacts, 173
Group conversations, 495
Instant messaging, 174
Mood messages, 493
Profile, 492
Screen sharing, 502
Status, 491
VoIP calls, 501
Skype for Business, 509, 510
Recording online meetings, 511
Scheduling online meetings, 511

Taking control, 511
Skype for VoIP Calls, 501
Slack, 552
Slide Layout, 382
Slide Pane, 373
Slide Show
Running, 398
Setting up, 397
Viewing, 398
Slide Sorter, 383
Slide Thumbnails, 375
Slide Transitions, 394
Slides
Animating objects, 392
Deleting, 382
Inserting new, 381
Rearranging, 383
Transitions, 394
Slides Tab, 372
Smart Phone Hardware, 54
SIM card, 55
Smart Phones, 50, 95
Keyboard / Dial pad, 55
Pictures, 133
Touch screen capability, 50
SMS. See Short Message Service
SMS Text Messages, 484
Snapchat, 551
Social Engineering, 218
Reducing risks, 218
Social Media, 464, 549
Friends and friend requests, 550
Hashtag, 465
Hashtags, 464
Networks, 549
Why join, 551
Social Media Apps, 254
Social Media Network
Building the network, 550
Social Media Networks, 549
Popular, 551
Social Media Neworks
Advantages of closed network, 552
Open vs closed, 551
Software, 1, 147
Application Service Provider, 477
Bundling, 477
Cloud based, 147
Configuring, 156
EULA. See End User License
Agreement
Freeware, 477
Installing, 150
Licenses, 476
Locally installed, 147
Managing, 149
Monitoring, 223
Obtaining, 148
Open Source, 478
Open-Source, 3
Platform considerations, 148

Program defaults, 157
Programs, 1
Proprietary, 2
Registration. See End User License
Agreement
Repairing, 154, 155
Shareware, 477
Software as a Service, 477
System Requirements, 148
Troubleshooting, 236
Uninstalling, 153
Updating, 156
Windows Registry, 154
Software as a Service, 247, 477
Software Threats
Cookies, 444
Spam, 531
Spammers, 531
Speakers, 63
Speed and Storage
Capacity, 38
Measuring bandwidth, 40
Measuring capacity, 39
Measuring frequency, 39
Spelling, 293, 387
Split Bar, 373
Splitting Cells, 305
Sponsored Links, 473
Spreadsheets, 244
Spyware, 216
SQL. See Structured Query Language
Standard Pages, 454
Start Button, 11
Start Menu, 11
Start Page, 429
Starting a Windows Computer, 7
Status Bar, 266
Storage, 41, 42
Commonly-used devices, 42
External disks, 43
External location, 42
Flash drives, 43
Hard disks, 42
How much do I need?, 42
Internal location, 42
Optical disks or drives, 43
SD cards, 43
Tablets or Phones, 43
Streaming, 71, 435, 512
Structured Query Language, 354
Stylus, 53
Subfolders, 105
Subscriber Identity Module, 55
Subscribing to a Calendar, 541
Synchronous, 483
System Image, 232
System Requirements, 148
System Restore Points, 231

T

Tab Scrolling, 312

Tab Selector Box, 288
Table Relationships, 360
Table Selector, 303
Table Tools, 303
Tables, 303, 343
   Adjusting the width or height, 305
   Foreign keys, 360
   Formatting, 343
   Inserting, 303
   Inserting rows, columns or cells, 304
   Merging or splitting cells, 305
   Metadata, 356
   Modifying data, 343
   Relationship types, 361
   Relationships, 360
Tablets, 49
   Operating system, 49
   Touch screen capability, 49
Tags, 420
Taking Control, 511
Task View, 13
Taskbar, 13
   Action Center, 14
   Buttons, 14
   New desktop, 14
   Task view, 13
TCP/IP, 71
Telephone Network
   Business telephones, 98
   PBX, 98
Template, 315
Templates, 374
Text Messaging, 166, 485
   Etiquette, 486
   When is appropriate?, 485
Text Objects, 386
Tier 1 Providers, 412
Title Bar, 265
Toolbars
   Mini, 286
   Quick Access, 265
Total Row, 343
Touch Screen, 11, 53
   Limitations, 54
   Smart phones, 50
   Tablets, 49
Touch Screen Navigation, 28
Touchpad, 53
Trackbacks, 548
Tracking Changes, 307
Transitions
   Timing, 395
Transmission Control Protocol/Internet
   Protocol. See TCP/IP
Troubleshooting, 235
   Connection issues, 237
   Hardware, 236
   Software, 236
Twitter, 551

U

UAC. See User Account Control
Undo, 282, 321
Uniform Resource Locator, 418
Uninstalling, 153
Universal Serial Bus, 63
UNIX, 5
Update Categories, 33
Updates, 33
   Categories, 33
   Manually checking, 34
   Mobile operating system, 35
Updating, 156
Uploading, 76, 433
Upstream, 76
URL, 72, 418, See Uniform Resource
   Locator
USB. See Universal Serial Bus
USB Flash Drives, 64
USB Ports, 63
User Account Control, 151
   Elevation prompts, 151
User Accounts, 5
User Names, 213
User Profiles, 6

V

Validating Resources, 471
Video Apps, 255
Video Conferences, 489
Video Editing, 246
Video Ports, 59
View Buttons, 266
Views
   PowerPoint, 377
   Presenter view, 399
   Read Mode, 281
   Slide Show, 398
   Word, 281
Vine, 551
Virtual, 14
Virtual Personal Assistants, 32
Virtual Private Network, 414
Virtual Private Networks, 225
Viruses, 215
   Avoiding, 221
   Removing, 222
   Worms, 215
Vitual
   Keyboards, 51
Voice Mail, 99
   Configuring, 99
   Leaving a clear message, 100
   Mobile phone, 100
   Retrieving messages, 99
   Retrieving messages from mobile
      phone, 100
VoIP, 488
   Conferencing, 500
   Disadvantages, 488

   Using VoIP, 501
Volume or Network License, 477
VPN. See Virtual Private Networks

W

WAN, 72
Web Apps, 247
   Google, 248
Web Browser
   Searching, 459
   Settings, 430
   Tabs, 424
Web Browsers, 422
   Address bar, 422
   Boolean Operators, 463
   HTML Objects, 464
   HyperText Markup Language, 419
   Page rendering, 427
   Popular, 425
   Search engines, 460
Web Development, 245
Web Layout, 281
Web Pages, 419
   CSS, 420
   Database driven, 366
   Dynamic, 366
   HTML, 419, 420
   Hyperlinks, 421
   Static, 366
   Using a mouse, 454
Web Site, 419
Web Sites
   Blogs, 459
   Business, 459
   Copyright, 475
   Education, 460
   Evaluating information, 469
   Government, 459
   Index page, 451
   Media, 460
   News feed, 460
   Podcasts, 460
   Reference links, 460
   Social networking, 459
   Types, 459
   Validating information, 471
   Wiki, 460
Web Standards, 451
   Navigation bar, 453
   Standard pages, 454
   Widgets, 453
WebEx, 489
Wide Area Networks. See WAN
Widgets, 453
Wi-Fi, 72
   Handheld device, 88
   Infrastructure, 86
WI-FI
   Ad-hoc, 85
Wi-Fi Protected Setup. See WPS
Wikis, 549

7500-1 v1.00 © CCI Learning Solutions Inc.

Window
- Moving, 110
- Scroll bars, 111
- Sizing, 110

Windows, 4
Windows 10 Mobile, 28
Windows Apps, 159
Windows Backup and Restore, 228
Windows Desktop, 9
Windows Registry, 154
Windows Store, 159
- Finding an app, 162
- Microsoft Account, 160
- Siging in, 160
- Signing out, 165

Windows Updates, 33
- Manually checking, 34

Wire Connections
- Advantages, 82
- Disadvantages, 82

Wired Connection
- Shared Printer, 83
- When to use, 82

Wired Connections
- Ethernet, 80

Wireless, 66
- Bluetooth, 66
- Compatibility, 67
- LAN, 86
- Modems, 78
- Routers, 79

Wireless Connections, 85
- When to use, 87

Wireless Fidelity. *See* Wi-Fi
WLAN
- Connect on Mac, 88
- Connecting, 87
- Handheld device, 88
- Network printer, 89

Word
- Align text, 286
- Column break, 292
- Columns, 292
- Contextual errors, 294
- Create from a template, 273
- Creating a new blank document, 272
- Cropping pictures, 302
- Customizing views, 281
- Cut, copy or paste, 282
- Drag and drop, 283
- Find and replace, 295
- Formatting text, 285
- Grammatical errors, 295
- Line spacing, 286
- Manipulating pictures, 300
- Margins, 289
- Office Clipboard, 283
- Opening documents, 273
- Orientation, 289
- Page numbers, 291
- Page setup, 289
- Paragraph spacing, 287
- Pictures, 298
- Preview and print, 296
- Print Settings, 297
- Repeat, 282
- Selecting text, 269
- Sizing pictures, 301
- Spelling errors, 293
- Table Selector, 303
- Table Tools ribbon, 303
- Tables, 303
- Tracking changes, 307
- Undo, 282
- Wrapping text around pictures, 301

Word Processing, 242
Workbook, 312
Workbooks, 314
- Close, 318
- Creating new blank, 314
- Opening, 317
- Previewing, 348
- Printing, 348
- Saving, 316
- Template, 315

Worksheet, 313
- Entering data, 313

Worksheets
- Moving around, 314

World Wide Web, 419
- Internet, 419
- Web pages, 419

Worms, 215
WPS, 89

Y

Yammer, 552
YouTube, 551

Z

Zoom, 378
Zoom Slider, 266